T0342108

LABOR IN THE AGE OF FINANCE

Labor in the Age of Finance

PENSIONS, POLITICS, AND CORPORATIONS FROM DEINDUSTRIALIZATION TO DODD-FRANK

SANFORD M. JACOBY

PRINCETON UNIVERSITY PRESS

PRINCETON & OXFORD

Requests for permission to reproduce material from this work should be sent to permissions@press.princeton.edu

Published by Princeton University Press
41 William Street, Princeton, New Jersey 08540
6 Oxford Street, Woodstock, Oxfordshire OX20 1TR

press.princeton.edu

All Rights Reserved

ISBN 978-0-691-217208
ISBN (e-book) 978-0-691-217215

British Library Cataloging-in-Publication Data is available

Editorial: Joe Jackson and Jacqueline Delaney
Production: Erin Suydam
Publicity: Kate Hensley (US) and Kathryn Stevens (UK)
Copyeditor: Karen Verde

This book has been composed in Arno

Printed on acid-free paper ∞

Printed in the United States of America

10 9 8 7 6 5 4 3 2 1

To Paula and the Six Tantes

CONTENTS

ABBREVIATIONS

ACTWU	Amalgamated Clothing and Textile Workers Union
AFL-CIO	American Federation of Labor and Congress of Industrial Organizations
AFR	Americans for Financial Reform
AFSCME	American Federation of State, County, and Municipal Employees
CALPERS	California Public Employees' Retirement System
CALSTRS	California State Teachers' Retirement System
CII	Council of Institutional Investors
CTW	Change To Win
CTWIG	Change to Win Investment Group
CWA	Communications Workers of America
EFCA	Employee Free Choice Act
ERISA	Employee Retirement Income Security Act
FASB	Financial Accounting Standards Board
HERE	Hotel Employees and Restaurant Employees Union
IBEW	International Brotherhood of Electrical Workers
ICCR	Interfaith Center on Corporate Responsibility
ILO	International Labour Organization
IRRC	Investor Responsibility Research Center
ISS	Institutional Shareholder Services
LIUNA	Laborers' International Union of North America
NLRB	National Labor Relations Board

NYCERS   New York City Employees' Retirement System

PBGC   Pension Benefit Guaranty Corporation

REIT   Real Estate Investment Trust

SEIU   Service Employees International Union

TARP   Troubled Asset Relief Program

UAW   United Auto Workers

UFCW   United Food & Commercial Workers

ULLICO   Union Labor Life Insurance Company

UMW   United Mine Workers

UNITE   Union of Needletrades, Industrial and Textile Employees

USW   United Steelworkers

LABOR IN THE AGE OF FINANCE

Introduction

THE 1970S AND 1980S were a disaster for America's labor movement. Gone were nearly one out of three members from private industry, once the heart of organized labor. Critics charged that unions had become dinosaurs: archaic and doomed. The one bright spot was state and local government. But the gains there did not stop the loss of numbers—and power—in the corporate sector.

Facing slow extinction, leaders of several unions decided the time had come for a do-or-die struggle to renew and rebuild. There then occurred a burst of activity, including the restructuring of unions, new ways of organizing, and more money allocated to underwrite the effort. Part of the rebuilding involved the use of union pension assets as leverage to add members in the private sector. Capital was harnessed to restore labor's strength.

The engagement with finance had two other purposes. One was to shore up pension plans that were a crucial feature of union membership. The other was to make financial institutions and public corporations more accountable, transparent, and public-minded. The attempt resonated with a century of liberal ideas for reconciling corporate power with democracy. The chain stretched from Louis D. Brandeis to Adolf A. Berle, and on down to John Kenneth Galbraith, Saul Alinsky, and Ralph Nader. By exercising their shareholder rights, union investors affected the governance of the nation's largest corporations even as labor faded from within them.

In the background was financialization, a transformative economic force. The financial sector's share of GDP nearly doubled from the 1970s to the eve of the financial crisis. Corporations acquired the characteristics of commodities, bought and sold by speculators. The irony is that workers' pension funds supplied some of the capital that fueled financialization.[1]

Labor's financial turn came on the heels of a shareholder revolt led by public pension plans like the California Public Employees' Retirement System

(CalPERS) and informed by ideas emanating from financial economics. Investors shook off their decades-long passivity and pressed executives to prioritize their interests, what is called shareholder primacy. There were three main demands: tying CEO compensation to stock performance, orienting executives and corporate boards to shareholders, and lowering the barriers to acquisitions. It was an assault on the postwar system under which corporations balanced the interests of diverse stakeholders—executives, employees, and shareholders—without privileging any one of them. Now, shareholders told CEOs to do more for them or lose their jobs.

For the financial turn to succeed, unions needed allies like CalPERS. Of necessity this meant supporting the tenets of shareholder primacy. It was odd behavior for labor unions. But if you're down and nearly out, the ends could be made to justify the means.

The traditional pressure tactic—the strike—and the legal protections for union organizing had lost effectiveness by the 1970s. Employers shed their reticence to replace striking workers and to fire union supporters. An alternative approach emerged called the corporate campaign. Corporate campaigns rely on forces external to the workplace to compel employers to recognize a union, or make bargaining concessions, or settle a strike. They often include shareholder activism and other finance-based tactics to pressure a company's directors, business partners, and creditors. These contributed to an uptick of members in industries such as healthcare, lodging, building services, and occasionally industries beyond the service sector.

In the shareholder realm, labor's signature issue was executive compensation. Unions charged that lofty executive pay was the result of a rigged system. CEOs made out like bandits—in fact sometimes they *were* bandits—while workers' wages flatlined. Unions filed pay-related shareholder proposals at a broad range of companies, not only where they sought more members. Pulling back the curtain on the pay-setting process drove a wedge between executives and workers and allowed unions to raise issues like inequality. The shareholder forum was capacious. Topics that the law kept off the bargaining table, such as takeovers and executive remuneration, were capable of being addressed when unions acted as shareholders.

The claims of shareholder primacy—that shareholders owned the corporation and that their interests should be paramount—led to a wealth transfer from labor to capital. For the most part, however, restraining shareholders was not on labor's agenda, other than admonitions to invest for the long term.

Unions were slow to criticize mounting payouts to shareholders. The seeming embrace of shareholder interests caused some European trade unionists to be dubious of what their American counterparts were up to.[2]

There is a cottage industry of people who study inequality's causes. The widening pay gap between executives and workers, and between educated and less-educated workers, are well-researched topics. Less often considered is the relationship between inequality and the creed of shareholder capitalism. As economist Thomas Piketty observes, inequality is "ideological and political rather than economic or technological." It is a point that runs throughout this study.[3]

Historians only recently have begun to reckon with the economic events of the twenty-first century, a period of widespread laxity in business ethics.[4] Not once but several times during the 2000s, executives at some of America's leading corporations were revealed as malefactors of great wealth, a phrase first used by Theodore Roosevelt in 1907 during an earlier era of excess. Business's damaged reputation offered an opportunity for unions.

In banking, the malefactors caused a financial meltdown in 2008. Because of its newly acquired expertise, labor had a hand in fashioning the legislative response to the crisis, the Dodd-Frank Act. Washington was one place where unions still had some sway. But the final version of Dodd-Frank failed to punish the bankers, which left voters disappointed and angry. The appearance of Occupy Wall Street shortly after President Obama signed Dodd-Frank blindsided unions. Occupy's protests on behalf of the 99 Percent received more media attention than labor's own marches and demonstrations. Occupy Wall Street marks a boundary between history and current events. It is the terminus of this study, although an epilogue is provided.

———

The late Lloyd Ulman, a distinguished economist, once told his students (I was one of them) that unions had three types of power at their disposal. Two were rooted in the labor market: organizing power and bargaining power. The third was political power. An increase in any type of power strengthened the other two. Over the last fifty years, there's been an ebbing in all of them, particularly in the labor market. Industries with once-high union density, such as manufacturing and transportation, have experienced huge membership losses. Three times—during the Carter, Clinton, and Obama administrations—labor

TABLE I.A. Union Membership and Density, 1973–2019

	Private-Sector Density (%)	Private-Sector Membership (millions)	State and Local Government Density (%)	State and Local Government Membership (millions)	All Wage and Salary Density (%)	All Wage and Salary Workers Membership	Privat All (%
1973	24.2	14,954	n.a.	n.a.	24.0	18,089	83
1983	16.5	11,980	37.9	4,744	20.1	17,717	68
1997	9.7	9,363	38.2	5,717	14.1	16,110	58
2008	7.6	8,265	38.5	6,839	12.4	16,098	51
2019	6.2	7,508	35.3	6,087	10.3	14,567	52
			Change (%)				
1973–2019		(−50)		n.a.		(−19)	
1983–2019		(−37)		28		(−18)	

Source: Barry T. Hirsch and David A. Macpherson, "Union Membership and Coverage Database from the CPS," Georgi State University, www.UnionStats.gsu.edu.

fought without success to rebalance the laws that diminished their power. Three times they failed.

Bargaining power can be gauged by the divergence between union and non-union pay. Economists Barry Hirsch and David Macpherson find a steadily narrowing gap between unionized and comparable private-sector nonunion wages: 26 percent (1983–1992), 24 percent (1993–2002), 21 percent (2003–2012), and 20 percent (2013–2018). In other words, about a quarter of the union wage premium vanished between 1983 and 2018. Because the promise of higher wages is a selling point for joining unions, the premium's decline diminished labor's organizing power.[5]

Another measure of bargaining power is labor's share of a corporation's financial resources, whether the latter is measured as value-added, earnings, or economic rents. The portion paid to workers has fallen in line with deunionization. In manufacturing, union contraction is responsible for a third of the reduction in value-added received by production workers.[6]

Labor's political power did not decline as sharply. Writing in the 1960s, political scientist J. David Greenstone observed that unions had become the Democratic Party's most powerful interest group. Unions, he said, brought new voters into the party, formed alliances with key constituencies, and provided resources for electoral campaigns. It made unions what Greenstone called an "interest aggregator" of the party's diverse voters.[7]

During the following decades, labor was a crucial part of the Democratic coalition. "Even with a depleted labor movement," wrote journalist Thomas Edsall in 2014, unions provided to the Democrats "about 5 million votes they would not otherwise have." No group worked as hard as organized labor to elect Barack Obama in 2008. Coordinating mobilization at the grass roots was Working America, an organization created by the AFL-CIO to build support for labor-backed candidates. To persuade voters and to raise turnout, union volunteers visited ten million households—union and nonunion—and made 70 million phone calls. The AFL-CIO reached out to its white male members, who voted for Obama by a margin of 18 percentage points, whereas their non-union counterparts voted against him by almost the same margin.

Unions still serve as aggregators for the Democrats, albeit less so than before. They now compete with the party's other interest groups. They can achieve their political goals if they share objectives with these groups. But Democrats from swing states are wary of helping unions, and unions feel that the party is unresponsive to their needs. According to Steve Rosenthal, a former political director of the AFL-CIO, "The unions basically have become an ATM for Democrats. There is a sense of taking unions for granted, no place else to go, don't need to do much for them."[8]

It was difficult for unions to transform their political clout into remedies for their organizing problems. Out of the quandary came a search for new sources of power. Sociologist Nathan Wilmers has identified several strategies that unions recently have pursued, such as working with immigrant and community organizations and accepting into the labor movement quasi-union groups such as workers' centers. The loss of members made stark the choice between business as usual and the need for new approaches. With their pension funds, unions found a source of power outside the labor market to augment their power within it.[9]

———

Corporate governance refers to the rules that structure the relationships among executives, boards, shareholders, and employees. Executives make operating decisions, but the board hires them, sets their pay, and reviews their strategic plans. Shareholders vote to approve takeovers and board nominees, and they can petition the board with advisory proposals on a restricted range of topics. Employees lack formal channels for influencing executives and boards, unless they unite to form a labor union in the same fashion that owners amalgamate their shares. On the sidelines are creditors, who become more important if the firm faces bankruptcy. Joining them on the sidelines are customers, suppliers, and the public. Governance arrangements are created by the actors—private orderings—and by legislatures, regulatory agencies, and the courts. Different sets of rules produce different apportionments of the corporation's wealth to those who have a stake in it. Money and power lie at the heart of corporate governance.

There is variety in governance systems. Governance in the United States is different now from what it was following the Second World War; Germany's and Japan's systems are not the same as in the United States. Within a country at any point in time, companies cluster around particular governance practices, but there are always deviations.

In an important study of corporate governance, political scientists Peter Gourevitch and James Shinn analyze the coalitions that "set the rules of the corporate governance game." They develop a model with three groups: workers, owners, and executives. Based on their preferences, the groups can form alliances (owners-workers, owners-executives, executives-workers) or play the game on their own. Each group is riven by cleavages, which Gourevitch and Shinn acknowledge but do not dwell upon. Taking stock of the cleavages makes the game more complicated but also more realistic.[10]

Owners: At the height of exuberant stock markets in the 1990s, it seemed that everyone was buying shares or receiving stock options from their employers. One financial journalist wrote that America had "democratized" share ownership. The rhetoric was as overheated as the markets; ownership was far from being widespread. It was the affluent who held most of the shares in public corporations, either directly or through retirement plans. Among US households in 2016, the top 1 percent owned 53 percent of all stocks and mutual funds. For the top 10 percent, the figure was 93 percent. Included in the top 1 percent are corporate insiders—executives, founders, and inheritors—who, as we will see, hold substantial stakes.

The bottom half of households own no stock whatsoever. In the three deciles above them are households who own stock—including in their retirement plans—but seven out of ten of these households have holdings worth less than $10,000. In other words, stock markets are mostly irrelevant for 80 percent of US households except to exacerbate wealth inequality.[11]

The picture changes when a household member participates in a traditional defined-benefit pension plan, a privileged group comprised of around a sixth of corporate employees. The stock held in those plans does not belong to them, but it is their deferred wages that helped to purchase it. For private-sector plans, the stock was worth roughly $45,000 per participant in 2017.[12]

Pension plans are part of a larger universe of institutional investors. The biggest are mutual funds and exchange-traded funds (ETFs), whose equity holdings dwarf those of pension plans. Institutions also include banks, insurance companies, and endowments. They differ systematically in their approach to investment and corporate governance. The upshot is that "owners" are a motley group with diverse preferences. Alliances are structured with different configurations around different issues.[13]

Workers: Through their pension funds, workers participate, indirectly, in corporate governance at companies whose shares are owned by the fund. A route by which covered workers can influence governance is via a pension fund's trustees. So-called multiemployer pension plans, for private-sector union members, have an equal number of trustees representing employers and the union. State and local pension plans usually permit participants to elect some of their trustees. On the other hand, the trustees of corporate plans—also called single-employer plans—are banks and investment managers and may include executives and directors.

Because of widespread pension coverage and the size of their pension plans, state and local government employees have greater influence over corporate governance than most of the people employed by those companies. Public plans could be indifferent to the situation facing workers in the private sector. But they also could be powerful allies. Around four in ten state and local employees belong to unions, which means that they have some commonality with their private-sector counterparts.[14]

Union membership is another channel through which workers can affect corporate governance and the allocation of corporate wealth. Research shows an inverse relationship between a company's cash holdings and the wages that result from collective bargaining. Also, if a firm is unionized, executive pay is reduced. Thus, worker preferences in corporate governance and the ability to potentiate them vary depending on income, pension coverage, and union representation. Like owners, workers are diverse.[15]

Executives: There are divisions among executives too. CEOs who have risen through the ranks have greater sympathy for fellow lifers—and less for shareholders—than do CEOs hired from the outside. Executives behave differently depending on whether they are engineers, attorneys, or MBAs, and whether their backgrounds are in finance, marketing, or technology. The size of executive stock holdings affects business decisions and the board's composition.[16]

———

For most of the twentieth century, the worlds of finance and labor spun in separate orbits. They drew nearer as the century came to a close and a new one began. It was an era when finance was driving the economy, and unions adapted to the moment. Finance-based pressure tactics, which included shareholder activism but went beyond it, became a regular part of campaigns to add members. The recurring corporate scandals of the 2000s, which angered the public and investors, put the wind at labor's back. After the banking crash, labor's regulatory agenda drew on its financial turn. It was a pretty good showing for an alleged dinosaur.

1

Labor, Finance, and the Corporation

1890–1980

WE THINK we live in an era of unprecedented financialization, but we do not. In 2003, economists Raghuram Rajan and Luigi Zingales published the article "Great Reversals," in which they showed that financialization has ebbed and flowed over time. My labels for these waves are industrialization (1890–1929), the New Deal (1933–1973), and neoliberalism (1974–present). Financialization waxed during industrialization, waned during the New Deal, and expanded again under neoliberalism. Three of their four measures of financial development—one way of measuring financialization—are dominated by stock markets: investment financed by equity issues, stock market capitalization, and the number of listed companies. It's a narrow definition but useful for this study.[1]

It is striking to see how historical measures of inequality correspond with swings in financial development. Union density (that is, membership adjusted for total employment) moves in parallel. The record shows a causal relationship.[2]

Corporate ownership similarly has swung back and forth: from high concentration among a minority during industrialization—when founders, their families, and investment banks owned the new industrial giants; to dispersion during the New Deal, as stock ownership by the affluent became prevalent; and then back to concentrated ownership in our own time, when large blocks of stock are owned by institutions such as mutual funds and pension funds.

Ideas about corporate governance mirrored changes in ownership. During industrialization, there was a shift from laissez-faire beliefs in the prerogatives of property to a Progressive view that corporations had public responsibilities, including to their employees. The New Deal was the heyday of managerialism, when executives and, to a lesser extent, unions, were key governance actors; corporations were less engaged with their shareholders. After 1980, however, powerful institutional investors pressed for owner-dominated governance.[3]

Among labor's main accomplishments in its heyday was the democratization of pensions in the private sector. Defined-benefit pensions went from being the prerogative of a select few before the New Deal to covering 45 percent of private-sector workers in 1979. For the most part, the participants were adult men who belonged to unions, people whose pensions coincided with stable jobs. Participants in corporate retirement plans weren't much different from their counterparts working in government, where jobs also were stable and pensions a standard feature of employment. Jobs like that aren't entirely missing in the private sector today, but they've changed and are harder to find.[4]

Organized labor wasn't much involved in taming finance in the New Deal years, even though unions were crucial for committing the nation to full employment and social welfare spending. The situation changed after 1970, as pension fund assets grew in preparation for the retirement of the baby-boomer generation and shifted into higher-return assets like stocks. It was around then that labor and finance began to intertwine.

This chapter is an overview of the history of labor and finance during Rajan and Zingales's three periods, laying the groundwork for subsequent chapters. The story plays out against changes in corporate governance and ownership, union power, and pension provision.[5]

Labor Meets Finance

During the late nineteenth and early twentieth centuries, two economic issues roiled the nation. One was the gold standard; the other was monopoly. Among those challenging concentrated economic power was Louis D. Brandeis, who became a US Supreme Court justice in 1916. One of the most influential minds within the Progressive movement, Brandeis was often a friend of organized labor, although also interested in alternatives such as employee representation plans. Within the labor movement, there developed a modest engagement with incipient financial development, notably in labor banking.

Gold and Monopoly

After the Civil War, the first protests against financial markets were those related to banks and the gold standard. Gold favored lenders, not debtors. Urban workers joined small business and rural populists in opposing a gold-backed currency that they blamed for depressions and ruinous debt. Groups arrayed against the gold standard ran the gamut from the Greenback Party, predecessor to the populist People's Party, to labor groups such as the Knights of Labor, the American Federation of Labor (AFL), and the Western Federation of Miners. They hewed to the ethos that direct producers were the source of value, whereas financiers were speculative parasites. In the midst of a devastating depression that began in 1893, the AFL's national convention endorsed bimetallism, which would expand the money supply and stimulate the economy by exploiting the country's supply of silver, much larger than that of gold. Then, in 1896, the AFL supported William Jennings Bryan for the presidency, the man who famously said that the nation had been nailed to a cross of gold.[6]

These same groups also protested monopoly power. But when it came to antitrust law as a remedy, labor parted ways with its gold standard allies. The AFL's Samuel Gompers tried to block the Sherman Anti-Trust Act of 1890 because he thought it would lead to unions being declared conspiracies in restraint of trade.[7] Indeed, unions were hit with lawsuits and injunctions against strikes and boycotts, draining their resources. A less anticipated result of the Sherman Act was the merger movement that began in 1895, which drove industrial concentration to even higher levels. A subsequent antitrust law, the Clayton Act of 1914, sought to remedy the defects in the Sherman Act. Because the Clayton Act contained an explicit exemption for unions, Gompers declared that the act was "the Industrial Magna Carta upon which the working people will rear their structure of individual freedom." President Woodrow Wilson, who signed the Clayton Act, picked up part of the labor vote. Then the courts quickly found ways to use the act against organized labor.[8]

Louis D. Brandeis

Stock markets were not of great importance in the first half of the nineteenth century, when, with the exception of the railroads, shares were held by founders and their families. But as the economy industrialized, secondary markets for stocks began to develop. New legal doctrines advanced shareholder rights, including limited liability, which protects a company's investors from being sued for the company's misdeeds.

Stock trading had become popular, a game that unscrupulous brokers enticed people to play. When stock speculation went awry, it could bring the economy to its knees, as during the panic of 1907, which was followed by crusades against brokerage houses. New York Governor Charles Hughes organized an investigation of speculation on Wall Street. Congress considered no fewer than nineteen bills regulating the trading of futures and options and convened its own investigation in 1912. Leading the inquiry was a representative from Louisiana, Arsène Pujo. The Pujo Committee blamed investment banks for insinuating themselves into the corporate governance of companies they financed, a tactic they used to drive up share prices and enrich themselves.[9]

The Pujo Committee was of great interest to Louis D. Brandeis. Before joining the Supreme Court, Brandeis wrote several works critical of Wall Street's growing influence over the economy. He savaged investment banks—"the money trust"—in a series of essays published in 1914 as *Other People's Money and How the Bankers Use It*. Brandeis drew on evidence gathered by the Pujo Committee that disclosed how banks like National City and J. P. Morgan put their own directors on boards and used interlocking directorates to enhance coordination within nominally competitive industries. Banker-directors "apply a false test" in making their decisions, said Brandeis, by always asking, "What will be the probable effect of our action upon the market value of the company's stocks and bonds, or indeed generally upon stock exchange values?" When banker-directors zeroed in on stock prices, he said, their short-term decisions had negative long-term consequences for the corporation. Maintenance expenditures, for example, might be deferred in favor of paying dividends if these actions would sustain stock prices. Brandeis favored directors who would ask, "What is the best in the long run for the company of which I am director?"

To change the situation, Brandeis made the typically Progressive recommendation for more "publicity," by which he meant regular reporting of information to investors. In an oft-repeated phrase, he remarked, "Sunlight is said to be the best of disinfectants." The sentence preceding the sunlight quip is less often quoted: "Publicity is justly commended as a remedy for social and industrial diseases." For Brandeis, transparency was not an end in itself but a way of attuning corporations to the public interest.[10]

Brandeis looked forward to the replacement of the self-made proprietor by professional managers then being turned out by the new business schools at

Dartmouth, Harvard, and other universities, whose curricula taught young as-
pirants new methods of scientific management and "publicity." Business was
becoming a profession "pursued largely for others and not merely for one's self,"
he wrote. The injection of contemporary social developments into an otherwise
dry discussion of corporate governance was consistent with the Progressive
legal view that, because the corporation was "a social creation, a creature of law,
government, and prevailing conceptions of legitimate exchange," public concerns were relevant to private enterprise.[11]

What about an employee role in governance? According to economic historian Richard Adelstein, Brandeis believed that "corporations could be made
responsible only by labor's participation in its decisions." The closest Brandeis
came to putting this idea into practice was the union–management agreement
he designed after a general strike by the Ladies' Garment Workers' Union in
1910. Known as the Protocols of Peace, it included an elaborate arbitration
system, restrictions on subcontracting, gathering of price and wage statistics,
and use of scientific management for designing work methods and setting pay.
Brandeis enthusiastically supported union participation in governance and
new employee representation plans in nonunion companies. In 1906, he had
a hand in designing the Filene Cooperative Association for the eponymous
Boston department store. It included a provision for the eventual transfer of
nearly half of the company's stock to employees. Over the course of the
century, Brandeis's ideas would be a touchstone for liberals concerned about
corporate power and democracy.[12]

Labor Banking

The AFL was silent when it came to discussing the impact of finance on workers
during the new century's wave of financial development. Gompers was nothing if not cautious, and his predilection was to avoid rhetoric that might brand
him as a radical. There were exceptions at the local level, and in states such as
Wisconsin, where unions supported the Progressive Senator, "Fighting Bob"
LaFollette Jr., who opposed "Wall Street dictatorship" and demanded nationalization of banks.[13]

The labor movement's socialists were similarly censorious. Eugene V.
Debs—trade unionist and the Socialist Party's five-time candidate for
president—lampooned what he called "the Junkers of Wall Street." When J. P.
Morgan died shortly after testifying before the Pujo Committee, the socialist
press celebrated the event as a victory for the working class. Left-wing labor

intellectuals were familiar with *Das Finanzkapital* (*Finance Capital*), an influential book published by Rudolf Hilferding in 1910. Hilferding, a prominent socialist and member of the early Weimar government, argued that capitalism had been transformed by the concentration and centralization of banks and their domination of the corporations that they financed. He called the banking system a fraudulent kind of socialism because it "socializes other people's money for use by the few," a phrase anticipating the words of Louis Brandeis.[14]

In addition to unions, Brandeis was an enthusiast of cooperatives, credit unions, and building and loan associations, which he called "people's banks." Farmers and workers, he said, were "learning to use their little capital and their saving to help one another instead of turning over their money to bankers for safekeeping, and to be exploited."[15]

The first union to broach the idea of a labor bank was the Brotherhood of Locomotive Engineers (BLE), which was not a member of the AFL. From 1912, when the idea surfaced, until 1915, when it became a definite plan, the BLE's president, Warren S. Stone, studied cooperative societies in Europe. The union wanted to create a bank providing members with loans at lower rates, and invest their savings at higher rates, than offered by ordinary banks. When it opened in 1920, the bank retained 51 percent of the stock and sold the rest to its members. Investors who wanted to liquidate their holdings had to promise to sell shares back to the bank. Very rapidly the BLE expanded into a chain of twelve banks around the country. They invested in coal mines, laundries, and office buildings, and provided mortgages to members. Using bank funds, the union developed the beach town of Venice, Florida, as a retirement community for its members. It also opened a New York securities company that competed with Wall Street. According to the BLE, it was better at handling investments than the "unscrupulous persons [who] were selling wildcat stock to members of the union, more especially to the widows of the members."[16]

Labor banking took off in the 1920s. Unions wanted safe places to invest their funds, obtain loans for striking locals, and earn dividends to underwrite their activities. The labor banks shunned anti-union companies as customers and favored "fair employers." Sometimes the banks were founded by several unions, as with the Federation Bank of New York, whose stock was owned by 126 organizations. William Green, president of the AFL, established the Union Labor Life Insurance Company (ULLICO) to "shake workers loose from employer-sponsored insurance systems," a hallmark of welfare capitalism.

At the movement's peak in 1926, there were nearly forty banks whose resources reached $130 million, worth around $2 billion today. Half of them participated in the Federal Reserve System. Because several banks were owned by railway unions, their locations followed the tracks across the United States to small towns like Bakersfield, California and Three Forks, Montana. Other bank-owning unions included the Flint Glass Workers, Printing Pressmen, and several from the clothing industry: the Full Fashioned Hosiery Workers, the Ladies' Garment Workers, the Fur Workers, and the Weavers, among others.[17]

The Amalgamated Bank founded by the Amalgamated Clothing Workers was the best known of the labor banks. Branches in New York and Chicago opened in 1922. On opening day in Chicago, "thousands of tailors came to greet their bank and deposit money." In New York, the opening was celebrated with bands, parades, and speeches. The New York branch took in $2.6 million in deposits within several months after its opening. The Amalgamated Bank drew on a tradition of mutualism among its immigrant customers. It underwrote an alternative financial universe of affordable apartment buildings, low-cost loans and mortgages, and insurance benefits.[18]

There were critics of labor banking from within the labor movement. Senior officials of the AFL, including Gompers, felt that the BLE and other unions had oversold its benefits and overreached financially. The AFL was annoyed that the two leading labor banks were associated with unions outside the AFL. Within the Clothing Workers, the communist faction at first thought labor banking would serve as "a weapon against capitalist bankers," but in 1927, the Third International in Moscow told American communists to oppose labor banks because they were a ruse perpetrated by labor leaders and bourgeois economists "trying to make the working class believe that by investing their savings in labor banks and through purchasing stocks, the workers could gain influence, control, or even ownership, in capitalist industry."[19]

Then things started to collapse. Even before the Great Depression, labor banking had begun to implode as a result of poor management and unsound investments. When the banks failed, union members lost heavily. By 1931, only seven labor banks remained, the Amalgamated Bank being among the survivors.[20]

Owners of the Corporation

The 1920s began with a spectacular explosion on Wall Street that killed thirty-eight people. Although the perpetrators were never found, blame was cast on those who had raged against finance capital during the previous decade: anarchists and socialists. It happened at the time of the Palmer Raids, when thousands of suspected radicals—all immigrants—were arrested and some deported.

Wall Street quickly recovered, and the decade brought booming stock markets and economic exuberance. Union membership, however, sank to rock-bottom levels that allowed investors and managers to help themselves to larger portions of the returns generated by rising productivity. The annual ratio of wages to value-added in manufacturing was constant between 1899 and 1914, and then, from 1915 to 1929, it fell by 12 percent. Adolf A. Berle Jr., then a young lawyer, said that "common stockholders . . . were draining the corporation of money that should go to labor."[21]

Stock trading took off after World War I as Wall Street brokers sought to persuade moderately affluent individuals to purchase shares. Historian Steve Fraser says that the bull market of the Roaring Twenties became an icon of the era: "Ticker tapes not only appeared in beauty parlors and in railroad depots, but on ocean liners. . . . New radio shows and newspaper columns . . . sprouted up everywhere to appease the hunger for investment advice." The expanding bubble led Harvard University economist William Z. Ripley to castigate banks for what he called the "financialization" of the economy, the first time the word had ever been used. Looking back on the Twenties, the *Saturday Evening Post* presciently said in 1929 that "buying [of shares] was not based on reasoning but simply on the fact that prices had risen; a rise led the public to expect more and more returns. . . . Excessive anticipation of growth and earnings . . . always leads to depression and unemployment."[22]

While investors were thrilled by the expanding bubble, union leaders hunkered down as an employer's anti-union offensive decimated organized labor. The Garment Workers, for whom Brandeis had designed the Protocols of Peace, lost 70 percent of its members over the course of the decade. The further labor fell, the more it seemed that the citizenry lionized businessmen. Rising income inequality was a well-known fact—it peaked in 1929—although the AFL had little to say about it, nor about Wall Street's role in producing it. Only at the midnight hour, six months before the 1929 crash, did the AFL warn that failure to regulate stock markets was causing deleterious effects on wage earners and economic growth. When tax figures for 1929 were released, the AFL called attention to the fact that the bulk of income gains since 1927 had gone to the top brackets. It blamed persistent wealth inequality on stock ownership, stock speculation that benefited the rich, and the sloughing off of corporate wealth to investors.[23]

Berle and Means

In 1927, Adolf Berle Jr. and Gardiner C. Means teamed up to write what would become a classic study of corporate governance, *The Modern Corporation and Private Property*. Means, a graduate student in economics at Columbia University, came from a generation that had embraced institutional economics. Berle was a graduate of Harvard Law School who had worked for Brandeis's law firm briefly before Brandeis left for the Supreme Court. Brandeis was Berle's mentor in absentia, and, as is often the case, Berle built on Brandeis's ideas while differentiating his own from them. Whereas Brandeis thought that corporations and banks had grown too large—he called it "the curse of bigness"—Berle and Means did not think that scale necessarily was harmful. To them, these features were inevitable and superior to small firms engaged in cutthroat competition.[24]

The Modern Corporation and Private Property had two parts, one written by Means, the other by Berle. Means supplied a wealth of data on industrial concentration and ownership of the nation's largest companies. During the 1920s, he found, ownership became more dispersed as smallholders were drawn into equities by the era's infatuation with the stock market. Thus, ownership passed "from people of large incomes to those of moderate means," who were passive investors uninvolved in the company's affairs.[25]

As a corporate lawyer, Berle had witnessed instances in which business insiders—executives, directors, and bankers—had abused their fiduciary duties by enriching themselves at shareholders' expense. A seemingly benign development, stock ownership by the middle class left no one on the scene to prevent what he termed "corporate plundering." Later, Berle and Means cited the finding that one-third of the nation's wealth was produced by two hundred corporations dominated by 1,800 men. This, they wrote, could lead to "oligarchy." With executives left in charge of untold wealth they did not own, how would theft on a grand scale be prevented? The authors prescribed the famous dictum that executives should act as trustees for shareholders: "By tradition, a corporation 'belongs' to its owners," which required that executive actions be taken "for the *sole* benefit of the security owners."

The dictum begged the question of enforcement. Berle thought that stock exchanges, particularly New York's, would develop standards to prevent executives from doing anything that undermined shareholder interests. The rest would be up to lawyers hired by large investors. But if wealthy investors were able to sue, then oligarchy might be less of a problem than Berle and Means made it out to be.[26]

E. Merrick Dodd Jr., a Harvard law professor who also had practiced in Brandeis's firm, published an influential essay in 1931 that challenged Berle's ideas. In a Brandeisian argument, Dodd asserted that business had obligations not only to stockholders but also to employees, customers, and the public. Dodd's solution to incipient oligarchy—and social unrest—was to have broad-thinking, educated business leaders act as stewards of the corporate commonwealth, men like Gerard Swope and Owen D. Young, both from General Electric. Dodd decisively rejected Berle's shareholder primacy in favor of a public-minded, albeit patrician, alternative.[27]

Berle and Means, perhaps with Dodd in mind, referred to the view "held by certain students of the field . . . that the control of the great corporations should develop into a purely neutral technocracy, balancing a variety of claims by various groups and assigning to each a portion of the income stream on the basis of public policy rather than private cupidity." Writing on his own in a rejoinder to Dodd, Berle said "you cannot abandon emphasis on 'the view that business corporations exist for the sole purpose of making profits for their stockholders' until such time as you are prepared to offer a clear and reasonably enforceable scheme of responsibilities to someone else." If management had to balance competing interests, it would lead to "the massing of group after group to assert their private claims by force or threat." Labor would be "invited to organize and strike," and it would end in "economic civil war." Indeed, a civil war started in 1932. Later, after corporations made it to the safe harbor of the postwar era, the world looked more like Dodd's than Berle's.[28]

The New Deal

The Great Depression impoverished workers and farmers and reached into the middle class. Out of this arose a broad political coalition—much wider than what had existed in 1896—that swept Franklin D. Roosevelt into office. The stock market crash was on everyone's mind, as was the belief that speculation and graft had caused it. Politicians blasted Wall Street as "a plutocratic elite." Rumors swirled that the Federal Reserve Bank, which was reluctant to reflate the economy, was under the control of the J. P. Morgan bank.

Among the largest movements of the Depression decade were those led by right-wing populists like Louisiana's Senator Huey Long and Father Charles Coughlin. Long attacked the nation's unequal distribution of wealth—"concentrated in the hands of a few people"—and tied it to the "God of Greed [worshipped] by Rockefeller, Morgan, and their crowd." For Coughlin, bankers and financiers were the chief obstacles to social justice. He demanded remonetization of silver and nationalization of the Federal Reserve Bank. Wall Street's reputation was in tatters.[29]

Father Coughlin's heated rhetoric attracted millions of adherents from the same groups that had elected Roosevelt. Coughlin had close ties to the Detroit labor movement, including what would become Homer Martin's anti-CIO faction in the United Auto Workers (UAW). A few other union officials, such as attorney Frank P. Walsh, became Coughlinites. The priest, a skilled orator, connected a worker's problems to abstruse financial forces: "Your actual boss, Mr. Laboring Man, is not too much to blame. If you must strike, strike in an intelligent manner, not by laying down your tools but by raising your voices against a financial system that keeps you today and will keep you tomorrow in breadless bondage."[30]

In 1932, the Senate Banking Committee created a commission to inquire into the causes of the Depression. Led by its chief counsel, Ferdinand Pecora, the commission revealed a host of problematic practices that Wall Street had foisted on the new shareholders of the 1920s. One was "touting," in which banks released seemingly impartial information about a stock to push its price up or down to pay off the banks' speculative bets. Another was the "sucker pool," wherein brokerages "sent out invitations all over the country to small brokers requesting them to take a share; enthusiasm is spread among the invitees and they are properly made to feel the favor being done them." Pecora made a scapegoat of Charles E. Mitchell, chairman of the First National City Bank, the predecessor to Citicorp. Testifying in the Senate, Mitchell was publicly humiliated by Pecora's claims that he violated the law while receiving compensation of over $3.5 million from 1927 to 1929. The Pecora commission, responsive to popular antipathy to Wall Street, anticipated Roosevelt's embrace of financial regulation.[31]

The first move toward financial reform was the Banking Act of 1933, better known as Glass-Steagall. It required the separation of investment banking from commercial banking, a slap at banks like National City and J. P. Morgan. Then came the Securities Act of 1933, the Securities Exchange and Banking Acts of 1933 and 1934, and the Investment Company Act of 1940, all of which mandated extensive disclosure of financial data, including the compensation of a bank's top three earners. Here were rays of Brandeisian sunlight.[32]

The financial industry shrank after the Depression, along with its public image. As historian Steve Fraser notes, the proportion of Harvard Business School graduates choosing Wall Street as their first position fell from 17 percent in 1928 to 1 percent in 1941. Not until the 1980s would MBAs become as prevalent on Wall Street as they had been in the 1920s. European nations introduced their own financial rules, limiting opportunities for regulatory arbitrage. The world's industrialized nations experienced what John Ruggie calls "a common thread of social reaction against market rationality," resulting in the quiescence of global stock markets for forty years. Harry Truman played on anti-finance sentiments in his 1948 presidential campaign by attacking Wall Street's "gluttons of privilege," reminding voters that, during the Depression, the Democratic Party "drove the money changers out of the temple and brought a new life to our democracy."[33]

The Bretton Woods Treaty, signed in 1944 by more than forty nations, addressed the criticism that unregulated currency markets had contributed to the Depression. Although the treaty negotiations did not include organized labor, important union leaders such as the presidents of the Auto Workers, Walter Reuther, and of the Clothing Workers, Sidney Hillman, endorsed the treaty. Bretton Woods, they hoped, would reduce isolationist tendencies on the Right and communist influence on the Left. Liberals and labor thought managed exchange rates would protect Keynesian spending to maintain full employment from speculators betting against currencies. The Congress of Industrial Organizations (CIO), comprised of left-leaning unions in the mass-production industries, campaigned to win public support for the treaty. After that, however, organized labor had little to say about financial regulation except when it came to taxes or when it periodically denied that union wage gains were responsible for gold outflows. The withdrawal would last for more than forty years.[34]

The labor movement scored a trifecta in the 1940s and 1950s. Membership, strikes, and political influence—labor's sources of power—flourished as never before. With the ideology of self-regulating markets discredited, the labor movement advanced an array of social programs: the GI Bill, higher minimum wages, and better unemployment insurance (although unions abandoned national health insurance in favor of employer provision). To pay for it all, labor sought redistributive taxation. Union economists familiarized themselves with the tax code's details: during the war, when they opposed a sales tax in favor of higher taxes on corporations and the wealthy, and after the war, when they demanded closing tax loopholes benefiting the rich. Gradually, workers secured a larger slice of corporate earnings that previously had gone to executives and investors. The share of income received by the top 1 percent fell steadily from the 1930s through the mid-1970s—broadly, the New Deal era— followed by a steady climb back up to levels not seen since the 1920s.[35]

A symbol of labor's power was the collective bargaining agreement that Walter Reuther negotiated with Charles Wilson of General Motors (GM) in

1950. Known as the Treaty of Detroit, it contained a promise from the UAW to eschew strikes during the contract's five-year term. In return, GM instituted a pension plan, promised to keep wages in line with the cost of living and, on top of that, to grant an "annual improvement factor" representing productivity increases. In other words, workers were guaranteed an inflation-adjusted share of an ever-larger pie. The remainder went to shareholders and executives, modest by today's standards, and the rest was retained for investments or held for a rainy day. Reuther and his staff met regularly with senior executives of the auto companies, a level of access that few shareholders enjoyed.[36]

Pensions

The Treaty of Detroit's pension plan came after a decade of growth in corporate pension coverage. Employers hoped that retirement provision would give them an edge in winning the loyalties of American workers, for whom economic security had become paramount after the depression. During the Second World War, pension coverage rose by over two million persons, facilitated by new tax laws and the exemption of pension contributions from wartime wage controls. Companies unilaterally adopted the new plans, whereas unions for the most part were passive observers. But then came *Inland Steel*, a pivotal 1949 Supreme Court decision which held that employers had to negotiate with unions over pension plans.

Employers had refused to bargain because they sought to demonstrate that they and not unions were the guarantors of old-age security. Also, unilateral control allowed for unconstrained benefit and administrative decisions by the company. But immediately following the *Inland Steel* case, the UAW pressed Ford Motor to negotiate what became a landmark pension agreement. Among its features was joint control: The company and the union would have an equal number of trustees overseeing the pension fund. The Treaty of Detroit came soon after the Ford agreement, and in the 1950s pension plans proliferated throughout the labor market.

Labor argued that pension assets were deferred wages, not a gift from employers, entitling employees a voice in their administration. Employers were bitterly opposed to this. Joint administration disappeared at Ford, while other companies did not adopt it. Inevitably, there were abuses—such as overinvesting in the company's own stock. A study published in 1961 found that 15 percent of single-employer plans under collective bargaining had their investment decisions made exclusively by the employer. Many but not all of these issues were unaddressed until Congress passed the Employee Retirement Security Act in 1974. Over the years unions made periodic demands for joint control, but companies drew the line against it.[37]

The earliest pension plans existed in the civil service and in monopolistic industries such as railroads and public utilities. Plans were less prevalent in manufacturing until the 1920s, when insurance companies began selling annuity plans to employers. Yet the uptake was modest: Only 2 percent of large corporations offered retirement benefits in 1929. Even in these firms, employees could be denied benefits if they had a break in their service, and, when they did receive a pension, the amounts were so meager that some preferred to keep working. The Depression revealed that numerous pension plans were actuarially unsound, leading either to their discontinuation or a requirement that workers contribute to what previously were noncontributory plans. The poor design and scarcity of employer-provided pensions was an impetus for government to step in with its own pension plan, Social Security.

The situation was different in the AFL's craft unions, where there was a history of mutualism and wariness of employer paternalism. Craft unions had pension plans of their own that they controlled. An estimate is that they covered one in five union members in 1930. In 1946, John L. Lewis, president of the United Mine Workers, led a national strike to obtain a health-and-retirement plan for coal miners paid for by the owners of the nation's unionized mines. Although the participating coal companies had some say, they received only one of three trustee positions. Conservatives in Congress were alarmed at the prospect of Lewis using the plan's assets as a "war chest" to finance strikes. They inserted into the anti-union Taft-Hartley Act of 1947 a provision that multiemployer benefit plans must have an equal number of trustees from both sides. From then on, multiemployer plans also were called Taft-Hartley plans.[38]

Shareholders Ascend

Deciding who would control pension funds was a microcosm of the bigger question of how power would be exercised in public corporations. To find out what was going on, a team of eminent economists—including Carl Kaysen, Seymour Harris, and James Tobin—interviewed a cross-section of executives from major corporations of the mid-1950s. The executives professed governance principles not much different from what Dodd had recommended. They viewed themselves as having "four broad responsibilities: to consumers, to employees, to stockholders, and to the general public. . . . In any case, each group is on an equal footing; the function of management is to secure justice for all and unconditional maxima for none. Stockholders have no special priority; they are entitled to a fair return on their investment but profits above a 'fair' level are an economic sin."[39]

The Kaysen team found that the concept of management rights, which originally referred to production decisions that management reserved for itself, free of union influence, had acquired an additional meaning: freedom from shareholders. Instead of shareholders weighing in on whether earnings would be distributed to them or reinvested, executives arrogated the decision to themselves. The National Association of Manufacturers said, "That's how the American system works."

Shareholders weren't treated shabbily. Companies kept dividends on a formulaic trajectory, an investor's version of the Treaty of Detroit. Yet shareholders were placed alongside, instead of above, the corporation's other stakeholders, and executives would broach no interference. Kaysen's team explained that management rights with respect to shareholders were "designed to defend for management a sphere of unhampered discretion and authority which is not merely derivative from the property rights of owners." Given their freedom to make decisions, did executives turn into oligarchs? They did not. Executive pay remained remarkably flat from the Second World War through the late 1970s.[40]

A new generation of liberals offered their own interpretations of the postwar corporation. In his 1952 book *American Capitalism*, economist John Kenneth Galbraith cautioned against business leaders having too much authority; government and organized labor should provide "countervailing power" against managerial autonomy. Galbraith was attuned to the sway of modern corporations in markets and politics, and, sounding a bit like Berle, called them ogres of economic power. Sociologist C. Wright Mills lampooned Galbraith for failing to see that countervailing force was ineffectual against a powerful elite. It was Yale political scientist Robert Dahl who defended Galbraith. In *Who Governs?*, his classic 1961 study of New Haven, Dahl depicted a pluralist community comprised of competing interest groups who continually shifted alliances and kept each other from monopolizing power.[41]

What about shareholders? One thing was clear: Berle had gone out of style. Dahl questioned the claim that shareholders should have primacy in executive decision-making: "Why should people who own shares be given the privilege of citizenship in the government of the firm when citizenship is denied to other people who also make vital contributions to the firm? The people I have in mind are, of course, employees and customers, without whom the firm could not exist, and the general public."[42]

The Sixties

As soon as it seemed a consensus had been reached about corporate governance, cracks began to show. President Dwight D. Eisenhower's famous farewell address to the nation, delivered in 1961, warned that during the Cold War a "military-industrial complex" had taken hold of government and that only constant vigilance—"an alert and knowledgeable citizenry"—would check abuses of power. The next year, Students for a Democratic Society (SDS) released the Port Huron Statement, its founding manifesto. Criticizing large institutions and counterposing "bureaucracy" and "democracy," the SDS argued that the "basic structure of distribution and allocation . . . is still determined by major corporations with power and wealth concentrated among the few." Even the average citizen felt similarly: Survey data show that, in the mid-1960s, a "confidence gap" opened between the general public and leaders of business, government, and labor. The public regarded business as too powerful in politics and indifferent to any interests other than its own.[43]

As the civil rights and antiwar movements heated up, criticism of big business became more forceful. Antiwar protesters probed the ties between corporations and the military. With church support, the North American Congress on Latin America (NACLA) was formed in 1966 to conduct research on corporations accused of human rights abuses in Latin America. Two NACLA researchers, Steve Abrecht and Michael Locker, went on to found the Corporate Data Exchange, a consultancy providing financial data to social justice organizations, including unions. Both men later became consultants to the Steelworkers union. Following that, Abrecht took charge of organizing for the Service Employees International Union (SEIU), while Locker consulted for unions over employee buyouts.[44]

NACLA and the Corporate Data Exchange, as well as other New Left groups, conducted what was called "power structure research" to document how elites controlled American politics and corporations. An epitome of the trend was William Domhoff's widely read book, *Who Rules America?* First published in 1967, it unearthed a wealth of data endorsing Mills's assertion that elites were in control. Domhoff analyzed ties between corporations, banks, insurance companies, and mutual funds. He concluded that interlocking board directorates and other coordinative institutions ensured the economic and political dominance of business leaders and the rich.[45]

Saul Alinsky

The situation took a surprising turn when a self-described radical and community organizer, Saul Alinsky, went to Rochester, New York in 1967. Alinsky wanted to help African Americans fight for good jobs at Eastman Kodak. Although it was the city's largest employer, the workforce was mostly white. To get Kodak's attention, he hatched a plan to embarrass its executives by disrupting the annual meeting. Alinsky asked the Unitarian Universalists' General Assembly to give him the church's Kodak proxies in order that he and others could enter the meeting. The church pledged all of its stock. As the news spread, other liberal denominations assigned their proxies to Alinsky. In an interview, Alinsky said, "By the purest accident, we'd stumbled onto a tactical gold mine. . . . I'd never seen the establishment so uptight before, and this convinced me that we had happened onto the cord that might open the golden curtain shielding the private sector from its public responsibilities."[46]

Alinsky dreamed of starting a new group, "Proxies for People," which would train individuals—the "army of small investors"—to become shareholder activists. Reflecting on the Kodak experience, he told an interviewer that shareholder activism

> can become a springboard to other issues in organizing the middle class. Proxy participation on a large scale could ultimately mean the democratization of corporate America. . . . Pat Moynihan told me in Washington when he was still Nixon's advisor that "Proxies for People would mean revolution—they'll never let you get away with it." It *will* mean revolution, peaceful revolution, and we will get away with it in the years to come.

Alinsky was far from naïve. When asked whether he intended to take control of major corporations, he replied:

> No, despite all the crap about "people's capitalism," the dominant controlling stock in all major corporations is vested in the hands of a few people we could never get to. We're not even concerned about electing four or five board members to a 25-member board, which in certain cases would be theoretically feasible. They'd only be outvoted by management right down

the line. We want to use the proxies as a means of social and political pressure against the mega-corporations, and as a vehicle for exposing their hypocrisy and deceit.[47]

Ralph Nader

Ralph Nader was another critic of corporate power. With his staff of Nader's Raiders, he published study after study showing that business leaders lacked accountability, which gave them freedom to abuse their power.[48] Large corporations, said Nader, had failed to meet their social responsibilities and had corrupted government, when they should be serving the public interest. In 1965, Nader published a best-selling book, *Unsafe at Any Speed*, which revealed how automobile companies had purposely neglected to put safety devices in their cars that might have saved thousands of lives every year. Companies like GM and DuPont were indifferent to the public interest, he said. Nader thought that assertive investors had the potential to reduce corporate insularity and negligence.

At the end of the 1960s, Nader launched a "Campaign to Make General Motors Responsible" (Campaign GM), demanding that the company take more responsibility for reducing air pollution and making highways safer. Nader's group submitted nine shareholder proposals seeking reform of GM's board. The car maker was asked to create a shareholder committee on social responsibility; expand the size of its board and add more women, minorities, and consumer advocates; and appoint a greater number of independent directors. Although similar shareholder demands barely raise an eyebrow today, James Roche, chairman of GM's board at the time, said that Campaign GM was "trying to challenge the entire system of corporate management in the US." GM asked the Securities and Exchange Commission (SEC) for permission to omit the resolutions from its proxy materials and was granted removal of seven of them. To garner votes for the two remaining proposals, Project GM appealed to institutional investors such as universities and public-employee pension plans. They received few votes from GM's shareholders.

After that, the Nader groups mounted other campaigns challenging business. One target was the state of Delaware, where DuPont had its headquarters. Ridiculing Delaware as a "company state," Nader's group issued a report showing the enormous influence DuPont had over the state's courts and elected officials. The situation there was much different from the competing groups Dahl had observed in New Haven. A 1971 Nader-sponsored conference on corporate governance led to the formation of a new organization, the Corporate Accountability Research Group. It culminated in the publication of Nader's tome on reforming business, *Taming the Giant Corporation*.

A change that Nader thought would make corporations more accountable was to take away Delaware's quasi-monopoly on issuing corporate charters and to transfer the responsibility to the federal government. Were charters granted at the national level, he argued, Delaware's pro-business courts would lose control and there would be an end in the race to the bottom by states competing for the charter business. He envisioned that the government would set minimum standards of accountability in areas such as campaign finance contributions and offshore tax havens.

To align business objectives with the public interest, Nader and his followers sought "social audits" to disclose a corporation's social impact. Like Brandeis, Nader saw transparency as a precursor to public-mindedness. Another recommendation was a requirement that company directors be entirely independent of management. Nader called for a new group of full-time professional directors, each of whom was assigned responsibility for monitoring a specific corporate constituency including shareholders, employees, and consumers. A related objective was to add more women and minorities to corporate boards, which, according to Nader, were "homogenously white, male, and narrowly oriented." To extend constitutionalism to the workplace, Nader formulated an employee bill of rights that would include a right to privacy and whistleblower protection.[49]

In 1979, Nader and his associate Mark Green announced the Corporate Democracy Act (CDA), with the intent of making companies more accountable. The following year two liberal Democrats—Senator Howard Metzenbaum (Ohio) and Representative Benjamin Rosenthal (New York)—introduced legislation resembling the CDA. Boards would have a majority of independent directors and their own independent staff. There would be proxy access, by which board candidates are nominated by shareholders. To minimize interlocking directorates, no director could serve on more than two boards. Specialized board members would oversee the relationship between a firm's performance and nine different factors that affect it, including employee well-being, shareholder rights, and consumer protection. Firms would have to disclose their twenty largest stockholders, their hiring records by race and gender, the number of workplace injuries, and impending plant closures.

To rally support for the CDA, Nader—who had a habit of spawning new organizations—created Americans Concerned about Corporate Power, which had support from a broad spectrum of labor, religious, and consumer groups. Among the figures supporting Nader were John Kenneth Galbraith and environmental activist Barry Commoner. With foundation support, Americans Concerned About Corporate Power, under its director Michael Schippani, an organizer on leave from the Amalgamated Clothing Workers, made plans for "Big Business Day" rallies in April 1980 in 150 cities. Consumer and environmental groups and the AFL-CIO Executive Council gave their endorsements, and prominent labor leaders spoke at the events. William H. Wynn, president of the United Food & Commercial Workers, predicted that "Just as the 1950s scrutinized the labor movement and the 1970s big government, this day will mark the 1980s as the decade to correct the abuses of big business." Green stressed that the goal was not government regulation but "self-regulation" by citizens and grassroots community organizations, including unions. Wynn probably liked Green's rhetoric. Although private-sector unions were dependent on state protection, they carried in their DNA a wariness of government and an affinity for voluntarist private orderings.[50]

Divestment

As the Vietnam war drew to a close, activists from religious, civil rights, and student groups began protesting the apartheid system in South Africa. Church endowments and faith-based pension plans created the Interfaith Center on Corporate Responsibility (ICCR) in 1971 to monitor American firms operating in South Africa, with the idea that their collective financial clout would shame companies from propping up an apartheid state. The ICCR organized private meetings between religious investors and executives and coordinated shareholder activism. General Motors and other companies faced proxy resolutions to disinvest from South Africa. Although the resolutions received few votes, their real purpose was to put a company in the public eye. Management's desire to avoid negative publicity gave the ICCR bargaining power, as would later occur with union investors. The group began building relationships with institutional investors, including government pension plans. In 1982, CalPERS and several investors affiliated with ICCR offered a South Africa–related resolution at Xerox's annual meeting. At the time, CalPERS (the California Public Employees' Retirement System) was the nation's largest pension plan.

Meanwhile, student protesters took a different tack—exit instead of voice—calling on universities to divest from companies that refused to leave South Africa. They demanded that university presidents resign any director-ships that they held in companies doing business there. David Rockefeller of Chase Manhattan told other executives, "It is scarcely an exaggeration to say that right now American business is facing its most severe public disfavor since the 1930s. We are being assailed for demeaning the worker, deceiving the consumer, destroying the environment, and disillusioning the younger generation."[51]

The movement spread to other places and issues. A group of African American students at Harvard held a sit-in to protest the university's failure to vote for a shareholder proposal asking Gulf Oil to report on its activities in Angola. Harvard's president, the labor lawyer Derek Bok, contacted other institutional investors—chiefly universities and foundations—to establish an organization that would provide information on what now was routinely called "corporate social responsibility" issues. The Investor Responsibility Research Center (IRRC) produced a steady stream of reports, initially pertaining to South Africa but later including the marketing of baby formula in Africa, animal experi-mentation, weapons production, and executive retirement benefits. Several of these became the subject of shareholder proposals, usually asking for more information about a company's social impact. The IRRC periodically recom-mended to members that they demand more information from companies in which they invested, submit proposals, and in other ways leverage their finan-cial assets to advance social goals.[52]

Pension Funds and Organizing

The late historian Judith Stein termed the 1970s "the pivotal decade," the pe-riod when the New Deal coalition began to fall apart, laissez-faire ideas resur-rected themselves, and companies stepped up attacks on unions. Labor was powerless to stem the flow of industrial jobs to the South and outside the United States and unable to reverse their membership losses. It was becoming a less important part of the Democratic Party, something that was unthinkable a decade earlier. Indeed, it was a Democrat, Jimmy Carter, who first deregu-lated union strongholds in the transportation and energy industries.[53]

The situation went from bad to worse in the 1980s, as downsizing and dein-dustrialization accelerated. With the loss of labor's strength came a dwindling of strikes, related in part to employer threats to move jobs to other countries

or hire permanent replacements. Wage norms turned from "pushiness" to passivity as unions made concession after concession to save jobs. Now pay
increases began to diverge from productivity gains. Companies replaced de-
fined- benefit plans with individual accounts—401(k)s—that shifted risk to
employees. The Treaty of Detroit was breaking down.

The public sector was one of labor's few bright spots. After 1960, the number
of union members employed by government rose steadily, thanks to changes in
state and federal laws. Nearly half of all union members now are in the public
sector, up from less than a fifth in the early 1970s (see table I.A in the introduction).
Some of the nation's largest unions—including the Communications Workers
of America (CWA), the Service Employees International Union (SEIU), and
the Teamsters—have members in both the public and private sectors.[54]

Not long after taking office, President Ronald Reagan sent a message to
organized labor: He fired more than eleven thousand government-employed
air traffic controllers after they went on strike in 1981. In the private sector,
labor's win rate in representation elections steadily fell. When a union did win
an election, management intransigence prevented the negotiation of a first
contract. Unions complained bitterly that the National Labor Relations Board
(NLRB) had failed to stop a steep increase in illegal anti-union behavior. The
AFL-CIO demanded legislation to make labor law more even-handed but
failed to secure it. Not all of the blame rested on management. Unions spent
less on organizing in the 1970s than they did in the 1950s.[55]

Corporate Campaigns

The traditional model for gaining new members was to rely on professional
organizers to build support for a union and seek an NLRB election when more
than a majority wanted representation. The problem was, the old model wasn't
working. New organizing methods were required, and one of them was the
corporate campaign.

At the beginning of Stein's pivotal decade, one of the first corporate campaigns took place at Farah Manufacturing of El Paso, Texas. The American
Clothing Workers Association (ACWA), beset by declining membership,
sought to organize clothing factories transplanted to the South, which long
had been the elephant's graveyard of union organizing. Farah aggressively
fought the union, which led to a twenty-one-month strike by four thousand
Farah employees. Jack Sheinkman, then secretary-general of ACWA, oversaw
the campaign and spearheaded the union's move into financial activism, relying in part on the expertise ACWA had built up through its ownership of

Amalgamated Bank. At the time of the Farah strike, Sheinkman was chairman of the bank's board of directors.

Sheinkman lobbied Wall Street's stock analysts, emphasizing Farah's shaky condition. Whether because of these problems or Sheinkman's activities, Farah's stock price fell. He also started a national boycott of Farah products. ACWA reached out to the social investing world, which sympathized with the plight of the company's poorly paid Latina employees. Shortly before a 1974 shareholders' meeting, the ICCR filed a proposal demanding that Farah make public the gender and racial composition of its workforce. After a few more prods and continued damage to its image, Farah conceded representation to the union.[56]

Several years later the union took aim at a bigger target: J. P. Stevens, a textile company with plants scattered across the South. The Clothing Workers recently had absorbed the Textile Workers to create the Amalgamated Clothing and Textile Workers Union (ACTWU). Since 1963, the Textile Workers had been trying to organize the company's 44,000 employees. Stevens's belligerent managers, however, frequently crossed the line into unlawful behavior, for which it was repeatedly fined by the NLRB. Sheinkman understood that taking on a company like J. P. Stevens—"the citadel of anti-unionism in the South"—would require substantial resources.

Sheinkman, now president of ACTWU, hired a young organizer named Ray Rogers to lead the Stevens campaign. Inspired by Alinsky's impromptu tactics, Rogers identified three groups who might be persuaded to take action on the union's behalf: first, the public—customers and civil rights, religious, women's, and community organizations. Rogers put together a boycott against Stevens products and supplemented it with a nationwide public relations campaign, in which the ACTWU hammered home Stevens's discrimination against female and nonwhite employees.[57]

The second was government. ACTWU brought federal pressure to bear by complaining about the company's employment discrimination and violation of environmental regulations. A third, in Rogers's words, were "the institutions heavily tied to Stevens' financial interests through interlocking directorships, large stock holdings, and multi-million-dollar loans." They included some of the nation's leading financial institutions: Manufacturers Hanover Trust, Metropolitan Life Insurance Company, and New York Life, all major creditors of J. P. Stevens. Rogers openly embarrassed Avon's CEO David Mitchell, who sat on both Hanover's and Stevens's boards. Mitchell resigned from both. The main objective, however, was Metropolitan Life, which held $100 million of Stevens's debt. After ACTWU threatened to run two dissidents for the company's board, Metropolitan Life's CEO, Richard Shinn, told the chairman of J. P. Stevens, Whitney Stevens, to settle with the union. Observers credit Shinn with getting Stevens to capitulate.[58]

Early in the Stevens campaign, ACTWU held demonstrations outside the company's annual meeting. Then it persuaded hundreds of people to buy a share of Stevens's stock to enable them to attend the meeting and protest from the inside, a reprise of Alinsky's tactics at Kodak. In attendance was Coretta Scott King, the widow of Martin Luther King. Union supporters offered several resolutions alleging that company profits were suffering as a result of its disregard of laws covering discrimination, health and safety, and union organizing. They demanded that Stevens tell its investors about its labor and equal employment opportunity policies. Rogers turned for support to institutional investors, including those affiliated with the ICCR and retirement plans. Several public-employee plans—from liberal states like California, Connecticut, New York, Ohio, and Wisconsin—supported the shareholder resolutions.

In 1980, Whitney Stevens signed an agreement granting union recognition at seven plants and promised the same terms at any other plant that ACTWU organized over the next eighteen months. The victory demonstrated the potency of financial activism. The quid pro quo was that the union had to call off its troops, as specified in what came to be known as "the Ray Rogers clause":

> Subsequent to the date of this agreement, the union will not engage in any corporate campaigns against the company. Accordingly the union will not in any manner attempt to effectuate the resignation of members of the board of Stevens or to effectuate the resignation or removal of Stevens executives from the boards of directors of other corporations, or to restrict the availability of financial or credit accommodations to Stevens.[59]

Attracting the attention of top executives was far from easy. ACTWU had to find out who were the company's business partners and who purchased its products, many of which were not sold under the J. P. Stevens name. Rogers hired consultants, like Michael Locker, with research skills and business acumen, who uncovered the company's financial and organizational structure, the identities of major investors, its profit centers, government contracts, and the social networks of its senior executives and directors. The campaign was labor-intensive, with thirty-one staffers, including Bruce Raynor, who eventually became president of the union, and William (Bill) Patterson, who first worked on the United Farm Workers' grape boycott led by Cesar Chavez. Patterson later would become a leader of labor's financial turn.[60]

In 1978, authors Jeremy Rifkin and Randy Barber published an influential book, *The North Will Rise Again: Pensions, Politics, and Power in the 1980s*. They noted the decline in union membership and the decimation of labor's redoubt in America's industrial heartland. Rifkin and Barber saw a remedy in the billions of dollars in Taft-Hartley pension funds, not to mention trillions in public pension funds. The authors recommended that these assets be invested in local development projects to revive the Rust Belt. The idea of using pension funds more strategically was in the air. In 1977, Democratic Senator Lee Metcalf (Montana) urged organized labor to stop the managers of their pension funds from investing in corporations with "antebellum attitudes toward workers."

That same year, the AFL-CIO national convention adopted resolutions urging pension funds to invest in construction projects employing union members and to move their assets to financial institutions "whose investment policies are not inimical to the welfare of working men and women." "Labor," said one journalist, "plans to use its billion-dollar clout as pressure on banks, insurance companies and asset managers to refrain from investing in corporations [where] labor is striking or attempting to organize." The logic was simple. As William Winpisinger, president of the Machinists union, explained, "If you got a choice of [investing pension funds] between Kodak and Xerox, for example, why take Kodak, when there's not a union member present in the whole goddam place. . . . We should go with Xerox," a unionized company.[61]

Masterminding ACTWU's organizing strategies was Bill Patterson, who had a knack for finding a company's vulnerable spots. For example, in 1987 the union was unable to reach a first contract with Echlin Inc., an auto parts manufacturer. Instead of risking a strike, the union zeroed in on the company's health and safety problems, especially its handling of asbestos, for which Echlin had been investigated and fined earlier in the year. At the shareholders' meeting, ACTWU and its campaign partner, the Carpenters, sponsored proposals demanding the appointment of a committee to study the health hazards and liabilities associated with the company's asbestos use, an early instance of organizers using regulatory profiles to find violations that could be used against a firm. The proposals received between 22 and 31 percent of shareholder votes, a decent initial showing. Patterson hired several permanent staff to analyze a firm's financial data and relationships. He had the idea for creating what was called the LongView Fund as an investment vehicle for Taft-Hartley plans. Launched in 1992 by Amalgamated Bank, which still was owned by ACTWU, LongView engaged with its portfolio companies on corporate governance and social issues. Of Patterson's many ideas, LongView was one of the best.

ACTWU and the Carpenters joined forces again in 1990 to go after Kodak. The firm recently had been levied with criminal penalties for toxic chemical leaks at its Rochester, New York factories. The union filed a proxy resolution demanding that Kodak create permanent committees on worker safety and environmental quality. Calling this their "Proxies for Health Campaign," the resolution alluded to other environmental scandals, such as the *Exxon Valdez* oil spill of the previous year, which had cost Exxon billions. Patterson said that Kodak had to change its decision-making "in ways which increase shareholder value," possibly the first time that someone from the labor movement had endorsed the new financial mantra.[62]

In 1989, partly in response to the *Valdez* disaster, environmental organizations and socially responsible investors created CERES, which relied on shareholder activism to promote exemplary environmental practices. CERES produced a ten-point platform known as the Valdez Principles, whose primary demand was for corporations to disclose more information on their environmental impacts. That year CERES offered twenty-three shareholder resolutions, mostly directed at chemical and energy companies. A founding member of CERES was the AFL-CIO's Industrial Union Department, an early instance of a green–labor alliance. Major public pension plans—including CalPERS, CalSTRS (California State Teachers' Retirement System), and the New York City pension funds—endorsed the principles and participated in CERES. Patterson understood that raising environmental issues at Kodak would garner support from CERES members.[63]

Another problem for labor were leveraged buyouts (LBOs), which became prevalent in textiles during the 1980s. At Cannon Mills, an LBO by financier David Murdock resulted in mass layoffs and raiding of the pension fund to finance the deal. Patterson, who by then had become ACTWU's national field director, went after the banks that underwrote Murdock, including the Continental Bank of Chicago. ACTWU petitioned the Federal Reserve Bank to protest Continental's acquisition of a small Arizona bank on the grounds that Continental had violated the Community Reinvestment Act. The Fed blocked the acquisition. ACTWU tried to embarrass J. P. Morgan, a major lender to textile firms, by publicizing the bank's activities in South Africa. The union formed a coalition with ten anti-apartheid church groups who filed shareholder resolutions at Morgan.[64]

The largest corporate campaign of the 1980s—a joint effort of the United Food & Commercial Workers union (UFCW) and the SEIU—took place at Beverly Enterprises, a nationwide chain of nursing homes that employed

60,000 low-paid workers. In the past, SEIU relied on conventional NLRB procedures for union elections. Beverly had responded by unlawfully threatening union supporters and dismissing union activists. Whenever the union won a representation election at a Beverly nursing home, management would contest the results through a labyrinth of lengthy legal appeals and refuse to bargain in good faith. Only one in four election wins resulted in a collective bargaining agreement. There was a clear need for an alternative to the organizing approach supervised by the National Labor Relations Board.[65]

SEIU launched the Beverly campaign in 1982, two years after John Sweeney became the union's president. Led by a talented organizer, Andrew Stern, the union experimented with new organizing tactics that circumvented the NLRB. One way was to pressure management by publicly questioning patient care quality and legal compliance. It caught the attention of nursing home regulators in several states. At a Beverly shareholders' meeting in 1983, SEIU sponsored a resolution to establish a committee to monitor patient care. Although it failed to win majority support, some institutional investors voted for it. The approach was tactically brilliant: It highlighted management's irresponsibility, strengthened employee support for the union, and demonstrated to management that, if institutional investors hopped on board, fighting the union might be costlier than imagined. SEIU also relied on its political influence to contest Beverly's attempts to license new nursing homes and to use municipal bonds to pay for them.

In 1984, Beverly threw in the towel, pledging not to oppose SEIU and to create a joint labor–management committee on patient care. But the agreement failed to hold. The fight between SEIU and Beverly continued for years.

Other unions emulated the Beverly approach. To assist their campaigns, the AFL-CIO published two manuals: on conducting corporate investigations (1981) and on what it called "coordinated comprehensive campaigns" (1985). It sponsored a 1988 conference featuring Joe Uehlein, one of the AFL-CIO's savviest organizing strategists, who emphasized that "power is not only what the union has, but what the company thinks it has."[66]

Shareholder Primacy

From 1980 through 2007, the United States experienced a fifteen-fold jump in the value of its financial assets. Contributing to the rise were the pensions and other retirement savings of the baby boomers. Equities held by defined-benefit pension funds were the fastest-growing portion, rising from 4 percent of the value of all domestic equities in 1960 to 27 percent in 1990.[67]

With the swell of assets came calls to remake corporate governance. Shareholder primacy was back in fashion. One could say that the revival began with the celebrated libertarian economist Milton Friedman. His best-selling book *Capitalism and Freedom* (1962) took aim at the managerialist philosophy that Kaysen and his colleagues found prevalent. The problem, according to Friedman, was that managerialism gave too much leeway to executives to decide how to spend the company's money. Executives, he said, had a single responsibility: to enrich shareholders by maximizing stock prices. Friedman said that his formula rested on two caveats: that markets were competitive and that they were free of deception. They are what economists call "heroic assumptions," more honored in the breach than the observance.[68]

Two decades later, economists like Harvard's Michael Jensen refined and extended Friedman's ideas while ignoring his caveats. Putting shareholders first, they said, would lead to higher productivity and shake off America's industrial malaise. Executives were overpaying workers and wasting funds on unprofitable acquisitions. They enlarged their companies not out of business necessity but because it justified higher salaries and created career opportunities for themselves. Only shareholders, not other stakeholders, deserved primacy because, it was alleged, they are the firm's "residual claimants"—they stand last in line if a firm goes bankrupt and thus have the most to lose were the worst to occur.[69]

The reappearance of shareholder primacy had an economic rationale, although some proponents, like Friedman, intended primacy as a rebuke of the liberal view that corporations were socially embedded. Wealthy conservatives such as Richard Scaife and John M. Olin understood the stakes and financed the dissemination of libertarian ideas about business through think tanks, universities, and educational programs for judges and attorney generals.[70]

Two influential critics of primacy doctrines are Margaret Blair, an economist and legal scholar at Vanderbilt University, and the late Lynn Stout, who taught law at Cornell University and UCLA. They observe that, in the real world, companies operate as a team that includes executives, employees, creditors, suppliers, and shareholders. Each team member has made firm-specific investments that are nonseparable, meaning that the firm can't create value without contributions from all of them: Everyone rises or hangs together. It is unlikely that team members will invest unless there is a neutral mediator to divvy up what's produced by the team. In practice, this entity is the board of directors. If the board consistently favors shareholders, it will be difficult to hold the team together. Shareholders, then, are *not* principals, and executives are not their agents. A telling fact is that two-thirds of firms planning to go public adopt some kind of anti-takeover provision, according to Blair and Stout, to "reassure the firm's managers and employees that their futures rest in the hands of the board of directors, rather than with shareholders." Later, Stout added that "shareholders are only one of several groups that can be described as 'residual claimants' or 'residual risk bearers.'"[71]

An alleged advantage of shareholder primacy is that it offers a single maximand: the price of a company's stock. But shareholders are not a unified body with common interests: Some buy and hold for the long term, like pension plans that invest in index funds, while others are transient speculators. Some investors are diversified, others are not. Even institutional investors—banks, pension plans, insurance companies, mutual funds, and so on—have different objectives that depend on their time horizons and portfolio structure. If shareholders possess divergent interests, says UCLA law professor Iman Anabtawi, maximizing shareholder value is as complicated as using other maximands.[72]

———

When Friedman wrote in 1962, individuals directly owned 85 percent of shares in US corporations. What he failed to reckon with was the then-ongoing shift in ownership from individuals to institutions. Thirty years later, the growth of retirement savings and mutual funds had led to institutions owning the majority of shares. With this came the power to mold corporate governance to their liking, and what they liked was shareholder primacy.

2

The CalPERS Era

A TRANSFORMATION IN STOCK ownership was underway during the 1970s. Pension plans bulked up their holdings, followed by mutual funds. Come the following decade, the public plans, epitomized by CalPERS, began to flex their muscles. They would mount a head-on challenge to postwar institutions of corporate governance.

This chapter considers the causes of activism's emergence. Shareholder primacy—as an economic norm and a set of practices—took hold of investors and conventional wisdom. Woven throughout the chapter is a critical analysis of the activist agenda and its consequences for players competing in the corporate governance game. The chapter ends with a primer on pension funds for those unfamiliar with them.

The Early Days

Robert A. G. Monks, a pivotal figure in the rise of pension fund activism, was a Harvard graduate and moderate Republican businessman who had supported attempts to make Harvard invest responsibly in South Africa. Although ambivalent about divestment, he believed that shareholders had a responsibility to encourage corporations to behave ethically wherever they did business. Precisely what constituted ethical behavior was not clear, however. For Monks, it did not mean a managerialist model in which companies were responsible to suppliers, customers, employees, and communities. While companies might consider these groups, he said, their primary accountability was to shareholders. In turn, shareholders, particularly large institutions, had a responsibility to be active "corporate citizens."[1]

During this era of hostile takeovers, institutional investors frequently failed to vote their proxies, which Monks considered a dereliction of duty. Those investors, said Monks, should "take the lead in proposing and passing provisions which ensure, before takeover battles occur, that all [takeover defenses] are submitted either to the shareholders or to an outside committee for their approval," a formulation that bypassed boards and, he argued, would result in greater value for investors. Monks had a bully pulpit, first in a two-year stint in the mid-1980s as head of the federal government's Office of Pension and Welfare Benefit Programs, which supervised the nation's private pension plans, and later as an owner of the proxy advisory firm, Institutional Shareholder Services (ISS).[2]

What was special about institutional investors? Monks said that their long-term liabilities gave them the perspective to weigh short-term gains carefully, like those from a hostile bid, against a company's long-term needs. In addition, institutional owners were "an adequate proxy for the national interest" because they indirectly represented millions of citizens.[3]

Monks had his detractors. Management attorney Martin Lipton called him "the quintessential shareholder activist seeking maximization of shareholder value in the short run." Louis Lowenstein, a Columbia University law professor, saw Monks as a utopian idealist. When Monks said that activism was "a cooperative long-term arrangement between managers and owners," Lowenstein replied that Monks failed to see the reality—that institutional investors were "playing a short-term speculative game." Despite his critics, Monks remained steadfast in advocating his ideas.[4]

Another important figure was Jesse "Big Daddy" Unruh. As California's treasurer from 1975 to 1987, Unruh was a trustee of both CalPERS and Cal-STRS (California State Teachers' Retirement System), the state's giant pension plans. Unruh was a wheeler-dealer in Sacramento and a liberal Democrat who'd written a landmark anti-discrimination law. It was during his tenure that CalPERS co-sponsored a proposal demanding that Xerox terminate its dealings with South Africa and in 1987, CalPERS stopped investing in corporations doing business there. Unruh's combination of calculatedness and conscience stamped CalPERS and CalSTRS. In recent years, CalPERS has asked companies to report on their liabilities associated with climate change and to improve their records on human rights. Phil Angelides, California's treasurer and a member of the CalPERS board, commented, "People in the investment industry often want to put up a wall between [social investing and performance] but they are related."[5]

CalPERS transformed itself in the 1980s from a sleepy organization with much of its portfolio invested in bonds to an active shareholder with large equity holdings. Thirty years earlier, state and local pension funds had only a tenth of 1 percent of their assets in stocks. Over time the proportion increased, although California had a requirement that constrained stock holdings to 25 percent of the CalPERS portfolio. After the limit was lifted in 1984, the equity allocation rose steadily.

The year 1984 saw the Bass brothers of Texas make a hostile bid for oil giant Texaco. To stave them off, Texaco paid a premium of $138 million for the Bass shares—an instance of greenmail. Unruh wasn't opposed to the bid but he was infuriated by management's reaction to it, which benefited some shareholders but excluded others, one of them being CalPERS, even though the pension fund was the company's largest investor. He unsuccessfully tried to block the payoff. Unruh drew two lessons from the episode: Executives don't care about long-term shareholders, and public pension funds needed to fight back.[6]

Unruh convened meetings that led to the formation of the Council of Institutional Investors (CII) in 1985. Its founding members were large public pension plans from around the nation. Among CII's first accomplishments was to produce a "shareholder bill of rights" demanding that executives consult with major shareholders, give equal voting rights to all, and appoint independent directors. Later, CII would seek reforms in the proxy process to make it easier to file dissident proposals. Robert Monks, who spoke at CII's first conference, promised Unruh to seek Republican support for CII to prevent the impression that it was merely "some Democrats trying to backdoor socialize [American business]." Working with Unruh was an attorney named Sarah Teslik, who became CII's first director. CalPERS lent staff and provided financial assistance to CII. It was a small world, but the assets involved were anything but. A Wall Street executive said of CII, "[I]f the institutions start speaking with one voice, they could become a financial OPEC."[7]

Present at the beginning was New York City's comptroller Harrison Goldin, who oversaw the city's pension plans. Goldin and Unruh, with ties to the labor movement, invited the Carpenters union, which had some big multiemployer plans, to join CII. Unruh, however, believed that the individuals representing CII's member plans should not be union activists but instead the experts who staffed them.

Collective Clout

By the mid-1990s, CII had grown to ninety-nine members, of whom the dominant group were fifty-one state and local pension plans. Other members included twenty multiemployer plans, four union staff plans (including the

AFL-CIO and the Steelworkers), two endowments, and twenty-two corporate plans (including General Motors, Hilton, Kodak, and Pfizer). CII also had as nonvoting members a number of securities and law firms, all eager to obtain business from the plans.[8]

Charles Valdes of CalPERS invited corporate plans to join the council. Labor, however, feared that having corporate members would undermine CII's assertiveness, suspecting that they would share with other firms confidential information presented at CII's biannual conferences, where members presented their blueprints for the coming season of shareholder meetings.[9]

Union activists like Bill Patterson of the Teamsters successfully prevented corporate-plan representatives from holding leadership positions in CII. After several years, the corporate plans threatened to withdraw, which was not an empty threat as they provided the bulk of CII's dues. With the help of CalPERS, an additional chairmanship was created for corporate plans, the compromise being that Patterson would be the co-chairman. Each type of plan set up its own caucuses.[10]

Close to a hundred corporate plans founded their own organization in 1985—the Committee on the Investment of Employee Benefit Assets (CIEBA). Primarily a lobbying group, CIEBA could be put to other uses, as when several CEOs of member companies launched a letter-writing campaign in 1987 urging other members to back management in proxy contests. Michael Useem found that corporate plans were one-fourth to one-half less likely than state and local plans to support shareholder resolutions directed against management. When it came to proposals permitting shareholders to vote on golden parachutes, there was zero support from corporate plans, whereas nearly 90 percent of public plans favored them.[11]

In the postwar years, the United States was portrayed as having relatively dispersed ownership as compared to countries like France, Germany, and Japan, where blockholders—singly or combined—owned enough shares to affect a company's behavior. But by the 1990s, the United States had its own form of blockholding: the shares owned by large institutional investors, especially pension funds and giant financial services corporations like Fidelity.

CII's pension funds alone accounted for around 5–6 percent of US equities. If they acted in unison—and allied with other institutional investors—they might obtain a majority of shareholder votes. Institutional holdings weren't evenly distributed but instead were concentrated in the largest 1,000 corporations, which accounted for 60 percent of shares at market value. In other words, an alliance of activist investors might easily double the 5 percent of shares considered the threshold for blockholding. What we know about block-holders in other parts of the world is that they extract value from the firms they own. The same proved true of the new blockholders, who marched under the banner of shareholder primacy.[12]

CII was put to an early test by events at Phillips Petroleum. T. Boone Pick-ens, one of the era's iconic raiders, attempted a hostile takeover that the com-pany deflected by buying his shares at a premium. A few months later, another raider—Carl Icahn—also went after Phillips. To protect the company, Martin Lipton devised the infamous "poison pill": Should anyone acquire more than 30 percent of outstanding stock, shareholders would be allowed to convert their stock to debt, leaving Phillips overleveraged and a less attractive target. Icahn extended to shareholders a juicy tender offer developed by Michael Milken's firm, Drexel Lambert, the originator of junk bonds. In the end, CII members favored Icahn and opposed management's anti-takeover strategy.

CII was then challenged by events at General Motors that began in 1986. H. Ross Perot, a GM board member, had for several years attacked the car maker for strategic errors in response to the upsurge in Japanese vehicle imports. GM's CEO, Roger Smith, decided to oust Perot from the board and paid $750 million to buy back Perot's stock. Perot resigned, but, instead of going quietly into the night, he kept up attacks on management. Harrison Goldin invited Perot and Smith to speak at a CII meeting. Smith infuriated members by send-ing his underlings. Goldin hinted that maybe Smith should be the one removed from his post as board chairman.

Under pressure, Roger Smith resigned in 1990 to be replaced by Robert Stempel, an engineer and GM lifer. Activist investors, including some of CII's public pension plans, soon forced Stempel out and replaced him with Jack Smith, who, despite being an insider, heard the message that investors were sending. Soon thereafter Smith raised shareholder payouts and expanded the use of stock-based compensation for executives. The corporate world was un-settled by the prospect of shareholder challenges to management. An execu-tive said there were still "some hard-core boards and CEOs who have that old Victorian feeling that shareholders should be seen and not heard."[13]

CII engaged with legislators and regulators around the issue of shareholder rights. Sarah Teslik would regularly get calls from both parties in Congress seeking information about investor concerns. She led a successful attempt to permit pension plan representatives to sit on creditors' committees at bank-rupt companies. Teslik found that companies were prepared to fight back against attempts to change the balance of power using dirty tricks like "leaking bad things about me to the press, and they will do that with shareholder money." CII provided advice to members about participating in shareholder litigation as it did with several derivative lawsuits.[14]

CalPERS was the most visible and vocal member of the CII in its early days. Dale Hanson, who became CEO of CalPERS in 1987, thought that the best way to raise portfolio returns was to demand that companies adopt governance practices favoring shareholders. He identified three main governance problems: the clash between shareholder interests and executive priorities, the failure of directors to be independent of CEOs, and the inability of shareholders to select directors more to their liking. Richard Koppes, the CalPERS general counsel, saw CII's role as "to goad the boards into doing their job. Boards cannot run companies. They cannot micromanage. But they can criticize business strategy and executive compensation."[15]

Among the forces driving the public plans was the need for sufficient assets to pay for baby-boomer retirements. One must be careful here, however, in assuming that public pension activism neatly correlated with funding needs. The peak years of activism coincided with the stock market's ebullience. State and local plans had funding ratios (the assets needed to cover future liabilities) of over 90 percent during the 1990s, and, although there was underfunding, it was unevenly distributed across states and localities.[16]

Pension plans liked index funds. They provided a cheaper way of tracking the market than directly owning shares. Aside from their low cost, index funds offered political cover for pension trustees, who could defend poor returns by saying, "We're not any worse than the market average." Pension plans cited index funds as justification for their activism. Reforming corporate governance, they said, was the only way to improve returns on index funds, whose individual holdings they were unable to sell. Among state and local plans, the indexed portion of their stock portfolios doubled between the mid-1980s and mid-1990s.[17]

CalPERS initially challenged companies with the most egregious governance practices. Later it aimed at those with governance defects *and* poor stock performance. Only those in the bottom performance quartile (measured over five years) were targeted because they could not argue, as better performers might, that "if it ain't broke, don't fix it." From the bottom quartile, a group of fifty was selected (the "Failing Fifty") based on additional screens: low scores on a corporate governance index and high levels of institutional ownership. The index favored board independence, separation of the CEO and chairman positions, and stock-based executive pay. CalPERS culled from its Failing Fifty a "focus list" of around a dozen firms where it intended to file proposals and meet with boards and management. The media widely broadcast this list, which contained names of blue-ribbon firms such as Alcoa and American Airlines. Note that the methodology created the impression that poor governance caused poor performance, although, as we will see, evidence to prove the assertion is ambiguous.[18]

Complaining that proxy rules were stacked against active owners, CalPERS sought broader shareholder rights at Boise-Cascade, demanding that the corporation revise its rules to give dissident proposals a better chance. It asked Hercules Chemical, Whirlpool, and others to keep proxy voting confidential. At Avon, Sears, and Texaco, it demanded the creation of shareholder advisory committees composed of large, long-term shareholders who would be invited to private meetings with directors. In a number of cases—including at American Express, IBM, K-Mart, Kodak, and Westinghouse—CalPERS led highly publicized and successful campaigns to remove CEOs.

Business leaders were furious. As Hanson put it, confronting directors and CEOs "was equivalent to flatulence in church." In 1988, the Business Roundtable's corporate governance committee met with Hanson and other pension managers in an attempt to dampen their activities. Some business leaders turned to California's Republican governor Pete Wilson for help. In 1991, Wilson responded with a scheme to tap CalPERS's holdings to close a state budget deficit and to replace its board with his own appointees. Hanson asserted that "[Wilson] made a promise to business that he will put a more compliant board in there so we will not be so active in corporate governance." Wilson saw an opportunity to diminish the power of the state's public unions.[19]

Although California voters rejected the Wilson plan, it put a damper on CalPERS. Now, instead of publicly mentioning a target, CalPERS first sent a confidential letter asking to meet with the company. At the same time, it would discreetly put into motion the machinery for a shareholder proposal. If management and the board agreed to go along with CalPERS, even partially, CalPERS promised to withdraw the proposal. When none of the firms cooperated with CalPERS, it released their names to the media and threatened to vote against their incumbent directors. Among them were IBM, Salomon Brothers, and Time Warner.[20]

An important point to keep in mind is that shareholder resolutions are merely advisory ("precatory"). Even if the vote is 90 percent in favor, management need not change anything. There may, however, be a resubmission. Experts differ, but the consensus is that a vote against management that receives 20–30 percent support will invite scrutiny from proxy advisors who tell institutional investors how to vote. A close vote is in the range of 40–60 percent and it will cause management and boards to be concerned. Anything above that is a slap in the face for the company.

CalPERS's tactics reflected the idiosyncrasies of Hanson and Koppes. Other big pension plans, such as CalSTRS and the New York plans, were not nearly as media-oriented or forceful.[21] After Hanson left CalPERS in 1994, followed by Koppes, CalPERS preferred to work behind the scenes. This disappointed activists like Monks, who rued Hanson's and Koppes's absence: "I'm sorry they're not around to push the envelope with me." It also bothered Koppes, who, two years after leaving CalPERS, said, "Five years of going to the press and now they don't go. You don't hear about CalPERS. If you don't keep the constructive tension, that's unfortunate."[22]

The people then running CalPERS, including president William Crist and general counsel Kayla Gillan, disputed Koppes's claim that CalPERS had lost its bite. Said Crist, "What we do now at CalPERS and have done for the last number of years is we'll talk a lot . . . [so] there are many companies that never make the focus list and never make the press, because between the time we start talking to them and the time we do that [publicly mention their name] they change."[23]

The Cookbook

In 1994, CalPERS codified its principles of corporate governance. Others were doing the same thing: CII and TIAA-CREF in the United States; the Cadbury, Greenbury, and Hampel committees in the United Kingdom; and the Organization for Economic Co-operation and Development (OECD). The codes were disseminated through organizations like CII and the International Corporate Governance Network, which CalPERS created when it was ramping up its international portfolio. There were nuances that distinguished the codes, but for the most part they contained the same ideas. I call these codes "the cookbook" and their specific recommendations "recipes." Although the era's cookbook often was portrayed as protection for shareholders, the claim had its limits. Institutional shareholders, like blockholders, sought privileges that would not extend to smallholders.[24]

Shareholder primacy was the matrix from which the recipes derived. They covered the main areas of corporate governance: takeovers, boards, executive compensation, transparency, and shareholder rights. CalPERS intended to grade companies on its principles, publicize the results, and prod recalcitrants to change. The idea met with a barrage of criticism. A *New York Times* analysis of Fortune 1000 companies found that only Texas Instruments met all of CalPERS's criteria. In its own statistical analysis, the *Times* did not detect any pattern linking governance recipes to stock performance. In 1998, CalPERS published a revised document that dropped several controversial ideas (such as a limit on the number of directors older than seventy).[25]

CalPERS experienced blowback outside the United States. The guidelines proved a tough sell in countries where governance did not follow Anglo-American assumptions. When William Crist went to Paris in 2000 to promote the CalPERS principles, the president of France, Jacques Chirac, said that French workers were being asked to make sacrifices simply to "safeguard the benefits of . . . California pensioners."[26]

The cookbook's proponents claimed that its adoption raised stock prices. Did the recipes produce these results? The evidence, as noted, is inconclusive, and sometimes negative, as shown in the following sections. Note that most of the studies discussed here use stock price as the performance criterion, measured over the brief period covered in event history analysis.

The late Lynn Stout made mincemeat of the claim that stock price (or the return on equities, ROE) was the most appropriate measure. Stock prices do not incorporate private information that managers keep from others, driving a wedge between price and the firm's actual value. Writing after the dot-com and Enron-era scandals, Stout had good reason to think that informational asymmetries were pervasive. There are myriad other ways to measure performance besides stock prices, including return on assets (ROA) or investment (ROI), economic value-added (EVA), efficiency, and stakeholder-type measures like the Balanced Scorecard. Because the cookbook's authors intended it as stimulus to share prices, it's relevant to draw on studies that evaluate the relationship.[27]

Takeover Defenses

Reducing takeover barriers was a key objective of shareholder activism. Takeover-related recipes included the right to vote on poison pills and golden parachutes, the right to call takeover-related shareholder meetings, and the elimination of staggered boards (also called classified boards).

There is empirical support for these ideas. A widely cited study by Harvard's Paul Gompers and colleagues finds a strong positive relation between an index of twenty-four governance recipes (almost all contained in the CalPERS cookbook) and stock returns during the 1990s. The study grouped the items into five categories, most of them takeover-related. Correlation is not causation, and it's possible that better-performing companies adopted the recipes because they had fewer concerns about hostile bids. A replication study by Lucian Bebchuk, also at Harvard, and his colleagues found that only six of the items in the Gompers index are related to financial performance. Of those, four have to with shareholder voting rights, while the other two relate to takeovers: eliminating poison pills and voting on golden parachutes. Bebchuk later found that any significant association between shareholder returns and the removal of takeover barriers disappeared after 1999.[28]

Other studies do not support a relationship between stock returns and the removal of takeover defenses. Economists Sanjai Bhagat and Brian Bolton reanalyzed the Gompers and Bebchuk indices and found that none of their components was associated with future stock returns. The inference is that takeover defenses have not only costs but benefits. While some poorly performing companies might improve following a takeover, on average, one year after a buyout, returns fell.[29]

Boards

Another part of the cookbook seeks to draw boards away from CEOs and closer to shareholders. Here the recipes include a greater number of independent directors, separating board chairs and CEOs, independent board chairs, a majority of independents on key board committees, majority voting (versus plurality voting), and declassified boards (allowing replacement of an entire board). (See table 2.1.)

Findings about the correlation between these recipes and shareholder returns are inconclusive at best.[30] So-called independent directors tend to be current and former CEOs or other highly paid individuals. Social similarity causes deference, clubbiness, and conformity; directors are reluctant to say that the CEO is overpaid. Moreover, independence is no guarantee of competence. When independent directors from major corporations attended a workshop at the University of Chicago, only 32 percent were able to supply correct answers to a basic accounting test. One of the questions asked for a definition of retained earnings, which fewer than 20 percent answered correctly.

TABLE 2.1. Voted Corporate Governance Proposals by
Topic, 1996–2012*

BOARDS [30%]	1,355
Majority vote to elect directors	342
Independent board chair	341
Cumulative voting	241
EXECUTIVE PAY [28%]	1,247
Advisory vote on pay	226
Link pay to stock performance	156
Restrict executive pay	120
TAKEOVERS [33%]	1,494
Repeal classified boards	563
Redeem or vote on poison pills	318
Shareholder right to call special meetings	185
OTHER [9%]	393*
TOTAL	4,489

Source: Georgeson, *Annual Corporate Governance Review (ACGR)*.

* The table shows the number of voted governance-related
proposals by category for S&P 1500 companies. Figures in brackets
are a category's share of proposals.

Jay Lorsch, Harvard Business School professor and an expert on corporate boards, criticizes the recipes for board independence as mechanistic. He writes that "independence is more than a legal definition[;] it's a psychological condition." A director's willingness to challenge management requires an atmosphere that blends assertiveness with cooperation. To get there, boards need directors who have an ability to communicate, manage conflict, and tolerate dissent. Inside (non-independent) directors have been shown to be more committed to their directorial duties than independents and more knowledgeable about the firm's idiosyncrasies, especially those that aren't easily quantified.[31]

Inside–Outside

Activist investors lauded companies that hired outsiders to replace CEOs promoted from within. Outsiders were hailed as "corporate saviors," a phrase coined by Harvard Business School professor Rakesh Khurana. Ostensibly, outsiders would find it easier to implement drastic cutbacks because they had no allegiances to a company's business units and their employees, or to other managers. In 1980, fewer than 5 percent of all CEO successors in the 850 largest

US corporations had come from the outside. The proportion of outsider CEOs increased to 10 percent in 1995 and then up to 30 percent in 2005. Raiders fighting for control were the harshest critics of insiders, people who might oppose them. Carl Icahn said, "What's going on in companies all over the country these days is absurd. It's like a corporate welfare state. We're supporting managers who produce nothing. No, it's really worse than that. Not only are we paying those drones not to produce, but we're paying them to muck up the works."[32]

Unfortunately, the belief in saviors is wishful thinking. Shareholder returns generally are higher during an insider's tenure, as was the case in nine of the twelve years from 2000 to 2011. Mobile outsiders are less willing to tackle difficult problems if the results will not become apparent before they leave for a new position. Even when there are benefits to hiring an outsider, they are reduced when members of the top management team depart after an outsider is hired, a frequent occurrence. It takes time to bring replacements up to speed; in business, time is money.[33]

Executive Compensation

The idea of compensating executives with stock-based pay instead of salaries received strong support from prominent economists like Michael Jensen and Kevin J. Murphy. "Corporate America," they wrote in 1990, "pays its most important leaders like bureaucrats." Tying pay to stock prices and firing CEOs if they failed to raise them were, they said, "the most effective tools for aligning executive and shareholder interests." Institutional investors seconded the idea. Jon Lukomnik, then the deputy comptroller for New York City's plans, said, mistakenly, that "shareholders just don't own a piece of paper but actually own the company. The whole thing is you don't want management to have a different set of incentives financially than the shareholders have. You want to align the business of managers with shareholders so they both prosper together." The 1990s marked the moment when stock options replaced salaries as the main component of executive pay.[34]

Whether stock-based pay leads to higher share prices is a vexed issue. While some studies find a positive association between stock returns and the portion of executive pay based on share prices, others find the relationship to be weak or null. A downside to stock-based pay is the incentive it creates for executives to manage earnings to raise the value of their stock options, along with problems like options backdating. A recent literature survey concludes, "The failure to document a consistent and robust relationship between executive pay and equity returns has frustrated scholars and practitioners for over three quarters of a century."[35]

Transparency

Active owners of all stripes demanded that companies supply more and better data of all kinds. Opaque compensation methods allowed executives to pad their pockets, while inadequate financial reporting hid poor results and manipulated earnings, a prime example being Enron. Transparency consistently has been found to improve various measures of performance, including efficiency. Transparency is the most potent part of the cookbook, as Brandeis understood. However, it is uncertain whether it is best achieved by regulation or through private orderings.[36]

Shareholder activists had deep convictions that the cookbook was effective even if studies failed to confirm it. Said William Crist, "There's so much contradictory evidence. I don't believe in any of the studies. I believe [corporate governance reform] is working. Maybe it's an act of faith, but we're changing corporate culture. More competition. More efficiency. Not boards sleeping or playing golf and drinking fine wines." Yet while professing disdain for research, CalPERS was quick to publicize studies showing positive results from its activism.[37]

Activism's Consequences

CalPERS often cited a study by Wilshire Associates, an investment advisor to CalPERS, showing an improvement in shareholder returns at companies it targeted, a phenomenon labeled "the CalPERS effect." Wilshire Associates first conducted the study in 1992 at CalPERS's request and repeated it several times in later years.[38]

However, other studies were less favorable to CalPERS and to activism more generally. Yale law professor Roberta Romano distinguished between activism based on proxy proposals and that based on nonproxy activity such as focus lists, private letters, and direct negotiations. The relationship between proposals and share performance is insignificant in all studies Romano reviewed. The evidence on nonproxy activity is inconclusive.[39]

Buybacks

For most of the twentieth century, dividends were the preferred method for returning cash to shareholders. Share repurchases, also known as buybacks, were another way of accomplishing this. The SEC first approved their use in 1982, despite previous SEC concerns that buybacks could be used to manipulate share prices. John Shad, the head of the SEC at the time, was a Reagan appointee and former executive at E.F. Hutton, a Wall Street brokerage. Shad liked buybacks because he believed they lifted share prices. At CII's first meeting in 1985, he told the audience that shareholders were "the principal constituency the commission was created to serve." What he didn't mention was that buybacks also benefited brokerages.

After the rule change, buybacks increased and then took off in the mid-1990s. The timing is telling: Rising payouts were associated with the ascent of shareholder primacy. They were largest at companies whose dominant owners were institutional investors with portfolios combining indexed and actively traded shares. Pension funds are an example. The trend continued over the following decades, and buybacks grew more important as compared to dividends.[40]

A problem with buybacks were stock options tying executive bonuses to earnings-per-share (EPS) targets. Because buybacks arithmetically raise EPS and often are followed by a jump in share prices, they allow CEOs to spike their pay while keeping investors happy. Buybacks were the apotheosis of financialized corporate governance.[41] But as economists are fond of saying, there's no such thing as a free lunch. The money for buybacks had to come from somewhere. Higher payouts were associated with lower levels of investment, R&D, wages, and employment.[42]

Consider Home Depot, which regularly bought back its shares. In 2017, buybacks amounted to $22 billion, or a little over $13,000 per employee. That year the median Home Depot employee earned $21,000, slightly below the poverty line for a four-person household. Even if only half those buybacks had gone to Home Depot workers, their earnings would have risen by more than 40 percent. There was nothing unusual about Home Depot among the S&P 500.[43]

What was good for shareholders wasn't always good for a company's long-term health. When GM announced its first major buyback in 1987, this at the behest of activist investors, analysts urged the automaker to retain the funds to finance development of energy-efficient vehicles. However, the head of New York City's pension fund, Harrison J. Goldin, celebrated GM's decision: "This is a dramatic demonstration of the company's new commitment and concern for shareholders. And as far as we're concerned, this is a good sign." By then, the finance people had come to dominate GM's upper echelons, displacing those from production and engineering. The same happened elsewhere.[44]

Under pressure from CalPERS and corporate raider Kirk Kerkorian, GM again bought back $13 billion of its own stock in 1996 and paid an additional $13 billion in dividends. Stephen Yokich, president of the Autoworkers union, said that Kerkorian's plan to siphon cash out of GM was of concern to the union. It was money that GM could reinvest or share with its workers, who, since the late 1970s, no longer received annual wage increases tied to productivity, as under the Treaty of Detroit. Yokich was right to have been wary. In the 1996 agreement with GM negotiated by the Autoworkers, starting pay was cut by 20 percent.[45]

Toyota, like other Japanese companies, took a different approach. Like GM it had sizable cash holdings. Foreign investors, including CalPERS, demanded that Toyota hand over some of its cash to them. The company's president, Hiroshi Okuda, told them that shareholder interests would be best served if Toyota invested the money in research and development (R&D). Toyota went on to develop the Prius hybrid and it improved its vehicles across market segments. In comparison, GM filed for bankruptcy in 2009.[46]

The one sure thing that the cookbook produced was more power and money for shareholders and, via stock-based pay, for executives. A study by a group of economists from Berkeley, MIT, and NYU finds that from 1989 through 2017, corporations created $34 trillion of real equity wealth. Nearly half of it was a reallocation from workers to shareholders. When unions were present in a corporation, they curtailed the size of its buybacks. But unions did not exist in most companies.[47]

Hostile Takeovers

The 1980s were when savvy corporate raiders like T. Boone Pickens and Kirk Kerkorian developed a new way of getting rich. They realized that with relatively little of their own money, they would be able to take control of a company by buying up its stock at a premium. The money for paying shareholders to tender their shares came from several sources: the acquisition's own cash, junk bonds that later would be paid back with debt heaped on the company, and assets from the pension fund. The next step was selling parts of the company, which often went for a premium.

Hostile takeovers took the business world by storm. About one out of four major corporations received hostile bids during the eighties. Often they were multidivisional (M-form) companies or their cousin, the conglomerate, whose multiple units would individually be put on the block. Historian Alfred D. Chandler Jr. and economist Oliver Williamson once had lauded the efficiency of M-form corporations of the postwar era. But a different view, put forth by President Reagan's Council of Economic Advisers in 1985, was that using takeovers to break up companies would "improve efficiency, transfer scarce resources to higher valued uses, and stimulate effective corporate management."[48]

When boards rejected hostile bids, their justification was to protect a corporation's long-run competitiveness from the raiders' short-term predation. Eliminating those defenses and reorienting boards to prioritize shareholders were crucial for the raiders, but first the courts had to be persuaded. Initially, in the *Unocal* decision (1985), the Delaware courts granted boards the discretion to consider a bid's impact on "constituencies" including creditors, customers, employees, and the community—not only shareholders. There were legal scholars who agreed. At law, wrote Melvin Eisenberg, the board "is conceived to be an independent institution, not directly responsible to shareholders in the manner of an agent." Directors, said Lynn Stout, have "the discretion to pursue goals other than shareholder value. . . . [M]aximizing shareholder value is not a requirement . . . just one possible corporate objective out of many."

But a year later, in the *Revlon* case (1986), the court placed tight constraints on boards. If a takeover were inevitable—an end-game situation—the board's obligation was to secure the highest offer from the bidder, full stop.[49]

Workers had reason to be worried about hostile takeovers. Layoffs, according to a study by economists Sanjai Bhagat, Andrei Shleifer, and Robert Vishny, accounted for perhaps 11–26 percent of the takeover premium. Fifteen percent of hostile takeovers, twice the level for friendly takeovers, were followed by raids (reversions) on allegedly overfunded pension plans within the next two years. Reversions added another 11 percent to the takeover premium.

Then there were pay cuts. After Carl Icahn took over TWA, pay cuts effected a transfer from employees to shareholders amounting to one-and-a-half times the takeover premium. Unionized workers were hit hard after a takeover. As Harvard economists Andrei Shleifer and Lawrence Summers found, "shareholders gained primarily because stakeholders lost." As with buybacks, this was value reallocation, not value creation. It is what shareholder primacy was all about.[50]

Active owners, including pension funds, greased the skids for hostile bids. CalPERS had ties to the California labor movement and had union members on its board. Yet, although CalPERS officially preferred companies to raise shareholder returns without layoffs, it was not averse to takeovers that led to downsizing and asset divestitures. Patricia Macht, a CalPERS official, told the *New York Times*, "There are companies that are fat, that have not taken a good look at the number of employees they need." Yet downsizing did not boost productivity, which was its alleged rationale.[51]

Pennsylvania was considering a tough antitakeover law in 1990. A group of nine CII pension plans—including CalPERS and CalSTRS—opposed the bill and threatened to sell their shares in corporations based in Pennsylvania should it be enacted. According to disgruntled managers, the public plans welcomed hostile bids and were quick to sell their shares if offered a sufficiently juicy premium. "One good stock killing and they look pretty good for the year," said an executive from Pennsylvania.[52]

Managers allied themselves with unions to lobby for legislative protection against the "barbarians." More than thirty-five states adopted anti-takeover laws that applied to corporations chartered in their state (even Delaware adopted a law, mindful that companies might incorporate in a different state if they felt Delaware was insensitive to their needs). The laws were passed at the behest of companies fearing hostile bids. They differed in their details— some imposed waiting periods for asset sales and others permitted poison pills. But they all relied on *Unocal's* protection of stakeholder interests.[53]

The states that enacted the toughest constituency laws on average had relatively high union-density rates. They were places where labor had friends in government and decent jobs to protect. At the federal level, labor joined with the National Association of Manufacturers to seek federal restrictions on hostile takeovers. Employees, said one investment banker, "have been extraordinarily loyal to management in takeover attempts."[54]

Not all takeovers were hostile. About a third were leveraged deals by the firm's own executives—so-called management buyouts (MBOs)—with financing provided by pension fund reversions and debt. As compared to the situation after a hostile takeover, employees did not fare any better when left to the tender mercies of their bosses. For example, after its MBO, Safeway, the supermarket chain, laid off 63,000 workers (some were rehired into part-time jobs at lower pay). Safeway's CEO said that union concessions were easier to obtain after the MBO than before. The typical MBO candidate was the same as that for a hostile takeover: a company with steady cash flow and unrelated parts that could be sold to raise cash. Part of the firm's cash was used to pay off debt, part went to the deal's advisors, and part went to the corporation's new owners. The evidence does not show that MBOs produced long-term gains in operating efficiency. The primary effect was to redistribute internal resources.[55]

Preemptive worker buyouts occasionally occurred, financed by an employee stock ownership plan (ESOP). Pension assets would be used to capitalize the ESOP, which left some pension plans holding over a third of their assets in company stock, risky for a retirement plan but a deterrent to hostile takeovers. With stock options and careful strategies, managers sometimes ended up owning half of an ESOP's equity. Critics labeled them "MESOPs": management enrichment stock ownership plans.[56]

It's easy to be cynical about executives and their spokespersons, like attorney Martin Lipton, who claimed that management was sensitive to employee concerns. Sounding more like Ralph Nader than a management attorney, Lipton said that corporations were quasi-public entities that should be run for the benefit of long-term shareholders, not for take-the-money-and-run investors. Similarly, in 1990 the Business Roundtable issued a statement on "Corporate Governance and American Competitiveness" which said that in addition to shareholders, corporations had other stakeholders to whom they were beholden. It listed employees, customers, suppliers, creditors, communities, and "society as a whole." These pronouncements were the last gasp of managerialism, an ideology that would fade as executives aligned with shareholders.[57]

Remnants of managerialism are found in some family-controlled companies. They have greater employment stability and fewer layoffs than comparable firms. The differences reflect the family's greater concern with its reputation and its willingness to give up short-term gains to insure that the company will remain a going concern for future generations. Privately owned firms may exhibit similar characteristics. SAS, a private software company, is well known for its generous employee benefits, flexible working hours, and job security. Asked about his firm's generosity, the CEO-founder said, "At many companies the focus is not on the employee or the customer but on the shareholder. The outlook is not for long-term growth but for the next quarter. In today's Wall Street–driven business environment, I think it's difficult for many people to see how employee turnover or employee morale can impact a company's performance over a long period of time. . . . It all comes back to the fact that I don't need to justify SAS's benefits to thousands of shareholders."[58]

A Primer on Pension Plans

Private and public defined-benefit pension plans are less popular than in the past, but they still own 11 percent of the nation's equities, with public plans holding around twice as much as private plans. Shares in US companies owned by defined-benefit pension plans are worth a lot of money, over $3 trillion in 2018.[59]

The labor movement did not invent defined-benefit pensions, but it made them more popular as well as more generous. Access to a defined-benefit pension is one of the main advantages of being a union member, to a greater extent than higher wages. Union members in the private sector are seven times more likely than nonunion workers to participate in a DB plan. The union-nonunion

TABLE 2.2. Pension Plans: Employee Participation Rates (Percentages), 2017*

	Defined benefit	Defined contribution	Either or both
PRIVATE SECTOR			
Union	66	44	82
Nonunion	9	45	47
All Private	15	44	50
STATE AND LOCAL GOVERNMENT			
Union	80	12	83
Nonunion	69	19	77
All Civilian Workers	23	40	54

Source: BLS National Compensation Survey, https://www.bls.gov/ncs/ebs/benefits/2017.

*The figures are for employees of all organizations within a sector, broken down by union status within the sector.

difference is smaller among state and local government employees, where DB plans existed long before government workers were allowed to bargain collectively. (See table 2.2.)

Defined-benefit (DB) pension plans are being replaced or supplemented by defined-contribution (DC) accounts such as 401(k)s that bear an individual's name. Pushing the DC alternative are employers who no longer want the responsibility of offering what is, in effect, retirement insurance; they'd prefer to shift the risk of having adequate retirement funds onto their employees. Conservatives believe that it's better, morally, for individuals to take personal responsibility for their retirement security. Economists favor the defined-contribution approach because it makes it easier for workers to switch jobs without losing their unvested benefits. The financial industry likes DC accounts because they yield higher profits than DB plans. Yet, there are flaws with the DC approach that make it inferior to DB plans for retirees. The most serious problem is that lower-wage workers are unable to accumulate adequate assets in their 401(k)s to finance their retirements. The median account balance of those nearing retirement was $92,000 in 2014.[60]

Taft-Hartleys

There are around 1,400 multiemployer DB pension plans (so-called Taft-Hartley plans) offered by groups of unionized companies. They have 10 million active and retired participants. The plans are co-administered by employers and unions. Those with over ten thousand participants make up 14 percent of all multiemployer plans, but they have 80 percent of the participants. They tend to be found in industries that once competed on a local basis and where small employers were unable to afford plans of their own. Multiemployer plans are prevalent in transportation, retail, and construction. Employers are dropping out of them, which means that currently employed workers are supporting ever-larger numbers of retirees. Some carry sizeable unfunded liabilities and have been forced to seek assistance from the Pension Benefit Guaranty Corporation (PBGC). It is these plans—the union plans—that were the initial base for labor's forays into shareholder activism.[61]

One of the largest Taft-Hartleys is the Teamsters' Central States plan. As a result of UPS's withdrawal in 2007, the plan is perilously underfunded. But there is a different Teamsters plan, the Western Conference. It is the nation's largest Taft-Hartley, with nearly 600,000 members. Before the pandemic, the plan was in good health. Other large Taft-Hartleys include two from the UFCW (500,00 members and $10 billion), an SEIU plan associated with its giant Local 1199 in New York City, and the SEIU's Master Trust, made up of three pension plans. The Master Trust had as one of its trustees the late Steve Abrecht, who was also in charge of SEIU's capital strategies. It's an indicator of the close connection between the union's pension plans and its organizing activities.[62]

The 2008 financial meltdown decimated pension funds, including Taft-Hartleys. Some of them folded and were taken over by the PBGC, which led to steep cuts in the monthly benefits promised to participants. Other plans found themselves with severe underfunding. At their trough during the financial crisis, multiemployer plans had only half the assets needed to meet their liabilities. After stock markets recovered, the average funding level for multiemployer plans was back up to 85 percent. A minority remained in critical condition, with less than half of the assets necessary to pay current and future retirement benefits.[63]

In the past, some Taft-Hartleys did the bidding of corrupt union leaders. The most infamous example was Jimmy Hoffa, president of the Teamsters, who took money from the Teamsters' pension funds and invested it in Las Vegas casinos and hotels tied to organized crime. But that was sixty years ago; since then, stricter federal oversight has reduced although not eliminated these problems.[64]

The AFL-CIO provides socially beneficial investment opportunities for its multiemployer plans. The Housing Investment Trust (HIT), established in the late 1960s, invests multiemployer assets in building low-income and affordable housing. HIT has financed in excess of one hundred thousand housing units during its existence, many for communities in need. It was one of the first to build in downtown New York City after 9/11, and the same was true on the Gulf Coast after Hurricane Katrina. The projects all are built by union members. The AFL-CIO also provides multiemployer plans with a real estate vehicle known as the Multi-Employer Property Trust (MEPT) and a related program, the Building Investment Trust (BIT), which invests in commercial properties.[65]

Single-Employer Plans

Single-employer (corporate) pension plans exist in both union and nonunion companies. The fact that executives appoint trustees or even serve as trustees themselves can be problematic because companies do "not necessarily [act] in the interest of members of the pension plan." Members of manufacturing unions associated with the former CIO usually are enrolled in single-employer plans. In the past, there were some tragic plan terminations. The largest occurred at Studebaker in 1963, when more than four thousand workers lost their promised benefits. It led Congress to enact the Employee Retirement Income Security Act (ERISA) in 1974 to protect private pensions. At the same time, it created the PBGC. Although state and local plans are not covered by ERISA, they are subject to analogous state laws.[66]

In 1958, Walter Reuther, president of the Autoworkers union (UAW), asked Ford Motor to invest a part of the company's pension assets in housing for its workers. The union argued that the assets belonged to employees and should benefit them before as well as after retirement. Ford refused the request, saying that doing so was contrary to the plan's fiduciary responsibilities. There was another reason for Ford's intransigence: "Legal considerations aside, we remain fully opposed, as we have been consistently in the past, to broadening the scope of our negotiations with the UAW to embrace the broad social fields that you envision." The UAW was forced to accede.[67]

Staff Plans and Reserve Funds

Nearly every unit of a union—national, regional, and local—has a pension plan for it staff. The largest of these have assets of several hundred million dollars. Staff pensions are a type of single-employer plan. Unions also have financial assets of their own—strike funds, operating reserves—part of which is invested in equities. An advantage to using the union's own assets for activism is that they are not subject to the same fiduciary rules governing pension plans. The AFL-CIO, for example, often uses stock held in its reserve fund as the basis for its activism. Unions had a total of $23 billion in directly controlled assets in 2014.[68]

State and Local Plans

Pensions for state and local employees date back to the late nineteenth century, when the civil service system was being established. An early plan, founded in 1894, was for New York City's teachers. By 1913, twenty-five states offered pensions to firefighters and police. Today, the state and local plans number around twelve thousand, many of them small. The five largest—CalPERS, CalSTRS, the New York State Common Retirement Fund, the Florida State Board of Administration, and the New York City Employee Retirement System (NYCERS)—account for around a fourth of total state and local pension assets. The governance structure of the state and local plans is varied; the trustees can be elected officials, political appointees, individuals elected by current and retired employees, or all three. In "blue" states like California and New York, the trustees from government often are Democrats, and some trustees have union backgrounds; in "red" states, the officials tend to be Republicans and there are few or no union trustees.[69]

Economist Peter Drucker thought that the accumulation of pension assets would bring socialism to the United States. Like Karl Marx, Drucker defined socialism as ownership of the means of production. Drucker was wrong. Pension funds are far from owning the nation's public companies, and they use their stock to promote a shareholder-centric system of corporate governance. Nonetheless, the labor movement relied on pension capital to boost its organizing and bargaining power, something that Drucker failed to anticipate.[70]

3

Labor's Shares

JOHN POUND—academic, investor, and CalPERS advisor—was at the center of shareholder activism's early days. In 1994 he declared, "The movement is over. Things are beginning to look more like a partnership between shareholders and corporations. We have gone beyond polemical debates."[1] Pound spoke at the moment when the activist baton was passing to union investors, who were less inclined to trust corporations.

This chapter examines the evolution of labor's financial turn. Like their public counterparts, union funds relied on the cookbook to find common ground with other investors and to raise returns on their holdings. Not infrequently they had a collateral interest: to add new members. In several industries—including hospitals, hotels, and building services—unions drew on experiences like Beverly to mount corporate campaigns that incorporated shareholder activism and other financial strategies. The ultimate goal was a collective bargaining agreement, a type of governance model that gives workers greater standing than under shareholder primacy.

At the end of the chapter, we examine how labor tweaked the cookbook to make it more compatible with a pro-worker approach to investing. The principles of transparency and accountability were invoked to press mutual funds to report their proxy votes and companies to reveal their political donations. Both involved changing the balance of power—in markets and in politics.

Don't Mourn, Organize

During the first term of Ronald Reagan's presidency, union leaders began to acknowledge that imports and union busters weren't the only causes of falling membership; problems also existed within labor's house. Several labor leaders committed themselves to reversing the decline, a group that included George

Becker of the Steelworkers, Morton Bahr of the Communications Workers, Jack Sheinkman of the Clothing and Textile Workers, and John Sweeney of the Service Employees.

When Sweeney became SEIU's president in 1980, the economy was experiencing job growth at the bottom and top but contracting in the middle of the wage hierarchy. The bottom was dominated by service workers in hotels, fast food restaurants, and office buildings. Their jobs could not be shipped abroad, but in some respects they were more difficult to organize than industrial workers.

Whereas once it had been public pension officials who warned, "[I]f you snub shareholders, we will get in your face," increasingly the threats came from union investors. The year 1995 marked a turning point. John Sweeney became president of the AFL-CIO, and the number of shareholder proposals from union plans surpassed those from public plans.

Sweeney and his lieutenant, Andrew Stern, understood that a side benefit of active ownership was access to corporate executives who normally would have no contact with unions. Regarding a shareholder proposal, a representative of a union pension plan explained, "What was actually the most significant part was not so much the resolution or the voting but the ongoing dialogue that ended up happening." Addressing a group of pension plans, Sweeney asked, "Help us to speak to management power with a voice loud enough to reach into the rarified atmosphere of the board room."[2]

Like other investors, union shareholders began the engagement process by notifying the company of their intention to file a proposal. If the company refused to discuss the issue seriously, the union likely would go ahead and submit. A study of an activist hedge fund in the UK found that the company's response was confrontational about 40 percent of the time, collaborative around 20–25 percent of the time, and otherwise was a mixed reaction. If a vote were held and received strong backing, a previously uncooperative company might become more accommodating.

Engagement was not necessarily belligerent. Damon Silvers, associate counsel for the AFL-CIO, said that "the labor movement may be uniquely suited to being the voice of investors on governance issues because we are not afraid to have a fight. In collective bargaining, it is both adversarial and relational. . . . [Y]ou don't get to the table without a fight. But then you sit across from the company and work out all kinds of different things on a daily basis. So [labor's shareholder activism] is confrontational and deeply relational at the same time."[3]

Shareholder activities related to strikes and contract negotiations were problematic as compared to membership campaigns. Beth Young, an advisor to labor unions, explains:

> Strike situations and to some extent bargaining situations do not fit well with the longer term time horizon that you need for this work. So, for example, if you're doing a shareholder proposal, you have to put it in about five months before the annual meeting. That means you have to start working on it, locating the sponsor, and drafting the proposal. So what you're looking at is a situation where you're doing something eight months in advance of when it will come to a vote. There's a high-level of anxiety about that delay. It means that we might be in a strike or we might be at an impasse in bargaining in the spring or summer or whatever. . . . So having that long time delay in there is just not comfortable in those very charged situations."[4]

Unions had diverse motives for shareholder activism, as reflected by the types of companies where they filed proposals. The largest group was made up of underperforming companies where labor had no collateral interests. Another group were companies in which there were collateral interests related to bargaining or organizing.[5] Of these, there were four types: nonunion companies that might become organizing sites in the future, such as chain retailers (for example, Home Depot and Walmart); firms where there were active membership campaigns (like HealthSouth, Marriott, and Oregon Steel); companies that had ties to a target corporation (Arden Realty and Boston Properties, whose office buildings hired cleaning contractors); and unionized employers with whom labor sought leverage in collective bargaining (such as Anheuser-Busch and Coca-Cola).[6]

Basing activism on the cookbook was critical to forming coalitions between unions and other investors. The cookbook, said an observer, "levels the playing field and . . . creates a common language for engagement." If labor had a gripe with a company, a cookbook proposal was sure to gain votes. According to Beth Young, sometimes union investors asked, "What would get me the highest vote? I don't have a story I want to tell, I don't have an issue I want to resonate with my members, I just want to get the highest vote . . . to put the hurt on the company." Takeover barriers were a perennial favorite because other institutional investors regularly voted to knock them down.[7]

The cookbook was no guarantee of success. An example was the nine-month strike by the Mine Workers Union (UMW) in 1989. Seeking to pressure the company, Pittston Coal, the UMW submitted a shareholder resolution demanding that Pittston rescind a poison pill and give shareholders the right to vote on future takeover defenses. Another proposal demanded that a committee of independent directors with no ties to management be the arbiter of future restructuring and asset sales. Leading the effort was the UMW's militant young president Richard Trumka, who hired a professional proxy solicitor and put substantial resources into the campaign. But with a strike underway, the UMW had difficulty getting help from the public plans, even though its proposals came from the cookbook. "We're the owners, not the managers," said Michigan's treasurer, whose state pension funds were among Pittston's largest shareholders. "We monitor the union situation closely, but we don't want to take sides."[8]

Corporate Campaigns

Starting in the 1970s, employers grew ever bolder in flouting the National Labor Relations Board's (NLRB) rules on conduct during organizing campaigns. Firing union activists was an unlawful but effective way to intimidate workers; the penalties were trivial. Over one-third of those who voted against a union said they did so because of management coercion. Other anti-union tactics included the filing of endless legal objections with the NLRB, even after the union had won the election. The delays might last several years and sap support for the union.[9]

Neutrality and card-check agreements circumvented employer bullying and the flawed NLRB election process. If a neutrality agreement were signed, the employer was expected to provide organizers with access to the worksite, foreswear retaliatory dismissals, and prohibit anti-union communications by managers and supervisors. Organizers then asked workers to sign cards saying that they authorized the union to represent them. When the union had a solid majority of cards, it would present these to the employer and ask for a contract. This was card check. Most neutrality agreements required the employer immediately to initiate bargaining if the union could show majority support. Some agreements stipulated that an arbitrator would fashion a settlement should the parties fail to reach one on their own.

The trick was getting the employer to sign an agreement. Unless pushed, few employers willingly consented. Even requests from a foreign government might not work, as in the case of Nissan. The French government was part owner of Nissan through its partner Renault and unsuccessfully tried to persuade the Japanese car maker to accept a neutrality agreement with the UAW at its American plants.[10]

Lessons had been learned from the earliest days of corporate campaigns. One was that a company would be more inclined to sign a neutrality agreement if the union publicized its anti-union stance to investors, consumers, and community groups. Also, the firm's financial partners could serve as a goad. To obtain an agreement, unions offered carrots, too: promising not to openly disparage the company—the Ray Rogers clause—or mount any protests against it, and, in the case of one agreement, foreswear from these activities "anywhere in the world." Not infrequently unions vowed to help the employer's business in return for an agreement. In Las Vegas, the Hotel and Restaurant Employees (HERE) promised to make job classifications more flexible and to work with local healthcare providers to contain costs. SEIU put its political connections to work by lobbying for cooperative companies to receive government contracts, or lobbied against those who resisted.

If a neutrality agreement were obtained, it raised the likelihood of union recognition and a first contract. Between 1998 and 2003, less than 20 percent of new private-sector union members were added through the NLRB elections process. Most of the other 80 percent joined as a result of neutrality and card-check agreements. The agreements doubled the win rate as compared to an NLRB election.[11]

Following Beverly, there was an uptick in the number of corporate campaigns as part of a broader attempt at union renewal. Securing a neutrality agreement was their usual objective, and most of them relied on financial activism as a tactical element. The first step was to understand a corporation's business relationships: major investors, directors and their business ties, creditors, suppliers, customers, and competitors. SEIU, UNITE, HERE, and other organizing-oriented unions began hiring former Wall Street analysts, real estate experts, and MBAs to conduct the research. They studied a company's interactions with government, for example, whether it had public contracts whose renegotiation the union might threaten. In Boston, for instance, SEIU testified against a group of hospitals seeking state bonds to finance new facilities, while in Indianapolis it urged local governments to cancel their contracts with a janitorial company it was seeking to organize.

Contacting regulators about health or environmental violations was damaging to a firm's reputation, as Bill Patterson tried to do at Kodak. In a campaign at Tenet Healthcare, a hospital chain, SEIU's Master Trust joined two faith-based retirement plans in filing shareholder resolutions against Tenet's use of supplies containing harmful chemicals.[12]

Corporate campaigns were closely associated with the unions that left the AFL-CIO in 2005 to create Change to Win: the Carpenters, the Food and Commercial Workers, the Hotel and Restaurant Employees, the Laborers, the Teamsters, SEIU, and the clothing and textile workers (which after its merger with the Ladies Garment Workers became UNITE.

Building Services

SEIU led the era's boldest campaign, "Justice for Janitors." In line with a broader outsourcing trend, building managers had shifted from direct employment of cleaning workers to hiring them from an array of private contractors. Organizing janitors was difficult. Each contractor had its employees dispersed around a city, the work sites contained only a handful of workers, turnover was high, and jobs often were part-time. Some contractors were small, privately owned firms that flew beneath the radar, while others were giant multinational corporations. SEIU decided that the best tactic would be to identify building owners and have them ask their contractors to sign neutrality agreements. Often the owners of large office buildings were Real Estate Investment Trusts (REITs) with substantial investments from pension funds.[13]

Justice for Janitors (J4J) originated in Pittsburgh in 1985. The campaign spread to Denver and Washington, DC, then to San Diego and Atlanta, and Los Angeles. Other cities included Boston, St. Louis, San Jose, Milwaukee, Vancouver, and Houston. Justice for Janitors reached out to a group ignored by many unions at the time: workers situated at the bottom of the labor market. It portrayed itself as a movement for social justice, turning for support to elected officials and to community, immigrant, and faith-based organizations. J4J was led by Stephen Lerner and Jono Shaffer, both talented organizers.

J4J demanded higher wages for janitors, who often received only the minimum wage. It also sought pensions and health benefits, which were rare in the industry. In Houston, the campaign began in the late 1980s, failed during the 1990s, restarted in 2002, and finally succeeded in 2005, after nearly twenty years. Backers included the mayor, half the City Council, members of Congress, and eighty clergy, including Houston's archbishop. There were marches, demonstrations, civil disobedience, posters, and T-shirts. The union mobilized public opinion and a sometimes fearful and often exploited workforce. SEIU signed up five thousand janitors; as in other cities where it was successful, the result was a significant improvement in wages, working conditions, and benefits.[14]

Cleaning contractors mounted fierce resistance. Hence, it was crucial that landlords take responsibility for their contractors' behavior. In Atlanta, the dominant owner of office buildings was the Portman Companies, which offered REIT investments to large public pension funds. Portman bitterly fought SEIU, including multiple lawsuits and complaints to the NLRB. In response, SEIU asked friendly state and local plans to tell Portman not to oppose the union and, if Portman refused, to refrain from doing business with it. The same occurred in Washington, DC, where CarrAmerica owned buildings through REITS in which CalPERS and other public funds invested. SEIU called for a national boycott of CarrAmerica, a tactic repeated elsewhere. In Denver, where a property management company was fighting the union, SEIU went directly to CalPERS, which owned the building outright, and the pension plan replaced the company.

SEIU turned to public pension plans to adopt its "Responsible Contractor Policy" requiring that cleaning contractors servicing properties they owned be required to obey labor laws and provide fair wages, health insurance, and pensions. SEIU said that the policy would benefit investors by providing better-quality services. CalPERS agreed to the policy in 1994 for buildings where it was the majority owner, and other state and local plans followed suit.[15]

On Los Angeles's affluent Westside, half of the largest buildings were owned outright by pension funds and another 21 percent by REITs in which they had investments. In Houston, pension funds owned around a third of the commercial buildings. CalPERS and CalSTRS gave crucial assistance to SEIU's campaign in Houston, where Hines Interests, a REIT, controlled the market. CalPERS owned a sizable chunk of Hines.

In addition to behind-the-scenes lobbying, SEIU's own pension plans filed shareholder resolutions. At Boston Properties, a REIT with office buildings in major cities, an SEIU proposal demanded that the company declassify its board of directors, a staple of the cookbook. The union launched an online website providing information to investors about business problems facing Boston Properties. It tried to embarrass the company's CEO, Mortimer Zuckerman, a major donor to the Democratic Party and later, a confidante of Barack Obama, by contrasting Zuckerman, one of the four hundred richest people in America, with part-time workers who cleaned Boston Properties' buildings at low pay and without health benefits. The Carpenters' pension plan lent assistance by asking Boston Properties get rid of four directors who failed to win majority support from shareholders.[16]

Another tactic was going after the companies whose offices were cleaned by contractors. SEIU focused on Silicon Valley icons who cared about their public image, firms such as Apple, Hewlett-Packard, and Intel. During the 2002 uproar over options expensing at tech companies, the union claimed that Intel's cleaning contractor, Somers Building Management, failed to pay decent wages and benefits. It criticized Craig Barrett, CEO of Intel, who was vulnerable to shareholders opposed to his leadership of the anti-expensing movement. The Carpenters plan and the AFL-CIO reserve fund sponsored proposals to get rid of Intel's stock options in favor of other types of stock-based awards. The Carpenters' proposal received a majority of votes. By 2008, SEIU had built up enough momentum in Silicon Valley to call a janitors' strike at the valley's blue-ribbon corporations, including Intel.[17]

Major owners of US real estate included foreign pension funds in the Netherlands, Sweden, and the United Kingdom. Some assisted SEIU, but not always. CarrAmerica's largest shareholder was ABP, the giant Dutch pension plan for teachers and other government employees. Despite its progressive image, ABP was among the last holdouts in agreeing to SEIU's responsible contractor policy. SEIU staffers traveled to the Netherlands to line up support from Dutch unions and to plead its case with ABP. Back in Los Angeles, SEIU was up against ISS, a multinational janitorial corporation headquartered in Denmark. It brought a group of Danish labor leaders to Los Angeles for a study tour in the hope that they would return home and lobby ISS. Eventually, twenty thousand janitors in Los Angeles and the Bay Area joined SEIU.[18]

SEIU relied on internal resources to back its efforts. The union had three big multiemployer plans of its own: a Master Trust and plans from two large union locals: 1199 (healthcare) and 32BJ (building services). One estimate is that their assets totaled over $13 billion. All were managed from the national office. Because SEIU has many of its members in state and local government, the union possessed several channels for lobbying public plans to back its activities in the private sector. Justice for Janitors was SEIU's great success story.[19]

Hospitals and Nursing Homes

In the mid-1990s, SEIU took on Vencor, a nursing home operator headquartered in Kentucky. SEIU had several collective bargaining agreements with Vencor and wanted more of them, although the company was seeking to dislodge the union. Then Vencor announced that it planned to merge with another nursing home operator, Hillhaven Corporation. When SEIU put up a website with a "shareholder alert" opposing the deal, it was regarded as an innovative application of a novel technology, the Internet. The website laid out in detail reasons that the merger would be disadvantageous to Vencor shareholders. Six months later, the parties reached a settlement that included a neutrality agreement.[20]

Columbia/HCA was a scandal-ridden for-profit hospital chain, whose facilities SEIU sought to organize. The first action came in 1997, when SEIU joined forces with LongView Funds on a proposal asking Columbia/HCA to rid itself of a poison pill it adopted without a shareholder vote. SEIU phoned all of the company's major investors for their support. Coming from the cookbook, the proposal received over 60 percent of the votes. SEIU salted the shareholder meeting with union supporters. A nurse criticized poor patient quality at Columbia/HCA, telling the CEO, "You are sacrificing long-term value for short-term gain by cutting down on staff, medical, supplies, and services." A year later, Andy Stern, SEIU's president, sent a letter to Columbia's board informing it that the Master Trust was seeking to replace two incumbent directors seen as subservient to the CEO. SEIU's candidates included a former SEC employee and a former government health expert. The union formed a rump shareholders committee that included CalPERS, NYCERS, and LACERS (the pension plan from Los Angeles County). In a separate action, ten public plans and LongView joined SEIU in a derivative lawsuit charging Columbia's management with fraud.[21]

Hotels

Las Vegas. The Hotel and Restaurant Employees union was another pioneering practitioner of financial activism. Whereas Los Angeles was where J4J had its greatest success, for HERE it happened in Las Vegas. Las Vegas had some unique characteristics favoring the union as compared to building services: a small of number of large employers; a more stable and geographically concentrated workforce; and an already-organized membership base that provided a steady supply of picketers and other activists. "A well-paid, dignified workforce can often fight harder to retain its position than a poorer, more discouraged one," an observer noted. Unlike office-building owners, the hotels directly employed their workers. HERE's victories transformed Las Vegas into "the last town in America where the white working class fully understands that unions can make a big difference in their lives," said a local labor leader.[22]

The Culinary Workers, HERE's Las Vegas local, had around sixty thousand members, of whom twenty-two thousand joined between 1988 and 1998, the first stage of organizing, and an additional twenty thousand later on. The Culinary Workers local devoted a whopping 40 percent of its budget to organizing versus 3–4 percent for the average union local. HERE also had considerable assets at its disposal. The Culinary Workers' pension fund was worth $1 billion and, as HERE drifted closer to UNITE (they merged in 2004), it obtained access to Amalgamated Bank's investment managers and the Long-View funds. The merger raised the size of UNITE HERE'S research group to almost one hundred people. In addition, the union had several capable strategists, one of them being John Wilhelm, who oversaw the Las Vegas campaign.[23]

Before the merger, HERE's research staff was under the direction of Matt Walker, a protégé of Bill Patterson's who had worked with Wilhelm since the late 1980s (and, like Wilhelm, is a Yale graduate). An early victory occurred at the MGM Grand Hotel, which opened in 1993 with the CEO announcing that he would never sign a labor contract. The union found a leverage point in the directors of MGM's parent corporation who sat on the boards of other companies averse to controversy. What also helped was that the parent's owner was Kirk Kerkorian, who had saddled the firm with substantial debt. Thus, he was susceptible to the union's behind-the-scenes discussions with creditors. Kerkorian, a pragmatist, overrode his CEO, accepted a neutrality agreement, and the union won a card-check election in 1997.

However, not everyone in HERE was enamored of the emphasis on financial tactics. HERE's Jeff Fiedler, the union's expert on corporate campaigns, took a side swipe at the financial experts on Walker's staff: "They think you do this stuff top down and the workers don't matter. These kids didn't get out there in organizing campaigns, don't go out there on strikes. They think they can look up on the Internet, get a little bit of fucking information, and collapse the company." The situation was a long way from the 1950s, when Jimmy Hoffa disparaged college-educated staffers as eggheads and longhairs. But the disdain has never completely disappeared.[24]

Despite HERE's strength on the Las Vegas strip, several hotels had succeeded in fending off the union. Although most were publicly held, their ownership was concentrated in the hands of a founder or their family. Among them was philanthropist Sheldon Adelson, whose Venetian Hotel was the last major nonunion holdout on the strip. Adelson and his family owned 90 percent of the Venetian's parent company. Owners like Adelson had longer time horizons than ordinary CEOs and quick-buck investors like Kerkorian, a factor that sustained their willingness to fight wars of attrition. When faced with this determined opposition, said one HERE staffer, "Picket lines just aren't that effective." Neither was financial activism.[25]

A tough nut to crack was the Santa Fe Casino Hotel, whose employees voted in favor of union representation in 1993. The situation was a typical example of the NLRB's shortcomings. The NLRB supervised the election, certified it, and rejected Santa Fe's repeated legal appeals; yet workers were unable to obtain a first contract. Picketing and a boycott had no discernible effect. The parent corporation was publicly traded, but 70 percent of its stock was owned by CEO Paul Lowden and his family. Since the late 1980s, Santa Fe had been under close scrutiny by a HERE research staffer, Courtney Alexander, yet another Yale graduate whose financial experience began with the South African divestment movement. Alexander immersed herself in Santa Fe's financial minutiae: its expansion plans, its lenders (one was a bank for which Lowden's wife served on the board), and its debt structure.

Santa Fe slid into financial straits. It ceased paying dividends on its preferred stock in 1997 and then its shares were delisted. Alexander determined that Santa Fe was overleveraged, information that she shared with Wall Street analysts and the company's bondholders. As Lowden traveled around the country to meet potential investors, the union would be outside the meeting room distributing its own reports. Alexander held a conference call with creditors, after which Lowden said that Santa Fe was "under siege": "They go to your bondholders and try to bring you to your knees." Major investors, even those unsympathetic to unions, credited HERE with providing valuable intelligence. For her part, Alexander asserted a "commonality" between minority shareholders and workers: "Employees went four years without raises. Investors haven't gotten their dividends." HERE sent letters to the company's shareholders outlining its case for replacing two board members with independent candidates. Yet despite pulling out all the stops, the Santa Fe campaign fizzled. In 2000, Santa Fe sold its Vegas casino to Station Casinos, which immediately laid off all of Santa Fe's former employees and refused to promise preferential rehiring.[26]

Station Casinos owned hotels that employed ten thousand nonunion employees. The children of Station's founder controlled more than a third of the company's stock, and its CEO, the founder's son, held a million stock options that were reissued and repriced several times. The Culinary Workers prepared a detailed report that it sent to Station's shareholders, alerting them of the substantial hit to earnings that would occur when the unexpensed options were exercised, which, it said, would cause a wealth transfer from shareholders to the family.

HERE submitted proposals to revoke power from the family and its friends on the board: to get rid of the staggered board and supermajority voting provisions and to rescind its poison pill. "Yes" votes on the submissions ranged from 25 to 33 percent, the highest being the pill's rescission. At least a third of the "No" votes came from the family. When HERE resubmitted the following year, the vote increased to 47 percent in favor. But then, in 2007, the owners took Station Casinos private, which eliminated shareholder activism as a strategy and netted the family somewhere between $600 million and $1 billion. However, the deal saddled the company with massive debt. In 2009, with the nation's financial crisis in full swing, Station declared bankruptcy. HERE published a report claiming that the buyout had ruined the company. It urged creditors and the bankruptcy court to force the family to pump its own money back into the firm, and to stop fighting the union. The NLRB in 2010 issued a 127-count decision showing massive labor-law violations, the largest unfair-labor-practice case it had ever dealt with. The union kept fighting Station, drawing repeated attention to one of its largest creditors, Deutsche Bank. The union's luck turned in 2015 and in short order it organized five of the company's properties. The effort had taken years, as do many other corporate campaigns. They require money and commitment.[27]

San Francisco. With well over a hundred thousand employees, Marriott is among the largest employers in the United States. The Marriott family still owns part of the corporation. Over the years, Marriott has put a high priority on remaining nonunion. For years it did not have a single collective bargaining agreement at any of its US hotels. Despite staggering levels of on-the-job injuries among its housekeepers, Marriott offered skimpy health insurance.[28]

In San Francisco, HERE had a militant local that represented workers at many of the city's large hotels. University of Texas law professor Julius Getman said that by the mid-1990s, HERE had succeeded so well with card check as an alternative to NLRB elections that "hotels began to approach the union, offering card-check recognition before the union even requested it." But Marriott balked. In 1980, when Marriott announced that it would build its first hotel in downtown San Francisco, the union went to the company and secured a promise that Marriott would allow card-check recognition after the hotel was built.

When the hotel opened nine years later, Marriott reneged on its promise. HERE filed a lawsuit in federal court. The union was a constant presence at the hotel during the four years that the case was in the courts. Management lost on appeal, and the case went back to district court. As a new trial loomed, the union and the company negotiated a consent decree including neutrality and card check. Success for HERE came in 1996, after it received authorization cards from the vast majority of the hotel's nine hundred workers. At long last, Marriott surrendered. One industry expert called it a groundbreaking settlement. But the hotel's general manager in San Francisco obliquely signaled his intention to keep fighting when he said that the card check's results failed to indicate the employees' "true desires." After two years, HERE still did not have a first contract. At this point, the union turned to financial tactics to raise the heat on management.[29]

Marriott asked its shareholders in 1998 to approve the issuance of dual-class shares, which the company said was necessary to facilitate future acquisitions. Dual-class shares would give the Marriott family control in perpetuity. Although some financial analysts were leery of the plan, the company did not expect significant opposition. More than one-fifth of Marriott's shares were held by family members (the CEO was the founder's son), and its other owners were mutual funds that usually supported management. Walker, now assigned to San Francisco, nevertheless saw an opportunity because dual-class shares were one of the cookbook's bugbears.[30]

Walker worked furiously to build opposition to Marriott's proposal ahead of the annual meeting. First, he sent faxes to the company's 120 largest shareholders. Then he turned for assistance to the AFL-CIO's new Office of Investment. The AFL-CIO alerted a thousand Taft-Hartley managers and made the Marriott proposal a Key Vote for the 1998 proxy season. Walker also contacted CII, which spread the word through its weekly newsletter. There were several remaining nuts to crack. Walker telephoned prominent journalists at media outlets like the *Wall Street Journal* and *Newsweek*, sent letters to those who owned at least a thousand shares, set up a website, and paid a proxy solicitor to mail the union's counterproposal to all shareholders. Walker and Marriott met separately with the three main mutual-fund owners—Putnam, Fidelity, and State Street—and also with ISS, the proxy advisor. Later, ISS recommended against Marriott's plan. The dual-class proposal received 47 percent of the vote, a loss for the Marriott family and a major victory for HERE.[31]

Yet humbling the company in front of its shareholders did not lead to a contract in San Francisco, the same problem Walker had faced in Las Vegas. What followed was four more years of traditional tactics: a huge demonstration with 150 arrests; weekly protests and picketing in front of the hotel as well at other Marriott locations; a two-day strike; and a call by San Francisco's labor-friendly mayor, Willie Brown, for a worldwide boycott of the chain. In 2000, the NLRB alleged that Marriott had committed more than eighty violations of labor law.

Religious leaders were deeply involved. After the NLRB ruling, they convened an ecumenical forum about the dispute, held at San Francisco's largest church. Sensing an opportunity, HERE began reaching out to faith-based investors who were concerned with human rights violations in Myanmar, where Marriott had operations. HERE prepared a proposal for the 2002 shareholders' meeting demanding that Marriott adopt a human rights policy modeled on the ILO's core principles, which included the right to organize and to bargain. The proposal was cast as a response to Marriott operations in Myanmar, but it would also apply in San Francisco. (Human Rights Watch had earlier issued a report charging that the hotel's San Francisco policies were a violation of the ILO guidelines.) Again, HERE lined up support from ISS and CalPERS, along with its backing from social and faith-based investors. What finally tipped the balance was the destruction of the World Trade Center. In its aftermath, Bill Marriott and John Wilhelm met for the first time and jointly lobbied Congress to help save jobs in the nation's hospitality industry. Wilhelm and Marriott formed a pragmatic relationship that, according to Wilhelm, cleared the way for a four-year contract in San Francisco, signed a year after 9/11. Thus culminated a twenty-two-year struggle that demonstrated what a determined corporation was capable of achieving even in a labor town like San Francisco. It also showed that corporate campaigns, including financial tactics, had the capability of wearing an employer down.[32]

Bargaining

Financial activism related to collective bargaining was less prevalent. One union that tried it was the Steelworkers, who were in tattered condition due to numerous steel mill closures and the shift to nonunion mini mills. Despite multiple rounds of deep wage cuts and layoffs, the union had lost about half of its members. Strikes and other industrial actions had had no effect. The union turned to ESOPs, which at first looked like a promising option for saving jobs, but they failed to stop the downslide.

The Steelworkers represented workers at Ravenswood Aluminum in West Virginia. During a dispute in 1991, the company locked out 1,500 union members. Then it hired replacement workers and refused to bargain. Ravenswood's finances and ownership were shrouded in mystery. Intensive research by the Steelworkers, with assistance from the AFL-CIO's Joe Uehlein and others, traced Ravenswood's ownership back to a bank in Amsterdam and ultimately to Marc Rich, the fugitive financier then hiding in Switzerland. With help from global unions in Geneva, the Steelworkers reached out to friendly Swiss unions, who introduced the union to the mayor of the town where Rich was living and to Dutch unions who arranged a meeting with Rich's bank in the Netherlands. The Swiss mayor testified against Rich at a West Virginia State Senate hearing in 1992. Eventually, the Steelworkers concluded that Rich had set up his businesses in a way that left him "impervious" to direct financial pressure. The union tried indirect methods, like leafletting at a gathering of global metals traders. Staying out of the limelight meant a lot to Rich, who ordered his managers to lift the twenty-month lockout. As part of their agreement with Ravenswood, the Steelworkers promised to cease all public criticism of the industrialist, something that more militant trade unionists found appalling.[33]

Less publicized but similar events unfolded at Bayou Steel, one of the few mini-mill steel producers then under a collective bargaining agreement. When the company refused to bargain with the Steelworkers over its intention to contract out production to other firms, Bayou's union members walked off their jobs. The strike, which began in 1993, went on for nearly three years, during which Bayou Steel hired replacements. Concerned about never getting their jobs back, around 30 percent of the workers crossed the picket line. Facing an intransigent employer, the Steelworkers brought in the same team of financial experts who had worked on Ravenswood.

Three months after the walkout began, the union tried to enter Bayou's investor meeting in New York but was refused. Outside the room, it distributed reports to investors and analysts detailing the company's environmental and safety liabilities. Bayou canceled its 1994 annual meeting, following which the Steelworkers filed a lawsuit asking Delaware's Chancery Court to require Bayou to give the union a list of its shareholders. The Steelworkers had intended to submit resolutions critical of Bayou's board composition and the longevity of its directors. A year later Bayou filed a RICO (Racketeer Influenced and Corrupt Organizations) lawsuit, charging the Steelworkers as well as the AFL-CIO with securities fraud, extortion, and other actions. RICO lawsuits, originally intended to fight organized crime, gave Bayou Steel the opportunity to subpoena internal documents belonging to the Steelworkers and carried the risk of major financial damage should the union lose the case. The Steelworkers capitulated. Although Bayou signed a six-year contract in 1996, it rehired only 40 percent of the strikers.[34]

Labor's Cookbook

Taft-Hartleys often failed to vote their proxies. For Robert Monks, this was an abdication of "citizenship rights held by owners." Monks lobbied ex-colleagues at the Department of Labor to do something about the problem. In 1988, the department issued an advisory opinion known as the Avon Letter and then a related document, the so-called Monks letter. They said that proxy voting was a fiduciary responsibility and demanded guidelines to inform that vote.[35]

The AFL-CIO's Pension Investment Committee, chaired by John T. Joyce of the Bricklayers Union, released model proxy guidelines in 1991. The guidelines were intended for Taft-Hartley trustees, those who voted their proxies, and proxy advisors like ISS. They have been revised several times since then, although the core remains the same. The guidelines drew heavily from the cookbook, the gold standard of engagement. But they included items missing from the cookbook, such as a recommendation that executives be rewarded if their company invested in employees and provided a supportive work environment. This was followed by a proviso that proposals related to the recommendation should be reviewed "to ensure that they are in the shareholders' best interests and do not unduly interfere with the company's operation." It was an odd stipulation coming from a labor organization but reflected fiduciary constraints.

What made the cookbook tolerable for unions was its premise that executives could not be trusted, a good fit to the labor movement's gut instincts. Since the late nineteenth century, American employers were more aggressively anti-union than their European counterparts, an attitude that brought forth an equally aggressive anti-management strain in the American labor movement. There was an interlude during the decades of managerialism. When union power began to wane in the 1970s, so did corporate tolerance of what labor had wrought: job security, pension benefits, and steady pay increases. For union pension funds and for unions, "imperial executives" were to blame for what had been lost. This was the place from which Patterson's passion emerged, and also Rich Trumka's, who in 1995 had become the AFL-CIO's secretary-treasurer.

"What's driving it for labor," said one observer, "is a fundamental philosophical belief that management has a sinister reason for wanting to have classified boards and poison pills, which is to cover their own asses."[36]

Long Term

Nearly every page of every version of the guidelines contained the phrase "long term," sometimes several times on the same page, defined as a company's return on equity (ROE) over a three- to five-year period as compared to peers and to the broader market. Proposals were to be judged or justified by their long-term impact. The US Labor and Treasury Departments had said in 1989 that private pension plans did not have a fiduciary responsibility to vote in favor of takeover bids offering the greatest short-term returns. In a takeover situation, an outside offer could be rejected if, by disrupting corporate stability and continuity, it hurt the corporation's long-term interests. Proposals to declassify boards and to promote directorial independence, said the guidelines, "while generally desirable, had to be weighed against any tendency of these practices to induce myopic business decisions." The language was incorporated into the AFL-CIO's guidelines.

Later on, union investors offered their own ideas to encourage long-term thinking: tying up stock-based pay for at least five years after the recipient left the company, setting a minimum ownership period of at least six months until a shareholder would be allowed to vote, and limiting proxy access to those who'd held shares for several years. A long-term horizon for business decisions was a deterrent to bust-up takeovers and to hedge funds, as well as a good fit to the long-term liabilities of pension funds. It also undergirded worker training investments and the stability of jobs and wages.[37]

The emphasis on "long term" was an encouragement to other institutional investors. They were more likely to exercise voice—to become activists in search of cookbook-style governance changes—if they retained shares for at least several years, or so it was hoped. While professing their lengthy time horizons, public pension funds often failed to walk their talk. They actively traded a portion of their equities, around half between 1990 and 2013, with holding durations averaging around a year. A portfolio manager quipped that "Pension trustees can seem concerned about the long-term performance of their funds in one room and then they seem overly concerned about the short-term performance in the next office over."[38]

Accountability

Globalization was on many minds during the 1990s. United Nation's Secretary-General, Kofi Annan, wanted the UN to play a larger role in steering globalization in sustainable and socially responsible directions. In 2000, the UN created two new organizations to realize Annan's vision: The Global Compact for corporations and the Principles for Responsible Investment (PRI) for investors and asset managers. They asked signatories to pledge adherence to environmental, social, and governance (ESG) standards. The assumption was that having companies publicly endorse the UN's standards and report on compliance would lead to accountability. The social measures included the ILO's Labour Standards, while the tenets of corporate governance drew on the cookbook, with an emphasis on corporate boards. The PRI occasionally would prove helpful to labor's financial turn.

The AFL-CIO's guidelines were filled with calls for corporate accountability. But it was unclear precisely what this meant. Bill Patterson and Ron Blackwell, who would become the AFL-CIO's chief economist, drew a distinction between corporate social responsibility (CSR) and what they called "corporate social accountability." In their view, the problem with CSR—as with the UN's orientation—was its lack of enforcement mechanisms. Without them, CSR was little more than an appeal to the corporate conscience. Blackwell cited the food company, Chiquita Brands, which repeatedly had been accused of exploiting workers and suppressing unions in Latin America. Chiquita was the first American signatory to the Global Compact. For Blackwell, the solution was clear: collective bargaining, which he said was "the most important source of power in holding corporations accountable."[39]

Damon Silvers and Michael Garland, also at the AFL-CIO, were more inclined to the UN's approach, but they added a caveat. The ideal of disinterested, independent directors was flawed, they said, because directors, like executives, were poorly monitored. The best approach was to implement "real structures of accountability to shareholders," such as proxy access, which would permit long-term shareholders to nominate directors. They admitted that this solution was imperfect because "efforts to ensure managerial accountability to shareholders may appear to favor shareholder dominance." And therein lay the rub.[40]

Keeping a check on boards and CEOs via long-term owners was problematic because owners, too, lacked accountability. And collective bargaining was a theoretical desideratum, absent from most US corporations. Who, then, would ensure accountability and to whom would they be accountable? It was a conundrum that lay at the heart of the AFL-CIO's guidelines.

Socially Responsible Investing

A different route to accountability was socially responsible investing (SRI) through mutual funds and ETFs that invest in companies that meet ESG standards. Some funds screen out firms with low ESG scores; others seek those with high scores. There also are funds that avoid entire industries, such as tobacco, guns, and gambling. Ron Blackwell's view of SRI predictably was jaundiced: It "makes people feel good about themselves and allows them to exercise their conscientious feelings. That's good but it doesn't change those companies' behavior because there's no accountability." Accountability might come if a refusal to purchase a company's stock drove down its price, but in reality the relatively small size of the SRI sector as compared to the rest of the market left companies impervious. Blackwell added that there were issues that ESG principles couldn't address: "If I was going to screen on the basis of companies that didn't overpay their CEOs, I'd have trouble getting a diversified portfolio." Nevertheless, union investors regularly partnered with SRI mutual funds and SRI asset managers.[41]

Sunlight's Many Uses

Mutual Funds

The mutual fund industry was a roadblock to labor's activism. The industry had ballooned in size with the advent of IRAs and 401(k)s. By the end of 2007, it held a quarter of all US corporate equities. Dominating the industry were a few behemoths like Fidelity Investments and the Vanguard Group. Fidelity was the largest shareholder in one of every ten US corporations, and its stakes sometimes amounted to 10 percent or more of their shares.

Mutual funds did not have to disclose how they voted their proxies. It was an open secret that the funds routinely voted with management because they didn't want to compromise their lucrative business of managing corporate benefit plans. A quarter of Fidelity's revenue in 2001 came from benefits administration: direct fees (paid by the client company) and indirect fees (paid by the employees who invested in Fidelity mutual funds). None of the fund families wanted to bite the hands of the corporate customers who fed them.

Mutual funds were the most passive of passive investors. The late John Bogle, the founder of Vanguard, said that not a single mutual fund had ever sponsored a shareholder proposal opposed by management. Publicly the funds said nothing about corporate governance—neither shareholder rights nor boards nor executive pay—despite the common belief that those issues affected the value of customers' holdings. University of Michigan business professors Gerald Davis and E. Han Kim found that CalPERS always voted for independent board chairs and to permit shareholder votes on golden parachutes. Fidelity never did.[42]

As unions became active owners, they put mutual funds in their sights. The goal was to undermine the funds' reflexive support for management. Steelworkers president Leo Gerard told a gathering of pension fund activists in 1996, "We've got to rip the veil of secrecy off [from mutual funds] and start telling people what's going on." Come the summer of 2000, the AFL-CIO, the Teamsters, the Consumer Federation of America, and several others sent letters to the SEC seeking disclosure requirements for proxy votes by mutual funds. "Transparency, accountability, and full disclosure must be the watchwords," intoned Trumka. The major fund companies, including Fidelity, said there was no need for disclosure because their customers didn't care how they voted.[43]

The 2002 Sarbanes-Oxley Act, a response to Enron and other instances of executive malfeasance, contained provisions for enhanced financial disclosure and controls. Harvey Pitt, then the SEC chair, believed it was consistent with SOX to ask mutual funds to report their proxy votes. Another factor weighing on Pitt was the SEC's investigation of late trading by twenty-five big mutual funds to benefit their hedge fund clients. (New York Attorney General Eliot Spitzer conducted a separate inquiry.) After the SEC released for comment a draft of its disclosure plan, activists mounted a full-court press to sway the final vote. In the lead was labor—chiefly the AFL-CIO and AFSCME—followed by social investors and state and local plans. The AFL-CIO "flooded" the SEC with a record eight thousand letters. As the comment period neared an end, the AFL-CIO arranged demonstrations in front of Fidelity's headquarters and its retail sites in nineteen cities. At a location in Washington, DC, a leader asked the crowd, "Why is Fidelity fighting against corporate reform?" The crowd answered in a chant, "Rich and rude, we don't like your attitude."[44]

At the time, the labor movement was furious with Fidelity for supporting management at the Stanley Corporation, a venerable hardware manufacturer headquartered in New Britain, Connecticut. Stanley had been transferring production from the United States to Mexico and China, laying off skilled union members. In 2002, it even announced a plan to reincorporate in Bermuda. Shareholders were told that this would save the company $30 million. The AFL-CIO asked institutional investors to oppose the move—and had support from CalPERS—but a majority of shareholders approved it. Bill Patterson's office analyzed the proxy votes and, with information from an insider, realized that the only way management could have won was with support from Fidelity, a major investor. The AFL-CIO challenged Fidelity to report how it voted, but it refused. Later there was a rally in front of Boston's Faneuil Hall protesting Fidelity's secrecy, with a group of Stanley workers up from New Britain among the crowd. Patterson informed the protestors, "Fidelity is at the center of all these governance failures." Stanley later withdrew its relocation plan.[45]

Other Republicans besides Pitt favored a change. Michael Oxley, chair of the House Financial Services Committee, said that a disclosure rule would "continue our efforts to restore confidence" in America's financial institutions. The shoe dropped in 2003 when the SEC voted in favor of having mutual funds report their votes. Richard Trumka savored the moment: "I sat across the table with one of their heads and he vowed to go to hell and die before they'd ever change the way they do business. 'We'll never tell you how we vote.' I said, 'that's interesting. Never is a long time.' Four days later the SEC issued the order. They had a vested interest in keeping the system the way it was, you know, rigged."[46]

Mutual funds were back in the news when the Bush administration released a plan to replace part of Social Security with individual, self-managed accounts. Even if only 5 percent was diverted, asset managers stood to earn nearly $1 trillion in fees over time. Leading the campaign for partial privatization was the Alliance for Worker Retirement Security, which was created expressly for the purpose of privatizing Social Security. Led by mutual fund companies, the Alliance included other financial corporations, the National Association of Manufacturers, and the Business Roundtable. Several unions sent letters to the mutual fund companies demanding that they reveal any donations they'd made to the Alliance. Pickets went up outside the offices of Charles Schwab, State Street Corporation, and Wachovia Bank, who were known to be contributors.[47]

Mutual funds reverted to their old patterns after the publicity died down. A 2016 study found that business ties still influenced their proxy votes. The effect was strongest when shareholder proposals passed or failed by narrow margins, meaning that the funds were throwing their weight around to aid management. The larger fund families—Capital Group, Fidelity, and

Vanguard—voted with management against disclosure of political donations on three of every four proposals.[48]

Political Spending

Corporations spend a lot to ensure that their interests are represented in politics. There is a long-standing concern that corporate political spending crowds out less affluent voices, including the labor movement's.

Modern campaign reform began with the Federal Election Campaign Act (1971) that sought to regulate federal election spending. From the start, groups like Common Cause and Congress Watch, a Nader organization, saw the act as full of loopholes. After years of seeking to re-regulate campaign spending, Congress passed the Bipartisan Campaign Reform Act of 2002, known as McCain-Feingold, which barred corporations from contributing to political parties. However, they still could donate to independent political committees known as "527s." Some political expenditures are reported to the government, but the data are scattered in filings with the Federal Elections Commission, tax reports, and state agencies. None of it is standardized, and few companies provide user-friendly information to shareholders.

Industry associations, however, are allowed to contribute to candidates, political parties, and political action committees (PACs)—all without disclosure. The associations run the gamut from the Business Roundtable and the US Chamber of Commerce at the top to trade associations for nearly every industry imaginable, among the largest being the American Hospital Association, American Petroleum Institute, the National Retail Federation, and the Securities Industry & Financial Market Association. Corporations are not obliged to tell shareholders how these organizations are spending their contributions. The Supreme Court's landmark decision in 2010, *Citizens United*, removed limits on corporate spending during elections, setting off a national debate about corporate power in a democratic polity.[49]

The craw in labor's throat was the uneven playing field. Unlike corporations, unions are subject to broad disclosure rules, including annual reports detailing their political spending. Following a 1977 Supreme Court ruling, members of public employee unions were permitted to opt out from paying the portion of their union dues spent on political causes they did not support, and a 1988 ruling applied the same logic to private-sector union dues. With their political power constrained, unions sought to do the same to corporations.[50]

In the wake of McCain-Feingold, a search began for more disclosure than required by the law. The Center for Political Accountability (CPA), a small nonprofit, coordinated many of the early efforts, writing a model proposal demanding transparency and regular reports to shareholders about a firm's political activities. Labor, social, and faith-based investors began to file versions of the CPA proposal. Among the earliest were the Adrian Dominican Sisters, the Sisters of Mercy–Detroit, Green Century Capital, and SEIU, who all withdrew their CPA-style proposals after negotiating disclosure agreements in 2004 at five big corporations.[51]

Of particular concern to labor was the American Legislative Exchange Council (ALEC), a libertarian, pro-business organization that develops model legislation for states and localities. Over the years, conservative state legislators have submitted hundreds of bills written by the council. Because of ALEC's objections to environmental regulation and its support for oil and coal, it receives donations from oil and mining companies, as well as electrical utilities. Its deregulatory and tort reform advocacy attracts companies in healthcare and manufacturing. ALEC's anti-union mission is reflected in model legislation favoring right-to-work laws, hamstrings on government unions, and an end to defined-benefit pension plans for government employees.

In the 1990s, ALEC—and other libertarian groups like Americans for Prosperity and Americans for Tax Reform—began calling on state and local governments to convert pensions from DB plans to DC accounts. Doing so would reduce unfunded pension liabilities and the need to raise taxes. The groups, along with conservative academic economists, issued dire and overstated warnings about a coming fiscal disaster caused by the liabilities. Libertarians favored the DC approach because it involved individual—rather than collective—savings and was controlled by individuals rather than "bureaucrats." They also hoped that the effort would limit shareholder activism and weaken unions in the public sector.

ALEC's campaign led to some early successes. Two states got rid of their DB plans while thirteen others added supplemental DC accounts, some of them mandatory. Politics, not economics, was the best predictor of these changes. They most often occurred in "trifecta" Republican states, places where the GOP occupied the state house and controlled the legislature. After Republicans swept local governments in the 2010 elections, the number of Republican trifecta states increased and with that came new mandatory DC accounts for public employees.[52]

ALEC operated in obscurity for years and firms did not report their donations to it. The curtain was drawn back in 2011, when the council recommended a Florida-style "stand-your-ground" gun law in reaction to the shooting of Trayvon Martin, an unarmed black teenager. The National Rifle Association, one of ALEC's founders, favored the law. Communities of color were outraged, more so when they learned of ALEC's activities on behalf of voter ID laws. The revelations energized a movement to force business to be more forthcoming about its political spending.

In the background was a Republican Party loath to inhibit the flow of contributions from business to GOP causes and candidates. Then came *Citizens United*. The Supreme Court unwound parts of McCain-Feingold related to corporate political activity, holding it unconstitutional to prevent companies from spending on elections. The decision recommended private orderings: shareholders, not regulators, should be the ones to determine whether political contributions advanced their interests, and they had the option of removing directors of companies whose spending decisions they opposed. Five years after *Citizens United*, the discrepancy between the financial resources available to labor and business had grown huge. During the 2015–16 election cycle, business outspent labor by a ratio of 16 to 1. The same was true of lobbying. As reported by the *New York Times*, "All of the nation's unions, taken together, spend about $48 million a year for lobbying in Washington, while corporate America spends $3 billion."

Facing strong headwinds in Washington, unions shifted to private orderings instead. Between 2004 and 2012, there were 541 political-spending proposals related to disclosure of lobbying activity and contributions to industry associations and groups like ALEC. Most were withdrawn; when that happened, half the companies subsequently made a change. After *Citizens United*, the pace picked up. AFSCME and Walden Asset Management drew together forty investors who then filed and co-filed resolutions demanding disclosure. Included in the coalition were the New York City and State pension plans, the AFL-CIO, Change to Win, and dozens of faith-based and social investors.[53]

Universal disclosure would have to come through the SEC. From its inception, the Center for Political Accountability had petitioned the agency to regulate corporate political spending. CPA sent a letter to SEC chair William Donaldson in 2004 signed by a dozen state treasurers in charge of their state's pension plans. It asked Donaldson "to let the sun shine on corporate contributions, so that the tens of millions of shareholders in America's public companies can know how their money is being used in the nation's political life." On the heels of *Citizens United*, there was another run at the SEC.[54]

Mary Jo White, who took over the SEC in 2013, was in the hot seat, grilled about the issue by Republicans, executives, and industry associations on the one hand and Democrats and shareholder activists on the other. Worried that the SEC might lean the wrong way, House Republicans offered bills making it illegal for the agency to issue political disclosure rules. A representative of Americans for Prosperity—an advocacy group funded by the Koch family—ominously commented about White, "We're keeping an eye on her." The Democrats prepared pro-disclosure legislation, while the White House floated the idea of disclosure rules for federal contractors.

The *Wall Street Journal*'s editorial page called the disclosure campaign an attempt by "unions, left-wing activists, and their factotums . . . to vilify companies that disagree with them." On the other side, the *New York Times* said that changes were necessary "to protect democracy from the flood of money unleashed by the *Citizens United* decision." At the end of 2013, White announced that she was removing the issue from the SEC's agenda, blaming a heavy workload related to Dodd-Frank.

The move forced transparency proponents back into the realm of private orderings. Each year between 2014 and 2017 saw an average of sixty political disclosure proposals filed by social investors, and pension plans, especially from New York City and State. The effort yielded half-full, half-empty results. By 2017, 90 percent of the S&P 500 had policies addressing their election contributions. But half had no board oversight, and only 12 percent reported their federal lobbying expenditures. Few revealed spending at the state and local levels or names of lobbying organizations to which they contributed. Lucian A. Bebchuk and Robert J. Jackson, Jr. observed that "the quality of the information that large public companies have so far provided to investors through voluntary disclosure policies is generally low. Many of these disclosures make it difficult to ascertain the actual amount of corporate funds spent on a particular political issue as well as the recipients of those funds."[55]

The twinned campaigns for disclosure—of mutual-fund proxy voting and corporate political spending—reinforced each other, scored some successes, and modestly changed the balance of power in politics and corporate governance. The disclosure norm went back to Brandeis, traveled along the century's chain of liberal reckoning with corporations and democracy, and finally found its way into progressive shareholder activism.

Pushback

Attempts to shed light on corporate political activities were not well received by the business associations whose bread and butter was lobbying. In 2007, the US Chamber of Commerce sent letters to the heads of the SEC and the Treasury Department, as well as to the Department of Labor, charging that union pension plans were violating ERISA's provisions on fiduciary responsibility. The SEC and the Treasury did not reply. The Labor Department wrote to the Chamber, affirming that it was unlawful to use pension fund assets to promote union organizing, collective bargaining, or "myriad public policy preferences" if doing so sacrificed investment returns. The department released two interpretive bulletins addressing the same issues. Neither the letter nor the bulletins broke fresh ground; they were written to assuage the Chamber.[56]

The issue might have rested there had not Eugene Scalia, former solicitor for the Labor Department and son of the late Supreme Court Justice, published an opinion piece in the *Wall Street Journal* discussing issues raised by the Chamber. He singled out a "reported union plan" to encourage shareholder proposals seeking disclosure of contributions to organizations opposed to national health insurance. Scalia urged his former colleagues at the Labor Department to "conduct investigations and bring federal court actions when pension assets are misused" on activities inimical to their fiduciary responsibilities.[57] Scalia cited the recently completed dissertation of a University of Chicago graduate student that purported to show that union pension funds "systematically exercise their proxies to support labor objectives rather than simply to increase shareholder value."[58]

The Chamber next financed a report analyzing ten companies that had received political disclosure proposals from shareholders. The report concluded that there was "little to no evidence of measurable improvements" in the stock market or operating performance as a result of the proposals. The Chamber released a related study singling out proposals from union plans. After reading it, Representative Pete Sessions (R-TX) said that "Americans don't see all the angles unions are going after." Union investors, he claimed, were "interested in flipping the free enterprise system." Sniping at labor's shareholder pursuits also came from libertarian organizations like the Manhattan Institute and the Competitive Enterprise Institute.[59]

Researchers have found that labor's shareholder activism bears little similarity to the picture painted by libertarian and anti-union advocates. Shareholders give strong support to many of the proposals from union funds, including on the issue of political transparency. So do proxy advisors like ISS and Glass Lewis, who said that they would generally recommend a vote in favor of political disclosure. According to economist Andrew Prevost, although labor's activism "may be undertaken on behalf of the union's constituents, the market's assessment is that the benefits of activism more than offset the costs for majority-supported proposals at unionized targets."[60]

———

Labor's financial turn followed the change to which John Pound had alluded: the unleashing of shareholder power. Union investors grew more sophisticated and successful over time, despite numerous difficulties. The Manhattan Institute complained that nearly all shareholder resolutions not filed by individuals were coming from unions and investors with a social, religious, or public policy purpose. To which *The Economist* retorted, "But so what? Activists prevail only when they persuade a majority of shareholders that their ideas will make money."[61]

4

Breaking Barriers, Building Bridges

UNION-INFLUENCED PENSION PLANS had the will but not always the way to become shareholder activists. A big problem was the SEC, which historically was a brake on their efforts. Multiemployer plans had additional problems. Many were small and lacking expertise. After John Sweeney became AFL-CIO president, he put in place an infrastructure to encourage their activism. Union investors also reached out to players in the investing world—the big public plans, CII, and proxy advisors such as ISS.

Problems at the SEC

The SEC's proxy voting rules had for years been "stacked in management's favor," this according to Dale Hanson of CalPERS. But in 1989, CalPERS took the lead in challenging the agency, offering nearly fifty separate proposals to loosen up proxy rules. The Business Roundtable was adamant in its opposition and sent letters to the SEC and testified in Congress against the proposals, fearing a tidal wave of shareholder activism would challenge management's discretion. According to Bruce Atwater, CEO of General Mills and a Roundtable officer, "No one has said it point-blank, but a question that could come up is, 'What makes you think you know so much about our business?'"[1]

Instead of reflexively backing management, the SEC's chairman, Richard C. Breeden, a Republican appointee, surprised many by calling for a "shareholder bill of rights." Breeden accepted the argument made by Reagan-era economists that shareholder primacy would help revitalize American industry and do so without government interference. He rejected The Roundtable's claims that changing the agency's proxy policies would hurt corporations: "I think we have a hyperactive imagination at work here."[2]

The SEC amended the rules in 1992. Investors were now allowed to discuss such topics as their target lists, which the SEC had previously forbade. By coordinating their votes, large pension funds and their allies could become a type of blockholder. Investors were given permission to broadcast their views and strategies openly. In the past, the SEC's staff had vetted shareholder communications "like a bunch of Russian censors," said John Pound. Now, open statements became the norm. CalPERS began issuing its focus lists right after the new rules came out.[3]

Active owners still faced an obstacle—the SEC's ordinary business exclusion (OBE) rule, which permitted companies to omit from the proxy any proposal pertaining to routine business decisions. The rule, which went back to 1954, a time when management was fending off investor incursions, assumed that there existed a sphere of management decision-making in which shareholders should not interfere. The SEC's staff was empowered to decide what fell within OBE limitations. The terrain was broad: Shareholders usually were forbidden from offering proposals touching on social and political issues, the workplace, and, at one time, now-standard topics such as executive pay.[4]

The Business Exclusion Rule

Because OBE judgments are made on a case-by-case basis and because of political considerations—SEC commissioners are partisan—the SEC's OBE rulings have zigged and zagged over the years. The courts chastised the SEC in 1970 for allowing Dow Chemical to remove from its proxy a proposal to cease the manufacture of napalm. Sounding like Ralph Nader, the courts said that shareholder activism was "corporate democracy" in action and that shareholders had a right and duty "to control the important decisions which affect them as owners of the corporation." After that, the SEC permitted shareholder resolutions on human rights, South Africa, and Northern Ireland, to name a few.[5]

For the SEC, executive pay lay within the boundaries of ordinary business and was therefore off limits to shareholders. Among those annoyed by this was Senator Carl Levin, a liberal from Michigan, who berated the agency in 1991 for leaving shareholders "without recourse to challenge spectacular pay increases for dismal or even mediocre performance." Levin introduced the Corporate Pay Responsibility Act, which would require the SEC to allow pay-related proposals, this when executive excess was in the news. Breeden couldn't ignore Congress so, in February 1992, the agency sanctioned what Levin's act sought.[6]

Also contentious were so-called social proposals. In 1982, the SEC restricted them, this after President Reagan appointed new commissioners, including John Shad. Proposals related to the workplace were permissible but required to have an underlying public policy concern, like equal employment opportunity (EEO) or occupational safety. Confusingly, however, the agency changed its stance ten years later, this time in a more restrictive direction, and limited social proposals. Invoking the business-exclusion rule, it disallowed a demand from ACTWU and faith-based investors that Walmart produce a report on its EEO practices. In response, ACTWU's Michael Zucker blasted the SEC for "a Reagan-Bush approach to regulation." The second decision involved Cracker Barrel Old Country Store, a Tennessee-based restaurant chain that had been charged with discriminatory policies against gays and lesbians. Citing the exclusion rule, the SEC permitted Cracker Barrel to omit a shareholder proposal demanding that the company include sexual orientation in its anti-discrimination policy. NYCERS, which was the resolution's lead sponsor, also filed a lawsuit to overturn the SEC's decision. Although NYCERS won the first round, it lost on appeal.[7]

Amid continuing controversy, the SEC offered a new rule in 1997 that would overturn Cracker Barrel but broaden the OBE in other areas. Shareholder activists—from ICCR, public pension plans, and labor unions—were incensed, as were some members of Congress. At this point, Harvey J. Goldschmid, a Democrat and law professor (and later to be SEC commissioner), and Ira M. Millstein, a management attorney, convened a group of executives and activists to develop an alternative. The SEC reversed course: Proposals addressing significant social policy concerns would generally be permitted on the proxy. It was a victory for those seeking corporate accountability.[8]

Building an Infrastructure

Unions had high hopes after Bill Clinton's election in 1992. With Democrats in control of Congress, it was an auspicious moment for labor law reform. But Clinton and some congressional Democrats were reluctant to spend political capital on the issue. Two years later, Republicans took control of the House for the first time since 1954, thwarting labor's legislative agenda.

Within the labor movement many believed that the AFL-CIO's president, Lane Kirkland, should resign. High on the bill of particulars was Kirkland's failure to make organizing a priority for the federation; only with a larger labor movement, said John Sweeney, SEIU's president, would unions again be a potent force. Kirkland eventually agreed to leave but named as his heir apparent Tom Donahue, viewed as little better than Kirkland. Those seeking an assertive, growth-oriented replacement for Kirkland put their hopes in Sweeney, whose platform, "America Needs a Raise," put inequality front and center. It called for living wages and stepped-up organizing to "close the wage and wealth gap and restore respect to workers." Sweeney challenged the AFL-CIO's affiliated unions to pour money into organizing, calling it a crusade, and was elected federation president in 1995.[9]

It was difficult for the AFL-CIO to take the lead role in organizing. It's a federation of autonomous unions, each of which maintains sovereignty over workers in its jurisdiction. Although the federation under George Meany and Lane Kirkland provided resources to aid affiliates in their organizing attempts, it walked a fine line. The situation began to change after Sweeney's election. Setting an example for its affiliates, the AFL-CIO raised spending on organizing— from $2.5 million in 1995 to $30 million in 1997—about one-third of its total budget. It beefed up the budget of its Training Institute to cover the cost of hiring 1,000 new organizers and set up a program called Union Summer to draw college students into organizing. For the first time the AFL-CIO had an Organizing Department, within which was the Center for Strategic Campaigns. The center coordinated the corporate campaigns of affiliated unions. Adair Dammann, an SEIU organizer in the healthcare industry, observed, "In the olden days there'd never be this sort of support from the AFL. But my experience with Sweeney and the new AFL is that they are deadly serious about organizing."[10]

Sweeney and Trumka had been enthusiasts of financial strategies since their days as union presidents. They created three other units at headquarters that were more closely related to the financial turn: the Department of Corporate Affairs, the Center for Working Capital, and the Office of Investment, all intended to promote and coordinate pension fund activism. To head Corporate Affairs, Sweeney hired economist Ron Blackwell, someone who had cut his teeth under ACTWU's Jack Sheinkman. He next brought on board Bill Patterson and put him in charge of the Office of Investment. Like Blackwell, he was an ACTWU veteran.[11]

The Office of Investment

Bill Patterson immediately hired a staff of experts, prepared an update of the AFL-CIO's 1991 proxy-voting guidelines, and presented the revised guidelines to two hundred Taft-Hartley trustees and union leaders. Patterson sought to "whip Taft-Hartley plans into a more solid voting bloc." He also planned to educate the public about runaway executive pay.[12]

Patterson knew how to draw public attention and make executives squirm. An example was Executive PayWatch, a website that he and Blackwell created in 1997. It listed the compensation received by CEOs at each of the nation's four hundred largest public corporations. Visitors to the site could calculate how many years it would take to earn their CEO's annual compensation. PayWatch had data on a CEO's stock options and the directors who had approved generous grants to underperforming executives. It allowed users to send emails to corporate boards, pension and mutual fund managers, and to Congress.

Executive PayWatch was extremely popular, receiving over four million hits in its first year. For example, site visitors learned how many workers could be supported on Jack Welch's compensation of $40 million. The site also offered "GREED! The Executive PayWatch Board Game," which pitted a CEO with a starting salary of $1 million against a worker making $30,000. Each roll of the dice gave the CEO a chance for steadily larger raises and severance packages, whereas a worker received small gains only once in a while. The PayWatch site was meant to show that "we have spiraling inequality between the executive suite and the shop room floor," according to Brandon Rees of the Office of Investment.[13]

The shareholder submissions receiving the highest percentage of "yes" votes during the 1990s were those opposing staggered boards and poison pills, practices that deterred hostile takeovers. When unions offered proposals on these topics, they obtained votes from institutional investors, on average more than half. Once again, provenance did not matter. UNITE filed a poison-pill rescission to persuade a retailing company to improve working conditions at its foreign apparel suppliers; it received strong support from major investors. According to one of them, "we usually look at the merits of the proposal rather than the motives of the proponents."[14]

For decades, companies had routinely ignored proposals receiving a majority of votes. While with the Teamsters, Bill Patterson came up with a way around the problem: Submit binding resolutions that would become part of a company's bylaws. The first attempt was at the Fleming Companies, which owned supermarkets and transported food, and was a Teamsters employer and organizing target. Fleming earlier had refused to take action after nearly two-thirds of its shareholders voted in 1996 to remove a poison pill. The Teamsters went to court and filed a request to change Fleming's bylaws. After the union received a green light, Fleming caved. Although only a few issues are able to meet the legal requirements for bylaw insertion, the tactic gives shareholders a way around recalcitrant boards and executives. The Office of Investment became a resource for union investors wanting to draft binding proposals. The Hotel and Restaurant Employees sought a binding resolution in its dispute with Harrah's Entertainment, and the SEIU behaved similarly with Columbia/HCA.[15]

The Office of Investment began to issue an annual *Key Votes Survey*, a list of how asset managers had voted on proposals of concern to the union pension plans whose money they invested. Most involved cookbook topics popular with institutional investors: directorial independence, removing poison pills, and eliminating other takeover barriers. They also included proposals with a labor twist: tying CEO pay to a company's layoff history; opposing the conversion of a retirement plan from defined benefit to cash balance; asking companies to endorse universal healthcare; and disclosure of political contributions, equal-employment records, and compliance with global labor and environmental standards.[16]

The AFL-CIO used the voting data to create a report card grading dozens of asset managers. Many of the firms voted less than half of labor's positions; the figure was 20 percent in the case of J. P. Morgan. Several firms voted against all positions and received scores of zero. On the other side, there were asset managers who supported most or all of the key votes. Those with low scores were unhappy with the results, which they claimed were biased. There was a great deal of money at stake for the firms investing pension assets, and a number of Taft-Hartleys dumped asset managers who continued to receive low scores. Rich Trumka, who helped design the survey, said, "Those that have a record of flunking will be ultimately flunked."[17]

The Office of Investment periodically stepped in to aid affiliates. In one of the decade's most bitter labor disputes, the strike between the Steelworkers and Wheeling-Pittsburgh Steel, the union demanded a defined-benefit plan. The two sides were locked in a war of attrition that the Steelworkers appeared to be losing. Patterson went after the company's main shareholder, Dewey Square Investors, a subsidiary of the financial giant UAM. He threatened UAM with the loss of union pension investments unless it changed its "anti-labor position." Said Trumka, "If this is your philosophy, you shouldn't be managing union money." Dewey Square's president persuaded Wheeling-Pitt to settle with the union.[18]

Center for Working Capital

The Center for Working Capital (CWC) was responsible for public relations, tactical planning, and education of trustees. It published the *Investment Product Review*, which contained guidance for pension funds on worker-friendly investment products in real estate and private equity. CWC launched a quarterly newsletter, *Working Capital*, with information on proxy matters, financial markets, pension regulations, and investment options. According to the newsletter, the center was developing "long-term investment strategies which depend on partnerships among shareholders, employees, and communities." CWC convened a Capital Stewardship Forum attended by 150 asset managers, where John Sweeney warned them to be more cognizant of the AFL-CIO's *Key Votes* or pension funds would desert them.[19]

CWC held regional forums that brought together trustees from union and public plans, creating networks among people who often did not know each other. It sponsored four trustee-training courses administered by the National Labor College, which is affiliated with the AFL-CIO, with a curriculum covering fiduciary, pension, and securities law; corporate governance; and capital stewardship. Trustees received practical instruction on filing proposals and dealing with asset managers. The lessons on capital stewardship covered topics like promoting good jobs with ETIs and strengthening pension rights through legislation. The course also touched on how financial activism could help organizing efforts. The goal was to offer much-needed information in one place. As Ron Blackwell noted, "The culture of the financial industry is intimidating. The trustees are spirited off to conferences in Hawaii or wherever there is a golf course and the fear of God is put into them on their fiduciary responsibility. On top of that, these trustees are workers. They don't have the time to become experts or the technical and legal support to question the investing decisions. So we are providing that."[20]

In addition, the CWC sought to raise the number of public-plan trustees with union leadership experience. Early on, AFSCME and SEIU, with numerous members working for state and local governments, had lobbied to increase the number of seats designated for trustees elected by participants. SEIU stated at its 2000 convention that "trustees are the union's lead organizers in the financial community and the voice for our members on Wall Street." It is estimated that, ten years later, a third of state and local pension assets were held by plans with at least one elected trustee who had a union background.

SEIU had three trustee-members on the CalPERS board. Support from state and local plans was crucial to labor's shareholder strategy. SEIU assigned one staff member as a permanent liaison to every four large plans.

When SEIU and UNITE-HERE sought to strengthen the neutrality provisions of the CalPERS responsible-contractor policy, several REITs warned CalPERS that they would restrict its participation in future offerings if it took an aggressive stance on contractor behavior. At this point, SEIU brought a group of janitors to a CalPERS board meeting to tell their personal stories. As one observer commented, "It's extremely embarrassing when the trustees are hearing this. They have to say 'this is outrageous' and they truly are disgusted by it. They look over at the staff and say, 'How could you guys have fucked up like this and let us be embarrassed? Then the staff goes, 'we don't want to have that happen again. Let's figure out if we can make these property managers let the union in.'"[21]

Those critical of labor's activism groused that trustees belonging to unions had dual loyalties that tested the limits of their fiduciary duties. However, the evidence is not consistent with the claim. Having union members on pension fund boards is associated with better portfolio performance. Member-trustees care about pension fund performance because their own retirements are at stake. Economist Joel Harper found that "member-elected trustees are more focused on a stable, sustainable plan to provide future benefits as opposed to chasing higher returns through a riskier asset allocation." A different measure, the financial health of a state's pension funds, is positively associated with within-state union density.[22]

Occasional clashes occurred when different unions backed opposite candidates for the same board, but there was also cooperation. For example, SEIU and AFSCME worked together to get an AFSCME member, a librarian, elected by her co-workers to be a trustee of Ohio's $65 billion pension fund. She gave labor a 5-4 majority on the board. On another occasion, the two unions worked together to remove a CalPERS trustee, who, although a union activist, was viewed as inept. At NYCERS, a Teamsters trustee candidate was endorsed by an AFT trustee.[23]

A number of unions had their own trustee-training programs. SEIU's raised issues such as the negative effect of poor labor conditions on a firm's financial performance. During its campaign for responsible-contractor policies, it held trustee workshops on the real estate industry. AFSCME organized conferences to educate trustees from public plans on avoiding investments that would harm state and local employees.[24]

Long before unions initiated trustee training, other organizations had staked out the same terrain. The largest of these was the International Foundation of Employee Benefit Plans (IFEBP), a nonprofit organization. Taft-Hartley trustees could enroll in training courses, including several in conjunction with the Wharton School at the University of Pennsylvania. The IFEBP's annual conference drew over five thousand participants, trustees as well as asset managers seeking clients. Some of those in the public pension world were contemptuous of Taft-Hartley trustees, especially those from small plans, whom they alleged were ignorant of their responsibilities. Bill Crist of CalPERS was one such person. "The main weakness of the Taft-Hartley plans," he said, "is the trustees. There are perks to being a trustee. You get to go to meetings and get off your job. Just so many of them don't have a damn clue. They don't know a fiduciary from a golf course."[25]

The IFEBP occasionally irked the labor movement, as when it gave an award to the author of a book promoting 401(k)s a day before Sweeney told the audience at its annual gathering that 401(k)s were eroding retirement security. Even though the IFEBP's courses covered plain-vanilla tissues without any of the active-owner content that the CWC offered, the CWC could not compete with the larger and more established IFEBP, nor with the programs offered by individual unions. The CWC closed its doors in 2005.

Working the same terrain was the National Coordinating Committee for Multiemployer Plans (NCCMP), a lobbying organization that promotes the interests of Taft-Hartley plans. Its board is weighted toward the building trades. According to Steven Sleigh, formerly with the Machinists and later a director of Amalgamated Bank, the NCCMP's members had little interest in the likes of Bill Patterson. "The union pension fund guys say, 'We don't want to listen to those guys. They're a bunch of bull shitters.' So even within their own house, they have no credibility, because they're talking about things that, quite frankly, don't matter or tangentially matter." Sleigh's comments touched on the fact that union locals often were indifferent to organizing. They also spoke to tension between construction unions and other parts of the labor movement.[26]

Worker–Owner Councils

Ed Durkin was in charge of corporate affairs for the Carpenters union. He was an acerbic critic of the financial turn even though he was part of it. He cited as an example the AFL-CIO's failure to involve rank-and-file workers, as in the preparation of proxy guidelines. It was a valid criticism. However, individual unions made some efforts. The Teamsters occasionally brought groups of workers who owned their employer's shares to annual corporate meetings. The UFCW as well sought opportunities to involve the rank and file, although, as a UFCW staffer admitted, it was a challenge.

Durkin was more ambitious. He created "Worker–Owner Councils" made up of trustees from local Carpenters' pension funds in the same region. The most successful was the Worker–Owner Council of Washington State, representing assets of over $1 billion. Council members developed ongoing relationships with local firms whose stock they held to discuss mutual concerns, such as strengthening the region's economic health, and the benefits of hiring the union's well-trained members. One of those companies was Microsoft, which spent millions on local construction. In the early 2000s, the Carpenter's multiemployer plans in the northwest held a combined total of over 20 million Microsoft shares. The head of the council, Doug Kilgore, told trustees how to communicate with executives and directors in one-on-one meetings, something usually handled by attorneys and pension staff. Councils were created in other areas too. In Cincinnati, Durkin identified all of the Taft-Hartleys from the area's construction unions, mapped their investment ties to local firms, and then invited the companies to meet with the trustees. The building trades offered something potentially of value to employers—highly skilled workers— as well as a tradition of cooperating with management. Taft-Hartleys from lower-wage service industries had less on offer.[27]

Labor's Allies

Council of Institutional Investors

Taft-Hartley equity holdings were small as compared to public and corporate plans, so they needed allies if they were to be more than gadflies. The Council of Institutional Investors was a logical partner. Over time, Taft-Hartleys grew to be a quarter of CII's members, while the rest were split between corporate and public plans. The union plans needed backing from about half the state and local plans to sway the council. Among the most congenial were those from the top ten states in terms of union representation, notably California, with a union density rate of 20 percent, Connecticut (18 percent), and the giant, New York (27 percent).

As union investors learned the cookbook's language, it became easier to find supporters, even when the union had a collateral interest. According to

Beth Young, "If [labor funds] do a proposal that says, 'You should take our interests into account because it's the right thing to do,' you'll get no support. If you construct a plausible sort of logic chain that affects the financial well-being of the company, you can actually get some surprising amount of institutional support."

On a number of occasions, labor used its council relationships to pressure people and organizations with ties to state and local pension plans. For example, sitting on the board of an anti-union company was the CFO of a major asset manager that handled billions of dollars for public plans. CII's union members persuaded several public plans to contact the asset manager and threaten that, because of the CFO's directorship, it might pull their money.[28]

That's not to say that unions controlled CII; far from it. Teslik had tried for years to steer the council away from matters that she thought were unrelated to core investor concerns. Her goal was to maintain CII's reputation for impartiality and minimize divisions among its factions: union, corporate, and public plans, with the latter divided into those from red states (majority Republican) and those from blue states (majority Democrat). But reaching consensus was not always possible. In 1989, CII took a position in favor of investing pension funds in the junk bonds that financed LBOs, which union plans opposed but corporate and public plans favored.

Tension was built into the relationship between public and union plans. SEIU's Dennak Murphy said, "We have nearly 800,000 members, most of whom are in public employee retirement funds. The public funds take their money and buy stock in two or three thousand companies. Then a lot of those companies turn around and screw the workers [in those companies]." Once again, the "workers" belonging to state and local plans were not the same workers in whose companies the plans invested.[29]

Conflict periodically surfaced at CII between its "left" (union plans and public plans from blue states) and its "right" (corporate plans and those from red states). To steer clear of the right, Patterson tried to create a group of activist plans that would be independent of CII. Potential members were the signatories to a 2002 letter that the AFL-CIO sent to Unocal, the oil company, to protest its labor policies in Burma. Included among them were larger Taft-Hartleys, CalPERS, the New York and Connecticut funds, LongView, and USS, the British pension plan for university employees. Patterson denied that the group intended to compete with CII and said it simply would be "more operational," but the group never coalesced.[30]

CalPERS

When elected officials are close to the labor movement, unions can gain friendly voices on pension boards. In California, labor pulled out all the stops in 1998 to elect Democrat Gray Davis, who was to be California's first Democratic governor in sixteen years. As governor, Davis had the power to appoint several trustees to the state's pension plans, including CalPERS and CalSTRS, two behemoths. Sean Harrigan, a UFCW vice president, was appointed to the CalPERS board by Davis. The new state treasurer, Phil Angelides, another Democrat, received ex-officio seats on the CalPERS and CalSTRS boards.

CalPERS moved in new directions during Davis's tenure: divesting its tobacco stocks, protesting the high cost of AIDS drugs, and, at the urging of Angelides, a real estate developer, making sizable investments in local business and real estate to benefit the state's poorer communities. Angelides quipped that the Latino market in California was every bit as much of an emerging market as those in other parts of the world. Inspiring Angelides was "the double bottom line"—the idea that a firm's social impact had to be considered along with its financial performance. As for foreign investments, CalPERS put in place a "negative" screen prohibiting investments in nations that lacked basic human and labor rights, a policy that the California AFL-CIO helped to develop. CalPERS also joined the "Come Home to America" campaign led by nineteen major public and union plans who demanded that American corporations headquartered in foreign countries reincorporate in the United States, this after the Stanley Corporation–Fidelity Investments dispute. The issue joined governance issues (foreign incorporation hindered investor scrutiny) to government concerns (the companies reduced their taxes while laying off workers).

By 2002, all thirteen CalPERS trustees had a union background or were Democratic state officials. The labor faction was split, however. There were newly appointed trustees with a worker–owner agenda, like Sean Harrigan, from the UFCW; and then there was the Old Guard, people like Robert Carlson and Bill Crist, academics from the state employees' association who were trustees when the cookbook first was being formulated. The longer-serving trustees didn't want to deviate from the policies they'd helped develop. Politically cautious, they were leery of people like Angelides; however, they liked the idea of investing in construction projects based in California, which boosted wages and employment in the state.[31]

Harrigan was elected president of the CalPERS board in 2003. Many expected that he would tie the system's billions more tightly to labor's aspirations. Nine months later, Gray Davis lost the governorship to a Republican, Arnold Schwarzenegger. There was trouble on the horizon.[32]

The flash point was a 2003 dispute between several California supermarket chains and their unionized employees, members of the UFCW. Claiming that they had to reduce labor costs to compete against Walmart, the supermarkets demanded steep cuts in health insurance and locked out their employees in anticipation of a strike. Leading the employers was Steven Burd, the CEO of Safeway Stores. The UFCW denounced Burd, including in newspaper ads, and picketed dozens of Safeway markets. Then the CalPERS board stuck its neck out and called for Burd's resignation. As the dispute wore on, Harrigan sent letters to the companies, asking that they negotiate in good faith with the union. The letter stressed CalPERS as a long-term investor and said that "fair treatment of employees is a critical element in creating long-term value for shareowners." The AFL-CIO's Office of Investment hosted an analysts' call—sponsored by J. P. Morgan and Citigroup—about the strike that featured Bill Patterson and a vice president of UFCW. A retail analyst from Citigroup explained that her company became involved because "it's important for investors to understand the whole picture, even if they disagree with the union." One result of the call was Smith Barney's downgrade of Safeway stock.[33]

The US Chamber of Commerce charged that the labor movement had "hijacked" CalPERS and was trying "to advance its own agenda at the expense of shareholders." The donnybrook ended in December 2004, when Governor Schwarzenegger clipped CalPERS's wings and engineered Harrigan's departure. The president of the state employees' union said Harrigan's removal was a signal from business to "knock it off and leave CEOs alone." Harrigan was replaced by Rob Feckner, a former president of the California School Employees Association, who steered a more cautious course.[34]

Having CalPERS take sides in a labor dispute hurt union investors and CalPERS as well. Insiders—attorney Beth Young, for example—blamed Harrigan for "political thuggery [without] enough substance." Edward Durkin felt that Harrigan had been too abrasive and lacked an analysis of Safeway's business situation. Bringing management pain to bear was, in Durkin's eyes, counterproductive and squandered the credibility of labor's governance agenda.[35]

For CalPERS, Harrigan's departure was small potatoes compared to what Governor Schwarzenegger announced the following month: a ballot measure to convert California's pension plans to individual DC accounts. If voters had approved the measure, it would not immediately have eliminated CalPERS and the state's other plans, but their asset base and influence would have steadily diminished.

In promoting his scheme, the governor never mentioned Harrigan, labor trustees, or anything directly related to unions. Instead, he argued that California could no longer afford the cost and uncertainty of DB pensions. To make his point, he held a press conference with two Brinks armored trucks parked behind him. "Right now, our treasury is like the armored cars right behind me—the door's kicked wide open and the money's flying out and bleeding our state dry." Business leaders and conservative anti-tax groups launched an organization called Citizens to Save California, which lobbied to privatize the state's pension plans. Like the governor, the group was careful not to criticize unions directly; nor did it say anything about reining in active owners. But it was no secret that Republicans were furious at CalPERS for "pressing an aggressive union agenda under the banner of shareholder rights."[36]

Angelides blasted the ballot measure. In his opinion, its supporters didn't like CalPERS because they didn't like pushy shareholders, regardless of any labor agenda: "The old holders of capital—the old status quo—are very nervous about this discussion of capital and the larger context of what's good for the economy. They don't want these questions asked. They don't want the old order to be changed." California voters defeated the measure. Angelides opposed other Republican-led attempts to privatize state-provided services such as school transportation, the latter at the behest of SEIU.[37]

Conservatives who complain about the politicization of blue-state plans fail to mention similar politicization of plans from red states. For example, in 2003 the Florida State Retirement System (FSRS) put up nearly all the money for a private equity firm to purchase Edison Services, an operator of private schools that drew students from public schools. The FSRS had only three trustees: then-Governor Jeb Bush, who was its chairman, and two other Republicans. The previous year Bush sought reelection on a platform that included school vouchers, school privatization, and attacks on teachers' unions.[38]

The Interfaith Center on Corporate Responsibility

A steadfast ally of labor were faith-based investors belonging to the Interfaith Center on Corporate Responsibility (ICCR). From its anti-apartheid beginnings, ICCR went on to become a shareholder activist, submitting between fifty and two hundred proposals each year on the environment, tobacco, weapons, healthcare, debt relief, and human rights. Its membership of several hundred organizations includes endowments, pension plans, and investment funds associated with faith groups, and they have assets totaling over $100 billion. ICCR's support gave legitimacy to union funds when they said their concerns were ethically grounded.

According to the International Labour Organization, the right to join a union is a human right. ICCR and union investors cooperated to force multinational giants like Nike, Gap, and Disney to reform their foreign labor practices. The companies were sensitive about their reputation and alarmed by proposals mentioning them in connection to child labor, forced labor, prison labor, and suppression of unions. The proposals typically asked that the firm adopt the ILO's labor standards as well as codes of conduct for producers in their supply chains. But even though brand image was important to these consumer-facing companies, they were reluctant to act. ICCR regularly filed the same resolutions year after year. It worked with companies on developing their conduct codes, as at Disney, which adopted guidelines on worker rights following six years of being pushed.[39]

Union investors worked closely with ICCR on other labor issues. The Steelworkers teamed up with ICCR to demand that Alcoa offer a living wage to its Mexican employees. Religious and union investors criticized Kohl's and other retailers who sold garments manufactured by vendors in Nicaragua and El Salvador, where pro-union workers had been intimidated and fired. The Adrian Dominican Sisters and the Jesuit Conference submitted proposals asking Chevron and Halliburton to adopt policies on labor rights, as well as asking McDonalds to endorse the ILO standards.[40]

ICCR participated in labor's campaign to get Walmart to pay better wages and benefits and to stop harassing union supporters. An early action came in 1992, when ACTWU and three ICCR members (the Dominican Sisters of St. Catherine, the National Council of Churches, and the Unitarian Universalist Association) offered a resolution demanding that Walmart release data on the gender and race composition of its employees and report annually on the number of women and minorities in management. When Walmart refused to include the proposal on its proxy statement, a stance that the SEC permitted under the ordinary business exclusion, the four investors sued in federal court.

Walmart's CEO, Lee Scott, began meeting with ICCR members in the early 2000s to discuss labor conditions in the factories that supplied its stores. While Walmart drew the line at openly discussing its own employment practices, it did make changes to its supply-chain standards. Critics could charge that UFCW and ACTWU had collateral interests when they filed proposals at Walmart, but it was impolitic to say that the Benedictine Sisters of Boerne, Texas, should be prohibited from acting on their moral principles.[41]

ICCR also joined unions on conventional governance issues like executive pay. It asked six companies—including J. P. Morgan and Pfizer—to do what it later demanded of Enron: to report the pay gap between their CEOs and their lowest-paid workers. J. P. Morgan challenged the request at the SEC by claiming that the terms "lowest-paid worker" and "top executive" were ambiguous. Sister Pat Wolf of ICCR said she was "astonished": "This is obstructive and damaging to their image." Most investors were reluctant to vote for ICCR's social proposals, which frequently received support below 15 percent. It wasn't a deterrent to ICCR, which believed that starting conversations about the issues it raised mattered as much if not more than winning shareholder votes.[42]

Proxy Advisors

Reaching out to proxy advisors, who conduct research on thousands of domestic and international companies and provide voting recommendations to their clients, was another way for union funds to achieve critical mass. The giant in this world is Institutional Shareholder Services (ISS), which monitors tens of thousands of shareholder meetings around the globe every year. ISS was inclined to endorse union proposals if they were drawn from the cookbook. Precisely how many proxy votes are swayed by ISS is a matter of dispute. There's no doubt that the figure is substantial—somewhere around 6–13 percent at the low end and 40 percent at the high end. In some major fights, such as Hewlett Packard's acquisition of Compaq and the vote against CEO Michael Eisner at Disney, ISS's recommendations are credited with tipping the balance. More striking is the finding that no proxy proposal was ever successful unless ISS had given its approval. Although ISS had plenty of pension funds as clients, much of its revenue came from mutual funds who also were its clients. ISS wanted to be a thought leader on corporate governance, but it had to be responsive to the inclinations of its customers and its owners.[43]

Robert Monks, who founded ISS, envisioned the organization at the center of the shareholder movement. ISS circulated lists of corporations with negative governance practices, what it called NGPs. When communicating with pension clients, Monks urged them to submit proposals for eliminating NGPs that "unduly diminish owners' rights." The details have changed since then, but ISS today still adheres to the cookbook in making its recommendations. Governance expert John M. Richardson notes that "it's in ISS's interests to create a cookbook because it's easy to peddle. But if you are a fiduciary fund, you've got to take more of a nuanced approach . . . and look at things in a situational context." In the same way that the cookbook is a flawed predictor of performance, so too are proxy advisors. A recent study finds that proxy advisors "do not predict governance-related outcomes with the precision or strength necessary to support the bold claims made by most of these firms."[44]

Monks, as we have seen, was highly visible in the world of shareholder activism. In the early days, he worked closely with CII on proxy contests, especially those involving takeovers. He advised Richard Koppes and Dale Hanson at CalPERS and unsuccessfully tried in the mid-1990s to get CalPERS to invest in the business ventures he launched after selling ISS. Monks had better luck with the Wisconsin plan and with Hermes Asset Management, which until recently was owned by the BT (British Telecom) Pension Scheme. When Monks repurchased ISS, Hermes was a major investor in the deal. ISS repeatedly has faced charges that it has conflicts of interest.[45]

ISS had subsidiary parts serving different types of clients. It launched a division in 1998, Proxy Voting Services (PVS), which provided Taft-Hartleys with customized guidelines mimicking the AFL-CIO's. PVS provided a channel for Taft-Hartleys to communicate with other parts of ISS.[46]

ISS also had a Social Advisory Services division, most of whose clients were socially responsible mutual funds. Here too, its recommendations were different from its advice to mainstream investors. It developed voting guidelines that backed proposals promoting the ILO standards, broader codes of ethical conduct, and disclosure of plant-closing criteria. When IBM slashed employee pensions and retiree health benefits, an IBM employee group affiliated with the Communications Workers filed a proposal to restore their benefits. Social Advisory Services approved the measure, saying that IBM's new scheme "has resulted in negative public sentiment and poor employee morale, which in our opinion could have a material adverse effect on the company." On several occasions, ISS recommended to all of its clients, not only the SRI funds, that they vote yes on submissions requesting Nike and retailers like Dillards and Urban Outfitters to require their suppliers to adopt the ILO's labor standards. The Labor Policy Association, an anti-union group whose members are senior HR executives, blasted ISS for "carrying the water for organized labor."[47]

A third ISS unit was its corporate services division, which "provides corporations with insights into the concerns of institutional investors" and advises them on responding to shareholder proposals. ISS argued that the various sides of its business were managed with firewalls between them. But Graef

Crystal, the compensation consultant, said that ISS had "a severe conflict when they work both sides of the street." A decade later, attorney Ira Millstein said much the same thing: "If your governance is not getting a good grade, you go see them and they tell you how to get a good grade. If that's not a conflict, I don't know what is."[48]

———

Union investors were on a learning curve during the 1990s. They accumulated know-how, allies, and more favorable regulations. No sooner had the twenty-first century begun than the tech bubble burst. On its heels came Enron's bankruptcy and an uptick in newspaper stories mentioning "financialization." Now it was union investors who took center stage at shareholder meetings and other realms relevant to investors, including Congress.

5

From Exuberance to Enron

THE PACE OF FINANCIAL development quickened under President Bill Clinton. Like Prime Minister Tony Blair, Clinton sought to challenge the libertarian drift set in motion by their predecessors, Margaret Thatcher and Ronald Reagan. Their "Third Way" preserved a role for government as a market buffer, though less generous than what FDR's New Deal and the postwar Labour Party had wrought. Rebalancing meant a larger role for civil society and a shift of responsibility from government and business to individuals. A *Business Week* journalist captured the mood in a 1996 book, *The High-Risk Society*, which argued that by embracing risk, people would better succeed in an economy of rapid technological change. The same rhetoric appeared in *The Commanding Heights*, an influential book published two years later, which contended that globalization had rendered obsolete the claim that citizens needed governments to insure them against risk.[1]

Accompanying the decade's frothy equity markets was a mania for stocks not seen since the 1920s. America, one journalist wrote, had become a "Shareholder Nation: the Republic of Main Street capitalists who are revolutionizing markets, politics and business." The Third Way's leaders were infatuated with the transformative potential they saw in share ownership. Clinton's Labor Secretary, Robert Reich, favored worker ownership of their company's stock, as did Tony Blair, who made it part of his "stakeholder economy."[2] For Clinton, as well as for Blair and Germany's Chancellor Gerhard Schröder, embracing stock markets was an economic as well as a political strategy: a way of drawing better-off voters away from conservative parties.[3]

No sooner had the new century begun than stock markets deflated along with the previous decade's bombast. Investors lost billions. Much of the fault lay with sketchy tech companies and the Wall Street firms who had hawked their shares dishonestly. Less than two years later came the infamy of Enron, followed by a string of bankruptcies at other corporations where executives and auditors had committed wanton fraud. It was the first time in a long while that business—and stock markets—had been roiled by scandals of such immense breadth and audacity. Sensing an opportunity to dethrone imperial CEOS, union investors embraced shareholder activism as never before.

The Clinton Years

The 1992 presidential campaign took place in the midst of a recession. Middle-class anxiety ran high as corporate downsizing hit white-collar workers; news stories of mass layoffs, stagnant wages, and income inequality were everywhere. None other than the *Wall Street Journal* reported that the 2.5 million individuals at the top of the income distribution annually received more money than the 100 million people at the bottom. "That wasn't true in 1980," it observed. "Somehow this has to influence corporate esprit, worker morale, and thus performance." President George H. W. Bush took a disastrous trip to Japan before the election, accompanied by a dozen CEOs from major corporations, including GM's Robert Stempel and Chrysler's Lee Iacocca, who reportedly earned $4.5 million annually despite Chrysler's reputation for shoddy vehicles. The media paired this with the fact that Honda's CEO made less than $400,000, producing a far smaller pay gap than at Honda's competitors from the United States.[4]

Bill Clinton was better than Bush at feeling the nation's pulse. Said the *New York Times*, "When Bill Clinton wants to galvanize his audience, he thunders from the podium that the top 1 percent of families got 60 percent of the gains from economic growth during the 1980s and owns more wealth than the bottom 90 percent." Clinton needled Bush with a memorable phrase, "It's the economy, stupid." Bush's chief economic advisor, Michael J. Boskin, scoffed at Clinton's numbers. Measuring income shares in a mobile society, he said, was as meaningless as measuring which bubbles are at the top of the blender at a given moment. It was not a politically astute comment.[5]

Aiming his populist rhetoric at Republicans, Clinton blasted the Reagan and Bush administrations for "letting self-serving CEOs try to build an empire out of paper and perks instead of people and products." One of his campaign ideas was to eliminate corporate tax deductions for executive salaries exceeding $1 million, which earlier had been recommended by Congress but vetoed by Bush. The *Washington Post* thought that Clinton won the election in part by "riding a wave of public outrage about some fat executive paychecks and stock option grants." And Clinton kept his campaign promise. The 1993 Revenue Reconciliation Act contained an annual ceiling for tax deductions of $1 million each on the salaries of a corporation's five highest-compensated officers. The limit was more show than substance. The law stopped short of counting performance-based rewards like stock options toward the $1 million limit, the result of which was a gusher of stock-based pay.

Clinton thought it was possible to decrease inequality without raising taxes on the wealthy; the bottom would catch up by investing in stocks. During his first campaign he said, "The thing that bothers me is not that people make money. You know, I'd like to create more millionaires than Reagan and Bush did.... What we want is more income equality, and you want people to make money the old-fashioned way by investing it in our goods, our products and our services." There was a problem with Clinton's prescription. Affluent households had sufficient resources for handling the volatility associated with stocks. Not so those at the bottom, who neither owned nor could afford them. Their primary concern was paying off their debts. They did not embrace risk; risk embraced them.[6]

Pumping Up the Balloon

There was bipartisan support in the Clinton years for deregulating the financial sector. Congress enacted the Riegel-Neal Interstate Banking and Branching Efficiency Act (1994), which favored big banks; the Financial Services Modernization Act, usually called Gramm-Leach (1999); and the Commodities Futures Modernization Act (2000), which eliminated regulatory oversight of derivative products and hedge funds. Gramm-Leach repealed large parts of the Glass-Steagall Act, the Depression-era law that had separated investment and commercial banking. The vote tally was 362-57 in the House and 90-8 in the Senate. Of the forty-five Democrats in the Senate in 1999, thirty-eight voted for Gramm-Leach. Expert opinion—even of Democratic economists who would change their tune a decade later—was bullish on deregulation. On the day that Congress repealed Glass-Steagall, Treasury Secretary Lawrence Summers hailed the event: "Today Congress voted to update the rules that have governed financial services since the Great Depression and replace them with a system for the 21st century." For Clintonite Democrats, financial deregulation was an endorsement of the Third Way.[7]

Afterward, banks like Citibank and J. P. Morgan morphed into financial behemoths, laying the foundations for "too big to fail." Sandy Weill, for example, led Citibank, now Citigroup, into investment banking, insurance, and other industries. One side of a banking conglomerate floated new issues, while the other side peddled the offerings. While the economy seemed solid in the Clinton era, the passel of deregulatory legislation would come back to haunt it during the following decade.[8]

An ever-expanding hoard of retirement savings stoked the era's stock markets. Owners of 401(k)s and IRAs loaded up on shares and some began day trading on the Internet. Share-turnover rates nearly tripled on the tech-oriented NASDAQ exchange. Nobody wanted to miss out on what was a self-fulfilling bubble. Companies like Fidelity that administered retirement accounts plugged the virtues of stock ownership.[9]

Meanwhile, the portion of public pension portfolios invested in equities rose from 30 percent in 1991 to nearly 70 percent in 1999, a sizable bet on the bubble. A bank manager gushed that the US economy was only in the early stage of a transformation resulting from the Internet. Pension funds, like individual investors, allocated a larger share of their portfolios to risky assets: tech and micro-cap stocks and hedge funds.[10]

Labor for the most part was AWOL on financial deregulation in the Clinton years. The bubble had brought jobless rates down to levels not seen since the early 1970s. Flush with revenue, state and local governments sweetened pension benefits, not only in heavily unionized states but around the country. An exception to labor's silence came in April 2000, when the Federal Reserve Bank considered higher interest rates to deflate the bubble. John Sweeney commented cautiously: "Raising rates to cool the *possibly* [emphasis added] overheated stock market is wrong on the merits." Jobs were higher on labor's agenda than the bubble.[11]

Wondrous things were happening on Wall Street. The Dow Jones index rose by 40 percent between 1990 and 1994 and went up an additional 65 percent between 1995 and early 2000. Alan Greenspan, head of the Federal Reserve Bank, warned in 1996 that investors were being driven by "irrational exuberance," a memorable phrase that failed to cool the markets. Then Greenspan poured fuel on the fire by endorsing the claim that the United States had entered a "new era economy" propelled by high tech and financial services. Greenspan's pronouncement reassured investors and further inflated the bubble. The peak of the NASDAQ came in March 2000, after which the NASDAQ index fell 80 percent over the next two years.[12]

Scandals

The first years of the century were punctuated by corporate scandals, one set related to the dot-com crash and another following the Enron collapse. The scandals took some of the shine off the Third Way's infatuation with stock markets. The widespread illegalities highlighted the shortcomings in private orderings. "If Enron teaches us anything," wrote Penn law professor William Bratton, "it is to question the reasonableness of reliance on any corporate monitor."

Between 2000 and 2002, $5 trillion in paper wealth vanished when tech shares crashed. Pension funds were devastated. The New York State Common Retirement Fund alone lost $78 billion in the last six months of 2000. The popping of the dot-com bubble and ensuing scandals turned unions into vocal foes of financial deregulation. Testifying to Congress about the crash was a young lawyer working for the AFL-CIO, Damon Silvers, a graduate of Harvard's business and law schools, who was among the labor movement's most visible experts on corporate law and securities regulation.

In 2001, Silvers appeared at hearings of the House Financial Services Committee to discuss the damage caused to pension funds by rampant fraud. He noted the failure of stock analysts to provide honest appraisals of the companies they followed. When the NASDAQ was on a downward slide, only 2 percent of analyst recommendations were "sells." A different problem was a tendency for analysts to inflate earnings estimates and ignore how executives manipulated those figures. Silvers traced these problems to the collapse of "the Chinese wall between investment banking and analysis," a wall that had crumbled with Glass-Steagall's demise.[13]

Union investors came into their own after the tech bust and Enron. Now they initiated a greater number of proposals than other institutional investors, and a greater number went to a vote. (See figure 5.1.) The building trades—led by the Carpenters—accounted for many of the proposals coming from union investors. Public plans were shying away from proxies and relying on *sub rosa* pressure tactics instead. As compared to the previous decade, the public plans were two to three times more likely to meet with executives and boards and write letters to them. Some, like the State of Wisconsin Investment Board, gave up entirely on shareholder proposals because they felt that the process was too expensive and too controversial. Filing proposals became concentrated among funds from two of the bluest states, California and, especially, New York. They accounted for 90 percent of public pension proposals voted on from 2003 to 2012.[14]

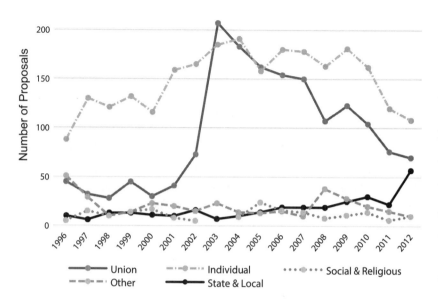

FIGURE 5.1. Number of voted corporate governance proposals, 1996–2112.*
(*Source*: Georgeson, *Annual Corp. Gov. Rev.*; Renneboog and Szilagyi, "The Role of
Shareholder Proposals in Corporate Governance," *J. Corp. Fin.* (2011))
*Does not include proposals submitted by two or more investor types.

Enron and Its Ilk

As the uproar over the tech crash faded, along came Enron. At the time of its
bankruptcy in December 2001, Enron employed more than twenty thousand
people. Enron investors lost over $10 billion between the peak of Enron's
shares in mid-2000 and its collapse eighteen months later. Large institutional
investors were diversified, which cushioned the blow, although the eight biggest public plans lost a combined total that exceeded $1 billion. Hardest hit
were Enron's employees because 60 percent of their 401(k) savings was invested in company stock. Enron froze those accounts in October 2001 but did
not prohibit executive stock sales, so senior executives—140 of them—cashed
in their options on the bankruptcy's eve, a money grab worth $744 million.
The *New York Times* described Enron as "the prime example of all the things
that were allowed to go wrong during the stock market mania."[15]

Congress's initial response came in December 2001, as Enron slid beneath
the water. Ernest Hollings, a Democrat from South Carolina and chairman of
the Senate's Commerce Committee, convened hearings. Appearing before the

committee was Damon Silvers, who zeroed in on the relationship between deregulation and the decimated 401(k)s of Enron's employees. Accompanying him was a group of former Enron workers, who put a human face on the disaster. Silvers argued that repeal of Glass-Steagall and subsequent banking consolidation had contributed to Enron's demise. Although it was the scheming of Enron's executives that captured the public's attention, Silvers reminded the Senate that major banks had played an important part. Based on research by the AFL-CIO's Office of Investment, he reported that the banks had lent shares to Enron while recommending its stock to investors. As Silvers told the senators:

> JPMorgan Chase and Citigroup were Enron's advisors and stood to earn large fees. Citigroup lent Enron more than $500 million, monies in part that came from federally insured commercial bank deposits. Citigroup's analyst at Salomon-Smith Barney maintained a Neutral-Speculative rating. JPMorgan Chase lent Enron $400 million, while its analyst rated the stock a Long-Term Buy all the way through November.

A month before the bankruptcy, when it was clear that Enron was doomed, the AFL-CIO and Amalgamated Bank privately urged Enron's directors to disclose the situation openly. Their entreaties were ignored.

In separate testimony to the House Financial Services Committee, Silvers fingered JP Morgan Chase for its recondite and likely unlawful Enron activities. The bank had disguised a loan to the Houston giant worth $1 billion as a derivative transaction. The funds were laundered through a special entity, Mahonia, set up to hide transactions between Enron and Morgan. Mahonia was headquartered on the island of Jersey, a tax haven similar to the Cayman Islands.[16]

More than a decade of deregulation seeded Enron's collapse. Glass-Steagall's repeal had created opportunities for bank analysts to promote shares of dazzling new tech companies, of which Enron was one. It was a return to the touting practices of the early twentieth century. As head of the Commodity Futures Trading Commission in 1993, Wendy Gramm, wife of Texas Senator Phil Gramm, exempted Enron's energy derivatives from the commission's supervision. After she left office, a grateful Enron gave her a seat on its board. Her husband sponsored the Commodities Futures Modernization Act (2000), which contained the "Enron loophole" that permitted the previously prohibited trading of energy derivatives.[17]

Before Enron, apostles of shareholder capitalism said that institutional investors with a commitment to "good governance" were the best way to keep an eye on executives and boards. But from 1995 through 1999, not a single institutional investor publicly criticized Enron's governance arrangements. (At Enron's peak, they held 60 percent of its stock.) Like many others, they were bewitched by the steady rise in Enron's share price and naïve about the governance structures they'd created. Enron, for example, could tick all the boxes in the governance cookbook: It had adopted recipes for director pay, board independence, and disclosure. Its audit committee included a distinguished professor of accounting from Stanford University. It was form over substance. Investors had no way to assess behavior; nor could they determine whether board members were conscientious, capable, and assertive. "All of a sudden the exemplar didn't look so shiny and bright anymore," said Ron Blackwell.[18]

Professional asset managers, including at pension funds, may have suspected something fishy, but the system worked against their taking action. Because asset managers were evaluated on their relative performance, none wanted to be below average, so none wanted to be the first to dump an overvalued but still-rising stock. Then, in herd-like fashion, they sold. Bill Crist, still chair of the CalPERS board, had a different explanation: He blamed the fund's losses on Enron's former CEO, Ken Lay, whom Crist called "Kenny Boy." Lay, he said, had hoodwinked CalPERS and other investors with multiple charm offensives. Before Enron crashed, CalPERS officials said not one critical word. Anat Admati, a finance economist at Stanford, points out that fraud and misconduct "may actually benefit shareholders, particularly if the misconduct remains hidden." The principals sometimes lack principles.[19]

CalPERS had conflicts of interest. In the early 1990s, CalPERS had cast its nets widely to find alternatives to stocks and bonds. It paid $250 million in 1993 to become a 50-50 investor with Enron for a limited private equity partnership called the Joint Energy Development Investments (JEDI), a name that was too clever by half. JEDI was managed by Andrew Fastow, Enron's CFO, who would spend six years in prison for his role in concealing Enron's losses. Because this was a partnership, Enron did not have to report JEDI's gains or losses in its consolidated financial statements. After four years, Enron signed a new 50-50 partnership with CalPERS, this time to the tune of $500 million. The corporation created a fund called Chewco, another Star Wars character, to buy out CalPERS's stake in JEDI, for which the California pension plan earned a hefty profit of $133 million. CalPERS reinvested part of the JEDI proceeds in Enron Energy Services. The Ontario Teachers' Pension Plan, an activist public fund, placed $156 million in a successor partnership named

JEDI 2. Thus, with help from public funds, Enron was able to conceal millions in losses, a fact that did not come out until the bankruptcy.

After Enron went bankrupt, CalPERS defended itself by saying it didn't have sufficient time to react to the company's problems: "Their [Enron's] demise was very quick." The statement implied that CalPERS knew nothing until the end, even though *Business Week* claimed that CalPERS long had an inkling but never blew the whistle. The monitor needed monitoring.[20]

Following Enron came additional downfalls: Martha Stewart and ImClone (December 2001), K-Mart (January 2002), Qwest and Global Crossing (February), Adelphia (April), WorldCom (May) investigations of Merrill Lynch and Dynegy (May), and Tyco (June). All involved accounting tricks, and the firms were, at least formally, cookbook adherents. Observers were alarmed by cumulative effects on markets of widespread deceit. *Business Week* opined that "at risk is the very integrity of capitalism."

When it seemed nothing worse could happen, the SEC on June 25, 2002, announced that it was filing a lawsuit against WorldCom for fraud, this four weeks before Sarbanes-Oxley was signed. The telecommunications giant went bankrupt shortly thereafter, leaving seventeen thousand workers jobless. In a move reminiscent of Enron, WorldCom executives liquidated their stock options before the company restated its earnings.[21]

Looking back three years later, SEC Commissioner William Donaldson said that the nation had gone through "a period not dissimilar to 1929." But this time, instead of jumping off ledges, executives jumped off sinking ships, cash in hand, leaving those behind to go down empty-handed. Labor hoped that the disparity would prove the relevance of unions to workers facing a high-risk economy. "We take very seriously our mission to take care of working people," said Damon Silvers. "We also want to make a point as to what can happen to workers when they don't organize." The companies that went bankrupt were nearly all nonunion.[22]

A month after Enron's bankruptcy, Reverend Jesse Jackson arranged for buses to take several dozen ex-Enron workers from Houston to Washington, DC to tell Congress of their plight. One woman said that almost all of her 401(k) had been invested in Enron stock. All she had left was $109 "and that will pay my light bill that's due Monday." Several Houston unions received calls for help from desperate Enron workers. The first responder was the AFL-CIO, which hired a lawyer to demand that Enron pay the full severance benefits promised to employees, including unused vacation days. On the heels of Enron's bankruptcy, each former worker received severance of $4,500, far less than they were due. But in bankruptcy law, severance payments are capped at $4,650 and after that all employee claims have to wait until creditors are paid off. Enron's creditors were seeking tens of billions, leaving little hope that workers would ever receive anything more. The AFL-CIO began a fax and mail campaign to have Enron's creditor committee do more for ex-employees. It brought in lawyers to negotiate on the workers' behalf. Nine months later, the creditors agreed to pay $29 million in additional severance benefits. Nothing like that had ever happened.

But at other companies, workers were less fortunate. WorldCom, like Enron, was a high flyer during the tech boom, and employees had invested 40 percent of their 401(k)s in its stock, now nearly worthless. As at Enron, employees were unable to collect the full amount of severance pay to which they were entitled. To rectify that, the AFL-CIO started a lobbying campaign to have the severance cap in bankruptcy raised from $4,650 to $13,500, the amount that Enron workers received from the settlement.[23]

There were hopes that debacles like Enron would bring white-collar employees into the labor movement. Job security was a concern. In the first half of 2002, the ten largest corporations filing for bankruptcy employed 430,000 people. Media reports about the travails of ex-Enron employees made stark the consequences of involuntary job loss and highlighted the deficiencies of the pension system. The shriveling of 401(k)s at Enron, WorldCom, and other stricken companies provided what journalist Steven Greenhouse called "political ammunition" for labor's fight to reverse the trend away from DB plans. A Harris Poll found just 26 percent of Americans believed that big corporations were honest in their dealings with consumers and employees. Seventy-nine percent thought corporate executives put their own personal interests ahead of workers and shareholders. A union organizer at IBM reported that "more and more professional people are seeing the value of union representation and a union contract."[24]

Richard Grasso, then CEO of the New York Stock Exchange (NYSE), claimed that only a few bad apples had tainted the barrel and that the United States still had "the finest system of enterprise the world has ever seen." Countering Grasso was a statement from the AFL-CIO's Executive Council, which said that problems were "not the product of a few bad people" but instead were "the systematic result of markets that once were well regulated but are now trapped in a destructive cycle where short-term financial pressures combine with greed." The AFL-CIO's statement also blamed the situation on "American corporate governance," which pointed in a different direction, to firms rather than markets, to apples rather than barrels.

Systemic re-regulation was not in the cards in 2002. Bill Patterson said the banking industry "had dug in their heels and was not going to move until all hell broke loose." That would happen six years later. During the interim, shareholder activists tinkered with corporate governance, through private orderings and legislation.[25]

Sarbanes-Oxley

As Congress fashioned its Enron response, shareholder activism was at a fever pitch. The Carpenters and fellow construction unions offered almost three dozen proposals related to auditors, who were blamed for hiding problems at Enron and other failed companies. Disney, for example, acceded to the Plumbers' union demand that it stop using its auditor, PricewaterhouseCoopers, for non-audit services, a conflict of interest that contributed to Enron's failure. Union investors submitted many other types of governance proposals, support for which was running higher than ever before. A representative from the Investor Responsibility Research Center said, "Unions, through their pension funds, have become some of the most articulate, far-reaching and successful of shareholder activists. Once again they've proven themselves to be on the cutting edge, identifying issues before other folks have thought of them." According to Louis Malizia of the Teamsters, companies were more willing to meet with representatives of union pension funds.[26]

The AFL-CIO wrote to twenty-one companies demanding that they remove Enron directors from their boards. It then asked the SEC to bar Enron's directors from serving on other boards, an effort that forced five out of ten Enron directors to tender their resignations elsewhere. Then the AFL-CIO petitioned the SEC to tighten the definition of directorial independence and force companies to disclose all ties between board members and management.[27]

Back on the Hill, Damon Silvers testified three additional times: twice in the House and once in the Senate. In his testimony, Silvers offered active ownership as a complement to legislation. To make it effective, he said, the SEC's help would be needed. He recommended that the SEC require management to *implement*, not merely consider, shareholder proposals supported by a majority. He asked that the SEC permit shareholders to nominate corporate directors—proxy access—and criticized the agency's OBE provisions, saying that the SEC should not take from shareholders the power to decide which issues belonged on the proxy. Joining Silvers was Sara Teslik, who expressed similar sentiments.

The Sarbanes-Oxley Act (SOX) dealt narrowly with the intermediaries between investors and executives: accountants, analysts, and boards. SOX required that all members of a board's audit committee be independent and have at least one member possessing financial acumen. It prohibited auditors from providing non-audit services to the same client, an idea first broached by the SEC in 2000 that was withdrawn after intense lobbying by the accounting industry. The CEO and CFO now had to certify personally the accuracy of a firm's quarterly and annual financial reports. SOX contained a provision for recouping (called a clawback) a senior executive's stock-based pay in the case of an accounting restatement arising from unlawful reporting. There were stiffer penalties for dishonesty, including incarceration for up to twenty-five years.[28]

Political scientist John W. Cioffi said that SOX crossed "a line that had impeded the reformers of the 1970s," namely, the government's right to intervene in a corporation's internal control systems. But the incursion was modest because SOX was more bark than bite. Omitted entirely were changes that most needed fixing, such as expensing options. Yale law professor Roberta Romano dubbed SOX "quack corporate governance." The law prescribed changes that research had found ineffectual, she said, such as having independent directors on the board's audit committee.

SOX's clawback rule was problematic. It could have been effective, but nobody knew because it was rarely used. "During SOX's first decade, when there were approximately 8,000 restatements, the SEC used the SOX clawback to recover funds from only six executives who were not alleged to have personally committed misconduct," this according to Harvard law professor Jesse Fried. SOX contained a section with a foreboding title: "White-Collar Crime Penalty Enhancement." But for ten years following its enactment, just five criminal cases were pursued.[29]

As the scandals unfolded, critics in the labor movement faulted John Sweeney, AFL-CIO president, for pulling his punches with business and banks. It wasn't until the day that President George W. Bush signed SOX that Sweeney swung hard.[30] Speaking at a rally in front of the New York Stock Exchange, he blasted executives as corporate criminals, robber barons, pirates, and criminals. Joining him were laid-off workers from Enron, WorldCom, and Arthur Andersen, Enron's now-defunct auditor. The rally was part of the AFL-CIO's national campaign "to hold CEOs and corporations accountable, eliminate conflicts of interest among accountants and financial analysts, abolish stock options for corporate leaders, secure retirement security of all workers and demand meaningful pension reform." It was a potpourri rather than a clear message.[31]

The Counter-Reformation

Sarbanes-Oxley was sufficiently lightweight that all Senate Republicans voted for it. The main opposition was in the House, where eighty-seven left-leaning Democrats voted "no" because they thought the legislation was too weak. Ron Blackwell, now the AFL-CIO's chief economist, labeled SOX a "diversionary bill" because it went no further than regulating intermediaries. The business community kept a low profile in the months following SOX. But between 2004 and 2006, by which time the catastrophes were fading and the stock market recovering, corporations tried to water down the new law. The Business Roundtable labeled SOX as "too strict," and its members met privately with officials from the White House, Office of Management and Budget, the SEC, Congress, and the Treasury Department to complain, this while the Bush White House refused to meet with union representatives.[32]

At congressional hearings labeled "The Sarbanes-Oxley Act 4 Years Later," business representatives took aim at the act's Section 404, which required CEOs and CFOs to sign a statement in the annual report certifying the adequacy of the company's internal control systems. Executives complained that compliance costs were onerous relative to the benefits, cost-benefit analysis being a standard dodge against regulation. Damon Silvers once again appeared before the committee, noting the billions that pension funds had lost. Nobody wanted needlessly expensive audits, he said, but the costs were a reasonable insurance payment: "Those who want to weaken Sarbanes-Oxley must answer the question—why should a company that cannot attest to the adequacy of its internal financial controls be able to offer its securities to the investing public?"[33]

A group named the Committee on Capital Markets Regulations sprung up to take the cudgels on behalf of Wall Street. Assembled in 2006, it included bankers, businessmen, and academics, several with ties to Treasury Secretary Henry Paulson. Chairing the committee was Glenn Hubbard, dean of the Columbia Business School. The group attacked Sarbanes-Oxley as burdensome for business and bad for the global competitiveness of the American financial services industry. It recommended limits on the liability of accounting

firms, tighter curbs on the SEC, and pulling the reins in on prosecutors. In-
tending to drag the situation back to where it was before SOX, the committee
was described by one legal scholar as "an escalation of the culture war against
regulation."

The AFL-CIO wrote a letter to Robert Pozen, a wheel in the investment industry. Pozen was a former Fidelity executive and chairman of MFS Investment,
a mutual-fund company that managed billions in pension fund assets. The AFL-
CIO criticized his membership in the Hubbard group, whose report it called a
"pre-conceived effort to undermine securities regulation." The letter noted that
the committee's funding came from Hank Greenberg, former CEO of AIG, a
company that the SEC had investigated for fraud the previous year (and which
would later contribute to the financial system's collapse). Separately, Damon
Silvers said that the committee's recommendations amounted to "protection-
ism for investment bankers—people who make, say, $50 million a year."

Weighing in on the issue were New York City's mayor Michael Bloomberg
and New York State's senator Charles Schumer, both friends of Wall Street.
Jointly they issued a report claiming that Wall Street was losing business to
foreign competitors because of Sarbanes-Oxley. Like the Hubbard group, the
report recommended rolling back the act. The attempt to water down financial
regulation coincided with the first signs that the markets were entering troubled waters. Housing prices were trending down, and subprime problems were
bubbling up. In a surprise tack, the SEC's new chairman, Christopher Cox,
defended SOX and distanced himself from the Hubbard group. Former SEC
chairman Richard Breeden drubbed the Hubbard committee's report as "a
bunch of warmed-over, impractical ideas. It is very elegant whining."[34]

Win Some, Lose Some

Winning severance pay for Enron employees and punishing its former directors had given unions "credibility on corporate accountability," as journalist
David Moberg put it. An example was the appointment of Damon Silvers to
the Investor Advisory Group of the Public Company Accounting Oversight
Board, a regulatory body created by Sarbanes-Oxley.

A week after SOX was signed, Ron Blackwell and Bill Patterson released a
plan to transform American corporations. With the public giving low approval
ratings to business, they wrote, labor had an opportunity to push for proxy
access, limits on executive pay, and a national commission to study the damage
caused by financial deregulation. "What is still uncertain," they wrote, "is

whether we use this 'post-Enron moment' to effect authentic corporate reform or whether the resistance of corporate insiders and their political allies will prevail and restore business as usual in corporate America."[35]

In the midst of all this, labor was jolted by a scandal of its own. A few weeks after Enron's bankruptcy, the *Wall Street Journal* reported that the CEO of Union Labor Life Insurance Company (ULLICO), Robert Georgine, had violated insider-trading rules three years earlier. ULLICO, a remnant of the labor banking era, still sold life insurance to union members but now also provided investment vehicles for multiemployer plans. The insider trades involved Global Crossing, a high-flying company from the bubble years that went bankrupt shortly after Enron. Georgine, a prominent figure in organized labor, for years had headed the AFL-CIO's powerful Building and Construction Trades Department. Along with Georgine, other ULLICO board members profited from the trades, including Doug McCarron, president of the Carpenters, and some former union presidents. Although John Sweeney had not participated in the trades, he sat on ULLICO's board when it approved a salary increase for Georgine from $900,000—itself a phenomenal amount—to $5.4 million. The salary, and the board's malfeasance, undermined labor's message at a critical moment. Sweeney asked for an internal investigation and disgorgement of ill-gotten gains. Georgine's profits were estimated to be at least $9 million, which eventually he paid back.

Republicans had a field day with ULLICO and sought to make unions appear no better than corporate crooks. A House committee headed by John Boehner convened hearings at which Georgine invoked his right against self-incrimination. Damon Silvers gamely tried to deflect criticism, arguing that, unlike Enron or WorldCom, ULLICO's employees did not suffer pension losses and that neither Kenneth Lay nor WorldCom's CEO Bernie Ebbers had returned any money. Yet the ULLICO affair was damaging. A labor expert quoted in the *New York Times* said, "It's bad enough when we see these shenanigans at Enron or WorldCom, but when union officials get involved in anything that has an appearance of impropriety . . . workers begin to question whose side they're on."[36]

The Building Trades

Studies of the US labor movement tend to emphasize service-sector unions like SEIU and devote less attention to those from the relatively conservative, relatively white-male construction unions, which account for one out of six

TABLE 5.1. Top Ten Sponsors of Governance Proposals, 1995–2011 (percentage of all voted labor proposals)*

1995–2002	2003–2011
LongView Fund (18 percent)	Carpenters (25 percent)
Teamsters (17 percent)	AFSCME (11 percent)
Carpenters (10 percent)	AFL-CIO (10 percent)
IBEW (9 percent)	Sheetmetal Workers (9 percent)
CWA (6 percent)	LongView Fund (8 percent)
Laborers (6 percent)	Laborers (8 percent)
UNITE (5 percent)	IBEW (7 percent)
AFSCME (5 percent)	Plumbers (5 percent)
Operating Engineers (4 percent)	Teamsters (4 percent)
AFL-CIO (4 percent)	Bricklayers (3 percent)

Source: Georgeson, *Annual Corporate Governance Review (ACGR)*.

* Voted proposals at S&P 1500 companies.

union members in the private sector. An important player in the financial turn was the Carpenters union. Under Doug McCarron, the union restructured to prioritize organizing in ways that mirrored SEIU's, despite the difference in their political orientations.[37]

Ed Durkin was the person in charge of shareholder engagement for the Carpenters. When it came to submitting proposals, he was prolific. The Carpenters had a greater number of them than any other union or institutional investor. (See table 5.1.) Durkin put together a voting coalition in the building trades and broadened the activist agenda with ideas for majority voting and setting executive compensation.

Durkin began his career in the early 1980s. His father had been a plumber who rose to become secretary of labor in the first Eisenhower administration. One of Durkin's formative experiences came in 1984, when Louisiana-Pacific demanded that its paper workers—represented by the Carpenters—take a 30 percent pay cut. Durkin instructed members to write letters to Louisiana-Pacific's main investors as well as to three dozen asset managers who did business with more than a hundred of the union's Taft-Hartleys. Later, Durkin worked closely with the Teamsters' Bill Patterson, as at Echlin and Kodak, and during the late 1990s he participated in monthly meetings of labor's financial experts—including Ron Blackwell, David Blitzstein, Damon Silvers, and Patterson—who debated "big think" ideas about transforming the financial turn into something greater than taking potshots at shareholder meetings.[38]

After the Carpenters withdrew from the AFL-CIO in 2001, there was a shift in Durkin's attitudes toward his former allies. He minced no words: "Labor has completely failed and wasted the past twenty years by not building a strategic vision of worker-ownership. . . . Labor had a lot of resources and ended up with a dead end." He faulted Patterson and others for pursuing collateral objectives that didn't add up to much. Lost was the opportunity to "articulate a worker-owner view that could guide activities. Nobody thought it through. And no one pushed it. No philosophy and no leadership." Durkin blamed other union investors for relying too heavily on the cookbook. He was one of the few involved with labor's financial turn to criticize the cookbook's empowerment of shareholders, positioning himself closer to management.[39]

Durkin wanted a center for the entire labor movement where union funds would pool data on their holdings, conduct research, and develop common strategies. In his view, the Office of Investment was not providing this. However, SEIU's Steve Abrecht suggested that Durkin didn't walk his talk because he shielded trustees of Carpenter funds from contact with CTW's financial staff. Abrecht wanted the Carpenters to share information on their investment managers, so, for example, if one fund had an issue with State Street, it could solicit support from other funds that did business with it. But, according to Abrecht, Durkin refused. A former SEIU staffer complained about Durkin's inconsistencies, charging that the Carpenters were the least willing of CTW's unions to be concerned about "anything other than the most immediate, self-interested, short-term tactical objectives."[40]

Doug McCarron was another nonconformist. He was disliked because he did nothing to stop Carpenters' locals from poaching members of other unions. When John Sweeney became AFL-CIO president—against McCarron's wishes—Sweeney told McCarron to cease the raiding and demanded that the Carpenters pay the substantial delinquent dues owed to the federation. Neither side compromised; McCarron reacted by pulling the Carpenters out of the AFL-CIO. There were rumors that McCarron intended to create a new federation comprised of the building trades. After Sweeney had been in office for several years, McCarron chided him for having failed to grow the labor movement. Unions that shared McCarron's views told Sweeney to do more. They were the germ for what would become Change to Win, of which the Carpenters would be a member. But after four years McCarron reversed course and led the Carpenters out of CTW, again over raiding complaints.[41]

McCarron's commitment to organizing went back to his pre-presidency days. He successfully organized immigrant drywall workers in Southern California during the early 1990s. After he became president of the Carpenters, the New England regional council hired three dozen organizers drawn from the rank and file. Over eight years, the council raised New England membership by around 25 percent. McCarron's style was autocratic. He forced local unions to amalgamate into regional councils that took away their autonomy. Centralization included the management of local union pension funds by the national union, giving headquarters control of over $40 billion in assets. Critics labeled McCarron's approach "corporate unionism" because he cozied up to builders and promised to cut deals for them if they hired the union's members.[42]

Although McCarron failed to create a building-trades federation, Ed Durkin succeeded in building a coalition of their Taft-Hartley plans. In the Taft-Hartley world, the construction industry has the greatest number of plans, and they tend to be in better shape than average. The initial step came in the 1980s, when Durkin combined the Carpenters' numerous Taft-Hartleys into a voting bloc. The informal all-trades coalition began in 2001, the year the Carpenters left the AFL-CIO. Six unions—the Electrical Workers (IBEW), Laborers, Operating Engineers, Plumbers, Sheet Metal Workers, and Teamsters—joined the Carpenters to coordinate their activities. "We work as a group in terms of targeting the companies," said Durkin. These unions were the leading shareholder activists of the century's first decade, at least as judged by the number of proxy submissions. Despite claims that wild-eyed radicals had hijacked shareholder activism, its largest constituency were multiemployer plans from politically conservative craft unions.

Durkin said that the group's philosophy was different from that of people in the Office of Investment who leaned in an anti-management direction. Instead, said Durkin, the coalition sought "the long-term success of the corporate enterprise . . . [and] the promotion of healthy and growing companies contributing to regional and national economic growth." The building trades had always been inclined to cooperate with management to a greater degree than other private-sector unions. They ran their apprenticeship programs jointly with employers, as with the training partnership between the IBEW and the National Electrical Contractors Association. Sometimes there were quid pro quos: construction jobs for union members in return for support of industry's political agenda. An example is the Pharmaceutical Industry Labor-Management Association (PILMA), half of whose trustees come from the building trades and the other half from large pharmaceutical companies that hire union workers to build their sophisticated manufacturing facilities. In the past, PILMA's labor representatives had backed lobbying positions taken by the drug industry—such as limiting caps on drug prices and preserving long-duration patents—that put them at odds with other unions.

Shareholder proposals from the Carpenters usually included a subset of firms where the union had collateral interests. A repeated target was the Pulte Group, a nationwide home builder. Nevertheless, Durkin had a reputation in the corporate world as someone who had sympathy for management. Like McCarron, Durkin had good relationships with business groups, including those from the construction industry as well as the US Chamber of Commerce, whose COO called Durkin "a thoughtful guy."[43]

Durkin was wary of public pension funds. He said they cared more about shareholder value than the workers employed by companies in their portfolio. An event that left an impression on him took place at Pacific Lumber, one of a number of West Coast mills employing Carpenters' members. Charles Hurwitz, a raider operating as Maxxam Company, bought Pacific Lumber in 1985 and loaded it with debt, precisely the moment that Jesse "Big Daddy" Unruh was sanctioning hostile takeovers. What irked Durkin was that CalPERS was one of Maxxam's largest investors. To meet its credit obligations, Maxxam skimmed $50 million from its pension fund. Pacific Lumber filed for bankruptcy twenty years later.[44]

Only by formulating a set of principles that transcended shareholder primacy, Durkin believed, could union investors eliminate the conflict between pension funds and corporate workers. Durkin thought he'd found a solution in cooperating with management: discussions with corporate officers to understand what was needed to achieve "regular and incremental improvements in management practices." If union investors went this route, they'd be forced to consider a company's business situation and strategy, according to Durkin. How this would redound to workers' benefit was never made clear, however, nor did Durkin articulate a larger vision.[45]

New Tactics

The drumbeat of executive misdeeds produced an angry mood among investors that ISS described as "shareholders gone wild." Proposals skyrocketed, as did meetings with corporate boards. Directors knew it was politic to be conciliatory, at least until investor outrage died down. If they tried to reach a compromise, investors might withdraw their proposals before they came to a vote, which happened to around one out of five proposals. For union investors, the negotiations that preceded withdrawals offered direct access to the company's inner sanctum.

Carin Zelenko, director of the Teamster Capital Strategies Department, said in 2008, "Five years ago we would never have gotten in a corporate boardroom. Now we're regularly meeting with corporate directors about substantive issues.[46]

Just Vote No

The Enron era brought a greater number of Vote No campaigns, in which investors withhold votes for individual directors, a group of them, or entire boards. Under the prevailing plurality voting system, shareholders do not have the option of voting "no": They can either vote "yes" or withhold their votes. In these situations, withholding can't prevent the election of a board nominee because he or she needs only a single "yes" vote to take office. Were anyone to claim that corporate governance is a type of shareholder democracy, plurality voting would be Exhibit A that it's not.[47]

The attraction of withholding is its low cost, much less than filing a proposal, which takes time to craft and must receive SEC approval. A Vote No campaign is quick to launch, bypasses the SEC, and can be started at any time up to a few weeks prior to the shareholder meeting. From 2004 through 2008, one out of six S&P 1500 companies experienced withholding of at least 15 percent of all votes cast.

Targeting directors was an activity in which public plans remained participants. They launched an equal number of Vote No campaigns as union investors. After Enron, CalPERS adopted a policy of withholding votes from any director approving auditors who also consulted for the company. In 2004, a tempestuous year, CalPERS withheld votes at 80 percent of the companies where it cast votes. "Withhold votes," said a consultant, "are changing the dialogue and changing the answers."[48]

When an individual director came under fire—as in about a quarter of Vote No campaigns—the reasons included failure to attend meetings, sitting on too many boards, or lack of independence from the CEO. If the board had approved CEO pay unrelated to performance, shareholders might withhold votes from every director sitting on the compensation committee. If a board repeatedly refused to implement previous resolutions receiving a majority vote, the entire board might be hit. ISS recommended withholding if a firm ignored majority votes for the same proposal in two of the previous three years.[49]

While some directors didn't care what investors thought of them, others found it unpleasant to be singled out. Joseph Grundfest, a Stanford law profes-

sor and former SEC commissioner, was an early advocate of Vote No campaigns because he believed that most directors were sensitive to public criticism. Beth Young, the labor lawyer, agreed: A Vote No campaign can make
directors "embarrassed, upset, or emotional. At that point directors are often
more willing to try to make something happen [to make a governance change
sought by investors]. They desperately want to get rid of the proponent at that
point. You have more power over them."

It was the SEC's 1992 proxy revisions that cleared the way for withholding.
CalPERS, ever the bellwether, embraced withholding. It was easier and less
controversial to punish directors than CEOs. Dale Hanson, then head of
CalPERS, put it succinctly: "We are no longer into CEO bashing. We are now
into director bashing." CalPERS and others began to ask their asset managers
things like "We are voting no on Mr. X. Will you do the same, not only for our
assets but all those you manage?"[50]

Union investors had long been in the business of targeting directors. When
he was at the Teamsters, Bill Patterson spoke at a Tenneco shareholder meeting and criticized one of its directors, business economist M. Kathryn Eick-
hoff, "for not contributing to shareholder value." After Patterson moved to the
AFL-CIO, the Office of Investment released a report detailing the business,
professional, and personal ties of nearly two hundred directors. Then it published a report on CEOs who had "close, often personal, ties to the very boards
that rubber-stamp their pay package." The AFL-CIO began including withhold recommendations in its *Key Votes* publication. One was for Richard Par-
sons, Time Warner's CEO, who chaired Citibank's compensation committee
when it awarded $44 million to Parsons's fellow CEO, Sandy Weill. Parsons
was listed on the Executive Paywatch site along with ten other directors who
sat on compensation committees.[51]

Labor's Vote No targets were neither more unionized nor more involved in
labor disputes than nontargeted firms. Union investors selected firms with
performance and governance defects, once again the CalPERS approach. The
most common rationales for withholding were an absence of effective linkages
between pay and stock performance and the failure to give shareholders the
right to vote on executive pay.[52]

Attacking directors at subpar companies didn't exclude selecting some from
companies where labor had collateral interests. Two examples from 2004:
First, at Cintas, a uniform supplier, the Teamsters and UNITE were trying to
organize the firm's 17,000 low-wage workers. The union launched a Vote No
campaign against the chairman, who was the father of the CEO and owned

20 percent of the company's shares. Then there was Comcast, a cable TV operator whose workers the IBEW and the CWA were trying to organize in the face of hard-knuckled opposition from management. The company's corporate governance was abysmal, with the CEO controlling one-third of the votes despite owning 1 percent of outstanding shares. Three weeks before the company's annual meeting, the AFL-CIO, IBEW, and CWA urged shareholders to withhold votes for the CEO/chairman and one other board member.[53]

Most directors were reelected after a Vote No campaign. But one shouldn't infer that withholding had no teeth. Sizable withholding is associated with an increased probability of CEO turnover, lower levels of executive compensation, and a reduction in the portion of CEO pay unrelated to performance. There are penalties for directors who are hit with Vote No campaigns; they are twice as likely to leave a board over the subsequent two years.[54]

While directors ran a risk in opposing investor demands, there was a different risk if they complied with them: being treated as pariahs by other directors. Two management scholars, James Westphal at the University of Michigan and Poonam Khanna at the University of Texas, examined "social distancing" on corporate boards. Their study identified directors who favor changes to weaken the CEO, such as separating chairmanship and CEO positions, creating independent nominating committees, and, ultimately, firing the CEO. Subsequently, at other companies on whose boards these directors serve, they are invited to fewer meetings with the CEO. They may be snubbed at board meetings by not being asked for their opinions or advice, and become the target of "exclusionary gossip whereby board members talk about other people and events with which the focal director is not familiar." Ingratiating behavior, however, improves the likelihood that a director will be appointed to other boards.[55]

———

The Enron years marked a change in the balance of power between investors and executives. Majority votes against management were way up; companies were more responsive to their angry shareholders, led by union investors. Forty percent of majority-vote proposals at S&P 1500 firms were implemented in 2004 versus only 16 percent in 1997. Yet there were still plenty of companies that ignored shareholder sentiment, especially when it came to paying executives. An official with the New Hampshire Retirement System asked, "Is it arrogant? Sure it is."[56]

6

Executive Pay

IN 2001, *Fortune* announced "The Great CEO Pay Heist." The magazine noted that four of the five most highly paid CEOs, whose companies' stock performance it characterized as "marginal to horrible," had received average annual compensation of $274 million during the previous five years. One of them was Disney's Michael Eisner. At Disney's 1997 shareholder meeting, the board approved a ten-year pay package for him worth $252 million, this in addition to a $90 million golden handshake for departing president Michael Ovitz. Nell Minow, a champion of shareholder rights, said that Disney had one of the worst boards in America.[1]

The AFL-CIO released a study charging that CEO compensation was the result of "pervasive cronyism" between executives and board members. Compensation consultants were quick to challenge the report, with one of them implausibly stating that, inside the board room, "You don't see much cronyism." Bill Patterson of the AFL-CIO disagreed: "Companies are giving out stock options no matter what the CEO does or what the company does." Patterson had a remarkable exchange with General Electric's CEO Jack Welch at GE's 1997 shareholder meeting. That year Welch received $21.4 million, including 320,000 options, this on top of 2.2 million unexercised options. Patterson asked Welch, "My question to you is, do these options motivate you to bring more ideas, commit more value and more time to the growth of the company?" "Absolutely," said Welch to laughter and applause. "Why stop at 320,000 shares?" said Patterson. "Why not double that? You would be more motivated." "I think that is a good suggestion for the board," Welch retorted, again to laughter. "They are all here."[2]

Soaring CEO pay was labor's signature issue. It spoke to a nation troubled by inequality and to investors appalled by misuse of corporate funds. As unions went on the offensive, the *Wall Street Journal* opined that the topic was "perfect for galvanizing workers." To brake CEO pay, labor fixed on a particular solution: say on pay. It gave investors the right to an advisory vote on the board's recommended pay package.[3]

Shareholder activism was a slow slog, company by company, vote by vote. It required time-consuming meetings and costly proxy solicitations, often to no avail because in the end, directors and executives were free to disregard investor sentiment. But these private efforts served as a nudge for government to devise market-wide laws that possessed enforcement teeth. Writing about Campaign GM, Berkeley political scientist David Vogel observed, "The extent to which demands addressed to the corporation anticipate the substance of subsequent government regulation of business is quite striking."[4]

Economics of Executive Pay

For decades, CEO compensation was remarkably stable, standing at about the same inflation-adjusted level from the end of the Second World War through the 1970s. This stability mirrored that of the total income share flowing to the top 1 percent. A change occurred during the 1980s, when compensation of CEOs increased by 55 percent. After that, things accelerated dramatically: CEO pay grew by 126 percent in the 1990s and by 125 percent from 2000 to 2005.[5]

Economists offer several explanations for executive pay's takeoff. The first—optimal contracting—asserts that CEOs are paid what they're worth. According to this account, changes in technology permitted the creation of a robust labor market for CEOs in which competition for scarce talent pushed up pay. Before the 1980s, allegedly, CEOs had skills that were specific to a single firm, which meant there was no incentive for other firms to hire them. What changed was the rise of MBA-CEOs, whose accounting and finance acumen could be used at any company. A related strand relates rising CEO pay to firm size. As scale increased, compensation went up because it was difficult to find people capable of managing large, complex organizations. A third is that changing dynamics between shareholders and executives had created an executive labor market. Shareholders preferred outsiders, and the competition to hire them led to higher pay.[6]

A different explanation turns on the relative power of shareholders, executives, and non-managerial employees to maintain or increase their share of corporate funds. In the past, workers relied on collective bargaining to stabilize their portion, as with the Treaty of Detroit, or to enlarge it. CEOs of unionized companies were paid less than comparable CEOs at nonunion companies. There were fewer buybacks when a union was present, so shareholders received less as well. Economists Richard Freeman and James Medoff found that in the early 1980s, profits were lower at unionized firms in concentrated industries, where there were rents to divvy up. Investors and executives were forced to share more of them with union members. The effect tended to zero at firms in more competitive industries.

As unions shrank and lost bargaining power, so did the size of the slice received by rank-and-file employees. Today, workers' earnings no longer track productivity; the gains go to CEOs and to shareholders instead. Shareholders have made out very nicely in recent years. So have CEOs. They receive greater than the percentage increase when stock prices rise; when they fall, their pay is rigid. There's nothing efficient here.[7]

Stock-based compensation offered myriad opportunities for executives to game the system, and the scandals of 2000, 2002, and 2008 provided plenty of evidence of self-serving behavior. Other factors, none of them optimal, drove CEO pay: rewards for "luck" instead of performance, an intentional lack of transparency, and compensation consultants who advised clients to pay their executives above average, producing a leapfrog effect. But what should CEOs receive? With so much of their compensation riding on luck and power, nobody really knew exactly what they were worth.[8]

Pay Proposals

Shareholder proposals on executive compensation mushroomed after Enron. (See figure 6.1.) Union investors were responsible for six out of ten pay proposals between 2003 and 2007, and they were more successful than other groups in obtaining majority support.[9]

Who were the targets of labor's shareholder resolutions? They were companies where CEO rewards were disproportionate to performance and whose CEOs served as board chairs. One study found "no evidence of union-related motives," and companies were equally likely to implement pay proposals from unions as from other investors. It was a sign that labor was swimming in the shareholder mainstream. Occasionally, union investors selected companies with labor disputes, but this had no effect on voting outcomes. The only situation in which union investors incurred a voting penalty was when the firm's employees were affiliated with the union sponsoring the proposal, which was not a common occurrence.[10]

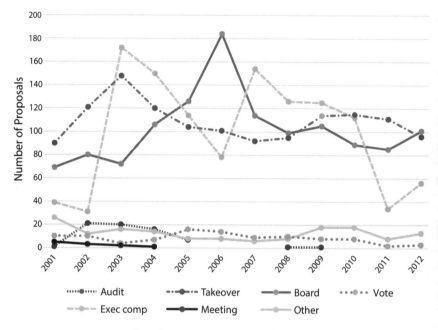

FIGURE 6.1. Number of corporate governance proposals voted on by topic, 2001–2012.* (*Source*: ACGR, for S&P 1500 companies)
*Includes proposals from individuals. "OTHER" includes proposals related to reincorporation, sale, and other miscellaneous topics.

Say on pay was the single most popular type of pay proposal. (See table 6.1.) There were numerous other kinds related to stock-based pay. To eliminate gimmicks, they called for options indexing, longer periods for cashing options, and eliminating options entirely and replacing them with other types of stock-based rewards such as restricted stock.

Disclosure related to pay-setting drew relatively few proposals and few votes. The picture completely changes if one classifies options expensing as a type of disclosure. There also were "social" pay proposals, a mixture of ideas for tying executive compensation to non-financial criteria such as employee satisfaction, environmental performance, and downsizing (cutting CEO pay after layoffs). The final category, "other," contains two items of note: "commonsense pay plans" and "pay for superior performance plans," both developed by Ed Durkin.[11]

Labor attorney Beth Young says that during the 1990s, "compensation had been considered a governance stepchild." State and local plans were wary of publicly criticizing how much CEOs were paid. Private meetings were preferable. The decade's bull market also mattered. CII's Ann Yerger said that her

TABLE 6.1. Compensation-Related Proposals: Number of Voted Proposals, Percentage Submitted by Union Investors, and Vote Tally by Sponsor, 2003–2012

	Proposals		Votes for Sponsor's Proposals			
	Total (n)	Union Investors (% proposals)	Individuals	Social, Religious, Other	SLPFs*	Union Investors
Stock-based Pay						
Abolish options	43	9	6%			6%
Eliminate accelerated vesting	15	93	42			37
Expense option at time of grant	107	93	47			49
End post-separation retention of equity pay	74	59	26	17%	29%	24
Require shares held after exercise	18	67		22	33	35
Performance-based pay system	136	85	17	19	21	24
Performance-based options	43	67	34		33	35
Performance-based vesting	9	100				34
Performance criteria for equity awards	27	41	26		30	42
Recoup if restatement	33	21	25			29
Performance/Time-based restricted shares	40	90	25			16
Miscellaneous	15	53				
Total stock-based pay [% of which union]	560	[69%]				
Percentage all proposals [% all union proposals]	47%	[57%]				
Advisory						
Approve, limit death benefits	21	90			39%	37%
Approve executive pay (Say on Pay)	225	30	40	42%	45	39
Approve future golden parachutes	105	74	44	42	66	54
Approve, disclose supplemental retirement plans (SERPs)	44	82	31	33		34
Approval stock-based pay	2	50	37			56
Miscellaneous	3	100				
Total advisory [% of which union]	400	[51%]				
Percentage all proposals [% all union proposals]	34%	[30%]				
Disclose						
Disclose executive compensation	45	7%	13%	3%	34%	51%
Highest to lowest paid	8	13	12			11
Pension fund reporting	9	11	31			30
Miscellaneous	1	0				
Total disclose [% of which union]	63	[8%]				
Percentage all proposals [% all union proposals]	5%	[1%]				

Continued on next page

TABLE 6.1. (*continued*)

	Proposals		Votes for Sponsor's Proposals			
	Total (n)	Union Investors (% proposals)	Individuals	Social, Religious, Other	SLPFs*	Uni Inves
Social						
Pay tied to environmental criteria	4	100%				6
Pay tied to social criteria	40	28	6%	8%		10
Total social [% of which union]	44	[34%]				
Percentage all proposals [% all union proposals]	4%	[2%]				
Other						
Adopt anti gross-up policy	10	90%			38%	43
"Commonsense" pay plan	26	100				8
Hire independent pay consultant	4	75			34	39
Restrict or limit executive pay	65	12	62%	26%		12
Miscellaneous	19	84				
Total other [% of which union]	124	[50%]				
Percentage all proposals [% all union proposals]	10%	[9%]				
ALL PROPOSALS	1203	56%				
ALL VOTES			24%	28%	38%	33
			n=341	n=138	n=51	n=6

Source: Georgeson, *Annual Corporate Governance Review (ACGR)*.

Note: Voting percentage of miscellaneous proposals not shown but is included in All Votes; voted proposals at S&P 1! companies.

* State and local pension funds.

members might care about executive compensation if the market were down but added, "Everybody's kind of fat and happy now."[12]

Stock Options

Stock options were not a new practice, although they were uncommon until after the Second World War. The Revenue Act of 1950 sweetened the tax treatment of qualified stock plans that caused an uptick in their usage. One of the earliest critics was the AFL-CIO's Industrial Union Department, which in 1959 issued a report called "The Stock Option Scandal." Stock options, said the report, "provide tax-privileged, risk-free profit opportunities unrelated in any meaningful way to executive performance and unchecked by effective stockholder control." These were prescient words, all the more so given that stock options counted for less than 5 percent of CEO compensation in the 1950s.[13]

Stock options were at the heart of shareholder capitalism, one of the cookbook's top two recipes (the other being the removal of takeover barriers). Shareholder activists had been enthusiastic about options. They were the key to undermining vestiges of a stakeholder approach and getting CEOs to prioritize investors. Said the AFL-CIO's Damon Silvers, "The managerial class gave up resisting the financial players and realized that it was better to play along with them. You got very rich by playing along with them . . . and stock options were a big part of that change." Economists liked options too. Harvard's Michael Jensen touted them as a market-based solution to the fading prowess of American industry. Getting rid of guaranteed salaries would encourage CEOs to become entrepreneurial.

Stock options, as intended, caused CEOs to take bolder steps. But there were unintended consequences. Executives "swung for the fences" and delivered erratic returns—big gains and big losses—with the losses exceeding the gains. Corporations whose CEOs received options larger than those of comparable firms experienced unexpectedly low stock returns. Related to risk-taking is the finding that stock options were associated with product safety problems because they promoted a lack of caution in CEOs.[14]

Options are like other incentive-pay schemes in that recipients eventually figure out how to game them. Law professors Lucian Bebchuk, Jesse Fried, and David Walker found that misuse of options was rife. That executives used options to garner more than their performance warranted was evident in their design: a host of clever features such as failing to index a company's stock gains to performance of its peers, offering in-the-money options (guaranteed payoff), reloading (breaking the pay-performance link by protecting options losses), hedging the company's own stock, spring loading (timing an options grant to precede positive news), repricing (replacing underwater options with new, above-water ones), and other tricks that were difficult to discern. A lack of transparency was intended, not accidental, something that the AFL-CIO first had flagged in its 1959 report: "The average person is caught in a maze if he attempts to obtain some idea of the value of stock options granted to specific individuals."[15]

Expensing Options

Options flowed like water because they were not reported as an expense when granted, thus overstating earnings. At WorldCom, earnings would have been 30 percent less in 2000 had its options been expensed. Options also reduced taxes. Companies received a tax deduction equal to the profit realized by employees when they exercised their options. It permitted high-tech firms like Microsoft and Cisco Systems to erase most of their federal taxes; Enron paid nothing for four years.[16]

Beginning in the mid-1980s, when options were starting to catch on, the Financial Accounting Standards Board (FASB), the US accounting standards setter, considered requiring companies to expense stock options to show the liabilities they were carrying on their books. The issue came to a head in 1993, after FASB released the draft of an expensing plan. Senator Carl Levin (D-MI) authored legislation to make expensing mandatory if companies took a tax deduction when options were cashed; they could have one but not both. The business community, with high tech in the lead, formed a united front against it.

The Clinton years were a time of boundless enthusiasm for Silicon Valley, and Congress shared the fervor. People were thrilled by companies like Microsoft, where, seven years after going public, stock options made millionaires of one out of five employees. Democrats from tech-heavy states in New England and California led the opposition to expensing. Senators Joseph Lieberman (D-CT) and Ed Markey (D-MA) savaged FASB's plan. By a lopsided vote of eighty-eight to nine, the Senate passed a nonbinding resolution asking FASB to halt its efforts, and so it did. Lieberman called this "a great victory for American business and workers," while Levin said that "honest accounting lost out to the pressure of the rich and powerful." In retrospect, Levin was closer to the truth. An accounting professor at Columbia University subsequently judged Lieberman's intervention as the first step on "the slippery slope that got us mired in the Enron swamp."[17]

CalPERS, which was susceptible to lobbying from the state's technology and venture capital firms, was firmly opposed to expensing and asked CII to remain neutral on the issue. The AFL-CIO's Karen Ignani asked FASB to adopt a compromise according to which corporations would not have to expense their options but would have to separately list on their financial statements their present value and the impact on stock dilution. Most CII members supported the compromise, although opposition from CalPERS and from CII's corporate pension funds kept CII from endorsing it. In 1997, Levin, this time together with Republican Senator John McCain (AZ), offered another bill to expense options. But the legislation went nowhere; by then, stock markets were in overdrive.[18]

A few years later came Enron, and options again were back on the political agenda. Senators Levin and McCain, now joined by new players like Representative Barney Frank, a liberal Democrat from Massachusetts, reintroduced expensing legislation in 2002. Republicans were dead set against it; instead, the GOP created the Senate Republican High-Tech Taskforce, with the express purpose of stymieing the push for expensing. Working with them was the International Employee Stock Options Coalition, a lobbying organization composed of technology companies. The party line was that expensing was technically unfeasible; there was no way to calculate the present value of option liabilities. Opposition to expensing included a phalanx of heavy hitters: President George W. Bush, Harvey Pitt of the SEC, and the nation's two main business associations—the US Chamber of Commerce and the Business Roundtable. The Technology Network (TechNet), another industry lobbying group, advised its members to have their employees write to FASB to explain how options had helped them buy a house or support an extended family.[19]

On the other side were prominent figures like Warren Buffett and Alan Greenspan, who claimed that business people were no greedier than in the past but that stock options had given them "avenues to express greed." A study by the Boston Consulting Group found that the value of stock options granted to CEOs at companies guilty of options-related fraud was 800 percent greater than those given to CEOs of comparable firms: "Nothing correlated so strongly with corporate fraud as the value of stock options—not the standard of the firms' governance, nor analysts' inflated expectations about their earnings, nor ego-boosting stories about their CEOs in the press."[20]

Sarbanes-Oxley (SOX) contained several provisions for regulating stock options. The law created the Public Company Accounting Oversight Board, over which the SEC had control, this in response to criticisms that FASB was too close to industry. But with a solidly Republican Congress and fierce opposition from corporations, expensing was kept out of the act. Labor was furious about the omission. On the day that the law went into effect, the AFL-CIO held a rally to kick off a nationwide campaign, "No More Business as Usual." John Sweeney denounced Enron's executives for cashing their options as the company went under. "They are thieves and they are stealing our hopes, stealing our dreams, and stealing our future," he declaimed. In a press release, Sweeney blamed stock options for driving up executive pay "to an obscene 410 times average workers' pay." However, compared to his rhetoric, Sweeney's recommendations were blandly technocratic. He told the rally that the number-one item on his agenda was expensing. The other was to prohibit executives from selling stock in their firm while in office, which, he said, would remove incentives for them to pump up their company's shares.[21]

Congress returned to executive pay several months after SOX became law. The Senate Commerce Committee, chaired by John McCain, convened hearings in 2003. The Arizona senator, by now a longtime critic of CEO compensation, was particularly incensed by the airline industry, which had received close to $4 billion from the government to tide it over through the drop in airline travel following 9/11. The subsidy was contingent on fixing what McCain called "insulting" executive pay levels, yet the airlines had failed to rein in compensation. Jack Welch was invited to testify but did not appear, nor did other highly paid CEOs like Michael Eisner (Disney) and Leo Mullin (Delta Airlines). McCain warned that the United States was "returning to a second Gilded Age" and that stock option misdeeds "give capitalism a bad name."[22]

Damon Silvers was among those who did appear. Playing to McCain, he noted that after 9/11, American Airlines had failed to disclose a scheme that included $41 million to protect executive pensions in case of bankruptcy. He said that generally the time frame for granting options was too short and led to risky decisions that hurt the interests of long-term investors like pension funds. FASB and the SEC had the power to do something about executive pay, Silvers asserted, but "they need the support of Congress." However, a greater principle was at stake than expensing, he contended: "Our markets will be damaged if after the events of the last two years it appears that our accounting standards are still being held hostage to the very political dynamics that prevented effective regulation in the 1990s."[23]

Business lobbying against a FASB expensing rule remained intense. The International Employee Stock Options Coalition collected signatures from more than forty members of Congress, including California representatives from both sides of the aisle, and sent them to FASB. The coalition, joined by TechNet, brought prominent executives to Capitol Hill. One was Oracle's Larry Ellison, another CEO who had thumbed his nose at McCain's committee. Representatives David Dreier (R-CA) and Anna Eshoo (D-CA) co-sponsored legislation to delay any FASB rule until the completion of a three-year study. In November, Senator Michael Enzi (R-WY), previously an accountant, introduced another bill to stave off a FASB standard, this one requiring that expensing be limited to a corporation's top five executives. With only a touch of hyperbole, Enzi said a FASB rule would kill entrepreneurial activity in the United States. Not to be outdone, John Doerr, the doyen of the venture capital industry, said to FASB's chairman, "I don't think there could be a worse time in America's economic history to adopt such a policy."[24]

In the midst of this back and forth, Microsoft broke ranks with an electrify-
ing announcement: It would abandon stock options for a mix of time- and
performance-based stock grants. The company had been preceded by Coca-
Cola, but Coke was not from the tech world, nor was it nearly as influential as
Microsoft. Richard Trumka sent letters to twelve major corporations, including Intel and Cisco, urging them to follow suit. Sounding more like the attorney he was than a tough-talking union chief, Trumka wrote, "I strongly encourage you to expense all equity compensation including previously granted
stock options, and to grant performance-vesting restricted stock to senior
executives instead of stock options." Bill Patterson labeled the Microsoft decision "a defection" and "the beginning of the end, though not the end," for
unexpensed options.[25]

On a parallel track, union investors offered numerous resolutions to compel
expensing. Corporations successfully bid the SEC to block them—as when
National Semiconductor said that a Carpenters' proposal was an accounting-
related and not pay-related matter and therefore covered by the ordinary business exclusion.

Despite negative sentiment in the business community, the SEC reversed
course and deemed expensing "an important social policy issue," hence, free
from the exclusion. Ed Durkin immediately announced that his building-
trades coalition planned to submit more than a hundred proposals and create
momentum to prod Congress and FASB to act. "Shareholder proposals," he
said, "provide an opportunity to weigh in while politicians are waffling."

Over 150 expensing proposals were filed in 2003-2004. Nine out of ten came
from union investors, most of them in Durkin's coalition, and they received an
average vote of 49 percent. Support reached 90 percent at Starwood Hotels
and 79 percent at Fluor. After the vote, Fluor immediately began to expense
options. Like other companies at this point, it could see the handwriting on
the wall. Fabrizio Ferri and Tatiana Sandino, accounting professors at Columbia and Harvard respectively, found that the mere submission of an options-
related proposal was associated with an 11 percent increase in the likelihood of
a firm voluntarily choosing to expense. When proposals received majority
votes at Fortune 500 corporations, they were followed by an average decrease
in CEO compensation of $2.3 million, a not insignificant amount.[26]

Cisco and Intel urged their employees to swamp FASB with anti-expensing
letters. Cisco executives knew that expensing would reduce the company's
earnings by more than a third. In response, the AFL-CIO created a form letter
stating that executives should be "ashamed for trying to hide the cost of stock

options" and posted it on the Paywatch site for visitors to send to FASB. The AFL-CIO was one of the founders of RestoretheTrust.com, a forty-member association of pension plans and other institutional investors that earlier had lobbied for Sarbanes-Oxley. The group devised its own form letter sent by nearly one thousand people that excoriated unexpensed options and the "exorbitant pay packages" that resulted from them.[27]

In the background was the steady drumbeat of corporate misdeeds. For example, the SEC sued HealthSouth for falsifying $2.7 billion in profits, following which the Justice Department indicted Richard Scrushy, the company's CEO, for money laundering, securities fraud, and other charges. It also accused Scrushy of forcing other top executives to commit fraud. This was one of the few criminal cases ever pursued for violations of Sarbanes-Oxley. Shareholders filed lawsuits charging Scrushy with insider trading connected to the sale of his stock options. That same year a cocky Jack Welch received his comeuppance when his divorce proceedings revealed a secret severance package that left General Electric on the hook for a luxury apartment, regular flower deliveries, and food service staff, among other eye-opening perks. The SEC criticized GE for failing to disclose the details of Welch's retirement deal. In contrast to the shareholder meeting where Bill Patterson drew hoots of derision from other investors, the 2003 meeting saw one shareholder stand up and say, "What we did for Jack Welch was absolutely disgusting."[28]

When it came to stock options, the SEC took a harder line than FASB. In 2003, the agency authorized a regulation giving shareholders the right to approve stock option plans. Shareholder consent also would be required before companies would be permitted to change the exercise price of outstanding grants.[29]

FASB finally adopted an expensing rule in December 2004. There then occurred a dramatic reversal in the popularity of options, from a weight of 49 percent in CEO compensation in 2000 to 12 percent in 2016. New types of stock-based pay replaced options. Because of congressional inaction, companies were still allowed to deduct an employee's gain, something that bothered Carl Levin nearly twenty years after he first flagged the problem. Ordinary employees were the one group that failed to recoup losses from the ebbing of stock options. During the NASDAQ boom, stock options were liberally distributed throughout high-tech companies, but because expensing raised their real cost, many fewer of these employees now received them.[30]

In the wake of repeated scandals, people realized that they'd been played. The source of management's misconduct, said economist Anat Admati, was "financialized corporate governance." It had encouraged opacity, fraud, and deception, particularly with CEO pay. Even Michael Jensen recanted his faith: "I recommend that a company never again issue another typical standard executive stock option. The vast increase in the use of options in managerial compensation plans in the last decade does not suffice to identify managers' interests with those of their stockholders and with that of society."[31]

Backdating

No sooner had expensing become law than a new problem arose: backdating. Backdating occurs when an option's grant date is reset to an earlier date. Doing this minimizes the risk associated with a falling stock price and raises the option's value. While not unlawful, failure to disclose violates accounting and securities laws. Backdating also overstates net income. If it's unreported but subsequently discovered, a financial restatement is required, which often reduces previously stated profits. A study by Erik Lie at the University of Iowa found that backdating had led to executives receiving "billions of [illegitimate] dollars." The *Wall Street Journal* reported Lie's findings in a March 2006 story that rocked the business world. The *Journal* created a website revealing corporations under scrutiny by the Justice Department and the SEC. It showed whether the CEO or directors had left the company and whether there had been an earnings restatement.

Of nearly eight thousand firms studied by Lie, almost 30 percent—more than two thousand from all industries, not only tech—had not reported backdating of options granted between 1996 and 2005. Most of them were forced to restate earnings. A few had credit downgrades and were temporarily delisted from stock markets. Several CEOs were indicted by the Justice Department. Some of the firms investigated for backdating would later be implicated in the subprime mortgage meltdown. Only sixteen months after a shareholder sued Lehman Brothers for manipulating grant dates, the investment bank declared bankruptcy.[32]

In 2006, the SEC circulated a plan to limit backdating through enhanced disclosure in proxy statements and annual reports, and to have the disclosures written in plain English. The plan left many dissatisfied. Demands on the SEC to take a stricter approach came in various forms, including proposals from union investors for longer holding periods for stock options (IBEW), a prohibition on vesting until performance criteria were met (AFL-CIO), and specified grant dates (LongView).

To keep the pot boiling, the AFL-CIO posted yet another form letter on Paywatch urging the SEC to require companies to disclose the formulas they used to calculate executive bonuses. Fifteen thousand site visitors sent letters to the agency, this out of a total of twenty thousand comments. The big public plans—among them CalSTRS, CalPERS, and the New York state and city funds—as well as CII and LongView, criticized the SEC's draft because it would shift responsibility for preparing compensation reports from the board's compensation committee to the CEO and CFO. The SEC rolled out its final regulations in July 2006, the biggest change in pay reporting since the Depression.[33]

Changes were on the way at the SEC. Business had long been unhappy with William Donaldson, the agency's chief. An investment banker and corporate liberal, Donaldson took his mandate seriously, too seriously for the business community. He came under fire from a range of critics, including the US Chamber of Commerce, Federal Reserve Chairman Alan Greenspan, and Treasury Secretary John Snow. Donaldson, said Snow, had engaged in "regulatory overreach." In the face of the attack, the SEC director "quit" before the final SEC regulations were released. Replacing him was Christopher Cox, a conservative former House member from Southern California. Several unions were dead set against his nomination. AFSCME said that Cox always sided with big business over investors and urged its members to complain to their representatives. In a letter to Senators Richard Shelby and Paul Sarbanes of the Senate Banking Committee, the AFL-CIO said that Cox had opposed nearly every part of Sarbanes-Oxley and alleged that he favored the immunity of CEOs to charges of fraud. Despite the SEC's new backdating rule, under Cox the pace of investigation was lethargic. Few executives were indicted, and only two went to prison.[34]

Another knock against Cox was his dark-of-the-night revision of stock option rules, a change put in place on the Friday before Christmas 2006. It permitted companies to spread the cost of a grant over several years instead of counting its value during the issuance year. Shareholder activists were furious. The Laborers, with $30 billion in its Taft-Hartley fund, said the change was all about optics; it would "make the numbers look smaller than they really are." CalPERS, CalSTRS, CII, TIAA-CREF, and the AFL-CIO loudly complained to the SEC. Barney Frank blasted Cox for offering a "Christmas eve gift to corporate America." Not surprisingly, the US Chamber of Commerce praised the revision, and even President Bush commended Cox for "making sure that the regulatory burden is not oppressive."[35]

It wasn't necessarily the case that Democrats were less tolerant than Republicans of those implicated by backdating. One of the era's most lucrative option grants went to Dr. William McGuire, the head of a Minnesota-based insurance company, UnitedHealth Group, who raked in more than $2 billion from illegally backdated options. The board, incredibly, had allowed McGuire to select the dates of his own grants, and he picked days on which the company's stock was at a low. Caught up in the mess at UnitedHealth was James A. Johnson, a UnitedHealth director and member of its compensation committee. Johnson was a bigwig in the Democratic Party. A native of Minnesota, he had managed Walter Mondale's 1984 presidential campaign. During the 1990s, he was Fannie Mae's CEO. Graef Crystal, an expert on executive compensation, twice rated Johnson among the nation's most overpaid CEOs.

After McGuire's backdated options came to light, the AFL-CIO's Office of Investment, under Trumka's purview, demanded Johnson's ouster from UnitedHealth's board. But several former Democratic senators lobbied John Sweeney to get Trumka to leave Johnson alone. Trumka backed off only after Johnson promised he would try to oust McGuire as UnitedHealth's CEO. McGuire resigned but kept $800 million from his compensation package. Johnson left too but retained the options he had received as a director, which were worth $175 million. He served on the boards of other companies affected by backdating scandals. Despite the baggage Johnson carried, Barack Obama selected him to serve on his three-person vice presidential selection committee, this at a time when Obama was calling for say on pay.[36]

Say on Pay

The SEC's 2006 regulations required companies to publicize grant dates for options and stock prices on those days and to report annually on executive bonuses versus an industry benchmark. But sunlight doesn't always disinfect. Some firms subsequently published the data in what the *Washington Post* called "gobbledygook." The newspaper asked three consultants to study Disney's annual report and decipher what Disney's CEO received. The figures ranged from $21 million to $31 million to $51 million. Disclosure, said Damon Silvers, "doesn't change the underlying dynamics to make boards more accountable to investors." To get accountability along with transparency, activist investors sought the right for shareholders to vote on executive compensation—say on pay. It would be an uphill struggle to obtain it.[37]

Controversy over executive compensation was not limited to the United States. The United Kingdom in 2002 adopted a say-on-pay law, which originated in the UK's governance cookbooks of the 1990s. Tony Blair backed say on pay as a way of addressing inequality without need for government expenditures. Almost immediately after the UK law went into effect, there was a donnybrook at the British pharmaceutical manufacturer, GlaxoSmithKline, when 61 percent of shareholders voted "no," a shock felt throughout investing world. Among Glaxo's shareholders was CalPERS. A month after the vote, Phil Angelides, California's state treasurer and a CalPERS trustee, joined the chief investment officers of six other state plans to press the SEC for a British-style law.[38]

Union investors introduced their first say-on-pay proposals during the 2006 season. Leading was AFSCME's pension fund, the driving force behind which was the late Richard Ferlauto. He left ISS's Taft-Hartley division in 1997 to join the AFL-CIO's Office of Investment, after which he was hired by Gerald McEntee, AFSCME's president. Among AFSCME's first targets were Countrywide Financial and Home Depot.

Countrywide was an interesting choice, the nation's third-largest lender of subprime mortgages. Its CEO and board chairman, Angelo Mozilo, received total compensation of $160 million, 6 percent of Countrywide's net income. Of that he realized an additional $119 million from exercised options and held additional options then worth around $200 million. These mind-numbing figures were sure to hit the outrage constraint. Said one consultant, "If you are going to pick on anybody, he would be a good guy to focus on."

In response to a say-on-pay proposal, Countrywide's board said that having shareholders vote on executive pay would hamper recruitment and retention of excellent senior executives. Ferlauto asked whether the board had to give Mozilo that much equity "to keep him happy and attached to the company? As a company founder, is he going anyplace?" The following year Countrywide reported losses totaling $3.9 billion, a canary in the coal mine for the financial meltdown.[39]

At Home Depot, shareholders were unhappy that the firm's shares had fallen 9 percent since 2000, when CEO Robert Nardelli was hired, as against a 185 percent increase at rival Lowe's Companies. Yet Home Depot paid Nardelli a total of $245 million during the five years after he became CEO, more than his Lowe's counterpart. On top of that, evidence surfaced that Home Depot's board had been backdating Nardelli's options for fourteen years.

AFSCME, joined by CalPERS, the Laborers, and the CtW Investment Group, urged Home Depot's shareholders to withhold votes from ten of the company's eleven directors. (The eleventh director was new to the board, and his name was Angelo Mozilo.) Demonstrators stood outside the general meeting, one of them wearing a chicken costume and an orange Home Depot apron. The demonstrators chanted, "Hey Nardelli! Your stock price turned to jelly!" Inside the meeting, Nardelli refused to respond to questions about his pay and enforced strict time limits on comments from the floor.

Home Depot didn't reveal its backdating schemes until after the general meeting. At that point, Richard Trumka sent an open letter to Bonnie Hill, a Home Depot director, demanding the board fire lead director Ken Langone and recoup all gains from backdated options. Hill agreed to meet with Trumka, promising "a hard look" at Nardelli's compensation. Home Depot was a non-union employer, where the UFCW recently had made several unsuccessful organizing attempts. Labor saw Home Depot as a steppingstone to Walmart. With its over 2 million low-wage employees, Walmart was the labor movement's mother lode. Companies like Home Depot and Walmart were what one labor journalist dubbed "the commanding heights of the service economy." Attacking Nardelli's pay tarnished management in the eyes of its employees.[40]

Corporations claimed that shareholders didn't deserve a say on pay because they were less well informed than directors, an argument for directorial discretion. The claim is a thin reed; boards can easily supply investors with information explaining the rationale for their pay decisions, as was happening in the UK. In ordinary times, institutional investors tend to support management in voting on executive pay. But the 2000s were not ordinary; the revelations of widespread illegalities had shaken investor confidence. What management really feared is what happened in 2011, after Dodd-Frank mandated say-on-pay voting: Glass Lewis, a prominent proxy advisor, recommended voting no in over one out of five say-on-pay votes; ISS advised a no vote in one out of ten.[41]

Take It to Congress

At the end of 2005, Barney Frank introduced "The Protection against Executive Compensation Abuse Act," intended to address "runaway pay" and "pay disparities" between executives and non-managerial employees. Its centerpiece was say on pay. Other provisions included mandatory clawbacks at companies forced to restate their earnings, a more stringent version than Sarbanes-Oxley's. With Jack Welch in mind, the legislation required companies to disclose the details of executive rewards, including perks like company-paid income taxes.[42]

The House held hearings on Frank's bill in 2006. The AFL-CIO's Brandon Rees testified in favor of it against powerful opposition. The Business Roundtable drubbed say on pay as "unwise and ultimately unworkable" and warned that it would lead to class-action lawsuits against executives. Regarding say on pay, the Roundtable warned, "If we adopted a system where small groups of activist shareholders used the process to politicize corporate decision-making, the consequences could very well be destabilizing." Frank's bill died, but it boosted his reputation as an expert in financial regulation, even taking him to Davos.[43]

Frank met with the media at the National Press Club after he became chair of the House Financial Services Committee in 2007. Over the next two years, his committee would hold hearings about the causes and consequences of inequality and flat wages. Frank believed that a "small segment" of executives had benefited from economic growth while the majority of Americans had not. According to David Smith, Frank's advisor, the decision to focus on say on pay was a reflection of "a new Chairman searching around for attention and getting stuff that was on the shelf and ready to go." Say on pay was easy to explain to constituents who saw a steadily widening income divide. Public opinion about big business had turned more negative than at any time since 1973. Smith said that Frank thought say on pay would appeal to the working-class voters who had put Bush in office for his second term.[44]

Democratic leaders understood that overhauling immigration and signing more trade agreements were off the agenda unless they responded to what journalist Robin Toner dubbed "the new populism." To retain the votes of the working class, the Democrats would have to tilt left in the upcoming elections. But as Toner reported, "Many on the left worry that the Democratic establishment is merely paying lip service." Say on pay was a good political issue: Who wouldn't like the idea of "voting" on the boss's pay? As a remedy for inequality, however, it was wanting.

Republicans recognized that they too were vulnerable to rising populism. President Bush gave a speech addressing inequality at Wall Street's Federal Hall following a surprise visit to the New York Stock Exchange in January 2007. He acknowledged that "a few extravagant pay packages" had "disgusted" millions of Americans. Said Bush, "The fact is that income inequality is real. It has been rising for more than twenty-five years." The audience of bankers and brokers reacted with silence but cheered when Bush said he would cut taxes.[45]

Corporations found it difficult to persuade the public that executives deserved what they received. Damaging to their cause were two astronomical severance payments—at Pfizer and Home Depot—that came to light in 2007. At Pfizer, the board awarded CEO Hank McKinnell severance pay worth nearly $200 million, even though the company's share price had fallen 43 percent during his five-year tenure. Shareholder anger caused McKinnell to retire from Pfizer a year earlier than intended. Ironically, Pfizer was a member of CII and a company with exemplary corporate governance, at least on paper.[46]

Robert Nardelli left Home Depot later that year. His going-away present was an exit package worth a head-turning $210 million. It was hubris on the board's part to give Nardelli that much money after his subpar performance and the backdating problem. Barney Frank released a scorching statement about Nardelli's exit package: "Some defenders of CEO pay argue that CEOs are rewarded for increasing the stock or the overall value of the company, but judging by today's market reaction, Mr. Nardelli's contribution to raising Home Depot's stock value consists of quitting and receiving hundreds of millions of dollars to do so." Breaking ranks with the business community, Charles T. Munger, business partner of Warren Buffett, predicted that say on pay "might dampen some of the excess." And a survey of chartered financial analysts (CFAs) found that three-fourths were in favor of it.[47]

Frank reconvened say-on-pay hearings. Although Bush said that he would not sign a bill containing say on pay, and most Republicans were opposed to it, Democrats were in control of Congress. Frank met with representatives from 130 pension funds at an event organized by CII and warned that if say on pay passed and directors were to "simply shrug off the votes, there could be more drastic reform." Even when three previous SEC chairs came out against Frank's bill, the Democrats had the votes, and it passed in April 2007 by 269-134.[48]

By then, candidates were on the hustings for the upcoming presidential election. One was Illinois Senator Barack Obama, who said say on pay would give shareholders "the power to debate and fight back against exorbitant executive compensation." Say on pay was a way of telling voters, "We feel your pain." Several hours after the House passed Frank's bill, Barack Obama introduced companion legislation in the Senate. Senators Hillary Clinton (D-NY) and John Edwards (D-NC), both candidates, backed the Obama bill, while on the Republican side John McCain (R-AZ), another candidate, said he supported say on pay as a concept but did not endorse a legislative approach. When Obama's bill died the following year, it wasn't Republicans who killed it. Instead it was Senator Christopher Dodd (D-NH), now chair of the Senate Banking Committee, who refused to hold hearings on the bill. Dodd too had thrown his hat into the presidential ring and had no desire to help Obama.[49]

AFSCME and Walden Asset Management, a social investor, created a coalition of shareholders to press companies for say on pay in tandem with Frank's efforts in Congress. It included state and local plans—from California, Connecticut, Boston, and New York City—as well as the AFL-CIO, Hermes Investment, Calvert Investments, Amalgamated Bank, and faith-based investors belonging to ICCR. The group submitted forty-four say-on-pay requests in 2007.[50]

With Congress, the SEC, and institutional investors nipping at their heels, companies showed a greater willingness to compromise than in previous years, not only on executive compensation but on other issues. The intensity of consultation between firms and investors was unprecedented. The head of CII, Patrick McGurn, said "We've never had a season that had so much activity going on in the wings and much less taking place center stage."[51]

Several companies reached out to the AFSCME-Walden group in search of a compromise. Led by the besmirched Pfizer, they called themselves the "Working Group on the Advisory Vote on Executive Compensation Disclosure." Included in the invitation-only group that met at Pfizer's headquarters in New York were twelve major corporations, weighted toward pharmaceuticals (Bristol-Myers, Colgate-Palmolive, and Schering-Plough) and finance (AIG, JPMorgan Chase, Prudential). The group had detractors in the business world, people who were wary of anything that might encourage say on pay. Martin Lipton distributed a letter disparaging the Working Group's ideas as "corporate governance run amuck" and proffered the usual criticism that directors should not be replaced by shareholders when determining executive rewards.[52]

Another group was dead set against say on pay. Co-led by the Carpenters and the US Chamber of Commerce, it included Citigroup and DuPont. Ed Durkin, again the renegade, had developed two alternatives to say on pay. His "commonsense pay plan" included a cap of $1 million on a CEO's salary, with other payments to be made in restricted shares instead of options. The plan rarely obtained more than 10 percent of votes cast, its Clinton-like cap being the kiss of death. Durkin then formulated the "pay-for-superior-performance plan," which called for benchmarking a corporation's stock returns—and CEO rewards—to the performance of its peers. This second plan fared better than the commonsense approach, averaging 30 percent of votes cast in the 2006 and 2007 seasons, but never came close to the popularity of say on pay. Durkin believed that activism should be based on "thoughtful investigative work on compensation plans" to see what would be best for the company and its shareholders. The goal, he said, was getting companies to take specific actions, such as benchmarking. According to Durkin, say on pay communicated little more than general dissatisfaction and did so in a disengaged way.[53]

Dodd-Frank

The global banking system reached the brink of collapse in September 2008. The initial response from the Bush administration was the Emergency Economic Stabilization Act, famous for its Troubled Asset Relief Program (TARP), which authorized the Treasury to spend up to $700 billion to purchase depreciated assets and to loan funds to failing banks. The quid pro quo was that the federal government had the right to monitor and direct the companies receiving its help. Twelve million people now had underwater mortgages, 7 million lost their homes, and employment fell by nearly 9 million persons. People were outraged, and, as in 1893 and 1932, they blamed bankers for their suffering. Stoking public anger were reports that rescued banks continued to spend lavishly. Merrill renovated its corporate offices, and Citigroup placed orders for corporate jets. People felt that bankers had reaped ill-gotten gains during the runup to the crisis, and they were right.

The financial crisis and associated scandals reignited say on pay. That fall investors prepared over one hundred say-on-pay proposals. Union plans divided theirs among corporations implicated by the financial crisis (like Bank of America), those where labor had no side interests (Apple and Lexmark), and those where it had collateral interests (CenturyTel, Walmart, and Windstream).[54]

TARP included restrictions on bankers' pay, some of the specifics drawn from shareholder resolutions. No bonuses were to be paid by companies receiving TARP funds unless they took the form of restricted stock and did not fully vest unless companies repaid their loans. Clawbacks would occur if the bonuses executives received were the result of inaccurate earnings statements. Loan recipients were told to eliminate incentive rewards that encouraged "unnecessary and excessive" risk-taking. TARP also imposed a cap of $500,000 on the tax-deductible compensation of senior executives.[55]

Two weeks before his presidential inauguration, President Obama announced the American Recovery and Reinvestment Act (ARRA). The legislation detailed plans for spending on infrastructure and aid to states. Title VII, however, spelled out "limits on executive compensation" for TARP participants. One of its requirements was for TARP companies to initiate say on pay. The president signed the legislation in February. Yet despite how voters felt about bankers' pay, shareholders seemed to feel differently. Only a handful of

TARP recipients received "reject" votes above 30 percent. At Goldman Sachs, 98 percent of the votes ratified the board's pay decisions.[56]

It remained uncertain whether Congress would extend say on pay to the thousands of companies not receiving federal aid. In May, Senators Charles Schumer (D-NY) and Maria Cantwell (D-WA) introduced a bill to make say on pay mandatory at all public companies, which Dodd then incorporated into his own legislation. It was still there when Congress voted on Dodd-Frank. By then, dozens of firms had voluntarily adopted the practice. On July 21, 2010, President Obama signed the Dodd-Frank Wall Street Reform and Consumer Protection Act. Say-on-pay voting commenced the following year, one of Dodd-Frank's first provisions to be implemented.[57]

As pay voting got underway, it appeared that business's dire warnings had been overblown. At Russell 3000 companies, 91 percent of shares were voted in favor of the board's recommendations. An article in the *Cornell Law Review* indicated this "showed strong support for existing pay practices." But insider holdings need to be considered. Their size varies, but estimates put them at around 21 percent of common stock in the average public company, and higher in some of the more problematic firms. Take Viacom, for example. In 2011, the board's pay recommendation was endorsed by 96.6 percent of voted shares, seemingly a resounding show of support for management. Yet much of Viacom was owned by its CEO, Sumner Redstone, his family, and Viacom executives. If one takes their shares out of the picture, two-thirds of Viacom's independent shareholders cast their ballots against management.[58]

Did say on pay change anything? On the investor relations side, it did. Companies held more frequent private meetings with large investors to discuss their concerns. But say on pay's effect on executive rewards is difficult to pin down. Some studies find that it raised the sensitivity of CEO pay to stock-price performance; others find that excess compensation (unrelated to performance) did not decrease following a say-on-pay vote, no matter how negative the vote. The AFL-CIO had been optimistic that say on pay would give shareholders "new tools to fight back [against] out-of-control CEO pay." But executive compensation continued its upward march. The *New York Times* financial reporter Jesse Eisinger judged say on pay an example of "toothless public regulations."[59]

Pay Ratios

Several months before Dodd-Frank became law, New Jersey's Democratic Senator Bob Menendez inserted a provision requiring companies to disclose in their annual report the ratio of the CEO's pay to that of the median employee. Menendez quoted Louis Brandeis's sunlight quip, adding that disclosure would encourage fairness of rewards. "Middle-class pay has stagnated while CEO pay has skyrocketed," he said.

Among the first to discuss pay ratios was management guru Peter Drucker in his essay, "Overpaid Executives: The Greed Effect," published in the 1980s when executive pay was starting to climb above the flat line of its postwar years while ordinary employees lagged behind. He warned that this would "disrupt the team" and make adversaries of executives and workers. Like others in those years, Drucker pointed to the Japanese, "our toughest competitors," where the distance between top and bottom was smaller than in the United States. "Yet their companies aren't doing too badly," said Drucker. CEO compensation mattered not only to those at the bottom but to higher-paid employees as well:

> Resentment . . . extends up into the ranks of professionals and managers. A large defense contractor, for instance, recently lost some 20 senior engineers and engineering managers—some of them men with 25 years of service in the company. Each quit for the same reason. Said one: "While our salary increases last year were held to 3 percent with the argument that any more would be inflationary, the nine people in the top management group voted themselves bonuses and additional stock options amounting to a 25 percent to 30 percent increase in their compensation—and that's simply dishonest." Needless to say, none of these men is "anti-business" or even mildly "liberal."

Drucker recommended that companies voluntarily adopt a preset multiple of CEO pay over lower-level employees in the range of 15:1 to 20:1. In 1978, the ratio stood at 30:1.[60]

The person who brought pay ratios to Congress was Martin Olav Sabo, a liberal Democrat from Minnesota. In 1991, when pay inequality was in the news, Sabo wrote the Income Equity Act, which would eliminate corporate tax deductions for executive pay in excess of twenty-five times that of the lowest-paid full-time worker. Relentless, he re-introduced the bill repeatedly, the last time in 2005 right before his retirement. He harbored no illusion that his legislation would pass but viewed it as a touchstone for debate and a way to draw national attention to inequality. Knowing the ratio, he said, "could "prompt business leaders to take a closer look at how they may be contributing to America's widening economic divide."[61]

Social investors picked up on Sabo's idea. United for a Fair Economy (UFE), a Boston-based advocacy organization with ties to social investors and unions, started a campaign called Close the Wage Gap. UFE identified CEOs whose compensation surged after layoffs and plant closures. Its leading "job shifter" was Jack Welch. GE's pay ratio, UFE said, was the result of a high numerator and a low denominator: Welch's bonuses rewarded him for shipping US jobs to Mexico. Together with a social investor—Franklin Research and Development (later Trillium)—UFE submitted resolutions at GE in 1998 and 1999, asking the company to set a cap on executive pay. The resolutions received below 6 percent.[62]

Social investors continued to press the issue. In 2006 Walmart faced a proposal submitted by ICCR on behalf of faith-based investors who included the Sisters of the Holy Names of Jesus and Mary. ICCR noted that Walmart's CEO received one thousand times the average pay of its "associates," who it said were contributors to Walmart's success and should be rewarded for that role. The AFL-CIO, however, was lukewarm to Sabo's approach. Like other union investors, it never filed proposals on the topic and played no apparent role in the Menendez proposal. But Menendez sat on the Senate Banking Committee, and Dodd needed his vote.

It's easy to understand how the provision found its way into the final legislation. It made up only eighteen lines out of Dodd-Frank's 2,300 pages, and there were bigger fish to fry. Implementation was left to the SEC, where employers kept it bottled up for several years. Despite its initial disengagement, the AFL-CIO began a letter-writing campaign demanding that the SEC take action. In a 3-2 vote along party lines, the SEC in 2015 approved collection of pay-ratio data. The first report using the figures was released by Representative Keith Ellison (D-MN) in 2018. By then the ratio stood at 278, nine times greater than in 1978.[63]

————

Investors had immense success in replacing executive salaries with stock-based pay. But repeatedly over the following years, they discovered the many ways executives could subvert their intentions. It sparked a second wave of shareholder activism, this time led by unions, that entailed a back-and-forth between private orderings and regulation. What resulted were several fixes to tighten the connection between pay and shareholder returns.

Executive pay wasn't only an issue for investors. It was bound up with public concern over the escalating disparities between the few and the many. Revealing how the system was "rigged," a word the union leaders used repeatedly, provided workers with further evidence that their bosses could not be trusted.

The same was true for voters. In the post-Enron and post-Lehman world, the malodorous details of executive pay-setting suggested that corporations did not act in the public interest. Bill Clinton, George Bush, and Barack Obama understood the political potency of CEO pay. So did Barney Frank, and so did the AFL-CIO. Riding the issue surely boosted labor's public image. Whether it helped unions in other ways is uncertain.

Despite the uproar over CEO pay and inequality, what CEOs were paid was small change compared to shareholders. In 2006, CEO compensation at the S&P 500 companies totaled $7.5 billion, whereas the companies distributed to their shareholders $432 billion as stock buybacks and $225 billion as dividends. It was often asked if executives received too much. The same was rarely asked of shareholders.[64]

7

Shareholder Democracy

AFTER ENRON, proxy access became the holy grail for union and public pension funds. It gives shareholders the right to nominate directors and place their names alongside the board's choices. Energizing the drive for proxy access were shareholders furious that boards had failed to protect their interests. An outsider on the board of a problematic company, someone truly independent, might persuade other directors to back away from obeisance to the CEO. Labor had high hopes for proxy access. The AFL-CIO's Ron Blackwell said, "It would be a very significant step. You're opening up the kitchen inside these companies. That's a dark secret. That's a place where the insiders really play inside ball. . . . That's why the Business Roundtable fought us to the wall on this."

Proxy access wasn't a new idea, but it was hotly contested because it challenged the balance of power within corporations. The search for proxy access circled around five venues—the shareholder forum, the SEC, Congress, the White House, and the courts. It eventually found its way into the Dodd-Frank Act.

Proxy access pitted business against shareholders, Republicans against Democrats, Congress against the SEC, and union investors against each other. As with say on pay, shareholder proposals and lobbying kept the heat on Washington to mandate a market-wide rule. AFSCME's Richard Ferlauto thought that say and pay and proxy access were related: A shareholder-nominated director could be a "hammer" on the board if shareholders rejected its pay recommendation. Proponents wrapped proxy access in democratic trappings; it was voting by constituents. The University of Delaware's Charles Elson, an expert on corporate governance, said proxy access would "make corporate democracy more real."[1]

The Rise of Proxy Access

Even without proxy access, shareholders had the right to nominate directors, although the barriers were high. Nominators had to pay all printing, mailing, communications, and legal expenses. Only 10 percent of public pension plans said that they had ever nominated a candidate. In companies with capitalizations above $200 million, there was an average of only twelve attempts each year to nominate individuals for board seats between 2001 and 2007. Said Joseph Dear, the CIO for CalPERS, "[C]ompanies can and do frustrate efforts to nominate directors."[2]

The SEC's staff had discussed a proxy access rule in 1942 that would have required companies to permit shareholders to place their nominees on the ballot. Business complained and the agency did not act on it. There was a permissible but watered-down alternative: to encourage the board's nominating committee to accept names from shareholders. Shareholder opinions merely were advisory to a nominating committee, whereas proxy access automatically placed a shareholder nominee on the ballot. Ralph Nader brought proxy access back with a shareholder resolution at General Motors in 1970, and it was included in the 1980 Metzenbaum-Rosenthal Corporate Democracy Act (see chapter 1). CalPERS offered an ersatz version in 1988, when it asked Texaco and three other firms to create a Stockholders' Advisory Committee that would permit their largest investors to weigh in on, although not nominate, board candidates. In those days, nominating committees remained few and far between.[3]

In 1990, when shareholders were feeling their oats, the United Shareholders Association, founded by raider T. Boone Pickens, sent a letter to the SEC asking for proxy access. Two years later, the SEC removed a range of barriers to shareholder activism, but proxy access was not among them. Following that, shareholders periodically offered access proposals and the commission permitted companies to omit them. Companies threw shareholders a bone and responded with nominating committees instead. CII's Sarah Teslik said, "Companies will fight back against allowing shareholders to nominate slates. They will watch my children, they will tap my computer, they will leak bad things about me to the press, and they will do that with shareholder money." But, she added, "The answer is, essentially, that we are the company. You are not."[4]

Another approach was to seek greater choice among board nominees. In 2000, a group called Responsible Wealth submitted a proposal at AIG to place on the proxy 50 percent more nominees than there were board vacancies. It was an idea that went back to Nader and General Motors. It wasn't proxy access, but foreshadowed it. The group brought its members to AIG's annual meeting dressed in colonial outfits and distributed cards saying, "A Declaration of Corporate Board Independence." CII supported the effort despite stiff opposition from management."[5]

Proxy access was starting to catch fire as Sarbanes-Oxley was being deliberated, too late for consideration. CII had just begun to debate whether the organization would endorse it, something that was adamantly opposed by its corporate members. To kick things into high gear, AFSCME launched a proxy access campaign in the fall of 2002. Gerald McEntee, the union's president, sent letters to 150 public pension funds urging them to support the campaign in the name of shareholder democracy, while Ferlauto exhorted shareholders to embrace proxy access to end an "Enronized" world of reckless managers and feckless boards. AFSCME submitted a mix of binding (amendments to corporate bylaws) and nonbinding proposals to Sears, Roebuck, Exxon Mobil, AOL-Time Warner, Eastman Kodak, and Bank of New York. Citigroup received only a binding proposal. The SEC disallowed all of them. The founder of AFSCME's corporate affairs office, Michael Zucker, said that proxy access would "take a fake democratic process and make it real," but the SEC wasn't listening.[6]

AFSCME appealed the SEC's decisions to its commissioners, joined by the AFL-CIO, CalPERS, and CII. CalPERS went even further with a 2003 petition to the SEC to create an absolute right for shareholders to nominate directors, that is, to mandate that all companies grant proxy access. Under the gun, SEC chairman William Donaldson announced in June that the agency would look thoroughly into the matter, much to the dismay of the business community. Then began a flurry of activity to sway the outcome. CII distributed flyers near Metro stations in Washington, DC, explaining proxy access and how to contact the SEC. The AFL-CIO, and other unions provided sample language on their websites for sending email messages to the agency.[7]

Led by the Business Roundtable, corporations launched a countercampaign. The Roundtable warned of the dire consequences of a proxy-access rule: "Special interest groups"—an allusion to social and union investors—might "hijack corporate management" and cause "divisive boards that have difficulty functioning as a team." To avoid this, the Roundtable wanted the board's nominating committee to be the arbiter of candidates. Again, Sarah Teslik correctly predicted that business would put up stiff resistance because proxy access would "rock the corporate world even more than charging options to earnings." When Damon Silvers appeared before a Senate committee investigating Enron, he reminded the senators that Enron had had an ostensibly independent board but forked over piles of money to its executives. Proxy access would end what he called "the North Korean model" of director elections. A management attorney at Dewey Ballantine offered a different view: "This is capitalism, not democracy. If I don't like how a company is run, it's really easy—I sell my stock."[8]

In July 2003, the SEC published a preliminary framework for mandatory proxy access, but it contained stiff prerequisites. Shareholders would be permitted to place an alternative nominee on the ballot only if, during the previous two years, the incumbent's "no" votes had exceeded 35 percent. Only investors who owned 5 percent of a company's shares and had held them for at least two years would be allowed to nominate. Not even the largest public plans held more than 0.5 percent of any single firm, but groups of shareholders would be permitted to aggregate their holdings to reach a threshold. In later years, after proxy access had become prevalent, a majority of firms permitted up to twenty investors to combine their holdings.[9]

Now that there was a concrete plan, the politicking became intense. The SEC received an unprecedented five hundred signed comments and nearly 12,500 form letters. Those from business were worded in strong language. The Roundtable filed an eighty-page comment with hundreds of pages of appendices. Shareholders, it said, had sufficient means at their disposal to affect a board's composition, such as withholding votes and making suggestions to a nominating committee. Again it claimed that the presence of a shareholder-nominated director would balkanize the board and disrupt its proceedings. Another criticism, this one the standard argument against regulation, was that, because any SEC rule would of necessity be "one size fits all," it could not take account of the particularities of different companies. Private orderings were a better way to go.

Most often heard was the hijack objection. Pfizer's Henry McKinnell, whom we met in the previous chapter, at the time was president of the Business Roundtable. In a letter to the SEC he warned that union investors in particular might place on the ballot someone who would "excoriate current management and . . . criticize . . . the management policies at the heart of [any] underlying labor dispute." One journalist quipped that he "hadn't heard so much power attributed to labor unions since the last Oliver Stone movie."[10]

Martin Lipton, whose firm represented Kodak, voiced yet another concern: that proxy access would force boards to pay less attention to non-shareholder groups such as employees, creditors, and suppliers. This reprised his ideas from the corporate constituency period. Skeptics thought that his professed concern for employees was disingenuous and that what mattered to him—and to his executive clients—was to keep management in charge. In a rejoinder filed with the SEC, the AFL-CIO turned the hijack argument around, claiming that executives themselves had interests and agendas beyond the corporation's performance. It added that, while good board relationships were important, preventing disasters like Enron mattered more.[11]

The United States was an exception when it came to proxy access. Other countries permitted it without experiencing the dire consequences predicted by its American opponents. The United Kingdom had it in place for over a century, and there was no evidence that it encouraged special interests or discouraged qualified people from serving as directors. The UK rule was not often invoked: an average of five times each year from 2011 to 2014, or one out of five hundred companies annually. In Australia and the Netherlands, countries with activist investors, proxy access existed but was rarely an issue.[12]

Unexpected support came from the Delaware Chancery Court. Chancellor William B. Chandler III and Vice Chancellor Leo E. Strine Jr. published a widely noticed article endorsing proxy access, which concluded, "The rhetorical analogy of our system of corporate governance to republican democracy will ring hollow so long as the corporate election process is so tilted toward the self-perpetuation of incumbent directors." Another distinguished advocate was Lucian Bebchuk of Harvard Law School, who said that proxy access would improve corporate accountability by removing the "effective monopoly" incumbent boards had over their own elections. On the skeptical side was Joseph Grundfest, who thought unions and pension funds wanted an SEC rule to obtain "megaphone externalities," the ability to draw attention to their causes even if their nominee stood no chance at the ballot box.[13]

Nominating Whom?

When asked what kind of director he would like to see on a board, Dan Pedrotty of the AFL-CIO's Office of Investment replied that it would be different depending on the type of company. Were it from the construction industry, a nominee might be a CEO from another construction company who'd been cooperative with labor in the past. Were it an insurance company, a world union investors knew less well, it might be an academic or a director on a different board who'd received strong support from active shareholders. Pedrotty emphasized that either type would have to be "someone who realizes that our pension funds have a significant long-term horizon, have concerns about real independence when they're negotiating a pay package . . . [and] who buys into the story we tell and the viewpoint we take on capital markets. Part of that is treating employees according to that long-term view." One person Pedrotty named as an ideal candidate was Warren Buffett.[14]

Rarely was it suggested that an employee or union representative might serve on the board, as with German-style codetermination and two-tier boards. American unions generally disliked the idea of employee-directors because it blurred the bright line between labor and management, something that meant more to American unions than to their German counterparts.

The TUC (Trades Union Congress, the UK's equivalent to the AFL-CIO) several times had floated the idea of placing an employee on a firm's compensation committee. Asked whether the same should happen in the United States, Pedrotty said that having genuinely independent directors had to come first. Employee representation, he said, was a long-term goal and perhaps not possible in the United States. Were union investors to push for an employee on the board, said Pedrotty, the Business Roundtable and the US Chamber of Commerce would say that it was proof that union investors cared only about collateral interests. Pedrotty's boss, Richard Trumka, took a different position. Then the AFL-CIO's secretary-treasurer, Trumka thought employees could serve as directors, but only if they were independent of management and had an interest in the corporation's long-term health: "We would have to train them, and we would have to make sure that they were qualified." But the AFL-CIO never advocated having employee directors as a routine practice.[15]

Employees sometimes received board seats following the creation of an ESOP, a situation in which the employees *were* the shareholders. It happened at ailing companies like Weirton Steel, United Airlines, and several others. A rare exception occurred when Chrysler was on the brink of bankruptcy and placed the UAW's president on its board. But this was done as a quid pro quo for steep wage concessions, and the arrangement lasted for only four years.[16]

Come 2004, the SEC still had not announced a decision. Several state plans—AFSCME, CalPERS, New York, and Illinois—filed a joint proposal for proxy access at Disney because they felt that the board had grossly overpaid CEO Michael Eisner. Optimism rose when the agency told Disney that it could not disallow the submission. But none of it came to fruition. A few months later the SEC nixed its own plan and reversed its position on Disney.[17]

The decision shocked activist investors. The about-face came around the same time as William Donaldson's departure from the agency. In his final months, Donaldson had flipped and flopped on proxy access to no one's satisfaction. A month after leaving office, he remarked that he'd been "surprised at the extent of doctrinaire thinking that was so rigid it couldn't accept the obvious conclusion that in a number of important areas we needed at least some mild regulation." He surely had the Business Roundtable in mind. When its president appeared before the Senate, he rejected proxy access, saying, "There is a misperception that corporations are democracies. In fact, they are not." Sitting next to him was Trumka, who quipped, "We do agree with Mr. Castellani that we have never found corporations to be democracies. We would like to change that, however." Trumka's remark was followed by laughter in the room.[18]

The window for proxy access closed in the face of the SEC decision and the waning of corporate scandals. According to Ron Blackwell, "The Enron thing and the WorldCom thing, as devastating as they were for those companies, it was an opportunity for corporate reform. We pushed it as hard as we could. But because of other winds blowing in the Republicans' direction, it was short-circuited." Not everyone was unhappy with the demise of the SEC's plan. Looking back, attorney Beth Young said the triggering mechanism had made the plan unworkable because it contained a one-year delay following a withhold vote before access to the proxy would be allowed: "People now claim that they were happy with it because it's more politically okay to say so. . . . But everyone hated it."[19]

Majority Voting

Majority voting took on new prominence as proxy access bogged down. By replacing the plurality rule, which allowed directors to serve on the board if they received but a single yes vote, majority voting would force companies to respect shareholder preferences. The Carpenters' Ed Durkin, a foe of proxy access, favored majority voting because he thought proxy access was adversarial and gave too much power to large institutional investors unconcerned with the fate of private-sector workers.[20]

Between 2004 and 2009, investors submitted over five hundred proposals for majority voting. Most likely to receive them were firms with poor economic performance and high levels of institutional ownership, the old CalPERS criteria. Those that went to a vote averaged 50 percent of votes cast. More than half came from union pension funds. Proposals drew strong support even when the sponsor had collateral interests. When the Teamsters demanded majority voting at FedEx, a firm the union had long been trying to organize, it received 85 percent of votes cast. Some companies opposed majority voting but others went along with it, believing it would stymie proxy access.[21]

Shareholders liked majority voting for a simple reason: It gave them more power. An uncontested director who did not receive majority support left the board 25 percent of the time; but if the company had a majority voting rule, it rose to 78 percent. Majority voting for directors had spillover effects. After a company adopted majority voting, it was more likely to implement other types of proposals receiving majority votes. The financial crisis sped up the dissemination of majority voting. In 2011, over 90 percent of the S&P 500 were using it, as compared to 16 percent five years earlier. One of the last holdouts was Apple, where CalPERS fought for three years until Apple caved.[22]

Regulatory Wrangling

When Barney Frank became the new chair of the House Financial Services Committee in 2007, the betting was that he would introduce proxy-access legislation. Indeed, no sooner had Frank stepped into his new post than he declared, "Shareholder democracy solves a lot of problems. We're not talking about a lot of individual cranks. We're talking about some fairly responsible people with a lot at stake. They're not interested in damaging a corporation. They're not interested in sacrificing profits for social issues." But Frank was busy with say on pay and put proxy access on the back burner. Said Frank, "You can't do it all at once."

Late in 2006, a federal court had overruled an SEC decision permitting AIG to keep proxy access off its ballot. Activists immediately responded. AFSCME and three public plans introduced a proxy access proposal at Hewlett-Packard, while CalPERS submitted one at UnitedHealth. Some companies responded by posting help-wanted ads on their websites for vacant board seats, including links to their nominating committees, in an attempt to placate investors.[23]

Finally, in the summer of 2007, the SEC put forth two options for a proxy-access rule. One was the original blueprint from 2003; the other, backed by its Republican commissioners, sanctioned proxy access but allowed boards the discretion to choose who would appear on the final ballot—the nominating committee approach. Activists were dissatisfied with both plans, whereas business representatives—who lobbied the Bush White House on the issue—backed the SEC's Republicans. Frank, annoyed by the SEC, told Chairman Cox to go back to the drawing table. There was intense lobbying from both sides over the next several months. Yet again the SEC was deluged with letters.

Only a few weeks later the SEC rejected both of its own plans and said companies would be allowed to deny shareholder access to the proxy, infuriating Barney Frank because Cox had not deferred the vote until an empty SEC seat was filled, a dodge reminiscent of his behavior on options expensing. John Sweeney alleged that Cox had succumbed to political pressure and taken away "a fundamental right." AFSCME thumbed its nose at the SEC and filed proposals containing a slight variant of proxy access, including at J. P. Morgan and Bear Stearns. Nobody could foresee that several months later Bear Stearns would collapse and be forced into a merger with Morgan. After Bear Stearns's demise, Richard Trumka said that its directors had failed to see the connection between lavish rewards to the CEO, Kerry Killinger, and his bets on subprime loans. Trumka said it showed the need for investor nominees on the board.[24]

The banking crash and the fall elections put proxy access back on the front burner. Also reappearing was Ralph Nader, running a fifth time for president. Nader touted proxy access and, as forty years earlier, he framed it as the democratic prerogative of shareholders. An oft-heard trope was the comparison of corporate election methods to those of totalitarian governments, as Damon Silvers had done with North Korea. A magazine for the pension fund industry selected a different comparison nation, saying "Corporate democracy has until now resembled nothing so much as the democracy of the politburo of the former Soviet Union, where an old-boy network selected Communist Party members for membership, and most stayed on it until retirement or death."[25]

After the Crash

Congress and the SEC

Shortly after Barack Obama took office, he appointed Mary L. Schapiro to chair the SEC. Although a reformer, Schapiro had credibility in the financial industry because of her prior service as an SEC commissioner and her subsequent position as CEO of the National Association of Security Dealers. During her Senate confirmation hearing, Schapiro noted that forty of the largest stock markets outside the United States allowed proxy access and added that the time had come for the United States to adopt "a well-crafted, rational approach."

Two previous SEC commissioners had recently announced support for it. The first was a Republican, Richard Breeden, who was chairman when Schapiro was a fellow commissioner. The other was a Democrat, Arthur Levitt Jr., who wrote an op-ed piece for the *Wall Street Journal* saying proxy access would "boost shareholder democracy." Schapiro hired as her senior advisor Kayla Gillan, an attorney who had worked at CalPERS for sixteen years.[26]

Under Schapiro, the SEC moved quickly on proxy access, and in April 2009 endorsed it. Then all hell broke loose. Marquee companies and seven of Wall Street's largest law firms sent an angry letter to the commission. The Chamber of Commerce made opposition to proxy access its signature issue, launching a grassroots effort urging small businesses to complain. One protester was the owner of Don's Tractor Repair in Wakefield, Kansas, who wrote, "If the companies I purchase parts from are caught up in expensive proxy contests, I am afraid they will not be able to deliver the parts that I need at a reasonable cost and in a timely manner."

On the other side, CII and major public and union plans had their own letter-writing campaigns. A group of eighty law and business professors co-signed a letter in favor. In June, the SEC created an Investor Advisory Committee stacked with access supporters. Of the fifteen members, at least nine had previously backed proxy access, including representatives from CII, the Consumer Federation of America, Domini Social Investments, and the AFL-CIO.

Union investors were taken aback when Ed Durkin released a six-page letter opposing the SEC plan. Again he complained that private-sector workers would lose out if proxy access came to pass because it would give too much power to institutional investors, among whom he mentioned Fidelity Investments. Durkin, ever the voluntarist, did not want to keep giving government a larger role in corporate governance. The better course, he wrote, was to "allow the private ordering process to develop a new and effective accountability mechanism," presumably majority voting.[27]

Senator Charles Schumer (D-NY) tossed a bomb in April 2009 when he announced what was dubbed the Shareholder Bill of Rights Act. Cosponsored with Senator Maria Cantwell (D-WA), it mandated proxy access along with say on pay. The bill made it to the Senate floor three weeks later, one day before Schapiro announced the SEC's new rule.[28]

Schumer had close ties to the labor movement, despite his allegiance to Wall Street, and labor repaid him for his loyalty. New York's unions, whether the building trades or SEIU, regularly endorsed Schumer. In return, he took up labor's causes, including the Employee Free Choice Act (EFCA). At the time Schumer released his shareholder bill, he was also meeting with Senate leaders to work out a compromise that would bring EFCA the votes needed for passage. John Sweeney and Andy Stern had easy access to Schumer, as did Damon Silvers, who never had difficulty getting through to the senator on the phone.[29]

For governance reformers, the mood was one of cautious optimism. Richard Ferlauto described the situation as "exciting and incremental at the same time." If Congress and the SEC were to deliver proxy access, he said, "shareholders will have brand-new extraordinary powers to assert their views." Sentiments such as these made business apprehensive. Most of Cantwell-Schumer was bothersome to them, whereas proxy access was alarming.[30]

Cantwell and Schumer persuaded Dodd to add the Shareholder Bill of Rights to his bill, after which CEOs streamed through Washington to excise it. The Roundtable said that stopping proxy access was its highest priority. At this point, moderate Democrats stepped in to thwart Schumer. Senator Thomas Carper (D-DE) joined a Republican senator, Bob Corker of Tennessee, in introducing an amendment to cut proxy access from the Dodd bill. Carper was a member of the New Democrat Coalition (NDC), a caucus from the party's center-right. Other Democrats opposed to proxy access included Senators Ted Kaufman of Delaware, Mark Warner of Virginia, and Evan Bayh of Indiana, all members of the NDC. Carper and Kaufman represented Delaware, whose revenues depended on adjudicating private orderings of the sort that Cantwell-Schumer undermined.[31]

Haggling over the final version of Dodd-Frank continued down to the wire. Come June, proxy access looked inevitable and the fight shifted to its details. Business sought to limit access to those owning 5 percent of shares for at least two years; the White House urged Senate negotiators to accept what business wanted. To get support from Senate Republicans and to please the White House, Dodd inserted the 5 percent threshold into the Senate bill.

Activist investors were enraged. CII sent an urgent email alert to its members asking them to directly contact White House advisor Valerie Jarrett. Were the new threshold to become law, claimed CII, it would "effectively shut out those large, long-term responsible investors—mainly public and union pension funds—most willing to engage companies and hold them responsible." CII also contacted House negotiators and importuned them to reject Dodd's revision. In Barney Frank they found a sympathetic ear. Frank said that there was "real angst" over the threshold and that 5 percent "is a lot to have to own." Under Frank, the House negotiators put up stiff resistance, and, in the end, Dodd-Frank said nothing about thresholds. The law kicked the issue over to the SEC, whose job it would be to craft a rule.[32]

In August 2010, a month after Obama signed Dodd-Frank, the SEC at long last released its proxy access plan. To deter hedge funds, proxy access could not be used to take over a company. To nominate, an investor would have to meet a 3-percent/3-year threshold. The SEC was ambiguous, however, regarding the number of investor groups who could amalgamate to reach it. Kathleen Casey, one of the two Republican commissioners voting against proxy access, offered a blistering criticism of the new rule, blaming activist investors for promoting "the paradigm of a power struggle between directors and shareholders." On the other side were CalPERS, CalSTRS, and the AFL-CIO, who praised the rule; the Teamsters called it historic. The betting was that activists would now challenge companies whose directors had been narrowly reelected, whose executives were overpaid, and whose boards had ignored shareholder proposals approved by majorities.[33]

Critics once again trotted out the hijack argument. The Chamber of Commerce said that the SEC "has given special interests the ability to hold the board hostage on narrow issues at the expense of other shareholders." Elsewhere the Chamber charged that proxy access would give union pension plans "greater leverage to ram through their agenda." With a touch of historical perspective, the *Wall Street Journal* invoked Saul Alinsky, and said that he'd won at the SEC. It labeled proxy access "a weapon to extract political concessions. . . . Activist groups and union-led pension funds will come knocking on a corporation's door threatening to run opposition candidates if, for example, the firm doesn't endorse ObamaCare or won't stop supporting the US Chamber of Commerce." However, a management attorney admitted that many public corporations were "breathing a sigh of relief" because the access threshold was a challenging one for investors to reach.[34]

Suddenly business associations stepped up their game. The Chamber and the Roundtable filed a lawsuit charging that the SEC had failed to perform a cost-benefit analysis—as required by law—to assess the effect of the access rule on efficiency, competition, and capital formation. The case was heard by the US Court of Appeals for the DC Circuit, the same court that produced *Citizens United*. Representing business was Eugene Scalia, who would return to undo other parts of Dodd-Frank.[35]

One year later the court ruled unanimously against the SEC, which during the interim had put the proxy access rule on hold. Justice Douglas Ginsburg, a conservative, blasted the agency for being inconsistent, opportunistic, contradictory, and unresponsive. He claimed that the SEC did not address the criticism that investors such as unions had objectives that "may well be greater than their interest in share value and [can] be expected to pursue self-interested objectives rather than the goal of maximizing shareholder value," the same charge Scalia had levied in 2008 (see chapter 3). Although the SEC had prepared a 160-page economic analysis, Ginsburg said it was inadequate in its quantification of the rule's costs and benefits. Ed Durkin, no friend of proxy access, echoed Ginsburg when he said that "good cost-benefit analysis is always a good thing in promulgating new regulations." He added, however, that the Roundtable's invocation of the hijack story "is the same old BS." The SEC decided not to appeal the decision.[36]

Back to Private Orderings

All was not lost. Although the court froze mandatory proxy access, it told companies that they could not exclude shareholder proposals to adopt it. With that, the door reopened to private orderings. But the court permitted companies to preemptively adopt their own plans for proxy access, which allowed them to reject a shareholder proposal. That's what many companies did, but the company-crafted plans were much weaker than those coming from shareholders. They erected tall barriers for nominator eligibility: in the number of shares owned, the number of amalgamations, and the number of nominations permitted each year. The company plans also required much lengthier ownership periods. And even when a shareholder proposal made it to a vote, mutual funds like Fidelity would oppose and sink it.

Matters changed in the 2015 season, when the number of proposals shot up. The catalyst was a gadfly investor who submitted an access proposal at Whole Foods. The company then adopted its own, more restrictive, plan and matters would have rested there had the SEC not stepped in. The agency said it no longer would allow companies to block shareholder proposals preemptively, thereby neutering corporate defenses.

Another crucial development was the Boardroom Accountability Project, launched that season by New York City's pension funds to promote proxy access. Overseeing the project was Michael Garland, who had previously worked for CtWIG and before that in the AFL-CIO's Office of Investment, where he wrote a 2004 article with Damon Silvers praising proxy access. The city's pension plan filed dozens of proposals that season, much as AFSCME had done with say on pay. Garland cleverly targeted companies that relied on a carbon-intensive business model, including coal-burning electrical utilities and oil companies. The following year the plan filed a similarly large number of access proposals, approximately one-third of the total two hundred submitted, as well as requests for binding bylaw changes at Cabot Oil & Gas and Noble Energy.[37]

The big mutual funds were in a quandary. They were on record in favor of sustainable development and corporate efforts to combat climate change. They were signatories to the Principles for Responsible Investment and similar statements. New York City's proxy access proposal at Exxon was a watershed, with 61 percent of shares voted in favor. BlackRock, State Street, and Vanguard all voted for it against management's wishes. BlackRock was pressured by its own shareholders, including Norway's sovereign wealth fund, which was its second-largest investor. The holdout was Fidelity, a privately owned company. But in 2017 it caved. Faced with a phalanx of owners, companies rushed to put plans in place. By the end of 2018, 70 percent of the S&P 500 companies had adopted proxy access, a stunning turnaround.

The New York City funds had backing from long-time activists like CalPERS and TIAA-CREF, but, with the exception of the Carpenters, union investors kept at a remove. Had they been more involved, it would have given ammunition to those who alleged that proxy access was a Trojan Horse for labor.

That didn't stop CtW Investment Group and IBEW from submitting a few proposals at companies where they had collateral interests, such as Walgreens, where the UFCW, a CTW member, had an organizing drive underway. It received 40 percent of votes, a good showing and evidence once again that investors were indifferent to collaterals.[38]

Was the *Sturm und Drang* over proxy access worth the effort? Once in place, proxy access functioned no differently than in Europe. As of 2019, it had been invoked only two times, once by a hedge fund, hardly what labor had in mind in its early enthusiasm for proxy access. In the future, proxy access may lead to a greater number of outside voices on boards, people less beholden to management, or it may not. David Smith, Barney Frank's advisor, thought that any transformative power of proxy access depended on factors that lay beyond it: "The world would be slightly better off . . . with less cumbersome proxy access.

But the world would not be transformed by [it] absent a unified ability to take advantage of it."[39]

———

Shareholder democracy was the banner under which union investors, joined by others, had demanded proxy access and say on pay. The customary vehemence with which companies opposed labor unions was a tipoff that management would put up a fight against any other group that threatened its control. With collective bargaining, the threat came from workers. With reforms such as proxy access and say on pay, the threat came from shareholders. On the eve of the pandemic, several bills appeared in Congress requiring employee representation on boards. There may yet be a unified ability to make proxy access transformative.

8

Organizing Finance

PRIVATE EQUITY rode the easy-credit wave associated with financialization. In the 2000s, the industry employed approximately five million people, about 4 percent of all US workers. Bringing some of those five million into the labor movement would be a coup. A different opportunity arose after the financial crash. Bank employees were traumatized as their employers tottered, which offered labor, specifically SEIU, another group of prospective members.

The Private Equity Industry

Private equity funds purchase companies, take them private, and hope to sell for a profit after several years—sometimes to a different private equity firm, sometimes to the public. The general partners invest money from the limited partners in a buyout fund with a fixed duration, usually ten years. Whereas private equity spent $91 billion on buyouts in 2000, the peak pre-crisis year was 2007, when $775 billion was pumped into over 2,500 deals. Private equity was a throwback to the leveraged buyouts of the 1980s, epitomized by the acquisition of Nabisco by KKR, the protagonist in the popular account of the incident, *Barbarians at the Gate*.[1]

Because interest payments are tax deductible, private equity—like hedge funds and venture capital funds—benefits from the tax code's favoring of debt over equity. Another advantage is that the acquisition's own cash is used to finance the debt; it's the reason that the industry likes companies with large, stable cash flows. There is also a tax benefit related to the 20 percent of the partnership's profits that the general partners traditionally receive called "carried interest." The government classifies it as capital gains, taxed at half the rate applied to ordinary income. In addition to carried interest, the partners take management fees from the companies it purchases to the tune of 2 percent annually. Partnerships are exempt from numerous regulations that apply to public corporations, including those related to transparency and investor rights.[2]

Similar to hedge funds and venture capital, private equity reduces its risk by owning a portfolio of companies, meaning that poor performance at some funds can be more than offset by lucrative successes at others. While two in twenty deals do not return any profits, five in twenty have returns above 50 percent. In short, a lot of money flows into the pockets of the general partners, which is why they include some of the richest people in the United States. It's also why private equity and hedge funds became a lightning rod for critics of inequality.[3]

Enthusiasts claim private equity raises value by bringing in a team of seasoned professionals to improve the efficiency of poorly managed acquisitions. Detractors say that operating improvements, if they occur, are but one source of private equity's profits. The main contributor is leverage. By saddling the acquisition with debt, the partnership need put up only a small part of its own funds to take control and can quickly earn its investment back. After that, all returns are gravy. Fidelity International's chief investment officer sniffed that private equity did little more than change a formerly public company's debt-equity ratio: "Performance over time will be driven by the same factors [as before the buyout]. The difference is leverage. Strip out the leverage and the correlation with quoted equities is tight." Others say that private equity doesn't consider a company's future beyond the date it flips the acquisition to a new owner. Harvard's Joshua Lerner, often a fan of private equity, says that there is a "fundamental conflict in private equity between taking steps that generate a good return for investors and doing things that are in the best interests of the companies."[4]

Private equity funds took part of their profits at the employees' expense. Purchases not infrequently were followed by wage cuts, downsizing, and intensified work. After a buyout, the partners might close a DB pension plan, skim off allegedly excess assets, and transfer remaining liabilities to the Pension Benefit Guaranty Corporation (PBGC). A British expert described pension funds as "catnip" for private equity.[5]

Investing in Private Equity

Asking how profitable private equity is would be the wrong question. An investor wants to know how profitable it is compared to other asset classes bearing similar risk. Although private equity appeared to offer higher returns, Oxford

University economist Ludovic Phalippou found that, on a risk-adjusted basis, private equity's returns from 2006 to 2018 were no higher than the S&P 500's. Why, then, did pension funds invest large sums in private equity? Phalippou attributes their behavior to asymmetric information. A feature of private equity is its opacity to investors. Lack of transparency made it difficult to calculate past performance, risk, and fees. High fees eat away at investors' returns, so, according to Phalippou, "[A] lot of effort is spent by private equity managers to ensure information [on fees and spending] remains as secret as the recipe for Coca-Cola."[6]

A key point here is that some private equity funds *are* profitable relative to stocks. Large pension plans get to invest in the best of them; smaller plans are left with the less desirable funds or a fund of funds. Either way, the outpouring of money from pension plans had all the earmarks of a stampede. It was said that state and local plans were desperate for yield because of unfunded liabilities. But there wasn't a neat correlation. Among public plans, Washington State and Oregon had the greatest portion of their assets in private equity, yet Washington had the second-best-funded public plan, and Oregon was in the top half.

Some deals put the public plans at loggerheads with union workers. An example was a food factory in New York City owned by Kraft. In 2006, Kraft sold the unit, Stella D'oro Biscuit Company, to a private equity investor, Brynwood Partners. Brynwood demanded steep wage and benefit concessions from Stella's unionized workforce. When negotiations with the union failed, Brynwood sold the factory to a public company, which moved production to Ohio and shuttered the New York plant. Much of the money in Brynwood came from public pension funds, including a large amount from the Pennsylvania State Employees' Retirement System, which covers thousands of unionized government employees. The connection between public pensions and private equity was hardly unique to Brynwood. As the public funds began to diversify into alternative investments in the 1990s, they would grow to become private equity's main investors.[7]

Taft-Hartley funds initially were cautious. With merely 0.1 percent of their assets in private equity in 1998, their allocation rose slowly over the next four years but still amounted to only 1 percent, a drop in the bucket as compared to state and local plans. The figure rose more rapidly after that, reaching around 5 percent on the eve of the financial crisis. Small multiemployer plans were prey to hard-sell tactics, like saying, "You really want to get in on this fund? I can leave open $200 million. But if you don't act by July 1, I've got a queue of five other people."[8]

State and local funds discarded their scruples when it came to private equity, which offered few rays of sunshine, little accountability, modest fiduciary protections, and no such thing as an independent board looking out for the limited partners. Private equity funds required that investors refrain from revealing information on fees and carried interest. A watchdog group sued CalPERS in 2004, demanding that it publicly disclose information about its private equity investments. Although CalPERS agreed to do so, it moved slowly. Ten years later a board member sent an open letter to the CEO of CalPERS, again complaining that it failed to publicize fees. Phalippou said that "CalPERS' total bill is likely to be astronomical. People will choke when they see the real number."[9]

A different type of recondite payment are so-called placement fees that hedge funds and private equity funds give to middlemen to pitch their business to pension funds. One example is the activist hedge fund Relational Investors, which paid a placement agent $17 million in 1993 to help get money from CalPERS. It paid off a couple of years later, when CalPERS invested $200 million with Relational. CalPERS did not report the placement fee until 2010, by which time the pension fund had about $1.5 billion in Relational. Placement fees weren't illegal, but they created the temptation to commit illegalities. CalPERS was forced to reveal the fees after discovering that several of its officials had unlawfully profited from the practice.[10]

To guide Taft-Hartleys into the private equity world, the AFL-CIO published a report in 1999 that evaluated and graded several private equity firms. The criteria revolved around worker-friendly policies: whether the firms fostered partnerships with their employees, including collective bargaining agreements, and whether they created or sustained decent jobs with decent pay. But it did not evaluate investment returns. Then the AFL-CIO published a second report, now focusing on private equity funds that invested in unionized firms, such as the Yucaipa Companies and KPS Partners. If an acquisition was in dire straits, these worker-friendly investors knew that the only route to profits would involve wage cuts and layoffs. However, the union usually would be part of the decision, and severance payments and profit sharing eased the pain of cost-cutting, something that other private equity funds rarely offered.[11]

Labor-friendly private equity funds frequently had general partners with ties to the labor movement. The wealthiest was Ron Burkle of Yucaipa, a former grocery worker and UFCW official from California. Unionized supermarkets were one of Yucaipa's favorite industries. Because Burkle invested $50 million to rebuild grocery stores damaged during the Los Angeles riots, the

AFL-CIO named him "Humanitarian of the Year" and he received a citation from the Los Angeles Labor Federation. Burkle was Bill Clinton's friend and a generous donor to the Democratic Party. All of this opened doors for Yucaipa. CalPERS and CalSTRS had $1.1 billion invested in the firm in 2009. Still, the overall impact of worker-friendly private equity was modest because there were few such firms and they were too small to absorb much pension money.[12]

Another private equity investor who once had ties to the Democrats was Wilbur Ross, who later became Donald Trump's secretary of commerce. Because he had good relations with the Steelworkers, when Ross sought to terminate an underfunded pension plan, he and Steelworkers officials went together to turn over the plan to the PBGC. Said Ross, "We found that if you approach the union with a realistic request—in that you are not cutting them [union members] just so management can live in the lap of luxury—and if you have a quid pro quo so that they can share in the profits, you get along reasonably well."

But not all unions were able to strike deals with Ross. In steel, the unions were successful; in coal, where unions were weaker, Ross refused to negotiate. The difference might explain why Steelworkers president Leo Gerard was more sympathetic to private equity than was Rich Trumka when he'd been president of the United Mine Workers. Gerard said that it was "easier for unions to solve discrete collective bargaining problems with private equity than with public companies." Yet Ross, like Burkle, was a businessman, not a philanthropist. He extracted $4.5 billion out of his steel acquisitions, about the same amount as retirees lost in health and pension benefits.[13]

Sometimes, blue-state plans were sensitive to the impact of their private equity investments on unionized workers. Hertz car rental was purchased for $15 billion in 2005 by three private equity funds: Clayton, Dubiler & Rice (CD&R), the lead investor, and two other funds, Carlyle and one from Merrill Lynch. Hertz had a large number of Teamsters members, who were worried about job cuts and the effect of the buyout—and the debt load that would ensue—on the company's future health. The Teamsters reached out to CD&R. When it refused to speak with the Teamsters, the union set in motion a Rube Goldberg series of network ties. First, it turned to the New York City Employee Retirement System (NYCERS), many of whose participants were union members and a trustee who was a Teamster. NYCERS then asked Merrill Lynch, a New York–based bank that did business with the city and state, to meet with the Teamsters and listen to their concerns. That same day a general partner from CD&R contacted the Teamsters. Later, a meeting of CD&R

and the Teamsters was held at Merrill headquarters, along with analysts and investors. After the deal closed, Hertz fired several thousand employees, although not union members. One thing is clear, however: Private equity managers did not (and often do not) reflexively pass on purchasing a firm because it was unionized. At Hertz, they were able to extract in excess of $2 billion between 2005 and 2007 alone. Because Hertz had difficulty meeting the debt obligations heaped on it by the buyout, it filed for bankruptcy in 2008, as the financial crisis took hold, and again in 2020.[14]

Continental Europe did not experience many LBOs until the late 1990s, whereas their prevalence in the UK and the United States familiarized British and American unions with private equity's business model. Thus, private equity's appearance shocked France and Germany. The era's most memorable words came from Franz Münterfering, chair of Germany's Social Democratic Party (SDP), who in 2005 said private equity investors resembled "swarms of locusts" descending on German workers and the country's midsized, family-owned companies. A few weeks later, Münterfering created a "locust list" of ten foreign-owned private equity firms. Critics viewed it as mere electioneering intended to bring back voters who had deserted the SPD because of the party's earlier enthusiasm for shareholder capitalism.

German labor and the SPD had something tangible to show for their resistance: a new law granting works councils the right to negotiate over buyouts. At the EU level, the socialist bloc in the European Parliament published a lengthy report on private equity in 2007, warning of its threats to the European social model. By a vote of 526 to 82, the Parliament asked the European Commission to draft regulatory legislation. Although the commission was friendly to finance of all kinds, the crash forced it to act. In 2011, it issued the Directive on Hedge Funds and Private Equity, which was bitterly opposed by British and American private equity funds. German unions, among others, charged that American unions were not sufficiently aggressive when it came to regulating private equity and hedge funds because their pension plans had billions of dollars invested in them.[15]

Hedge Funds

There was a thin line between private equity and certain types of hedge funds, so-called activist funds. Unlike private equity, these hedge funds do not seek to own companies, only to take stakes large enough to wield power and withdraw cash. They have a median holding period of less than two years for completed deals, shorter than the average for private equity. Pension funds that invested in hedge funds while criticizing short-termism were guilty of rank hypocrisy. But the returns were tempting.[16]

Consider Relational Investors. Its CEO, Ralph Whitworth, began his career with a six-year stint working for corporate raider and cookbook promoter, T. Boone Pickens. Relational's business strategy took a page out of Pickens's playbook. With money from its chief partners, CalPERS and CalSTARS, Relational would buy a company's shares, and then demand the sale of underperforming or unrelated units, and a board seat if the company resisted, all in the name of shareholder value. After divestment, Relational—like any other hedge fund—would pocket the cash and move on. Other times, it simply demanded that the company disgorge its cash on hand.[17]

Hedge funds took a toll on workers. Like private equity, the funds were associated with pension cuts and layoffs. When Relational acquired a hefty position in Timken Corporation, whose workers were represented by the Steelworkers, contributions to the pension fund dropped from a third of cash flow to near zero; capital investment was cut in half; and the portion of cash devoted to buybacks quadrupled. CalSTRS played a dual role. It was a Relational partner as well as a Timken shareholder. It sponsored a shareholder proposal to break up Timken, something unprecedented for a pension fund. One study concludes, "shareholder wealth gains from [hedge fund] activism are partly wealth transfers from employees."[18]

Private Equity and SEIU

Stephen Lerner came up with the idea for SEIU's "Private Equity Project" in 2006. Private equity had some vulnerabilities. Although the industry was flush with money, it was threatened by demands for regulation. In addition, Münterfering's portrayal of private equity as a predatory insect had gone viral and damaged its image, this when private equity firms were considering selling themselves to the public. They wanted nothing to reduce the asking price.

SEIU's president, Andy Stern, began meeting "quietly and cordially" with CEOs of the largest private equity firms early in 2007. Among those he conferred with were the heads of Blackstone, Carlyle, and TPG. Stern said he was "incredibly impressed . . . Compared to most of my meetings with company CEOs, they are much more businesslike, and have much more understanding of what we are trying to accomplish. I'm not saying that we agree. But they are much more calculating than they are ideological."[19]

There were good reasons for the industry to pay attention to Stern. Peter Dreier of Occidental College called him "the best known and most powerful union president in the country since the United Auto Workers' Walter Reuther." Stern had a close relationship with former community organizer and then presidential candidate Barack Obama. He was on good terms with powerful Democrats, including Senators Hillary Clinton and Charles Schumer, who came from SEIU's stronghold, New York.

Stern hoped to negotiate framework agreements with private equity much like those SEIU had obtained through corporate campaigns in the private sector. As he told leaders of the industry, "If you agree to a set of principles on how workers should be treated at the companies you buy, we'll give you a measure of political cover against your critics at home and abroad."[20]

To light a fire beneath recalcitrant private equity funds, SEIU published a report, *Behind the Buyouts*, that analyzed five major deals, including CD&R's Hertz purchase and Bain's buyout of KB Toys. The case studies showed that the deals were made profitable by squeezing workers and loading acquisitions with high levels of debt. Allegedly, SEIU included Bain as one of the case studies because its one-time partner was Mitt Romney, then running against Obama.

The report contained the principles Stern was discussing with the magnates of the private equity world. First, private equity would have to play by the same set of rules as public corporations: transparency and disclosure of risks. Second, workers should receive paychecks adequate to support a family, decent health insurance, and retirement benefits. As in earlier agreements with REITs, Stern wanted the private equity industry to adopt a responsible-contractor policy wherein portfolio companies would adhere to labor standards when outsourcing janitorial and security services. Third, he wanted workers to have a seat at the table when a deal was being negotiated as well as after an acquisition was made. The kicker was that "workers should have a voice at work— meaning the freedom to join a union using majority sign-up without interference from any party."[21]

In May 2007, Barney Frank's House Financial Services Committee convened a one-day hearing on private equity's impact on workers. Frank put inequality front and center. As with say on pay, Frank was responding to a surge of voter populism and positioning the Democrats for the next elections. The hearings, said Frank, would seek answers to such questions as "What are the implications of the very high degrees of profitability in many of these transactions on the growth of income inequality?" and do workers "find themselves disadvantaged" as a result of the deals? In his opening remarks, Frank pointed to the recent buyout of Tommy Hilfiger, the clothing manufacturer, where janitors making $19 an hour were fired and replaced by janitors paid $8 an hour. Earlier, he had told the industry, "If you start recognizing unions among the people who you have acquired as employees you would save yourself a lot of grief with the US economy."

Stern was the first speaker at the committee hearing. Making it clear that he wanted to change, not hurt, the private-equity industry, he said that private equity offered genuine opportunities to enhance an acquisition's value. The problem was the failure to share that value with employees. The industry earned more than enough money to continue to do well, to benefit investors, and to give workers some of the wealth, he said. He called on the industry to adopt SEIU's principles on private equity.

The prospect that Congress might decide to treat carried interest as income, which would boost tax rates significantly, was said to be "the industry's worst nightmare." SEIU played a cat and mouse game on the issue. Neither *Behind the Buyouts* nor Stern's testimony made mention of taxes. To suggest tax increases might have angered the industry sufficiently to queer any deals with SEIU. As Stephen Lerner said, "Let me be clear. We are not against private equity firms. We are agnostic. We are just challenging the private equity firm to define what role they are going to play in society. . . . We don't have a specific tax or regulatory proposal right now. What we are doing is raising a set of issues, and we don't know the solution." Lerner's reference to taxes was a clear signal: SEIU would refrain from throwing its weight behind tax increases if the industry played ball. And if not, watch out.[22]

The AFL-CIO

Less encumbered by organizing motives, the AFL-CIO was more forthcoming about taxes. Richard Trumka sent a couple of letters to the SEC saying that Blackstone was violating the law by claiming that it was a limited partnership despite the fact that over 40 percent of its investments were in securities. Trumka said it should be considered an investment company akin to a mutual fund. As such, it would be subject to reporting regulations, a fiduciary duty to investors, listing rules requiring a majority of independent directors, and an end to the carried-interest dodge.[23]

The AFL-CIO turned to Congress next. Representative Sander Levin, Carl's brother and also a liberal Democrat from Michigan, introduced a House bill two months later that would classify private equity firms as investment companies. In the Senate, Democrat Max Baucus of Montana, chair of the Senate Finance Committee, offered parallel legislation together with the ranking Republican, Charles Grassley of Iowa. Treasury Secretary Henry Paulson predictably was opposed. Of greater significance was opposition from New York's Senator Charles Schumer, who sat on the Senate's Finance Committee. He warned that higher tax rates would put the industry—and the nation—at a disadvantage relative to competitors elsewhere in the world. It was a familiar argument. Schumer always had to steer a course between Wall Street—his home state's main industry and a major donor to the Democrats—and New York's labor movement, the nation's largest.

Other Democrats were against Baucus-Grassley for the same reasons. They came from states where private equity firms as well as venture capital and hedge funds had their headquarters. In August, Schumer offered his own bill containing what the *Wall Street Journal* called a "poison pill" intended to sink Baucus-Grassley. By now, few expected that the Senate would do anything about carried interest. Left-leaning Democrats worried that the party's establishment was merely paying lip service ahead of the election. Although the House passed a bill in November 2007 to change the tax rules, it died in the Senate.[24]

Another bump in the road was the National Conference on Public Employee Retirement Systems (NCPERS), an organization representing five hundred public pension plans. It sent letters to Baucus and Grassley opposing their plan to raise taxes on private equity, which it said would cut into their returns. The AFL-CIO blasted NCPERS: "We have firefighters, teachers, and cops paying a higher tax rate than Steve Schwarzman," said Dan Pedrotty. "We think this is a rip-off and that the loophole should be closed." After having its arm twisted, NCPERS withdrew its letters but refused to openly criticize private equity's fee arrangements.[25]

Dodd-Frank

During the 2008 presidential campaign, candidates Hillary Clinton and Barack Obama both endorsed raising tax rates on carried interest. After he became president, Obama inserted a tax increase in his 2010 budget proposal and did so again a year later. Keeping the increase out of what would become Dodd-Frank was a strategy to avoid the Senate Finance Committee, where Schumer would have killed it. Then Max Baucus reintroduced his earlier bill in the Senate. Schumer insisted that Baucus's bill be extended to include all industries relying on carried interest, not only private equity, an unworkable idea. As Barney Frank put it, "The best way to avoid supporting what is doable is to insist on making it undoable. Schumer wanted to broaden the bill to death." Again, the Senate voted "no," including eleven Democrats; the justification was that the financial recovery was too fragile to risk a change.[26]

While the issue was being debated, Trumka and Silvers appeared several times on the Hill to back Baucus and similar legislation in the House. (Trumka had recently become president of the AFL-CIO.) They contrasted the jobs destroyed by private equity to the fortunes earned by the general partners. Change to Win and SEIU were barely visible. An exception was a 2009 plan written by SEIU and endorsed by Nevada's Representative Shirley Berkley (D) that would legally require private equity to invest in their portfolio companies any tax savings they achieved through restructuring their debt. Few took it seriously, seeing it as a tactical move by SEIU to arm-twist Las Vegas hotels owned by private equity.[27]

When it became clear that carried interest was a no-go issue, the AFL-CIO put its weight behind a bill from Senator Jack Reed, a Rhode Island Democrat, to require private equity and hedge funds to register with the SEC. In an op-ed in the *Wall Street Journal*, Trumka argued that registration would give the SEC and investors "full access" to information about them. The industry's lobbying arm, the Private Equity Council, fought the registration plan, as did lobbyists for Blackstone and Carlyle. They warned that retirees dependent on pensions would be hurt by anything that might cut into private equity's rate of return. Reduce those returns, said one lobbyist, "and you're changing Grandma's pension from her years as a schoolteacher."

The industry conceded to a modest registration provision in Dodd-Frank. For the most part, the change still left pension plans in the dark. As economist Eileen Appelbaum noted, there were no requirements to report portfolio holdings or financial performance. Despite escaping higher taxes, some industry leaders remained incensed about President Obama's previous support for a tax increase. Right after President Obama signed Dodd-Frank, Stephen Schwarzman gave a private speech dramatically calling the industry's fight against higher taxes "a war": "It's like when Hitler invaded Poland in 1939." The implicit comparison of Obama to Hitler had been made by several Republicans. News of the remarks didn't surface until a month later, at which point Schwarzman—later a Trump supporter—offered a tepid apology. Still, he was happy: Private equity had escaped higher taxes.[28]

In Search of New Members

Change to Win

As the private equity industry grew, the labor movement was splitting in two. Several of the unions that earlier had experimented with corporate campaigns banded together to create the New Unity Partnership in 2003. At first, the group functioned as a loyal opposition within the AFL-CIO, demanding that the federation prioritize membership growth. Led by Andy Stern, it included Terence O'Sullivan of the Laborers, Bruce Raynor of UNITE HERE (the two unions had merged the previous year), John Wilhelm from the former Hotel and Restaurant Employees, and Doug McCarron of the Carpenters (by then outside the AFL-CIO). Come 2005, the group had expanded to include Joe Hansen of the Food and Commercial Workers and James P. Hoffa from the Teamsters. That year the seven unions bolted from the AFL-CIO to create a rival federation, Change to Win (CTW).

Change to Win was reminiscent of the CIO's glory days, when militant industrial unions joined under one umbrella with a shared commitment to organizing. CTW had fewer unions than the AFL-CIO, which made it easier to coordinate the new group. As compared to the AFL-CIO, a higher percentage of CTW's budget went into organizing, whereas on a per-member basis, the AFL-CIO spent more on political campaigns.

CTW faced internal conflicts. Andy Stern's fights with his own locals angered some CTW members. There were others who didn't like UNITE HERE's president Bruce Raynor. Raynor, previously president of UNITE, and John Wilhelm, formerly head of HERE, had a pitched battle over jurisdiction, raiding, and ownership of Amalgamated Bank. Wilhelm also locked horns with SEIU, which backed Raynor in the fight over Amalgamated. Nearly everyone held Doug McCarron at a remove.[29]

Within CTW, SEIU was the union most committed to growth, some said at all costs. At SEIU's 2000 national convention in Pittsburgh, delegates adopted a resolution called the New Strength Unity Plan to add 300,000 members over the next four years. The goal seemed ambitious, but the union claimed to have already gained over 150,000 members during the previous four years. The convention approved an increase in dues of 40 percent to support organizing activities for SEIU's three divisions: healthcare, government, and building services. By 2005, the divisions were receiving $100 million for organizing. SEIU hired a large number of organizers and strategic researchers, including financial experts, until its staff totaled nearly five hundred in 2008. A related resolution passed in Pittsburgh, "Organizing Our Pension Funds to Work for Our Members," said, "We have only scratched the surface." By centralizing and streamlining operations and combining union locals into larger amalgamations, SEIU was prepared to do battle.[30]

Carlyle and Manor Care

There was a fit between industries where Change to Win's affiliates sought members and industries where private equity was prevalent. Listed in order of deal volume, they were building services and real estate (SEIU, Carpenters, Laborers), retail (UFCW), healthcare (SEIU), transportation (Teamsters), and hotels (UNITE HERE). The exception was financial services, but SEIU intended to change that. Labor in these service industries was a greater share of costs than in manufacturing, which was why private equity acquisitions prioritized wage and employment cuts. Five years after a private equity purchase, employment declined by 10 percent in service industries versus 2 percent in manufacturing. Slashing labor costs happened quickly. Wages fell by nearly 2 percent in the first two years after a buyout.[31]

SEIU had always included nursing homes in its jurisdiction. They were different from building services. The staff was occupationally diverse: a combination of nurses, less-skilled aides, and low-wage food and cleaning workers, groups that may not identify with each other. A plus for organizing, however, was that nursing homes were enmeshed in a regulatory web that played to SEIU's political connections. And because they served the elderly and infirm, any mistreatment could be seized on by the union to stir up public disapproval. "Andy harasses. It's a very clear strategy," said David Smith, who knew Stern well. "Andy harasses not particularly on corporate governance issues or even corporate behaviors you see; he harasses in order to try to convince folks that making him go away is what they want."

SEIU signed a neutrality agreement with forty-two California nursing homes in 2003. In return for unopposed workplace access, the union promised to put its political muscle to work for the industry. It successfully lobbied for higher Medicaid reimbursements for nursing home residents and, surprisingly, pushed back against health advocates seeking to tie state subsidies to indicators of care quality. (The agreement itself specified that the union was not allowed to report healthcare violations to state regulators.) SEIU also promised in writing to lobby for tort reform to limit the rights of nursing home residents to sue for neglect and abuse. Under these terms, the union added a total of three thousand members. When word of the deal leaked out, it alienated some of the union's allies and officials. Stern and Lerner were harshly criticized by a dissident SEIU official in California, Sal Rosselli, who said that they had made a lousy deal by bringing $1 billion more to the nursing home industry in return for weak agreements at only a handful of the state's 1,200 homes. At Beverly, SEIU's old nemesis, Stern sought a neutrality agreement in return for which the union would lobby to increase the payments Beverly received from Medicare and Medicaid. But Beverly refused.[32]

Nursing homes were attractive to private equity. They could be separated into two parts: the nursing home—the operating company—and a property company owning the buildings and land. As economists Eileen Appelbaum and Rose Batt point out, private equity funds will sell the property company to a real estate firm, distribute the cash to investors, and then have the operating company lease back and pay rent on what it previously owned, a type of bust-up. Minus its real estate, the operating company has relatively few physical assets, giving it less financial exposure in the case of lawsuits. Nursing homes also have a dependable source of cash flowing in from government. By 2007, private equity owned six out of ten of the nation's nursing homes.[33]

A major player in the healthcare sector was the Carlyle Company, founded in 1987 by David M. Rubenstein. It was among the largest private equity firms in the world, with over two hundred companies in its portfolio. In the beginning, Carlyle specialized in purchasing companies that manufactured defense products. Over the years, its trustees have included defense-oriented Washington insiders such as former president George H. W. Bush, former secretary of state James Baker, and former secretary of defense Frank Carlucci. Tellingly, its headquarters are in Washington, DC, instead of New York. Carlyle diversified in the 2000s, moving into telecommunications and healthcare. Carlyle had forty-nine managing partners who owned 94 percent of the firm. CalPERS owned the other 6 percent. Its limited partners included state plans from Delaware, Florida, Louisiana, Michigan, New York, Ohio, and Texas.[34]

Carlyle was offering a hefty $6.3 billion for Manor Care, a nursing home chain, a 20 percent premium over the company's s stock price. To minimize spending its own funds, Carlyle borrowed to finance its purchase, forced Manor Care to take responsibility for the debt payments, sold five hundred facilities to a REIT for $6.1 billion, and then leased back the properties. At this point, the partners were left with enough money to replace their initial investment of $1 billion. Carlyle owned the company free and clear and could count on receiving an annual flow of advisory fees. However, Manor Care now had to pay fees to Carlyle and rents to the REIT, which were equivalent to the interest on a $5 billion loan.[35]

SEIU had been trying to sign up Manor Care's sixty thousand workers since the 1990s. Come 2007, it had only a thousand members to show for its twelve-year effort. After purchasing Manor Care, Carlyle left in place the pre-buyout management team, a group that had fought unions aggressively, as the NLRB record showed. Now SEIU mounted a siege on several fronts. It held meetings with major pension funds that had invested billions in the company. It lobbied Congress to closely scrutinize private equity's impact on patient care. When Stern testified to Frank's committee in 2007, he warned that a highly leveraged buyout of a nursing home chain would "squeeze capital expenditures necessary to maintain and update vital medical equipment." In the fall, Representatives John Dingell (D-MI) and Barney Frank announced hearings on private equity's impact on nursing home quality. At SEIU's request, Senators Baucus and Grassley sent letters to private equity firms that operated nursing homes, seeking data on health and safety violations. SEIU's lobbying received a lift when the *New York Times* published a study showing that nursing home residents were worse off after their facility was purchased by private equity. One of the nursing home chains included in the study was Manor Care.[36]

Hearings were held in both the House and Senate. A professor at the University of California presented findings from another study showing that patient-related problems more than doubled after private equity acquisitions. Two lawmakers—Hillary Clinton (D-NY) in the Senate and Pete Stark (D-CA) in the House—asked the Government Accounting Office to investigate how ownership by private equity affected staffing levels and care. David Smith in Barney Frank's office approved of SEIU's attempts to sway Congress: "Should SEIU try to use the threat of political retaliation or intervention or simply pissing off the chairman of an important political committee in order to make Carlyle a better employer? Of course it should." But, he added, "It's a tactic; it's not a strategy [to improve patient quality]."[37]

SEIU met with local regulatory authorities, pressing them to require Carlyle to make commitments about staffing, quality of care, and workers' rights before approving transfers and licenses to the new owner. In Michigan, where Manor Care had twenty-seven facilities, the union mounted radio and direct-mail campaigns highlighting the company's record of health violations. One slogan was "Let's put money into caring for seniors, not into CEO's pockets." The state's long-term care ombudsman subsequently endorsed the union's charges. She reported that after Manor Care acquired the facilities, it shunned Medicaid patients because Medicare offered higher reimbursement rates and its patients had shorter stays. SEIU threatened Carlyle in at least five other states during the period preceding shareholder approval of the buyout, the period when Carlyle—in theory—would be most willing to cut a deal with the union.[38]

Agit-prop was part of the siege. Protesters, most of them Manor Care employees, marched in front of Carlyle's headquarters on Halloween dressed as "fat cat" CEOs holding bags of fake money. Others wore candy-bar costumes with names such as "King Size Paycheck" and "Loophole Savers." Then SEIU members wearing business suits crashed a meeting at the Waldorf-Astoria hotel where David Rubenstein was speaking. They held up a banner reading, "Why does he pay taxes at a lower rate than the hotel's doorman?" Said Steve Lerner, "There's always been a history of us doing really creative things to shed light on issues, which includes humor and absurdity." In a widely reported incident, SEIU protesters disrupted Rubinstein's keynote speech at a Wharton School conference on private equity. A Manor Care nurse got up on stage to declare she was worried that Carlyle would hurt patient care.[39]

On the eve of the financial crisis, public pension funds provided 27 percent of the capital invested in private equity. CalPERS had upped its private equity allocation and other state plans followed suit. Money also came from corporate and multiemployer plans. Enticing them into private equity (and hedge funds) was Congress, which in 2006 permitted private plans to put a greater portion of their money into those asset classes.[40]

After the Manor Care buyout went through at the end of 2007 without a deal for SEIU, the union asked public funds to disinvest in Carlyle. It persuaded California State Assembly Majority Leader Alberto Torrico to sponsor a bill that would bar CalPERS and CalSTRS from investing in private equity plans that took investments from sovereign wealth funds (SWFs) based in countries with a record of human rights abuses. The target here was Abu Dhabi's sovereign wealth fund, perennially criticized by human rights activists. The fund recently had purchased an 8 percent stake in Carlyle. In a professional-looking report, "Sovereign Wealth Funds and Private Equity," SEIU laid out its charges against Carlyle.[41]

CalPERS and CalSTRS opposed the Torrico bill, saying that they would lose $7.5 billion in the first three years alone were it enacted. In its own report, CalPERS argued that the bill would restrict it from investing in the best-performing private equity funds, which tended to be large ones that took investments from SWFs. Several California unions were against the bill, indicating SEIU's occasionally isolated position in the labor movement. On top of all this, Governor Schwarzenegger announced that he might use his veto power if need be. The bill died.[42]

SEIU then turned to Washington State, whose pension plan had a whopping 25 percent allocation to private equity worth over $12 billion. The union filed a citizen's initiative with the state legislature to limit the plan's investments in private equity unless they met specified "social criteria." The head of the State Investment Board complained that no private equity firm would do business with it were the proposal enacted. Again, the attempt flopped.[43]

A raft of people in the pension world were skeptical of SEIU's approach to private equity. Someone close to the AFL-CIO said that SEIU's political activities around private equity were nothing more than a bargaining chip to obtain neutrality agreements, and as such, "hardly something to emulate." Others cited SEIU's cavalier attitude toward yield-hungry pension funds. It was a charge Steve Abrecht confirmed: "Pension funds don't need to make 30+ percent returns on certain asset classes if, by doing that, they're putting the long-term stability of the financial markets at risk. I would prefer for private equity to make consistently 15–20 percent returns."[44]

After the Manor Care deal closed at the end of 2007, SEIU publicly questioned how the company would be able to fund its annual debt load and make a profit without cutting corners. The concern was spot on. Five years later, Manor Care launched a "cost-reduction program" and slashed the money it gave its homes to meet expenses. The results were disastrous: Staffing levels declined and serious health-code violations increased. Meanwhile, the Department of Justice was investigating Manor Care for telling nursing home therapists to "exploit elderly patients for profits."

In 2017, ten years after the buyout, Manor Care went bankrupt and defaulted on its loans. The nurse who had jumped on stage when Rubenstein spoke at Wharton said that shortly before the bankruptcy, Manor Care reduced staff at her facility from thirteen patients per nurse to eighteen. Creditors, including the landlord, took possession of its facilities. The deal decimated Manor Care, but Carlyle walked away intact, having taken out its equity—and profits—long before. One journalist described the bankruptcy as a "humbling experience" for David Rubenstein, as he was the man who had extolled the virtues of private equity in speeches and media interviews. When Rubenstein resigned, he claimed a net worth of $3 billion. There's no telling if the outcome would have been better had he approved a neutrality agreement, but it's possible.[45]

KKR

Kohlberg, Kravis, Roberts (KKR) was another target of SEIU's Private Equity Project. KKR was one of the big three private equity firms, along with Carlyle and Blackstone. Its portfolio companies had 800,000 workers in 2008, making it the second largest US employer after Walmart. Around one-fourth of KKR's companies operated in industries where SEIU had or sought members. The union's strategy for obtaining neutrality agreements from KKR was similar to Manor Care. With KKR, there was an added dimension: an international campaign.

One company of interest to SEIU was the Hospital Corporation of America (HCA), which KKR bought with other partners in 2006 for over $33 billion, making it the largest private equity deal until then. HCA, where SEIU already had some members, was the same firm the union had hit with lawsuits and shareholder actions several years earlier, when it was known as Columbia/HCA. KKR also bought US Foodservice, with 27,000 workers. With a corporate profile like that of other catering companies where SEIU had or sought members—Aramark, Compass, and Sodexo—US Foodservice was of interest to SEIU as well.[46]

SEIU tried to get KKR to sign on to its framework principles. Andy Stern met with CEO Henry Kravis, but to no avail. Using Lerner's "creative and absurd" tactics, SEIU poked at KKR. There was a demonstration outside Kravis's mansion on Long Island and a rally in Washington where protesters used wheelbarrows to carry "cash" from IRS headquarters to Carlyle's nearby office, depositing it in front of a stodgy tycoon figure. On a serious note, SEIU published a report, "Winners and Losers: Fallout from KKR's Race for Profits," which detailed the corporation's adverse effects on consumers, workers, and the environment. When KKR announced in 2007 that it intended to sell part of itself to the public, it handed SEIU an opportunity. The union warned public and union pension plans not to participate in the offering. Once again, it went to Washington State's pension plan. George Roberts, the "R" in KKR, gave a presentation to the state's investment board asking for even more money: $700 million on top of the $900 million the Washington plan had previously invested. As before, the Washington plan disregarded SEIU's entreaties and upped its investment.[47]

Global Outreach

Tom Woodruff, SEIU's executive vice president and director of CTW's Center for Strategic Organizing, was the visionary who guided SEIU's global campaigns. For a number of years, SEIU had been putting in place the infrastructure needed to mount international campaigns to assist organizing in the

United States. A key ally was UNI Global Union (UNI)—a Geneva-based federation of nine hundred service-sector unions representing over fifteen million workers around the world. SEIU hoped that UNI would help it obtain international framework agreements from multinational firms to respect organizing rights as contained in the ILO standards. UNI gave SEIU access to foreign labor movements, their pension plans, and the multinational corporations headquartered in their home countries. In food services, the largest companies included Sodexo (headquartered in France), and Compass Group (UK). In private security, there were two giant employers of guards: Securitas (Sweden) and G4S (Britain and Denmark). SEIU opened offices in Australia, the Netherlands, and the United Kingdom, each of them places with large occupational pension plans whose assets could, in theory, provide leverage for SEIU to use in its organizing.

Christy Hoffman, an SEIU attorney, went to Geneva in 2004 to head UNI's property services division and to negotiate framework agreements with multinational companies. There were allegations that there had been a non-hostile takeover of UNI by SEIU. Because many European labor federations regarded Change to Win as an illegitimate dual union, SEIU was closed out of organizations in which the AFL-CIO participated, including the Committee on Workers' Capital, the International Trade Union Confederation, and the OECD's Trade Union Advisory Council. UNI Global provided SEIU with alternative networks for international access. Ten years after Hoffman joined UNI, it had negotiated framework agreements with twenty-six multinational service corporations, resuscitating hopes raised during the 1999 Seattle protests for a new era of transnational labor solidarity. But the bar was higher for obtaining framework agreements from private equity firms headquartered in the United States.[48]

UNI and ver.di, the German service-workers union, organized an international conference in 2007 timed to coincide with the release of SEIU's report on KKR. UNI arranged a Global Day of Action to demand that KKR respect trade union rights and stop fighting the enactment of new tax rules. Demonstrations were held in cities around the world. UNI held a second conference to discuss labor standards for private equity and the possibility of creating a European works council for employees of KKR's portfolio companies. Michael Laslett, head of SEIU's London office, and Steve Lerner explained the KKR campaign. Yet among UNI's affiliates and even among its staff, support for the campaign varied. One staffer said that SEIU was "very blatant about saying 'we want KKR because if we get neutrality with them it delivers us a shitload of members.' . . . But UNI's goal is not to organize or die. The private equity thing goes so much further than just getting neutrality."[49]

SEIU also joined forces with the biggest labor union in the United Kingdom, UNITE, (unrelated to UNITE in the United States), as a way of reaching out to British pension funds about their KKR investments. SEIU recommended that the British funds seek from KKR full disclosure of its covenants, debt-equity ratios, and other items related to its acquisitions. With UNITE as its partner, SEIU had a way to ratchet up pressure on KKR of the sort it had tried in Washington State.[50]

Other British unions were wary of SEIU. UNISON, a union of UK public-sector workers, was the lead British union with regard to US-style shareholder engagement. UNISON officials thought that SEIU was overly tactical in its use of financial activism and intolerant of slower-moving strategies like responsible investing and governance reform. "The idea that building the union is a solution to everything the working class faces—I can understand it in the United States where you've got very low density, but when we've had very, very high density in this country and its syndicalism didn't really work for us. . . . You need to have some other constant in what you're doing." UNISON favored a long-range approach to reworking shareholder-company relationships and was concerned that SEIU was asking British labor's pension funds for information and access without considering the fiduciary risks or reciprocal benefits, criticisms also heard in the United States. A leader of UNISON complained, "What's in it for us? When is it going to come to fruition?" A representative of the Trades Union Congress expressed similar concerns about SEIU's aggressive tactics: "We don't like confrontational shareholder-company relationships in the UK." Yet there were British labor leaders who thought it helpful for the country's unions to be exposed to SEIU's organizing-oriented culture.[51]

The KKR campaign ended in 2010, when HCA signed a neutrality and card-check agreement with SEIU. The agreement applied only to a subset of HCA's hospitals; SEIU promised to stay away from other locations and refrain from negative campaigns against the company. HCA had previous experience with neutrality agreements, which in the past had yielded several thousand new SEIU members. The settlement was reached as KKR was preparing to take the company public.[52]

The Blackstone Group

Blackstone was the largest private equity firm in the world, founded in 1985 by Peter G. Peterson and Stephen A. Schwarzman. Its specialties were hotels, resorts, theme parks, waste management, and private security companies. Although its founders were conservative Republicans, Blackstone had ties to the Clinton administration and elsewhere in the Democratic Party. SEIU and UNITE HERE jumped on Blackstone when in March 2007 it too announced its intention to go public. At the time, several Blackstone acquisitions were of interest to the unions, including Hilton Hotels.[53]

UNITE HERE took a gentler approach to Blackstone than had SEIU with Carlyle. When Blackstone announced its purchase of Hilton, Bruce Raynor of UNITE HERE praised it. "We welcome this combination," he said. "We enjoy a positive partnership with Hilton Hotels. Blackstone has demonstrated its commitment to fair treatment for thousands of hotels workers." At the time, Hilton employed 15,000 of the union's members.[54]

Before the buyout, UNITE HERE and Hilton signed a "partnership for future growth," an agreement that traded management neutrality in a select group of cities in return for the union's promise to help Hilton obtain more customers. But the partnership came with no guarantee that Blackstone would honor it. Raynor went to someone who had the power to challenge Blackstone if need be: Barney Frank. After the buyout, Frank called Stephen Schwarzman and, as David Smith paraphrased it, said to him, "You guys just bought Hilton. Good. It would be great if you are nice to UNITE HERE." Blackstone wanted Frank on its side, given that he had the power to change the carried-interest rules. Blackstone promised to respect the previous neutrality agreement, perhaps calculating that it would be cheaper to permit the union to organize a limited number of additional hotels than to risk a tax increase, negative publicity, and boycotts. It intended to sell Hilton at some point, which turned out to be six years later.[55]

Within the union, Raynor had critics who felt that he had signed a "sweetheart deal" that brought new members without offering current members a say in the process. It was a charge made since the earliest days of the corporate campaign. Yet Raynor, like Stern, was certain that partnering with employers was the only way to grow the union's membership. Also like Stern, he viewed Schwarzman as a pragmatist. "These guys are not anti-union," Raynor said. "They're just pro-money."[56]

Meanwhile, SEIU had its eye on other companies owned by Blackstone: Equity Office Properties and Trizec Properties, who employed building service workers, and AlliedBarton, the largest security firm in the United States. In the months leading up to the IPO, Andy Stern met with Schwarzman more than once. SEIU launched a website to monitor the IPO process and arranged for UNI and a group of foreign labor leaders to meet with Blackstone representatives. The leaders threatened to go back to their home countries and ask pension funds there not to invest in the IPO. When Blackstone filed papers related to the IPO, it listed among the risk factors "agitating" by labor unions.[57]

Mergers and Acquisitions

Bill Patterson left the AFL-CIO in 2006 to head up the CTW Investment Group (CtWIG). It was a coup for the new federation and an indication that Patterson wanted a tighter connection between organizing and financial activism than had been possible at the AFL-CIO. After moving to CTW to head up its investment group, he focused on merger and acquisition (M&A) transactions, which were red-hot at the time. Negotiating with management over ordinary shareholder proposals was "a hollow process," he said, whereas M&As provided "a more serious opportunity to engage companies in their business plans." Shareholders paid attention to M&As, more so than other corporate decisions. A momentary surge of opposition might overturn a transaction on which management had spent many months and millions of dollars. Because the deals had deadlines, it gave Patterson greater leverage. CtWIG concentrated exclusively on financial deals in which CTW's unions had collateral interests.[58]

Patterson's previous employer, the AFL-CIO's Office of Investment, was not as closely involved with the organizing plans of its affiliates, who were numerous, fractious, and autonomous. Change to Win was a smaller and more cohesive group of unions committed to an "organizing first" agenda. CTW was less transparent than the AFL-CIO, making it easier to fly below the radar when formulating strategies and tactics.

In its first year, CtWIG was a whirlwind of activity, challenging a private equity buyout of Heinz, tender offers at Pilgrim Pride's and LaFarge, and a Rite Aid bid to acquire two drugstore chains with nearly two thousand stores. However, the transaction to which CtWIG devoted most of its energy was the potential purchase of Caremark, a prescription benefits manager, by CVS, a drugstore chain. CtWIG was the first to criticize the deal on the grounds that Caremark had accepted a lower premium than those offered in equivalent transactions. Patterson attributed the problem to the fact that Caremark's directors and senior executives would receive change-in-control payments regardless of the premium size. As in the old days, he blasted Wall Street and corporate insiders for furthering their own interests at shareholders' expense.[59]

CTW affiliates had skin in the game. The UFCW represented in-store CVS employees and pharmacists and sought to organize more of them. The Teamsters had members working at CVS distribution centers. Despite the collaterals, CtWIG's bid to stymie the Caremark deal was well regarded by shareholder-rights experts. One said, "It's great what they are doing. They're identifying transactions that need to be opposed, and they'll say things others won't."[60]

CtWIG mounted a "Vote No" campaign against two Caremark board members, including the lead director, Roger Headrick, and issued a report criticizing Caremark's backdating of their options. Patterson reprised these issues at an investment forum in New York attended by representatives of thirty-six asset management companies and an equal number of pension plans, public and Taft-Hartley. Headrick's "no" votes totaled 44 percent, but Patterson challenged the outcome. In letters to the board and the investment community, he charged that Headrick would have failed to receive a majority were it not for broker votes supporting him. Headrick was forced to resign, and CVS raised its bid for Caremark. Not long after, CVS proffered neutrality agreements to the UFCW, including one for five hundred stores in California.[61]

Organizing Banks

One of SEIU's more audacious campaigns involved bank employees. The financial crisis had caused multiple bank failures and involuntary mergers, leaving workers uncertain about their futures. There'd been layoffs throughout the industry, reaching 200,000 in the fall of 2008. Pay was low, with tellers earning around $24,000 annually, vastly less than what John Thain, CEO of Merrill Lynch, spent on curtains during a recent $1 million office renovation. Steve Lerner said that banks "represent the most extreme example of the unsustainable disparity between those on the top and the rest of us. Nothing illustrates this better than the simple fact that we could increase pay by $2.00 per hour and provide employer-paid health insurance for over 550,000 tellers with just 3.6 percent of the bonuses paid out to executives." Yet Lerner admitted that organizing banks was a "challenging effort." Less than 1 percent of bank employees belonged to unions, and previous attempts to sign them up had little success.[62]

The first public mention of a campaign occurred in December 2008, when someone leaked a memo SEIU had sent to ACORN, the community organization that was SEIU's steadfast ally. "Do you have ACORN members who work for banks or Freddie Mac/Fannie Mae?" it asked. "Banks we are most concerned about: Fannie/Freddie, BB&T, SunTrust, BOA/Countrywide, Wachovia/Wells Fargo, PNC/National City, Citigroup. We need to get a handle on who these workers are, working conditions, etc." Bank of America (BofA) was the bull's eye, with more than 150,000 employees. The media warned that BofA was planning "the Mother of all Layoffs" and would get rid of 30,000–35,000 workers over the next three years. SEIU put BofA in its sights.[63]

With the financial sector in disarray, it was easy for SEIU to find chinks in BofA's armor. SEIU zeroed in on questionable bonuses of $3.6 billion paid by Merrill in late 2008, after it was forced into a shotgun marriage with BofA. Anna Burger, chair of Change to Win, sent a letter to Neil Barofsky, the Treasury Department's special inspector general for the Troubled Assets Relief Program (TARP), asking him to investigate whether there were improprieties attached to the bonuses. The bonus pool at the merged banks amounted to one-fourth of their TARP funds, which meant that executives might lose a lot of money if Barofsky's audit found anything amiss. SEIU's Master Trust filed a proposal asking for the resignation of Ken Lewis, BofA's CEO and chairman of the board, from his chairmanship. SEIU put up picket lines in more than one hundred cities demanding that Lewis step down. Lewis's "no" votes totaled 50.3 percent, a coup for SEIU.[64]

SEIU went after other financial services companies, shaking up the entire industry. After it was revealed that AIG had handed out bonuses while it was on government life support, SEIU sent five hundred of its members to march through the streets of downtown Chicago chanting, "Hey, hey, ho, ho, where did all the money go?" In San Francisco, SEIU demonstrators gathered in front of a Wells Fargo branch and then marched to AIG's offices, with one person carrying a sign reading, "Asinine Incomprehensible Greed." Outside the Washington, DC offices of Goldman Sachs, protesters chanted, "Too big to fail, too big to exist." There were signs condemning Goldman for giving two hundred flu shots to its executives before the vaccine was made available to the general public. One woman shouted through a megaphone, "My grandchildren didn't get the flu shot, but the fat cats from Goldman Sachs did."[65]

The attacks widened. The SEIU Master Trust sent letters to the boards of twenty-nine banks demanding that they investigate whether previous executive bonuses had been based on faulty metrics, such as profits from now-worthless derivatives. The union threatened lawsuits if the boards failed to claw back ill-gotten gains. Outside the American Bankers Association's annual convention in Chicago, SEIU held three days of demonstrations followed by a march. Among the participants were twenty groups representing low-income communities with high unemployment and foreclosures. None other than the chair of the Federal Deposit Insurance Corporation, Sheila Bair, addressed the crowd, saying that she supported their demands and promising to mention them in her upcoming speech at the convention.[66]

Banks were in a tizzy. The American Bankers Association told its members to survey their employees to find out what was bothering them and to communicate the importance of the work they did. Morgan Lewis, a white-shoe corporate law firm, warned banks to prepare themselves for litigation and to ramp up their activity in employee relations and public relations. The Financial Services Roundtable (FSRT), another industry association, lobbied against the Employee Free Choice Act, which would have made bank organizing easier. Anna Burger sent a letter to FSRT demanding that it cease its lobbying. She also wrote to Barney Frank, who said publicly that FSRT's push to block the Employee Free Choice Act was "shameful."[67]

By 2010, SEIU's bank campaign had legs. Early that year demonstrations took place across California, and in Minneapolis and other cities. SEIU felt confident enough to approach several banks in search of neutrality agreements. Then two events occurred that put the brakes on the campaign. In April 2010, Andy Stern suddenly resigned as SEIU's president after fourteen years on the job. And in November, Mary Kay Henry, Stern's successor, put Stephen Lerner on paid leave. Henry felt that Lerner's media-oriented bank campaign was soaking up tens of millions of dollars without bringing in new members. It's possible that Stern too had lost confidence in Lerner's tactics. A year after stepping down, Stern reflected that he'd been too hard on private equity and banks. In an interview, he said, "Some of it was totally appropriate; other of it probably was a little bit out of hand." Bruce Raynor, always close to Stern, didn't think that this was a *volte face* for the former president: "SEIU under his leadership partnered with companies."[68]

Lerner was pushed further to the periphery after a recording of the talk he gave to a closed audience at Pace University found its way to the press. He had said that "we are in a transformative stage of what's happening in capitalism" and that labor should develop the ability to "put a boot in the wheel [to] disrupt how the system operates." The strategy, according to Lerner, was to bring down the stock market, take away bonuses, and make bankers struggle to become rich. He envisioned the equivalent of a rent strike in which homeowners and students would refuse to make payments on their underwater mortgages and student loans. Lerner wanted cities strapped by the crisis to stop paying off their loans unless banks renegotiated them. Not surprisingly, conservatives attacked hysterically. Glenn Beck said Lerner's plan was "economic terrorism," while Jason Chaffets, a Republican from Utah, asked Attorney General Eric Holder to investigate Lerner. With Lerner out of the picture, SEIU's bank campaign was dead.[69]

The Limits to Growth

As with earlier corporate campaigns, SEIU's organizing methods during the 2000s were disparaged by critics from within the labor movement who charged that affected workers knew nothing about negotiations between union leaders and corporate executives over framework agreements. Because of secrecy, they were unaware when the union had traded neutrality for limits on the number of people to whom an agreement would apply, usually a mere 10–20 percent of a company's workforce. Neither did they did know about any side promises the union may have made, such as no-strike guarantees or foreswearing derogatory remarks about management. One healthcare agreement allegedly included a gag order prohibiting employees from raising patient care issues. Jane McAlevey, a former SEIU organizer, charged that SEIU's "shallow" organizing and mobilization left members with "only the most tenuous relationship" with their union: "The union becomes nothing more than the contract and the contract is only engaged when the worker files a grievance."[70]

A source of these problems was what John Wilhelm labeled SEIU's "growth at all costs model." Another critic was John Borsos from SEIU's West Coast renegade healthcare local that had a bitter fight with the national union. Borsos felt that all SEIU's leaders cared about was getting first contracts; there was no long-term vision for member participation. He compared this to union pension funds that consider only the short term and ignore time-consuming activities like trustee education.[71]

A related factor was SEIU's centralization, which, he said, shifted resources from local organizers to staff working in New York and Washington. This problem was inherent to all campaigns relying heavily on capital strategies: a staff-driven, instead of a membership-driven, approach to organizing. Borsos admitted that financial activism was helpful in membership campaigns at West Coast healthcare companies, but only when the firms were financially troubled and vulnerable. Capital strategies had less success with profitable firms unless they were combined with bottom-up mobilization.[72]

Andy Stern and Bruce Raynor rejected these "rank-and-filist" criticisms in favor of what they saw as *realpolitik*. Their methods had brought tens of thousands of corporate workers into the labor movement at a moment when other unions were shrinking. The bottom-up approach, while reminiscent of labor's glory days, was no longer feasible given the impotence of labor law in preventing illegal employer resistance. In Andy Stern's estimation, "The old ways aren't working, and we're trying to find different relationships with employers that guarantee workers a voice . . . The 1930s adversarial-type unionism isn't going to apply to nurses and reporters and childcare workers."[73]

SEIU's membership gains looked impressive. The union claimed that it had added over one million members from the mid-1990s through 2010. Skeptics alleged that the figures were puffed up because some gains came through mergers with other unions, others resulted from raids, and still others from the conversion of full-time jobs to a greater number of part-time positions. The charge was made repeatedly that SEIU sacrificed quality for quantity. The president of a small SEIU local in food services complained that SEIU was "putting growth in numbers ahead of any other consideration of what a union means in the lives of working people." Even if its gains were overstated, there's no gainsaying that SEIU was one of the few union success stories of the 1990s and 2000s, a period when other Change to Win unions found themselves struggling. A Cornell University study that examined Change to Win's affiliates found "no statistically significant difference in organizing success following Change to Win's implementation of new organizing strategies and practices, relative to the AFL-CIO."[74]

———

Private equity's centralization, with a relatively small group of people overseeing the purchase and sale of dozens of companies, mirrored the corporate campaign's staff-led approach. People like Andrew Stern or Bruce Raynor could sit down with someone like Stephen Schwarzman to discuss possible deals.

What gave SEIU and other unions leverage was private equity's dependence on pension fund capital, its plans to go public, and the industry's fear that Congress would take away the tax benefits that made its business model so remunerative. Private equity also had an image problem because of its super-wealthy general partners. In 2007, nearly three out of four Americans—the highest proportion since the early 1990s—agreed with the statement, "Today it's really true that the rich get richer and the poor get poorer." Then came the crash of financial markets, which brought other fish to fry.[75]

9

The Financial Crisis and Dodd-Frank

THE DEMISE OF BEAR STEARNS in March 2008 was a dress rehearsal for events that would take place five months later, when the global financial system verged on a meltdown. Lehman Brothers went bankrupt; Bank of America had to rescue Merrill Lynch; Berkshire Hathaway did the same for Goldman Sachs; and Freddy Mac and Fannie Mae were put into receivership. Polls showed that public confidence in Wall Street had reached its lowest levels in forty years. When people were asked to say the first word that came to mind after hearing "Wall Street," the top responses were "stock markets," "money," and "greedy." It was 1932 redux. The moment was ripe for re-regulating finance.[1]

The Great Recession was a disaster for working people and their retirement funds. State and local pension funds racked up losses of $1 trillion during 2008. Multiemployer funds were especially hard hit. Whereas two in ten were in endangered or critical condition in 2008, the figure jumped to seven in ten the following year. Because of yawning liabilities, some multiemployer plans were terminated and handed over to the PBGC, itself underfunded. Corporate plans suffered as well.[2]

A cause of many pension fund losses were collateralized debt obligations (CDOs), which the funds first began to snap up in the early 2000s. These derivative products had hidden within them chunks of high-risk subprime mortgages. The economy was awash in money, and bond yields were low. Pension funds were eager to diversify their credit portfolios and boost returns. But when interest rates began rising in 2006, so did foreclosures. With that, CDOs rapidly lost their value. The banks selling CDOs had promised astronomical returns but downplayed risk.

Even as Bear Stearns began to sink in 2007, it held a conference in a Las Vegas ballroom where it pitched CDOs to fifty public pension fund managers. A company salesperson promised a 20 percent annual return. She admitted, "I think a lot of people are confused about what this product is and how it works." It wasn't only pension funds that were in the dark. In the years leading up to the breakdown, nobody had monitored financial institutions to see if they had sufficient strength to meet their counterparty obligations should a crisis shake the markets. The notional value of derivatives worldwide stood at $648 trillion in June 2008. Warren Buffett had labeled derivatives "financial weapons of mass destruction." Not only were they the heart of the shadow banking system, they were the essence of financialization.[3]

The pension world was in denial until it was too late. In April 2007, the research director for the National Association of State Retirement Adminis- trators said public funds were sufficiently diversified that they faced "minimal exposure" should CDOs go south. In Orange County, California, which went bankrupt in the mid-1990s due to bad bets on derivatives, administrators of the county's pension plan said that this time around, they'd taken adequate account of risks attached to derivative products. But the county's treasurer, who was a new trustee for the plan, didn't buy it: "Fund managers wanted yield, so Wall Street sold it to them. The beauty of Wall Street is that they put lipstick on a pig."[4]

This chapter begins with labor's response to the financial collapse. It took place on the ground, with hundreds of protests, and in Congress, where labor's financial experts pressed Democrats to take a tough approach to Wall Street. The Dodd-Frank Act, the nation's most ambitious financial legislation since the New Deal, spelled out new rules for financial transactions. It also included mandatory governance standards that drew on the investor cookbook. After Dodd-Frank became law, it was attacked on the right by Republicans and banks, and on the left by Occupy Wall Street. Despite its brief existence, Oc- cupy Wall Street challenged the labor movement's approach to political mo- bilization and to inequality.

Before Occupy

The first reaction to the crash was an AFL-CIO demonstration on Septem- ber 25, 2008 in front of the New York Stock Exchange. Hundreds of union members gathered to oppose President George W. Bush's $700 billion bank rescue plan, announced the previous day. Organized by the New York City

Central Labor Council, the demonstration featured John Sweeney, the Reverend Jesse Jackson, and Randi Weingarten, president of the America Federation of Teachers. Signs read "Bail Out Main Street, Not Wall Street" and "No Blank Checks for Wall Street." Sweeney roused the crowd: "Our country is facing the biggest financial disaster since the Great Depression. But working people have been living this crisis with lost jobs, stagnant wages, crumbling schools, dwindling hopes for our children, and eroding healthcare and disappearing pensions." He demanded an independent panel to allocate the bailout funds and "real tough new regulations." The AFL-CIO again rallied outside the New York Stock Exchange on the one-year anniversary of its earlier protest. Now Richard Trumka rebuked banks for having "strangled commerce and killed jobs." The protests received but a glimmer of media notice.[5]

In its demonstrations, the AFL-CIO tied the banking collapse to the concerns of working people—problems like underwater mortgages, cutbacks in public services, and the lack of jobs. The spring of 2010 saw an upsurge of protests timed to coincide with the Senate's final deliberations over the Dodd bill. In March, the AFL-CIO arranged two hundred "Make Wall Street Pay" protests around the country that took aim at six of the nation's largest banks. In brisk weather outside Buffalo's Bank of America branch, three union supporters dressed in business suits played poker beneath a sign reading "Gambling with Our Lives." In West Virginia, there was a rally outside a branch office of Wells Fargo. "We just want people to know that Wachovia and Wells Fargo are the names they need to remember," said Kenny Perdue of the state's AFL-CIO. Working America, the voter outreach arm of the AFL-CIO, ran a mobilization campaign dubbed "I am not your ATM." Its televised town hall drew a hundred thousand participants. Karen Nussbaum of Working America said, "What we're talking about now is the big banks and Wall Street and what they've done to Main Street over the last years. . . . This is not a complicated issue for people to understand."[6]

The culminating event occurred on April 29, when the AFL-CIO protested outside New York's City Hall. The venue was four blocks from Zuccotti Park, which would become the site of Occupy Wall Street's encampment. Addressing a crowd of 15,000, Trumka—now the AFL-CIO's president—said, "We're here for the folks who were played for suckers in the casino economy and will be silent no more." A middle-school teacher spoke about cuts in the city's schools and the injustice of "making our kids pay for this mess." Several speakers demanded that banks cease lobbying against beefed-up regulations. That day, SEIU ran online ads showing Republican Senator Richard Shelby

(AL) fishing for contributions at a gathering of the American Bankers Association.[7]

Silvers in the Spotlight

Attending to the financial system was a departure from labor's policy concerns of the previous seventy years. The AFL-CIO's expert in this area was Damon Silvers; without him, it's doubtful that the labor movement would have had the same influence on Dodd-Frank as it did. Silvers owed his position to labor's financial turn, having once worked for ACTWU's Jack Sheinkman, the person who led the way with the J. P. Stevens campaign. Patterson also had worked with Sheinkman, although Patterson started out as an organizer, and he stuck to the terrain where finance and organizing came together. For CTW, devoting resources to signing up bank employees was more important than lobbying to curb risky business financial strategies. But at CTW, as elsewhere in the labor movement, people relied on Silvers's ability to speak about finance with persuasive clarity.

The Troubled Asset Relief Program (TARP), Bush's response to the crisis, created a five-person Congressional Oversight Panel that held its first meeting three weeks after Barack Obama won the election. The chair was Elizabeth Warren, then still a Harvard professor. One of the four other slots was for someone nominated by the Speaker of the House, Nancy Pelosi (D-CA), and the Senate's majority leader, Harry Reid (D-NV). They selected Damon Silvers. The appointment insured that the AFL-CIO could press from the inside during the eighteen months of haggling that produced Dodd-Frank. Before joining the panel, Silvers wrote a briefing memo for the Obama-Biden transition team that traced the global crash to financial deregulation of the Clinton years, the same criticism he made at the time of Enron. In the memo, he castigated Treasury Secretary Hank Paulsen's bank rescue scheme, the final version of which was signed by President Bush early in October 2008. Silvers said it was a warmed-over "deregulatory wish list," a step back in time: "The financial crisis we are currently experiencing is directly connected to the degeneration of the New Deal system of comprehensive financial regulation into a Swiss cheese regulatory system where the holes, the shadow markets, grew to dominate the regulated markets." Among the holes he mentioned were hedge funds, private equity, and the derivatives packaged by financial institutions. Silvers made thirteen appearances in Congress over the next two years, including four visits to Barney Frank's House Financial Services Committee and four to Christopher Dodd's Senate Banking Committee.[8]

From the election through the signing of Dodd-Frank, Congress discussed banking problems but had less to say about their effects on ordinary Americans. Silvers told a House committee in 2009 that they should not ignore suffering in the heartland, stressing "an urgent need" to halt the rise of unemployment and home foreclosures and recommending a second, more job-targeted, stimulus plan and greater relief for homeowners. When Silvers appeared in front of another House committee a few months later, he said that long-term joblessness and foreclosures were "profoundly destructive phenomena. They damage the people who endure them in ways that go beyond the numbers. The parent who tells their child they will have to leave their home, their school, their friends and neighbors . . . suffers in a way that a spreadsheet cannot capture." In a panel discussion with journalist Robert Kuttner, AFL-CIO organizer Heather Booth, and other progressives, Silvers said that TARP would be a "process of regressive wealth redistribution" unless stock and bond holders took substantial haircuts. The idea put the AFL-CIO well to the left of Treasury Secretary Timothy Geithner and beyond the ever-cautious president himself.[9]

In June 2009, Geithner appointed Kenneth Feinberg to be the special master in charge of overseeing executive compensation at the companies receiving federal bailout funds. When one of them, AIG, announced that it would distribute bonuses worth millions, Feinberg averred he could do nothing because the bonus promises predated TARP. Geithner, Feinberg's boss, pronounced, "The government cannot just abrogate contracts." Privately he told someone, "This is not Bolivia." Retribution came from union and public pension plans, who tried to block the reelection of the director who chaired AIG's compensation committee. Geithner's handling of the TARP strictures on executive pay reinforced the view that bankers got off easy.

The failure to prosecute, much less punish, those who had committed fraud rankled the public. In 2010, Democratic Senator Arlen Specter of Pennsylvania, who recently had switched parties, convened a hearing to analyze the government's disinclination to go after bankers who had broken the law. In his testimony there, Silvers described "a public perception in the wake of events of 2008 that unfortunately has some justification that a small number of wealthy and powerful Americans did vast damage to our country and to the lives of millions of families. . . . A double standard with respect to willful illegal activity should not be acceptable in a democracy." He called Wall Street a place where "lying" and "cheating" were pervasive. Silvers blasted the Federal Reserve Bank of New York, where Timothy Geithner had recently been president, for its secretive approach to AIG's credit default swaps.[10]

A year later a bigger bombshell hit, right after the president signed Dodd-Frank. It was reported that seventeen banks had paid $1.6 billion in bonuses during the fall of 2008 *after* receiving bailout money. While admitting that the bonuses were "ill advised" and "showed poor judgment," Feinberg stated they were not in conflict with the public interest. (Federal auditors later found that Feinberg had been pressured by Geithner to circumvent pay caps.) The timing tarnished Dodd-Frank at its inception. Polls showed that three out of five respondents were in favor of having government limit executive compensation.[11]

Throughout all this turmoil, Damon Silvers was ubiquitous: appearing in Congress, at press conferences, and in front of regulatory bodies. Even the *Wall Street Journal* saw fit to interview him. And Silvers wasn't shy about criticizing the White House and the Treasury. He had a contentious relationship with Timothy Geithner going back to Geithner's days at the New York Fed. Often perceived as Wall Street's handmaiden, the New York Fed had a poor track record when it came to disciplining banks. Silvers said he wanted "strong, independent regulators," the word "independent" an allusion to the fact that two-thirds of the New York Fed's board was elected by member banks. He told the House Financial Services Committee that "the current structure of regional Federal Reserve Banks, the institutions that actually do the regulation of bank holding companies, where the banks participate in the governance, is not acceptable." What was needed, said Silvers, was a regulatory body that was transparent and accountable to the public, and the Fed was neither. For a while, Senator Dodd leaned in the same direction—against Obama's wishes—and considered splitting off banking regulation from the Fed's other activities.[12]

Americans for Financial Reform

In the spring of 2009, unions worked behind the scenes to organize an alliance to press for comprehensive financial reform. Meetings led to the founding of Americans for Financial Reform (AFR) in June 2009. AFR, made up of over 160 national and local organizations, had one foot in the labor movement and the other in community organizations. It included the Council of Women's Organizations, La Raza, the NAACP, the Urban League, and eight different consumers' groups. Additional members included the AFL-CIO, an Alinsky-influenced group—the Pico National Network, and Ralph Nader's Public Citizen. AFR had a $2 million budget, most of it from unions, though it was a pittance compared to spending by the financial industry.

AFR's president, Heather Booth, was a longtime community organizer from Chicago whose husband was an AFSCME official. She had previously served as president of Chicago's Citizen Action Program, created in 1969 by organizers from Saul Alinsky's Industrial Areas Foundation. Booth hired Lisa Donner as her deputy director. Donner was a Harvard graduate, ex-SEIU staffer, and for ten years head of ACORN's Financial Justice Center. The center was one of the earliest to warn about subprime mortgages.[13]

Robert Kuttner lamented the fact that only a few "technically savvy advocates for the public's interest in strong regulation of derivatives are actively engaged in the rule-making process." He cited Silvers, Heather Slavkin, and Michael Greenberger. Slavkin chaired the AFR's task force on derivatives regulation. She worked for the AFL-CIO and later headed its Office of Investment. Greenberger was a law professor and one-time administrator of the Commodity Futures Trading Commission (CFTC). When the SEC and the CFTC held hearings about derivatives, said Kuttner, "the first panel was 15 guys from Wall Street and Heather Slavkin. Behind each of them [from Wall Street] are another 15 lawyers and researchers writing the comments and doing the legwork." But labor and its allies had something that the banks did not: an ability to mobilize the citizenry. Without them, the efforts of progressive policy experts like Silvers, Slavkin, and Warren would not have packed the same punch. And that was the idea.[14]

Democrats Divided

Right after he took office, President Obama declared—with former Treasury Secretary Paul Volcker at his side—"Never again will the American taxpayer be held hostage by a bank that is too big to fail." Progressives such as those in AFR, however, trusted neither Obama nor Geithner to be tough enough on banks. In April 2010, when debate over the Dodd bill was at its peak, Senators Sherrod Brown (D-OH) and Ted Kaufman (D-DE) introduced an amendment to cap the size of the nation's banks. Known as the SAFE Banking Act, it would have limited liabilities at banks to 2 percent of the nation's GDP and 3 percent at non-banks. A megabank—one judged too big to fail—would not be allowed a share of the nation's insured deposits greater than 10 percent, and the assets of the six largest would be cut in size from 64 percent of GDP to 34 percent, the level in 2001. At a subsequent press conference with Brown and Kaufman, Damon Silvers, Heather Slavkin, and SEIU's Bill Regan spoke in favor of the legislation.

Standing against it were economic experts in the Obama administration, including Geithner and Lawrence Summers, director of the National Economic Council, as well as congressional centrists, who aligned with Geithner in their preference for modest regulation. Brown-Kaufman failed on the Senate floor, receiving sixty-one "no" votes, of which twenty-seven came from Democrats. In an exchange with an unidentified senator, Richard Trumka angrily said, "By voting against this amendment . . . [you] avoid addressing the problem of too big to fail institutions and leave our economy at risk of another financial crisis." Three years later, now-Senator Elizabeth Warren (D-MA) reported to the AFL-CIO convention that, by ignoring too big to fail, the Senate allowed the nation's four largest banks to accumulate assets that were 30 percent larger than at the onset of the Great Recession; the five largest held more than half of all banking assets in the United States.[15]

MIT professor Simon Johnson (also the former chief economist of the International Monetary Fund) blamed the administration for failing to pare down the size and power of major banks. When Obama told a group of bankers, "my administration is the only thing between you and the pitchforks," the implication was that people like Elizabeth Warren, Damon Silvers, and Sherrod Brown were leading a peasant's revolt, as Johnson put it. Brown complained that it was "pretty clear" [the administration] "has too much Wall Street influence." Wall Street donated less to Obama than to financier Mitt Romney during the 2012 presidential campaign, yet it still contributed one-third of Obama's campaign funds. As one J. P. Morgan executive said, "We may be pissed at Obama, but when it comes down to it, he was pretty good for our business."[16]

Size was one problem. Another was scope. The repeal of Glass-Steagall in 1999 demolished the Depression-era wall between commercial banking and investment banking. Now banks could trade risky derivative products like CDOs and invest in hedge funds and private equity. Banks seized the opportunity. Federal deposit insurance (and access to the Federal Reserve's credit facilities) reduced risks for banks as they plunged ahead. The arrangement had never been intended when the Federal Deposit Insurance Corporation (FDIC) was created in 1933.

Senator Blanche Lincoln (D-AR) offered an amendment to the Dodd bill that would prohibit banks from benefiting from federal assistance when trading derivatives. That is, it would force them to bear all of the risk. Among those speaking in favor of Lincoln's proposal was Damon Silvers, who told reporters that derivatives were "a major contributor to what went wrong in our financial system—that vast risks involved in multitrillion-dollar derivatives books were embedded within larger financial institutions." In the end, the industry succeeded in watering down but not eliminating Lincoln's amendment.[17]

The so-called Volcker Rule went much further. It would rebuild the walls that Glass-Steagall had taken down, by forcing banks out of the derivatives business entirely. The financial industry fought ferociously against its inclusion in the Dodd bill, claiming this would put them at a disadvantage when competing with foreign banks, the same complaint levied against Sarbanes-Oxley. Initially they succeeded; the bill called for a six-month study of the Volcker Rule before it could be adopted, which would give banks time to weaken it. Joining the banks in opposition to the Volcker Rule were Geithner and Summers, as well as Ben Bernanke, whom Obama had recently reappointed as chairman of the Federal Reserve Board.

When the Dodd bill was in its final stages, however, two liberal senators, Jeff Merkley (D-OR) and Carl Levin (D-MI), offered an amendment to immediately implement the Volcker Rule and do so in a way that would be difficult for future regulators to sidestep. Joining them in pushing back against the banks were Elizabeth Warren, labor representatives like Damon Silvers and Heather Slavkin, and others. As Dodd-Frank was going down to the wire, several of them met with President Obama, seeking his endorsement of Merkley-Levin. Damon Silvers was quoted in the Wall Street Journal saying that it was "critical" to restrict banking activities in the derivatives market, especially "in terms of whether we're addressing 'too big to fail.'" At the last minute, the amendment—now with backing from Obama, who originally had been ambivalent on the issue—made its way into the final legislation.[18]

Investors and Risk

It wasn't only bankers who had fueled systemic risk before the crash. Investors also were implicated. One reason was the structure of bankers' pay, which, as in the nonfinancial sector, had come to rest on the types of stock-based rewards that the cookbook prescribed. Another contributor were hedge funds. During the runup to the crisis, it was pension plans who had poured money into hedge funds.

Bankers' Pay

At the end of 2007, as warning lights flashed throughout the economy, Wall Street's five largest securities firms handed out $38 billion in year-end bonuses, even though the firms had lost a quarter of their equity value. Citigroup, faced with billions of losses related to CDOs, fired its CEO, Charles O. Prince III, that fall. Yet Prince received a $12.5 million bonus as he went out the door, this on top of nearly $70 million in unrestricted stock and one million stock options he took with him. Prince's severance package was chintzy as compared to the one received by Merrill Lynch's CEO, Stan O'Neal, fired at around the same time and for the same reason. O'Neal walked away with over $160 million in stock, stock options, and retirement benefits. A few months later, both men found themselves in front of Representative Henry Waxman's House Committee on Oversight and Government Reform, which was investigating Wall Street's pay practices. For Prince, the situation was reminiscent of Charles E. Mitchell—whose bank was a predecessor to Citigroup—when he faced the Senate Banking Committee in 1932.

Waxman asked Prince, "How can a few executives do so well when their companies are doing so poorly? It seems like everyone is hurting except you." After the crash, Citigroup and Merrill Lynch (now part of Bank of America) would become TARP beneficiaries. Bonuses in the financial services industry, said the AFL-CIO's Daniel Pedrotty, "are in our view a giant fraudulent conveyance, where money was paid out to executives at firms that were fatally undercapitalized."[19]

In the first months after Obama's election, shareholder activists were divided on whether to change pay practices in banking through legislation or private ordering. Charles M. Elson, the Delaware governance expert, recommended private ordering: "When the federal government gets involved, there are typically unintended consequences. It's better to do it internally than have the government do it." Like Elson, Patrick McGurn, special counsel to ISS, feared that intervention by Congress and the SEC would lead to an undesirable one-size-fits-all solution. But McGurn acknowledged that, as with Enron, the tools of private ordering—internal controls, transparency, independent directors, and shareholder activism—had failed to prevent questionable practices. "The federal government is going to fill the void," he predicted. He was right.[20]

Bankers' bonuses, paid as stock options, were tied to the bank's return on equity (ROE). It wasn't a quiet life, but it was a good one. Between 1979 and 2005, executives in financial services doubled their share of individuals in the top 1 percent, to nearly one out of every seven. They earned 250 percent more than comparable executives. Although some banks were enormous, size could explain only one-fifth of the premium.

With compensation based on ROE, according to Anat Admati and Martin Hellwig, there was an incentive to manipulate accounting methods and pursue riskier lines of business, what they termed "the ROE culture." Shareholders bore responsibility too, first as proponents of stock-based pay, and later for abetting bubbly stock gains in financial services. The rewards were too abundant to pass up, even if they were built on a house of cards. Months before his ouster, Charles O. Prince III said that the party would end at some point, "but as long as the music is playing, you've got to get up and dance."[21]

Sanjai Bhagat, finance professor at the University of Colorado, offered a different analysis of the relationship between risk and bankers' pay. He examined the case of bank "projects" (for example, new types of securities like CDOs) that have high returns in the early years and negative returns in the later years, and whose total net present value is likely to be negative in the long run. Only the issuer knows the risks associated with a project. Banks had risk management units, but they were underfunded and their opinions ignored by senior executives. Because bank executives held large numbers of shares, and options that either had no vesting requirement or that already had vested, the rational approach would be for them to cash out early on. Then they would come out ahead in the long term when returns dropped below zero, not least because it was a near-certainty that the government would rescue their bank if the fall was precipitous. Bhagat compared the large financial institutions receiving TARP funds with nonrecipients and found that TARP executives had liquidated their shares before the banking collapse to a much greater extent than other banking executives.[22]

In 2009, the House Financial Services Committee held a hearing on systemic risk. Among those appearing was Damon Silvers, who criticized the pay methods that had migrated from the cookbook to the banking sector. Reliance on stock options, said Silvers, "creates an incentive to focus on the upside, and be less interested in the possibility of things going really wrong. It is a terrible way to incentivize the manager of a major financial institution, and a particularly terrible way to incentivize the manager of an institution the federal government might have to rescue."[23]

Dodd-Frank embodied the belief that defective compensation methods in the financial industry had contributed to the exacerbation of systemic risk. Banks now had to report to regulators whether their incentive pay arrangements were leading to "inappropriate risks" that could cause material loss. Bankers, as one might expect, abhorred these requirements. But the risk-related rules turned out to be less onerous than expected. Four years after Dodd-Frank's signing, Anat Admati told the Senate Banking Committee that the act had failed to solve the problem of excessive risk-taking: "Compensation structures that reward return on equity, which are [still] pervasive in banking, effectively pay bankers to gamble at the expense of creditors or taxpayers. . . . Even shareholders may be exposed to risks for which they are not properly compensated. Few benefit, while the rest are harmed by this situation." The SEC, under pressure from President Obama to prevent bankers from taking "reckless risks," announced a plan for stricter pay rules, including for clawbacks of bonuses based on accounting fraud, a similar provision to one in SOX that rarely was enforced. Obama urged the agency to act as quickly as possible, but the banks ran out the clock; nothing was on the books by the time Donald Trump was elected. Shortly thereafter, the SEC dropped its plan. There were those who had been optimistic that the crisis-induced regulation of bankers' pay would have an impact stretching beyond financial markets. Lawrence Mishel, a savvy economist at the labor-backed Economic Policy Institute, said that "Wall Street led the way, and that's going to be reversed. We're going to see a decline in inequality." It was not to be.[24]

Hedge Funds

Hedge funds were implicated in the catastrophe. As early as 2005, MIT economist Andrew Lo warned that hedge funds were raising systemic risk. It was a lesson that should have been learned from the 1998 collapse of Long-Term Capital Management (LTCM), which brought financial markets perilously close to the edge. After LTCM's downfall, the SEC investigated hedge funds, but no consequential regulations were put in place. Hedge funds are highly leveraged entities. When financial markets change unexpectedly, the funds may be unable to cover their obligations. Nearly half the purchasers of CDOs were hedge funds. One way out is to unload assets, which weakens the value of assets held by others, causing a widening spiral of losses. In the case of hedge funds, those "others" are in the banking sector. Compounding the problem were hedge funds created by banks. Bear Stearns had two hedge funds tied to subprime mortgages. When they lost their value in 2007, it marked the beginning of the end for Bear Stearns, whose demise in March 2008 panicked the markets and heralded the oncoming disaster. David Skeel, a law professor at Penn, said that before the financial crisis, "hedge funds are best understood by what they are not. They are not regulated."[25]

A herd of pension plans stampeded into hedge funds during the early 2000s, hungry for yields. Everyone had heard of the wonders achieved with hedge funds by university endowments like Yale's. Pennsylvania's state pension plan, PSERS, increased its allocation eight-fold between 2001 and 2006, until hedge funds accounted for 27 percent of its portfolio. The following year PSERS had an overall return of 17 percent, an enviable amount.

Taft-Hartley funds, always cautious, were the last to join the party. Advisors to Taft-Hartleys, like Marco Consulting, endorsed hedge funds for its Taft-Hartley clients. In April 2007, with subprime mortgages already headed for disaster, Marco boasted that its recommendations had "worked out fabulously well." Yet the risk-adjusted returns on hedge funds were awful, "reliably lower than the return on the S&P 500 index," said one study.[26]

The AFL-CIO was worried. Trumka sent a letter in 2006 to Senators Richard Shelby (R-AL) and Paul Sarbanes (D-MD) expressing concern that the weakly regulated hedge fund industry was bamboozling pension plans. He asked that the funds disclose their fees and trading tactics and that steps be taken to mitigate the systemic risks they posed. The AFL-CIO staked out a position critical of public and multiemployer plans, a stance from which it previously had shied. Damon Silvers disparaged the plans for "pursuing this phantasm of sustained above-market return. What we are trying to do in this environment is to put some distance between the labor movement and the hunger of our [pension] funds for return. Some of our funds are very enthused about putting more and more money into private equity or more and more money into hedge funds. That's not where we are."[27]

Pension funds had an additional way of earning money from hedge funds: share-lending. When activist hedge funds wage a proxy fight, they can build a critical mass of shares by borrowing them from other owners (which is why share-lending peaks on the record date of the annual meeting). After casting their so-called empty votes, the hedge funds return the shares along with a fee. It's legal, but it doesn't pass the smell test.

Who loaned shares? The main providers were mutual funds and public pension plans. A survey from 2004 found that 80 percent of pension plans engaged in share-lending and of those funds, a fifth lent between 25 and 50 percent of their actively held shares. The money was not insignificant: in a single year CalPERS earned $130 million from the practice. Share-lending made mincemeat of claims that pension plans took proxy voting seriously. Again, Silvers berated them: "Absolutely every other pension fund thinks that it's absolutely fine to go criticizing folks in the City and on Wall Street for having shorted this and that but they then fail to turn around and say, 'Yes, but it was my lending them the stock that allowed them to do it. It was my hedge fund investment that encouraged all of this.' It's not even irresponsible. It's almost a-responsible, responsible-like without having to take responsibility."[28]

The crisis decimated hedge funds. As a record number folded, investors demanded their money back. Returns never again reached the levels of the pre-crisis years. PSERS—and other pension funds—suffered billions in losses on their hedge fund investments. They discovered the hard way that nobody in the investing world liked to discuss risk-adjusted returns, only returns. Some funds, like CalPERS, pulled out of hedge funds entirely. Others, still mesmerized by the phantasm, stuck it out.[29]

Indicting Investors

The Chartered Financial Institute's president, John D. Rodgers, boasted in 2014 that institutional investors had birthed a new economic system, "fiduciary capitalism," based on "long-term investing for the good of our world." It was a throwback to the Third Way, and it was wishful thinking. Long-term investing was slow to penetrate, even after more than twenty years of advocacy. The year before Rodgers's pronouncement, McKinsey surveyed over one thousand executives and board members and found that 79 percent felt pressure from large investors to demonstrate strong financial performance over a period of two years or less and that 63 percent said the pressure to generate strong short-term results had increased over the previous five years. Executives attributed the problem to their boards, while boards said they were merely relaying demands from shareholders. Short-term investors received disproportionate attention because they were the ones driving share prices, not buy-and-hold investors.

Another issue was the short-term biases of asset managers, whose performance reviews are based on annual results. State and local plans have the added burden of operating in a fishbowl; their annual returns are reported to legislatures, city councils, and the media.[30]

The institutions who own the bulk of US equities—including bank shares—are a diverse group. Sixty-one percent are quasi-indexers, including pension plans; 31 percent are transients, such as hedge funds and high-frequency traders; and 8 percent are dedicated investors. Among quasi-indexers, there is variation in the amount of time they hold on to their actively traded shares: somewhat longer for pension funds than mutual funds and endowments. Even so, two-thirds of all trades by pension plans between 1999 and 2009 were of shares held for less than a year.[31]

In 2007, the Aspen Institute published a report on "long-term value creation" that discussed how to curb managerial myopia. Representatives from thirty organizations contributed to it, including eight companies, the Business Roundtable, CII, the AFL-CIO, Change to Win, and three pension funds (CalPERS, New York State, and TIAA-CREF). The report recommended changing how CEOs were rewarded, such as requiring them to retain equity after leaving a company. Two years later, during the financial crisis, Aspen issued a second report, this time on investor short-termism. The report noted that, with a new administration and a Congress ready to legislate, the moment was ripe to do something about myopic shareholders.[32]

Sand in the Wheels

To encourage "patient capital"—a phrase not heard since the industrial policy debates of the 1980s—the second Aspen report recommended that capital gains tax rates be reduced progressively the longer an investor held a stock. The problem with the idea was that pension funds do not usually have to pay tax on their capital gains. As an alternative, it recommended an excise tax on stock sales; however, this was only briefly mentioned and never spelled out. The excise tax referred to levying a small fee on every financial transaction to discourage short-term trades. It is also known as the Tobin tax, after Yale economist James Tobin, who said the tax would "throw sand in the wheels" of destabilizing speculation. For obvious reasons, Wall Street hated the idea.[33]

European advocates of a transactions tax built on Tobin's ideas, urging that revenues from the tax be used to support public services; thus, the Tobin tax also is referred to as a "Robin Hood tax." On the Continent, the push for a transactions tax began with the Association for the Taxation of Financial Transactions and Aid to Citizens (ATTAC), a single-issue group created in 1998 by left-leaning economists in France. Attracting support from the French labor movement and from technocrats in the French government, even from former Prime Minister Jacques Chirac, ATTAC grew into a pan-European organization. France first adopted the tax in 2012; then Germany endorsed it but wanted it levied throughout the European Union and pressed the European Commission to take action. In 2011, the Commission released a plan "to make the financial sector pay its fair share" as recompense for the money spent on propping up banks. The commission predicted that the tax would raise huge amounts to support EU activities. But the financial industry strangled the attempt.[34]

In the United States, the Congressional Populist Caucus, led by Representative Pete DeFazio (D-OR) and Senator Tom Harkin (D-IA), unveiled legislation in 2009 called the "Let Wall Street Pay for the Restoration of Main Street Act," which had backing from the AFL-CIO and AFR. The bill called for a levy on stock transactions of one-quarter of 1 percent, half of which would be spent on deficit reduction and half to combat unemployment. The legislation, from which pension funds were exempt, would yield $100 billion in annual revenue, according to the Congressional Budget Office. The banking industry's main lobbying group, the Financial Services Roundtable, said that the tax would "strike at the very heart" of the American economic system. A more mundane reason Wall Street opposed the tax was that the industry's profits rose in tandem with trading volume. Within the Democratic Party, Wall Street bested the reformers. Timothy Geithner, firm in his opposition, said the tax made no sense unless it was levied globally. House Speaker Nancy Pelosi (D-CA) said it was not a priority for Congress. Thus, Robin Hood was absent from Dodd-Frank.[35]

The Cookbook

After months of congressional logrolling, the Shareholder Bill of Rights was embedded into Dodd-Frank, enshrining the cookbook as law. When it came to boards, companies were now required to tell shareholders why they combined the chairman and CEO positions, if they did. The act required the independence of a board's compensation committee and its compensation consultants, but in recognition of SOX's failures, stock exchanges were told to prepare criteria for precisely defining independence. Say on pay and proxy access were in the act. It also included the pay provisions previously discussed: disclosing the relationship between executive pay and share performance and reporting on the ratio of CEO-to-worker pay.

The situation annoyed management spokespersons. Martin Lipton, along with Jay Lorsch and Theodore Mirvis of the Harvard Business School, castigated the provisions in a *Wall Street Journal* opinion piece. The argument was classic Lipton: Management was not at fault for the subprime mess; the blame lay with short-sighted shareholders who had pushed executives to seek unsustainable returns. Meeting their demands drove "reckless risk taking" that had led to the disaster. "The stockholder-centric view of the current Schumer bill," they wrote, "simply cannot be the cure for the disease it spawned . . . [Its provisions] "enhance stockholder power and thereby would fuel the very stockholder-generated short-termist pressure that, in the view of many observers, contributed significantly to the financial and economic crises we face today." Shareholders may have paid a price, although, as Lipton pointed out, it was "employees who devoted their lives to building stockholder value [who] felt the pain acutely."[36]

Lipton was on to something. The parts of Dodd-Frank taken from the cookbook failed to pass empirical muster, including for the financial sector. Together with colleagues, René Stulz, a prominent finance economist, found that banks whose boards were shareholder-friendly before the crisis performed worse than others after it began. Maximizing shareholder wealth led them further up the risk-reward curve into aggressive securitization and derivatives trading. Banks whose CEOs were aligned with shareholder interests performed no better than others, and some evidence suggested they were worse. Because the United States had the most shareholder-friendly governance system in the world, its banks developed more serious problems during the crisis than those from nations with less powerful shareholders. In other words, shareholder primacy had toxic effects on the financial system. Ironically, however, its tenets undergirded parts of Dodd-Frank.[37]

Occupy Wall Street

Occupy Wall Street was born in New York City on September 17, 2011. The initial demonstration spontaneously morphed into nationwide and then global protests in over nine hundred cities. The participants tended to be young, educated, and either unemployed or stuck in low-wage jobs. Although stock markets were up, along with bank profits, unemployment rates for college graduates in 2011 were still twice as high as before the Great Recession; the situation was worse for those with less education. From the protesters' point of view, Wall Street's misbehavior had diminished their own prospects, yet Wall Street received and continued to receive government assistance. The stock portfolios of the wealthy recovered quickly. College graduates, however, had few assets and faced a jobless recovery that prevented payment of their student loans.

Occupy disparaged Dodd-Frank and blamed President Obama for its shortcomings. Protesters marched past the White House in early October with signs reading, "No More Wall Street White House." Occupy's signature slogan—"We Are the 99 Percent"—went viral globally. Marshall Ganz, longtime organizer, called it "a brilliant articulation of their position and what the movement is about."

Although critics said Occupy Wall Street's ideas were inchoate, protesters were consistent in blaming the nation's economic problems on three groups.

Heading the list was the top 1 percent. Protest signs said, "Tax the Rich a Lot," "Robin Hood Was Right," and "Not So Fast, You Greedy Bastards." Occupy also skewered the other two, bankers and politicians: "Banks Got Bailed Out, We Got Sold Out," "J. P. Morgan Is a Kleptomaniac," and "Our Politicians Are the Priesthood of Capitalism." Occupy was among the first to tie social media to mass mobilization. And it was a near-daily feature in the news.[38]

Where Occupy fell short, however, was in offering solutions. The Canadian group AdBusters, which was the first to call for the "occupation" of Wall Street, wrote a manifesto for Occupy. Among its demands were ending foreclosures, forgiving student debt, and a transactions tax. The manifesto also called for higher taxes on the 1 percent, with the revenue to be used for public services—the Robin Hood approach. But Occupy ignored the manifesto and, instead of highlighting the specific demands made by AdBusters, sought what Judith Butler, a Berkeley literature professor, called "impossible demands." Of Occupy's participants, Butler said, "Either they say there are no demands and that leaves your critics confused. Or they say that demands for social equality, that demands for economic justice are impossible demands and impossible demands are not practical. But we disagree. If hope is an impossible demand, then we demand hope."[39]

An offshoot of Occupy Wall Street was Occupy the SEC, which surfaced in 2012 with the release of a 325-page letter demanding that the agency immediately implement Merkley-Levin. Occupy the SEC, a small group of attorneys and renegade ex-Wall Street bankers, later published "Occupy Finance," a report that was distributed at a Zuccotti Park reunion. The group followed up their letter with a lawsuit to compel the SEC to stop dragging its heels. Another group spinning in Occupy's orbit was the Alternative Banking Working Group, which demanded that banks be forced to adopt higher capital adequacy ratios.[40]

Comedian Rodney Dangerfield's famous line "I can't get no respect" describes the different reactions to Occupy as compared to earlier events led by the labor movement. Labor's two New York marches garnered only around a dozen stories nationwide. But in the twelve months after Occupy surfaced, there were 29,000 articles mentioning it. Occupy's tactics were creative, funny, and unpredictable. Its protesters were young and edgy; unions were less so.

A way of gauging differences between the two movements is to count newspaper articles in the Factiva database for the three years after Occupy's emergence that mention the AFL-CIO or Occupy and also contain keywords related to finance, regulation, executive pay, and inequality. Both movements were associated with these issues but displayed different frequencies. For Occupy, the most common terms were inequality, followed by finance. For the AFL-CIO, executive pay and regulation were most frequent.[41]

When it came to inequality, influence flowed from Occupy to the AFL-CIO. Comparing the three years before and three years after Occupy, articles in the *Factiva* database that mentioned both the AFL-CIO and inequality rose fivefold. Two months after Occupy's appearance, the AFL-CIO sent out a memo advising unions to use Occupy's signature issue—the top 1 percent—in their communications. Yet the AFL-CIO continued to tie inequality to executive pay.[42]

The top 1 percent comprised not only corporate executives, but other groups too. Within the top 1 [.01] percent, 65 [45] percent of income derived from employment; 22 [33] percent from self-employment, small business ownership, and partnerships like law firms, hedge funds, and private equity; and 12 [22] percent from capital income, that is, from ownership of wealth. Focusing on the top 1 percent instead of lavish executive rewards implicated taxation, inherited wealth, and individuals not employed by corporations.[43]

Occupy wanted no part of electoral politics. In this respect, Occupy differed from the labor movement as well as its contemporary on the right, the Tea Party. Whereas young people had been hopeful and enthusiastic when President Obama ran for the first time, now they were cynical and disappointed. Electoral participation by those aged eighteen to twenty-nine declined sharply when Obama ran a second time. Nonetheless, Occupy produced some practical results, like keeping the transactions tax on the political agenda. It called for a "Bank Transfer Day," when individuals were supposed to pull their money out of private banks and deposit the funds into nonprofit credit unions; credit unions added over two million new customers as a result. Most of all, it channeled public anger—at a president who seemingly wasn't angry enough and at a system that had made the wealthy whole, unlike themselves.[44]

Occupy caught unions by surprise. Overnight it accomplished what they had tried but failed to do: mobilize youth. More than a few union leaders were wary of Occupy's anarchist tendencies, while Occupy members distrusted unions for fear that they might muscle in and impose different priorities. Despite the misgivings, unions participated in Occupy's activities and provided portable showers, meeting rooms, photocopying, and legal assistance.

Occupy offered lessons on reinvigorating the labor movement. Stewart Applebaum, president of the Retail, Wholesale, and Department Store Union, said that the labor movement "needs to tap into their energy and learn from them. They are reaching a lot of people that the labor movement has been struggling to reach for years." At the time, the average age of a union member was forty-five. At the AFL-CIO's 2013 convention, there were booths teaching union leaders how to use social media like Twitter and Facebook. Occupy even affected shareholder activism. SEIU, AFSCME, and several community groups came up with the idea of "99% Spring": to hold protests at shareholder meetings over corporate tax avoidance and executive compensation. Unions learned from Occupy, but Occupy failed to learn from labor about leadership, organization, and diversity. As a result, Occupy burned out rather quickly.[45]

Shredding Dodd-Frank

After President Obama signed Dodd-Frank, Richard Trumka heralded "a new day on Wall Street—one where working peoples' voices are finally being heard." Dodd-Frank had cut short a thirty-year trajectory of financial deregulation. No wonder the Business Roundtable said that the law "takes our country in the wrong direction." The final bill drew on TARP and its successor, made their provisions more rigorous, and extended regulation beyond the group of TARP recipients.[46]

Business failed to stop Dodd-Frank, but it received something in return for its estimated $1 billion in lobbying expenditures. Banks that were too big to fail were spared from downscaling. If a bank needed rescue, there would be bailouts first and repayment later, possibly stretching out for years. Lobbyists prevented the Consumer Financial Protection Bureau (CFPB), created under Dodd-Frank, from having authority over financial products such as stocks, insurance, and auto loans. And there was more.[47]

One of Dodd-Frank's flaws was that Congress handed over its implementation to a multitude of federal agencies. No sooner had the ink dried than Wall Street declared another war. The first four months were a blitzkrieg. Wall Street's lobbyists held over five hundred meetings with regulatory agencies. Defenders of Dodd-Frank logged only one-tenth as many. "The big banks have a ton of money to put toward this battle," said Heather Slavkin, "and the people who are fighting to reform just don't have the resources or the people." AFR had a staff of eight, and Republican gains in Congress made critics close to labor, like Damon Silvers, less visible.[48]

The 2010 midterm elections were a disaster for the Democrats, who lost control of the House and a greater number of congressional seats than any midterm election since 1938. After Spencer Bachus (R-AL) replaced Barney Frank as chair of the House Financial Services Committee, reformers lost an important access point. Bachus had the temerity to say that "Washington and the regulators are there to serve the banks." The new House introduced bills repealing parts or all of Dodd-Frank along with steep cuts in the budgets of agencies charged with fleshing out the law. When the CFTC sought additional funds to implement Dodd-Frank, President Obama recommended a budget increase of 80 percent, but the House cut its funds by a third. Damon Silvers, quoted in the *Wall Street Journal*, called the onslaught "an attempt to chip away at the first meaningful steps towards re-regulating our financial markets since the Great Depression." During the 2012 election season, Republicans savaged Dodd-Frank. Presidential hopefuls Mitt Romney, Rick Perry, and Jon Huntsman all called for its repeal. They blamed lingering joblessness on Dodd-Frank, which, they said, had dried up business lending.[49]

At the time, a survey of voters found that 83 percent wanted stronger rules than were contained in the act. But the GOP continued its assault on Dodd-Frank, made all the more potent after it took control of both houses of Congress in 2014. Congress cut the budgets of agencies charged with carrying out the act, especially the CFTC and the CFPB. Citigroup and JPMorgan Chase persuaded Republicans to insert a provision into the national budget that would repeal Blanche Lincoln's swap pushout rule. Citigroup wrote most of the provision.

Meanwhile, companies sought shelter from Dodd-Frank, as when Black-Rock asked the CFTC to let it opt out from derivatives trading rules. Via their industry associations, large banks demanded exemptions from the act's strictures on bonus deferrals. An important issue for the banking industry was to transfer responsibility for implementing Dodd-Frank from government to corporate boards, with the rationale that directors were better equipped than government to decide which employees should be covered by the new pay rules. Requests for self-policing went to the SEC, the Federal Reserve Bank's Governors, the FDIC, the Comptroller of the Currency, the FDIC, and other agencies. Bankers had 574 lobbyists working to protect their interests, two-thirds of whom were former federal employees.

A key strategy was to slow down the SEC's conversion of Dodd-Frank into specific rules. After the agency finally issued its Volcker rule guidelines in 2015, the banking industry asked the agency to give them five more years to comply.

There were numerous lawsuits. Eugene J. Scalia, who now represented Wall Street financial institutions, challenged the CFTC's rules on derivatives. He argued other Dodd-Frank cases as well, including an attempt to overturn the law's whistleblower rules and another involving a company's designation as "too big to fail." Scalia, relying on the cost-benefit argument he'd used against proxy access, won all but a single lawsuit. Harvey J. Goldschmid, a former SEC commissioner, saw these lawsuits as an attempt to undo in the courts what couldn't be stopped in Congress. Staffers at the SEC took to calling Dodd-Frank the "Eugene Scalia Full Employment Act."[50]

After Donald Trump took office, Republicans ruled the roost. Five Goldman Sachs executives worked in the White House and one, Steven Mnuchin, was the treasury secretary. All were keen on dismantling Dodd-Frank. Six months after Trump's election, House Republicans approved the Financial CHOICE Act, intended as the coup de grâce for Dodd-Frank. Its provisions included revocation of say on pay, the Volcker rule, the pay ratio rule, and pay-hedging disclosures. The bill said that only investors who held 1 percent of a company's stock for at least three years would be allowed to submit a shareholder proposal. The threshold would have deflated shareholder activism. The bill also required that all of Dodd-Frank's remaining provisions be justified by cost-benefit analyses. Not a single House Democrat voted for the CHOICE Act, just as Dodd-Frank had received no Republican votes in the House. The Senate never voted on the CHOICE Act, however. [51]

In testimony to the House Financial Services Committee in 2015, Damon Silvers presented his view of the previous five years. The Dodd-Frank Act, he said, had been a "compromise" and "definitely half a loaf." It failed to address too big to fail and the problem of banks setting the agenda for the Federal Reserve rather than the other way around. He complained of the act's slow implementation by the SEC.

In the years after Silvers spoke, the SEC remained sluggish in promulgating rules to implement Dodd-Frank, especially those related to executive compensation. Come 2017, by which time Donald Trump occupied the White House, a majority of the SEC's commissioners were Republicans keen to water down Dodd-Frank's intent. At the Consumer Financial Protection Bureau, Trump put in charge someone opposed to the agency's existence.[52]

Before the crisis, financialization was portrayed as the era's dominant mode of accumulation, one that touched all aspects of the economy, society, and daily life. Global regulation following the banking collapse, including Dodd-Frank's half a loaf, took some of the wind out of financialization's sails. As a share of total US profits, profits in the financial sector increased steadily from the 1980s through Dodd-Frank's passage, and then declined. Seven out of eight of the largest financial institutions had a lower return on equity in 2019 than 2005. Even Goldman Sachs, the icon of financialization, had become a less profitable company than before.[53]

Epilogue

THE FINANCIAL CRISIS was devastating for working people and for the labor movement. It took nine years for unemployment rates and household incomes to return to their pre-crisis levels. Unions lost 1.2 million members in the private sector between 2008 and 2012, after which numbers drifted back up but not to pre-crisis levels. The labor force expanded more rapidly, pushing union density down to rock bottom in 2019. That year, 6 percent of corporate employees belonged to a union, fewer than in 1929. The struggle to rebuild the labor movement was not for naught, however. It led to major changes in structure and strategy, including financial activism. Outcomes surely would have been worse otherwise. Still, unions were not where they hoped to be when they started down the road to renewal.[1]

Despite the odds, CTW and its affiliated unions pulled out the stops after the financial crisis. SEIU launched the Fight for $15 campaign as part of its drive to sign up low-wage workers in the fast-food industry. It led to one-day walkouts in over a hundred US cities in 2013. The strikes pricked the national conscience and were followed by minimum-wage increases in a string of blue cities and states. SEIU hoped that the campaign would pressure the parent corporations of chains like McDonalds and Chipotle into signing contracts that would cover their franchisees.[2]

The UFCW launched a parallel campaign at Walmart, whose food-retailing operations were a threat to the union's grocery workers. UCFW created a group separate from the union, Organization United for Respect at Walmart (OUR Walmart), which relied on social media to mobilize Walmart workers. There were orchestrated protests outside hundreds of stores on every Black Friday, as well as finance-based tactics. A group of OUR Walmart members went to the company's annual shareholders' meeting to distribute fliers, and CTW's Investment Group (CtWIG) sent letters to Walmart's board in 2014 and 2015 highlighting problems with its executive-pay practices.[3]

A dam broke in 2018 when companies in big-box retailing and fast food announced substantial wage increases—up to $11 at Walmart and $15 at Amazon. McDonalds promised that it would stop lobbying against increases in the federal hourly minimum wage, stuck at a paltry $7.25. With the unemployment rate below 4 percent, employers faced spot labor shortages and worker unrest, with more work stoppages in 2018 and 2019 than at any time during the previous thirty years. But the companies were tough nuts to crack. The full name of SEIU's campaign had been Fight for $15 and A Union, but only the first three words bore fruit. This was the conundrum. SEIU and the UFCW had spent heavily, yet they could not sustain the effort if it failed to bring more members and money.[4]

Unions had become wary of devoting diminishing resources to corporate campaigns. They were expensive, drawn-out wars of attrition. Employers had become less willing to sign neutrality agreements, and the results were disappointing as compared to earlier days. Following Donald Trump's election, SEIU cut its $300 million budget by 30 percent. The AFL-CIO now allocated but a tenth of its budget to organizing, well below the previous decade's levels. Two of SEIU's visionaries, David Rolf and Steve Lerner, announced that the postwar collective bargaining system was dead. There were mutterings within the labor movement that the best strategy was "fortress unionism," a retreat into blue-city redoubts where unions still had strength.[5]

Labor drifted away from shareholder activism focused on corporate governance. The portion of corporate governance proposals emanating from unions declined from 42 percent (2003–2007) to 28 percent (2008–2014) to 13 percent (2015–2018). After that it was only the AFL-CIO and the Teamsters who filed the bulk of labor's governance proposals, supplemented by a much larger number from union-friendly pension funds in New York City and State, both deep-blue places. The New York funds concentrated on proxy access and political disclosure, the latter a step removed from corporate governance.[6]

It was a change from the days when labor left a mark on corporate governance. Campaigns for say on pay and proxy access had been led by AFSCME, while nearly all shareholder proposals for majority voting came from the Carpenters and other multiemployer plans. Among institutional investors, it was union pension plans that had offered two out of three proposals seeking independent board chairs.

Pioneering activists such as Richard Koppes, who had helped design the original CalPERS agenda, and Peter Clapman, who had done the same at

TIAA-CREF, believed that shareholder activism was less urgent now that a majority of companies had embraced the cookbook. They co-authored a 2016 opinion piece in the *Wall Street Journal* announcing that "the shareholder rights agenda has largely been achieved since it began in the 1980s." There was evidence backing up their celebratory claim. Ninety percent of the S&P 500 firms now relied on majority voting and had adopted annual director elections instead of staggered boards. The number of companies combining the CEO and chairman positions had dropped by half since 2001. Proxy access was widespread. Merely 4 percent of the S&P 500 maintained poison pills, once the *bêtes noires* of the cookbook.

What Clapman and Koppes failed to ask was whether enhanced shareholder rights had changed CEO behavior. The evidence suggests that the effects were modest. In the decade after the financial meltdown, CEOs continued to receive compensation out of line with their firms' economic performance. Fair-value options remained understated, while generous golden parachutes endured. Companies still thumbed their noses at shareholder proposals and at their votes in director elections. Independent directors and say on pay not only failed to constrain CEO compensation but were associated with *higher* pay. And instances of executive misconduct still erupted, albeit less spectacularly. CEO dismissals for insider trading or accounting irregularities increased between 2012 and 2016, affecting one in twenty CEOs at the 2,500 largest US corporations.[7]

The cookbook didn't perform as promised because executives were able to subvert its intent. They could adopt the cookbook while cooking the books. Firms adopted the recipes, but it was difficult to monitor the spirit of their implementation. CEOs wanted the right to manage; shareholders were an interference. Longtime crusader Robert A. G. Monks captured the futility of the situation: "I've had so little tangible success . . . [as] I've tried to expose the illusion of corporate democracy."[8]

The relationship between CEOs and investors also had a cooperative side. The groups found common ground in the primacy of shareholder value. Stock-based pay was crucial for the alignment. Executives and investors also shared a focus on short-term gains. On average, CEO pay—the bulk of it based on stock performance—vests in one year; institutional investors hold their actively traded shares for around the same amount of time.

Workers, however, had a different relationship to the corporation. What's valuable to workers, especially those with lower wages, are such things as job stability, employer-provided training, and low-risk pensions. The practices are undermined by the myopia of CEOs and investors. Buybacks are another example of the disconnect. They enrich CEOs and investors but are associated with lower levels of employment, investment, and wages.

Buybacks were a tricky issue for the labor movement. They helped pension funds but not the vast majority of workers who owned little or no stock. There was an additional rift: The largest pension plans were in the public sector, whereas the money spent on buybacks came at the expense of private-sector jobs and pay. Yet unions mostly were silent when it came to buybacks.[9]

The situation changed around 2014, when buybacks returned to levels not seen since before the financial crisis. That year, William Lazonick, an economist at the University of Massachusetts, published a widely noted article in the *Harvard Business Review* outlining the problems associated with buybacks. The issue entered the zeitgeist when presidential candidate Hillary Clinton blamed buybacks for undermining investment and exacerbating inequality. Other critics included Democratic policy advisors at the Brookings Institution, along with Nobel Prize winner Joseph Stiglitz, professor at Columbia University and chief economist at the Roosevelt Institute. Stiglitz said buybacks were an example of inequality caused by "pre-distribution"—the way markets and firms allocate income before redistributive taxation and social spending. Buybacks at the S&P 500 companies between 2014 and 2019 amounted to $3.7 trillion, the equivalent of giving each employee of the five hundred firms an annual check for $21,500.[10]

Labor jumped on the anti-buyback bandwagon in 2016. The UAW Retiree Medical Benefits Trust (RMBT), with $60 billion in assets, launched the Share Buybacks Disclosure Initiative. Participating in the initiative were eleven organizations, mostly from the union investing world, including the AFL-CIO Office of Investment, Amalgamated Bank, CtWIG, Marco Consulting, and SEIU's National Industry Pension Fund. Absent from the group were CII and public pension plans.[11]

The Disclosure Initiative led to seven shareholder proposals in 2016 demanding that the companies exclude the effect of buybacks on EPS when determining CEO bonuses. Four came from the AFL-CIO and two from LongView. Those that went to a vote received weak support of 5–6 percent, and no additional proposals were offered. Large financial institutions that routinely voted with management—such as State Street, Vanguard, and BlackRock—opposed curbs on buybacks. BlackRock's stance was notable because its CEO, Larry Fink, had on several occasions criticized buybacks for undermining long-term investment. It was not the first time, nor would it be the last, that prominent business leaders failed to walk their talk. These reactions were cautionary. Reckoning with buybacks via private orderings would be an uphill fight.[12]

As the 2020 elections loomed on the horizon, buybacks again were on the Democratic agenda. The Reward Work Act of 2018, introduced by Senator Tammy Baldwin (D-WI), would completely prohibit open-market buybacks. Its co-sponsors included Brian Schatz (D-HI), Elizabeth Warren (D-MA), Kirsten Gillibrand (D-NY), and Bernie Sanders (I-NY). The last three were presidential candidates. The Baldwin bill contained a flaw: It lacked a guarantee that money previously spent on buybacks would be shared with employees. Other legislation made the link explicit. Senators Cory Booker (D-NJ) and Sherrod Brown (D-OH), also presidential candidates, offered separate bills requiring companies to pay "worker dividends" based on the size of any buybacks that they conducted. The various bills had the potential for putting a dent in inequality, but they lacked the universal reach associated with tax reform. To that end, Sanders and Warren sponsored their own bills to tax wealth above a certain level and restore progressivity to the income tax.

Behind the scenes, sponsors of buyback legislation worked with several labor groups, including the Communications Workers (CWA) and United for Respect, the successor to the UFCW's OUR Walmart. Stiglitz's Roosevelt Institute, with its own ties to the labor movement, also contributed. But CII—the voice of public and corporate pension funds—warned lawmakers to be cautious and not make it difficult for companies to "recycle excess cash back to investors." Buybacks help the US economy, said CII, because investors use the cash to invest in firms with better growth opportunities. CII misspoke. Money invested in stocks of growing companies is unavailable for investment, except for IPOs; it's simply exchanged between shareholders.[13]

That Congress had its attention on stock markets was more than politicking. Underway, or so it appeared, was an historic turning of the screw: the delegitimization of shareholder capitalism. We noted at the beginning of this book that the legendary University of Chicago economist Milton Friedman insisted that public corporations had a single responsibility: to maximize shareholder value. How ironic that nearly sixty years later it was another distinguished Chicago economist, Raghuram Rajan, who challenged Friedman's assertion, couching his objections in efficiency terms. Rajan said that employees were no less the company's residual claimants than shareholders. When employees invest in skills useful only to their current employer, "they are no longer commodity labor." Companies might occasionally have to let workers go, said Rajan, but "job cuts that boost shareholder value aren't warranted if they reduce the value of other core stakeholders more." The flaw with Rajan's ideas is that any corporation that departs from shareholder primacy will find its stock price beaten down by spooked investors. For that reason, said Elizabeth Warren, "You have to do it with a rule," that is, on a market-wide basis.[14]

The same year Rajan penned his essay, the Business Roundtable drew global media coverage with a three-hundred-word "Statement on the Purpose of a Corporation." The document stated that the Roundtable's members shared "a fundamental commitment to *all* of our stakeholders. . . . Each of our stakeholders is essential. We commit to deliver value to all of them." The corporations pledged to compensate employees fairly, provide them with benefits, train them, and treat them with dignity and respect. Shareholders were promised transparency, engagement with managers, and long-term value. The Roundtable's press release said that the statement "moves away from shareholder primacy [and] includes commitment to all stakeholders." Among the stakeholders mentioned in the statement, shareholders were listed at the bottom.[15]

Coming from CEOs of the nation's two hundred largest public corporations, the document was remarkable. It hearkened back to the era of constituency statutes and the Roundtable's 1990 declaration on stakeholders. As back then, CII said that the Roundtable's statement "undercuts notions of managerial accountability to shareholders." CII was right. After more than three decades of shareholder capitalism, CEOs still preferred that shareholders be seen and not heard.[16]

The Roundtable's statement was, in part, a reaction to the renewed interest in corporate reform. Warren's Accountable Capitalism Act called for federal chartering of corporations, which would make it a legal requirement that companies consider the interests of their multiple stakeholders. Warren's approach would hold Roundtable companies to their rhetoric. Another concern were Democratic proposals to put workers on corporate boards by giving them the right to nominate and elect directors: one-third of board seats in the Reward Work Act and 40 percent in the Accountable Capitalism Act. The legislation embodied a broad concept of accountability, one that did not rest exclusively on directors beholden to shareholders. A voter survey found a majority of individuals from both parties in favor of giving employees the right to vote for board members.[17]

For unions, putting employees on boards was second-best to collective bargaining, labor's preferred method for changing pre-distributive outcomes. In 2019, Democrats unveiled the Protecting the Right to Organize Act (PRO

Act). A fresh attempt at labor law reform, it would eliminate right-to-work laws and give employees the right to sue—and the NLRB the authority to levy financial penalties—if employers interfered with organizing attempts. The PRO Act was approved by every House Democrat early in 2020.

The PRO Act came as the percentage of surveyed individuals reporting approval of labor unions reached its third-highest level since 1970, with the greatest support coming from college graduates in the eighteen- to thirty-four-year-old age bracket. The group included those who graduated around the time of the financial crisis—the Occupy generation—and who on average received lower wages than previous cohorts in their demographic group. Gallup polls found that during the decade after 2008, younger adults' opinion of capitalism had deteriorated to the point that capitalism and socialism were equally popular among the age group. For the Roundtable's CEOs, the interest in socialism "is what really scares them," said the president of the Ford Foundation.[18]

Yet another plan—for "fair and sustainable capitalism"—came from Leo E. Strine Jr., an attorney at Wachtell, Lipton who recently had resigned as chief justice of the Delaware Supreme Court. Strine recommended ambitious changes in corporate governance to give workers a larger share of corporate wealth. His key reform was to establish board-level "workforce committees" to address gainsharing between workers and investors in public corporations and those owned by private equity. Strine included checks to prevent the committees from undermining unions, and he endorsed the PRO Act. He also addressed the fiduciary duties of institutional investors, which he wanted to widen to include consideration of beneficiaries' interests as "workers, parents, breathers of air, and citizens," something that union and social investors had floated in the past. Strine's omnibus plan wasn't just pie in the sky. In February 2020, Mark Warner in the Senate and Cynthia Axne in the House introduced the Workforce Investment Disclosure Act that contained several of his recommendations.[19]

The proposals—on buybacks, stakeholders, and unions—endorsed workers' claims to a larger share of the corporation's wealth and a voice in its governance. But with Republicans controlling the Senate and the White House, the legislation was aspirational. And even with a political realignment, investors and executives would fight tooth and nail to retain their perquisites. It had been fifty years since Ralph Nader advanced the same reforms to no avail.

Sometimes the impossible becomes feasible. Unexpected changes like the Great Depression and the financial crisis shook the corporate status quo. The pandemic registered high on the societal Richter scale. Will there come a turning point for labor? For neoliberalism's reign? For the allocation of power and money within corporations?

———

American unions became alchemists during the age of finance, seeking to transform the power of money into power for workers. The attempt bolstered the labor movement and brought a measure of corporate accountability. Organized labor, an institution whose origins lay in the nineteenth century, again had demonstrated an ability to adapt.

The financial turn wasn't heroic. Rank-and-file members rarely participated. Pursuing worker interests through financial activism led to strange bedfellows and the messy compromises of realpolitik. While labor never embraced the cookbook as gospel, it lent its imprimatur. The tradeoffs would have been less problematic had unions been stronger, pension funds better funded, and fiduciary rules more flexible.

The longue dureé of postwar capitalism rested on a commonweal of shared risk and prosperity, one of whose foundations was the labor movement. Ours is a meaner era. Its hallmarks are staggering inequality and flat incomes for the vast majority. Improving the situation will require a host of changes: to shareholder capitalism, the tax system, social spending, and more. In the past, organized labor raised living standards and shored up democracy. It can happen again. Studies find that recent inequality has led to greater public support for unions. And half of nonunion workers say they would vote for a union if given the opportunity, a sentiment that cuts across partisan lines.[20]

Corporations have always been riven by conflict. Executives, owners, and workers jockey for wealth in a war of all against all. For more than forty years, the winners have been executives and owners, sometimes both, sometimes only one of them. Workers usually have lost. If they are to gain a fair share, they will need help from unions, and unions will need help as well.

ACKNOWLEDGMENTS

I am grateful to the many colleagues and friends who helped me during this book's lengthy gestation: David Aboody, Thomas Altura, Eileen Appelbaum, Stephen Bainbridge, Rose Batt, Tony Bernardo, Sanjai Bhagat, Yuri Biondi, Margaret Blair, Alon Brav, Ian Clark, Simon Deakin, Diane Del Guercio, the late Ronald Dore, Christopher Erickson, Matthew Finkin, Carola Frege, Gerald Friedman, Carola Frydman, Teresa Ghilarducci, Paola Giuliano, Barry Hirsch, Michael Huberman, Charles Jeszeck, Thomas Kochan, Naomi Lamoreaux, Nelson Lichtenstein, James Livingston, John Logan, Leib Kaufman, Ruth Milkman, Miyajima Hideaki, John Marshall, Daniel J.B. Mitchell, Nakata Yoshifumi, Michael Oppenheimer, Daniel Pedrotty, Brishen Rogers, Emmanuel Saez, Saguchi Kazuro, Judith Samuelson, the late Lynn Stout, Suzuki Fujikazu, Cynthia Williams, Steven Willborn, Kent Wong, and Yoshida Shoya. If I have forgotten someone, please forgive me.

A special thank you to the interviewees, who generously shared their ideas and time.

Financial assistance was provided by the UCLA Anderson School, the UCLA Institute for Research on Labor and Employment, and the John Simon Guggenheim Foundation.

The staff at Princeton University Press is nonpareil. They include Peter Dougherty, Joe Jackson, and Brigitte Pelner. For help with preparing the manuscript, I thank Mary Lou Bertucci, Anne Holmes, and Karen Verde. I appreciate very valuable comments from the manuscript's readers.

This book could never have been written without the support and forbearance of my family: Susan Bartholomew, Alex Jacoby, and Maggie Jacoby. The dedication recognizes seven women who held me up with love when I needed a lift: Paula Alexander, Gertrude Halberstadt, Hilde Joseph, Helen Kanter, Hedy Kahn, Hilde Meyer, and Edith Weissfeld.

NOTES

Introduction

1. Thomas Philippon, "The Evolution of the US Financial Industry from 1860 to 2007: Theory and Evidence," NYU Stern working paper (2008); Greta R. Krippner, *Capitalizing on Crisis: The Political Origins of the Rise of Finance* (Cambridge, MA: Harvard University Press, 2011); Christopher Kollmeyer and John Peters, "Financialization and the Decline of Organized Labor: A Study of 18 Advanced Capitalist Countries, 1970–2012," *Social Forces* (2019): 1–30. Todd E. Vachon, Michael Wallace, and Allen Hyde, "Union Decline in a Neoliberal Age: Globalization, Financialization, European Integration, and Union Density in 18 Affluent Democracies," *Socius* 2 (2016): 1–22; McKinsey Global Institute, *$118 Trillion and Counting: Taking Stock of the World's Capital Markets* (2010). In this book, "union-influenced pension plans" include multiemployer plans with union trustees and the much larger state and local pension plans, some of which have trustees who are union members. "Union plans" are comprised of multiemployer plans and pension plans for union staff.

2. Daniel L. Greenwald, Martin Lettau, and Sydney C. Ludvigson, "How the Wealth Was Won: Factor Shares as Market Fundamentals," National Bureau of Economic Research, working paper 25769, April 2019.

3. Thomas Piketty, *Capital and Ideology* (Cambridge, MA: Harvard University Press, 2020), 12. On corporations and inequality, see Jason Furman and Peter Orszag, "A Firm-Level Perspective on the Role of Rents in the Rise in Inequality," Presentation at "A Just Society" Centennial Event in Honor of Joseph Stiglitz, Columbia University, 2015; Adam J. Cobb, "How Firms Shape Income Inequality: Stakeholder Power, Executive Decision Making, and the Structuring of Employment Relationships," *Academy of Management Review* 41 (2016): 324–348. It wasn't only in the United States where unions took a financial turn. Where there were sizeable occupational pension systems—for example in Australia, Canada, the Netherlands, Sweden, and the UK—unions to varying degrees experienced their own financial turn. There is much to be said about similarities and differences, although doing so would require a different study than this one.

4. An excellent historical account of the 2000s, but one that omits organized labor, is Adam Tooze, *Crashed: How a Decade of Financial Crises Changed the World* (New York: Viking, 2018).

5. Barry T. Hirsch and David A. Mcpherson, *Union Membership and Earnings Data Book: Compilations from the Current Population Survey* (Arlington, VA: Bureau of National Affairs, 2019), 21.

6. Andrew T. Young and Hernando Zuleta, "Do Unions Increase Labor Shares? Evidence from US Industry-level Data," *Eastern Economic Journal* 44 (2018): 558–575; Michael Elsby, Bart

Hobijn, and Ayşegül Şahin, "The Decline of the US Labor Share," *Brookings Papers on Economic Activity* (Fall 2013): 1–63. Many studies of "labor's share" problematically lump executives together with non-managerial employees.

7. J. David Greenstone, *Labor in American Politics* (New York: Alfred A. Knopf, 1969). Also see Taylor E. Dark, *The Unions and the Democrats: An Enduring Alliance* (Ithaca, NY: Cornell University Press, 1999); Samuel Issacharoff, "Democracy's Deficits," *University of Chicago Law Review* 85 (2018): 485–520.

8. Peter L. Francia, "Assessing the Labor-Democratic Party Alliance: A One-Sided Relationship?" *Polity* 42 (2010): 293–302; Timothy J. Minchin, "A Pivotal Role? The AFL-CIO and the 2008 Presidential Election," *Labor History* 57 (2016): 299–322; Donald W. Beachler, "Victory and the Promise of Reform: Labor and the 2008 Election," *WorkingUSA* 12 (2009): 265–277; Jan E. Leighley and Jonathan Nagler, "Unions, Voter Turnout, and Class Bias in the US Electorate, 1964–2004," *Journal of Politics* 69 (2007): 430–441; Matthew T. Bodie, "Labor Interests and Corporate Power," *Boston University Law Review* 99 (2019): 1123–1249. Rosenthal in Thomas B. Edsall, "Republicans Sure Love to Hate Unions," *New York Times*, November 19, 2014.

9. Nathan Wilmers, "Labor Unions as Activist Organizations: A Union Power Approach to Estimating Union Wage Effects," *Social Forces* 95 (2017): 1451–1478.

10. Peter Gourevitch and James Shinn, *Political Power and Corporate Control: The New Global Politics of Corporate Governance* (Princeton, NJ: Princeton University Press, 2005), 22–23, 67, 274–276. I prefer the term "executives" to Gourevitch and Shinn's "managers." Managers are a heterogeneous group, most of whom take rather than make orders, unlike executives. Occasionally I follow Gourevitch and Shinn in referring to shareholders as owners, although the usage is problematic. What shareholders own is stock, not the company itself. Simon Deakin, a scholar of corporate law at Oxford University, writes, "It is surprisingly difficult to find support within company law for the notion of shareholder primacy. We cannot do it by referring to the claim that shareholders 'own the company.' In law, shareholders do not 'own the company'; if we take the company to be the fictive legal entity which is brought into being through the act of incorporation, it is not clear in what sense such a thing could be 'owned' by anyone. Nor does the ownership of a share entitle its holder to a particular segment or portion of the company's assets, at least while it is a going concern." Deakin, "The Coming Transformation of Shareholder Value," *Corporate Governance* 13 (January 2005): 11–18; Deakin, "Reversing Financialization: Shareholder Value and the Legal Reform of Corporate Governance," in *Corporate Governance in Contention*, ed. Ciaran Driver and Grahame Thompson (Oxford: Oxford University Press, 2018), 25–41.

11. Donald Van de Mark and Beverly Schuch, "Wall Street Editor from Newsweek Discusses The New Rich," *CNNfn*, July 29, 1997; Jon Talton, "Jon Talton Column," *Charlotte Observer*, May 24, 1998; Edward N. Wolff, "Household Wealth Trends in the United States, 1962 to 2016: Has Middle Class Wealth Recovered," working paper 24085, National Bureau of Economic Research, 2017; Emmanuel Saez and Gabriel Zucman, "Wealth Inequality in the United States since 1913: Evidence from Capitalized Income Tax Data," *Quarterly Journal of Economics* 131, no. 2 (2016): 519–578. These figures do not include traditional pension plans, only 401(k)s, IRAs, and other individual accounts.

12. I assume an equity allocation of 50 percent in DB plans. Wolff, "Household Wealth"; US Department of Labor, Employee Benefits Security Administration, Private Pension Plan Bulletin Historical Tables and Graphs, 1975–2016 (September 2019).

13. On the variety of investor preferences, see Henrik Cronqvist and Rüdiger Fahlenbrach, "Large Shareholders and Corporate Policies," *Review of Financial Studies* 22 (2008): 3941–3976; Martijn Cremers and Ankur Pareek, "Patient Capital Outperformance: The Investment Skill of High Active Share Managers Who Trade Infrequently," *Journal of Financial Economics* 122, no. 2 (2016): 288–306.

14. http://www.pensionrights.org/publications/statistic/how-many-american-workers -participate-workplace-retirement-plans; Alicia H. Munnell and Dina Bleckman, "Is Pension Coverage a Problem in the Private Sector?" Center for Retirement Research, Boston College, April 2014, Number 14-7.

15. Sandy Klasa, William F. Maxwell, and Hernán Ortiz-Molina, "The Strategic Use of Corporate Cash Holdings in Collective Bargaining with Labor Unions," *Journal of Financial Economics* 92 (2009): 421–442; Robert N. Stern, "Participation by Representation: Workers on Boards of Directors in the United States and Abroad," *Work and Occupations* 15 (1988): 396–422; Rafael Gomez and Konstantinos Tzioumis, "What Do Unions Do to Executive Compensation?" Centre for Economic Performance, London School of Economics and Political Science, 2006.

16. Neil Fligstein, "The Intraorganizational Power Struggle: Rise of Finance Personnel to Top Leadership in Large Corporations, 1919–1979," *American Sociological Review* (1987): 44–58. Even the physical appearance of CEOs and directors affects relationships with investors. Joseph Taylor Halford and Scott Hsu, "Beauty Is Wealth: CEO Appearance and Shareholder Value," SSRN Working Paper 2357756 (2014); Philipp Geiler, Luc Renneboog, and Yang Zhao, "Beauty and Appearance in Corporate Director Elections," *Journal of International Financial Markets, Institutions and Money* 55 (2018): 1–12.

Chapter 1. Labor, Finance, and the Corporation

1. Raghuram Rajan and Luigi Zingales, "The Great Reversals: The Politics of Financial Development in the Twentieth Century," *Journal of Financial Economics* 69, no. 1 (2003): 5–50; Rajan and Zingales's fourth measure is the ratio of bank deposits to gross domestic product (GDP).

2. Thomas Piketty and Emmanuel Saez, "Income Inequality in the United States, 1913–1998," *Quarterly Journal of Economics* 118 (2003): 1–41; Wojciech Kopczuk and Emmanuel Saez, "Top Wealth Shares in the United States, 1916–2000," NBER working paper 10399 (2004); Thomas Piketty, *Capital in the Twenty-First Century*, trans. Arthur Goldhammer (Cambridge, MA: Harvard University Press, 2014), 316, 349; Stijn Claessens and Enrico Perotti, "Finance and Inequality: Channels and Evidence," *Journal of Comparative Economics* 35, no. 4 (2007): 748–773; Jesper Roine, Jonas Vlachos, and Daniel Waldenström, "The Long-Run Determinants of Inequality: What Can We Learn from Top Income Data?" *Journal of Public Economics* 93, nos. 7–8 (2009): 974–988.

3. Margaret M. Blair, *Ownership and Control: Rethinking Corporate Governance for the Twenty-First Century* (Washington, DC: Brookings Institution, 1995); Sanford M. Jacoby, "Corporate Governance and Employees in the United States," in *Corporate Governance and Labour Management*, ed. H. Gospel and A. Pendleton (Oxford: Oxford University Press, 2005), 33–58; Thomas K. McCraw, *Prophets of Regulation* (Cambridge, MA: Harvard University Press, 2009).

On blockholders, see Alex Edmans and Clifford G. Holderness, "Blockholders: A Survey of Theory and Evidence," *Handbook of the Economics of Corporate Governance*, ed. Benjamin E. Hermalin and Michael S. Weisbach (Amsterdam: Elsevier, 2017).

4. Bradley R. Schiller and Randall D. Weiss, "Pensions and Wages: A Test for Equalizing Differences," *Review of Economics and Statistics* 62 (November 1980): 529; Richard B. Freeman, "Unions, Pensions, and Union Pension Funds," in *Pensions, Labor, and Individual Choice*, ed. David A. Wise (Chicago: University of Chicago Press, 1985), 89–122. The cited figure is three times the current coverage level. See table 2.2.

5. John G. Ruggie, "International Regimes, Transactions, and Change: Embedded Liberalism in the Postwar Economic Order," *International Organization* 36, no. 2 (1982): 379–415.

6. Louis Hartz, *Economic Policy and Democratic Thought* (Cambridge, MA: Harvard University Press, 1948); Mark Roe, *Strong Managers, Weak Owners: The Political Roots of American Corporate Finance* (Princeton, NJ: Princeton University Press, 1994); David Montgomery, *Beyond Equality: Labor and the Radical Republicans, 1862–1872* (Urbana: University of Illinois Press, 1967), 445; Jonathan Lurie, "Commodities Exchanges, Agrarian Political Power, and the Antioption Battle, 1890–1894," *Agricultural History* 48 (1974): 115–125; Samuel Rezneck, "Unemployment, Unrest, and Relief in the United States during the Depression of 1893–1897," *Journal of Political Economy* 61, no. 4 (1953): 324–345; Irving Bernstein, "Samuel Gompers and Free Silver: 1896," *Mississippi Valley Historical Review* 29, no. 3 (1942): 394–400; Lawrence Goodwyn, *The Populist Movement: A Short History of the Agrarian Revolt in America* (New York: Oxford University Press, 1978), 278–284.

7. Gompers's misgivings were proved correct in the 1908 Danbury Hatters's case (*Loewe v. Lawlor*, 208 U.S. 274), when the Supreme Court ruled that secondary boycotts were unlawful, which entitled the plaintiff to triple damages as permitted under the Sherman Act.

8. Stanley I. Kutler, "Labor, the Clayton Act, and the Supreme Court," *Labor History* 3, no. 1 (1962): 19–38; Daniel R. Ernst, *Lawyers against Labor: From Individual Rights to Corporate Liberalism* (Champaign: University of Illinois Press, 1995).

9. Morton J. Horwitz, *The Transformation of American Law, 1780–1860* (Cambridge, MA: Harvard University Press, 1977), chap. 6; Morton J. Horwitz, *The Transformation of American Law, 1870–1960: The Crisis of Legal Orthodoxy* (New York: Oxford University Press, 1992), chap. 3.

10. Louis D. Brandeis, *Other People's Money and How the Bankers Use It* (New York: Stokes, 1914), 92, 203.

11. Louis D. Brandeis, *Business—A Profession* (Boston: Small, Maynard, 1914), 2; Jerry W. Markham, *A Financial History of the United States: From J. P. Morgan to the Institutional Investor* (Armonk, NY: M.E. Sharpe, 2002); Samuel Haber, *Efficiency and Uplift: Scientific Management in the Progressive Era* (Chicago: University of Chicago Press, 1964), 53–84.

12. Richard P. Adelstein, "'Islands of Conscious Power': Louis D. Brandeis and the Modern Corporation," *Business Historical Review* 63, no. 3 (1989): 614–656, at 622; Louis D. Brandeis, "Banker-Management: Why It Has Failed; A Lesson from the New Haven," *Harper's Weekly*, August 10, 1913; Brandeis, *Other People's Money*, 204; William Gomberg, "Union Policy Experimentation in a Volatile Industry," *Labor History* 9, no. 1 (1968): 69–81; Steven Fraser, *Labor Will Rule: Sidney Hillman and the Rise of American Labor* (New York: Free Press, 1991), 79–83; Brandeis, *Business—A Profession*, 1–12; Saul Engelbourg, "Edward A. Filene: Merchant, Civic Leader, and Jew," *American Jewish Historical Quarterly* 66, no. 1 (1976): 106–122. Also see Daniel

Nelson, *Managers and Workers: Origins of the Twentieth-Century Factory System in the United States, 1880–1920* (Madison: University of Wisconsin Press, 1996).

13. James Weinstein, "Radicalism in the Midst of Normalcy," *Journal of American History* 52, no. 4 (1966): 773–790; Cedric Cowing, "Sons of the Wild Jackass and the Stock Market," *Business History Review* 33, no. 2 (1959): 138–155; Julia C. Ott, *When Wall Street Met Main Street* (Cambridge, MA: Harvard University Press, 2011), 79, 113. There are exceptions to my generalization about the AFL. For example, Gompers wrote to Treasury Secretary William G. McAdoo in 1917 to complain that "the banking interests of all countries with control over credit agencies have a determining control of all industrial, commercial, agricultural, and mining operations." Gompers to McAdoo, Feb. 5, 1917, in *The Samuel Gompers Papers, Vol 10: The American Federation of Labor and the Great War, 1917–18*, ed. Peter J. Albert and Grace Palladino (Urbana: University of Illinois Press, 2007), 5.

14. Nick Salvatore, *Eugene V. Debs: Citizen and Socialist* (Urbana: University of Illinois Press, 2007); Daniel Bell, *Marxian Socialism in the United States* (Princeton, NJ: Princeton University Press, 1952); Steve Fraser, *Every Man a Speculator: A History of Wall Street in American Life* (New York: HarperCollins, 2005), 343–345; Howard Brick, *Transcending Capitalism: Visions of a New Society in Modern American Thought* (Ithaca, NY: Cornell University Press, 2006), 45; Rudolf Hilferding, *Finance Capital: A Study in the Latest Phase of Capitalist Development*, ed. Tom Bottomore, trans. Morris Watnick and Sam Gordon (Milton Park, Oxfordshire, UK: Routledge, 2006), 180.

15. Brandeis, *Other People's Money*, 220.

16. Princeton University, Industrial Relations Section, *The Labor Banking Movement in the United States* (Princeton, NJ: Princeton University Press, 1929), passim; Russell D. Kilborne, "The Labour Bank Movement in the United States," *Economica* 15 (1925): 294. By the time the BLE opened the Co-operative National Bank of Cleveland in 1920, another union, the Machinists, already had established the Mount Vernon Savings Bank in Washington, DC.

17. Princeton, *Labor Banking*, 104, 145, 227; Irving Bernstein, *The Lean Years: A History of the American Worker, 1920–1933* (Boston: Houghton Mifflin, 1960), 103–104; Edward W. Morehouse, "Labor Institutionalism: Banking," in *American Labor Dynamics: In the Light of Post-War Developments*, ed. J.B.S. Hardman (New York: Russell & Russell, 1928), 310–319; Richard Boeckel, *Labor's Money* (New York: Harcourt, Brace, 1923).

18. Susan Roth Breitzer, *Jewish Labor's Second City: The Formation of a Jewish Working Class in Chicago, 1886–1928* (PhD diss., University of Iowa, 2007), 219; Daniel Soyer, *Jewish Immigrant Associations and American Identity, 1880–1939* (Detroit: Wayne State University Press, 1997); Fraser, *Labor Will Rule*, 216–219.

19. Princeton, *Labor Banking*, 135.

20. Nelson, *Unemployment Insurance*, 89–92; Princeton, *Labor Banking*, 131–35; Bernstein, *Lean Years*, 338.

21. Beverly Gage, *The Day Wall Street Exploded: A Story of America in Its First Age of Terror* (New York: Oxford University Press, 2009); Kevin Phillips, *Wealth and Democracy: A Political History of the American Rich* (New York: Broadway Books, 2002): 43; Sanford M. Jacoby, *Employing Bureaucracy: Managers, Unions, and the Transformation of Work in the Twentieth Century* (Mahwah, NJ: Lawrence Erlbaum, 2004), chap. 6; Richard Kirkendall, "A. A. Berle, Jr., Student of the Corporation, 1917–1932," *Business History Review* 35, no. 1 (1961), 43–58, esp. 48–49.

22. Fraser, *Every Man a Speculator*, 391, 401; *Saturday Evening Post* quoted in Cedric B. Cowing, *Populists, Plungers, and Progressives: A Social History of Stock and Commodity Speculation, 1868–1932* (Princeton, NJ: Princeton University Press, 1965), 170.

23. According to the AFL, between 1927 and 1928, capital gains rose by 70 percent, dividends by 7 percent, and wages by 1.5 percent. At International Harvester—a bellwether corporation in its day—wages barely budged during the 1920s despite the firm's record profits. Irving Bernstein, *The Lean Years: A History of the American Workers, 1920–1933* (Boston: Houghton Mifflin, 1960), 63–65; Cowing, *Populists, Plungers,* 170–173; Robert Ozanne, *Wages in Practice and Theory* (Madison: University of Wisconsin Press, 1968), 49; Gardner C. Means, "The Diffusion of Stock Ownership in the United States," *Quarterly Journal of Economics* 44 (1930): 600.

24. After Berle became a consultant to the Temporary National Economic Committee (TNEC), created by Congress during the late 1930s to study monopoly in the American economy, he said that the committee "should not assume that all monopoly was bad, that cartels were necessarily harmful, that small business was necessarily competitive or necessarily humane, or that big business necessarily grew by predatory tactics." Adolf A. Berle Jr. and Gardiner C. Means, *The Modern Corporation and Private Property* (New York: Commerce Clearing House, 1932); Jordan A. Schwarz, *Liberal: Adolf A. Berle and the Vision of an American Era* (New York: Free Press, 1987), 51, 74, 135; Ellis Hawley, *The New Deal and the Problem of Monopoly* (Princeton, NJ: Princeton University Press, 1966), 307; 460–461; Brandeis, *Business—A Profession,* 189.

25. A recent analysis suggests that Means overstated his case. Better data show that the top 1 percent by wealth saw their holdings of all equities fall sharply between 1913 and 1919, but the figure went back up during the 1920s, recovering half of its decline and peaking in 1929. The long slide in the portion of all equities held by the top 1 percent began in the 1930s and continued until the late 1970s. TNEC also investigated blockholding, the ownership of a sufficiently large number of shares to grant control. Assessing blockholding's effects depends on the choice of an ownership level that confers control. Today as in the past, substantial blocks remain in the hands of families and founders. Family firms comprise over 35 percent of the S&P 500 and on average families own 18 percent of their firm's shares. Stock ownership calculated from data at http://gabriel-zucman.eu/usdina/ and Wojciech Kopczuk and Emmanuel Saez, "Top Wealth Shares in the United States, 1916–2000: Evidence from Estate Tax Returns," *National Tax Journal* 57 (2004): 445–487. Also see Mihir A. Desai, Dhammika Dharmapala, and Winnie Fung, "Taxation and the Evolution of Aggregate Corporate Ownership Concentration," paper no. w11469 (Cambridge, MA: National Bureau of Economic Research, 2005); Marco Becht and J. Bradford DeLong, "Why Has There Been So Little Blockholding in America?" in *A History of Corporate Governance Around the World,* ed. Randall Morck (Chicago: University of Chicago Press, 2005), 613–666; Maurice Zeitlin, "Corporate Ownership and Control: The Large Corporation and the Capitalist Class," *American Journal of Sociology* 79, no. 5 (1974): 1073–1119; Philip Burch, *The Managerial Revolution Reassessed: Family Control in America's Large Corporations* (Lexington, MA: Heath, 1972).

26. Berle and Means, *Modern Corporation,* 310–311; Schwarz, *Liberal,* 106–108, 135–140. Elsewhere Berle posited the same thesis: "All powers granted to a corporation or to the management of a corporation, or to any group within the corporation . . . [are] at all times exercisable only for the ratable benefit of all the shareholders as their interest appears." A. A. Berle Jr., "Corporate

Powers as Powers in Trust," *Harvard Law Review* 44 (1931): 1049. Curiously, Berle and Means had little to say about directors, who generally were held in low regard. Shortly before he became a Supreme Court justice in 1939, William O. Douglas—then chairman of the SEC—gave an address in which he excoriated corporate boards. Douglas called for their replacement by salaried, professional directors, the idea later picked up by Ralph Nader. William O. Douglas, "Corporation Directors" in Douglas, *Democracy and Finance* (New Haven, CT: Yale University Press, 1940), 46–55.

27. E. Merrick Dodd Jr., "For Whom Are Corporate Managers Trustees?" *Harvard Law Review* 45, no. 8 (1932): 1145–1163.

28. Berle and Means, *Modern Corporation*, 356; A. A. Berle Jr., "For Whom Are Corporate Managers Trustees? A Note," *Harvard Law Review* 45 (1932): 1365–1372. Although Berle was chair of the American Labor Party (ALP) and friends with David Dubinsky, the head of the International Ladies Garment Workers Union, he had little of Brandeis's idealism when it came to labor. The ALP merely was a vehicle for Berle's private ambitions. Means was similarly dispassionate about labor. He had been impressed by Josephine Roche's experiments in union–management cooperation at the coal company she owned, Rocky Mountain Fuel, and by the broad-mindedness of labor leaders who participated in code formulation under the National Recovery Act, but, after finishing the book with Berle, he never again wrote about corporate governance. Schwarz, *Berle*, 159–161, 292–293; Frederic S. Lee, "From Multi-Industry Planning to Keynesian Planning: Gardiner Means, the American Keynesians, and National Economic Planning at the National Resources Committee," *Journal of Policy History* 2 (1990): 186–212; Frederic S. Lee and Warren J. Samuels, eds., *The Heterodox Economics of Gardiner C. Means: A Collection* (Armonk, NY: M.E. Sharpe, 1992), 64; Robyn Muncy, *Relentless Reformer: Josephine Roche and Progressivism in Twentieth-Century America* (Princeton, NJ: Princeton University Press, 2015).

29. Regarding the silver standard, Coughlin contended that "God wills it—this religious crusade against the pagan of gold. Silver is the key to prosperity—silver that was damned by the Morgans." Members of the House and Senate pressured Roosevelt to send Coughlin to the 1933 London Conference on the gold standard, and in 1934 Congress passed the Silver Purchase Act, a mostly symbolic gesture. While "gold bugs" were around for years after the Depression, they regained respectability during the 1980s, when congressional Republicans and supply-side economists advocated for a new gold standard. William E. Leuchtenberg, *Franklin D. Roosevelt and the New Deal* (New York: Harper & Row, 1963), 101; Alan Brinkley, *Voices of Protest: Huey Long, Father Coughlin, and the Great Depression* (New York: Knopf, 1982), 113; Barry Eichengreen, *Golden Fetters: The Gold Standard and the Great Depression, 1919–1939* (New York: Oxford University Press, 1992); Daniel J. B. Mitchell, "Dismantling the Cross of Gold: Economic Crises and U.S. Monetary Policy," *North American Journal of Economics and Finance* 11, no. 1 (2000): 77–104.

30. Mitchell, "Dismantling the Cross of Gold," 103; Alan Brinkley, *Voices of Protest*, 140, 150, 171.

31. Michael Perino, *The Hellhound of Wall Street: How Ferdinand Pecora's Investigation of the Great Crash Forever Changed American Finance* (New York: Penguin, 2010); Vincent Carosso, "Washington and Wall Street: The New Deal and Investment Bankers, 1933–1940," *Business History Review* 44, no. 4 (1970): 425–445; James H. Mathias, "Manipulative Practices and the Securities Exchange Act," *University of Pittsburgh Law Review* 3 (1936–37): 104–119; James W.

Moore and Frank M. Wiseman, "Market Manipulation and the Exchange Act," *University of Chicago Law Review* 2 (1934): 46–77. At today's prices, Mitchell's pay was worth around $50 million. He later was acquitted of criminal charges.

32. Leuchtenberg, *Roosevelt*, 54–56, 60; Roe, *Strong Managers*, 42; Cowing, *Populists, Plungers*, 223; Charles R. Geisst, *Undue Influence: How the Wall Street Elite Put the Financial System at Risk* (Hoboken, NJ: John Wiley & Sons, 2004), 68; Paul Studenski and Herman E. Kroos, *Financial History of the United States* (New York: McGraw-Hill, 1952), 363; Herbert M. Bratter, "The Silver Episode: II," *Journal of Political Economy* 46, no. 6 (1938): 802–837; Hawley, *The New Deal*, 307; Burton A. Abrams and Russell F. Settle, "Pressure-Group Influence and Institutional Change: Branch Banking Legislation During the Great Depression, *Public Choice* 77 (1993): 697–705; Harwell Wells, "U.S. Executive Compensation in Historical Perspective," in *Research Handbook on Executive Compensation*, ed. Randall S. Thomas and Jennifer G. Hill (Northampton, MA: Elgar, 2012), 41–57. One estimate is that the disclosure rules restrained compensation among the top 2 percent of CEOs but otherwise did not reduce CEO pay. Alex Mas, "Does Disclosure Affect CEO Pay Setting? Evidence from the Passage of the 1934 Securities and Exchange Act," Working Paper, Princeton Economics Department, March 2016.

33. Fraser, *Every Man a Speculator*, 444–447, 473; Ruggie, "International Regimes," 387; Elizabeth A. Fones-Wolf, *Selling Free Enterprise: The Business Assault on Labor and Liberalism, 1945–60* (Urbana: University of Illinois Press, 1994), 49.

34. Ruggie, "International Regimes"; Patrick Renshaw, "Organised Labour and the U.S. War Economy," *Journal of Contemporary History* 21, no. 1 (1986): 3–22; Nelson Lichtenstein, *Walter Reuther: The Most Dangerous Man in Detroit* (Urbana: University of Illinois Press, 1995); Fraser, *Labor Will Rule*.

35. Studenski and Kroos, *Financial History*, 471; William L. Cary, "Pressure Groups and the Revenue Code: A Requiem in Honor of the Departing Uniformity of the Tax Laws," *Harvard Law Review* 68, no. 5 (1955): 745–780; Boris Shiskin, "Organized Labor and the Veteran," *Annals of the American Academy of Political and Social Science* 238 (1945): 146–157; Robert M. Collins, "The Economic Crisis of 1968 and the Waning of the 'American Century,'" *American Historical Review* 101 (1996): 396–422; Piketty, *Capital in the Twenty-First Century*, 316.

36. Lichtenstein, *Walter Reuther*, passim; G. W. Schwert, "Indexes of U.S. Stock Prices from 1802 to 1987," *Journal of Business* 63, no. 3 (1990): 399–426; Frank Levy and Peter Temin, "Institutions and Wages in Post–World War II America," in *Labor in the Era of Globalization*, ed. Clair Brown, Barry Eichengreen, and Michael Reich (Cambridge: Cambridge University Press, 2010), 15–49; Dalia Tsuk, "Corporations without Labor: The Politics of Progressive Corporate Law," *University of Pennsylvania Law Review* 51, no. 5 (2003): 1861–1912.

37. Jack Barbash, "The Structure and Influence of Union Interests in Pensions," Joint Economic Committee, Subcommittee on Fiscal Policy, Old Age Income Assurance, Part IV, December 1967, 60–97; Testimony of Jack Barbash in US Congress, Senate Committee on Labor and Public Welfare, "Labor Union Welfare Funds" (Washington, DC: US GPO, 1955); interview with Ron Blackwell, chief economist, AFL-CIO, March 2007, Washington, DC; Peter Gourevitch and James Shinn, *Political Power and Corporate Control: The New Global Politics of Corporate Governance* (Princeton, NJ: Princeton University Press, 2005), 217.

In preparing for the Obama presidency, an AFL-CIO study group recommended placing employees and retirees on the boards of corporate plans. On earlier occasions, unions sought to take unilateral control of a pension fund away from its corporate sponsor, as at bankrupt

Eastern Airlines in the early 1980s. Interview with Dan Pedrotty, director, AFL-CIO Office of Investment, November 2009, Washington, DC; Randy Barber, "Breaking New Ground: Pension Fund Bargaining at Eastern," *Labor Research Review* 1, no. 4 (1984): 75–92; Michael A. McCarthy, "Turning Labor into Capital: Pension Funds and the Corporate Control of Finance," *Politics and Society* 42, no. 4 (2014): 467.

38. Jacoby, *Employing Bureaucracy*, 39–40, 146–49; Sanford M. Jacoby, *Modern Manors: Welfare Capitalism since the New Deal* (Princeton, NJ: Princeton University Press, 1997), chaps. 3 and 6; Peter W. Seburn, "Evolution of Employer-Provided Defined Benefit Pensions," *Monthly Labor Review*, December 1991, 16–21; Steven A. Sass, *The Promise of Private Pensions: The First Hundred Years* (Cambridge, MA: Harvard University Press, 1997).

39. Francis X. Sutton, Seymour Harris, Carl Kaysen, and James Tobin, *The American Business Creed* (Cambridge, MA: Harvard University Press, 1956), 64–65.

40. Sutton et al., *Business Creed*, 84–88; Mary O'Sullivan, "Living with the U.S. Financial System: The Experiences of General Electric and Westinghouse in the Last Century," *Business History Review* 80, no. 4 (2006): 621–655; Carola Frydman and Raven E. Saks, "Executive Compensation: A New View from a Long-Term Perspective, 1936–2005," *Review of Financial Studies* 23 (2010): 2099–2138.

41. John Kenneth Galbraith, *American Capitalism: The Concept of Countervailing Power* (Boston: Houghton Mifflin, 1952); C. Wright Mills, *The Power Elite* (New York: Oxford University Press, 1956); Robert A. Dahl, *Who Governs? Democracy and Power in an American City* (New Haven, CT: Yale University Press, 1961).

42. Robert A. Dahl, *After the Revolution? Authority in the Good Society* (New Haven, CT: Yale University Press, 1970), 102; and Abram Chayes, "The Modern Corporation and the Rule of Law," in *The Corporation in Modern Society*, ed. Edward S. Mason (Cambridge, MA: Harvard University Press, 1959), 41, both cited in Ralph Nader, Mark Green, and Joel Seligman, *Taming the Giant Corporation: How the Largest Corporations Control Our Lives* (New York: W.W. Norton, 1976); Robert A. Dahl, "Business and Politics: A Critical Appraisal of Political Science," *American Political Science Review* 53 (1959): 1–34; Colleen A. Dunlavy, "Social Conceptions of the Corporation: Insights from the History of Shareholder Voting Rights," *Washington and Lee Law Review* 63 (2006): 1347–1388. For a contemporary take, see Kent Greenfield, "The Stakeholder Strategy," *Democracy* 26 (2012): 47–59.

43. https://www.eisenhower.archives.gov/all_about_ike/speeches/farewell_address.pdf, accessed November 16, 2018; Seymour Martin Lipset and William Schneider, *The Confidence Gap: Business, Labor and Government in the Public Mind* (Baltimore, MD: Johns Hopkins University Press, 1987); https://history.hanover.edu/courses/excerpts/111huron.html

44. Correspondence with Andy Banks, Teamsters, June 3, 2010; Jarol B. Manheim, *The Death of a Thousand Cuts: Comprehensive Campaigns and the Attack on the Corporation* (Mahwah, NJ: Lawrence Erlbaum, 2001), passim.

45. G. William Domhoff, *Who Rules America?* (Englewood Cliffs, NJ: Prentice-Hall, 1967).

46. "Playboy Interview: Saul Alinsky," *Playboy Magazine*, March 1972, 3, 59–78, 150, 169–173, 176–178 at http://www.freerepublic.com/focus/f-news/3451533/posts

47. Terry Anderson, "The New American Revolution: The Movement and Business," in *The Sixties: From Memory to History*, ed. David Farber (Chapel Hill: University of North Carolina Press, 1994); "Playboy Interview: Saul Alinsky."

48. Nader never defined "accountability" but often used it in conjunction with "responsibility." In his view, accountability would not occur by appealing to a CEO's conscience but by empowering stakeholders such as unions, consumers, and shareholders. Nader distrusted bureaucracy in any form and sought to expand accountability to government and international organizations. During the 1970s, he drafted what he called a Civil Service Accountability Bill and later took on the World Trade Organization. Ralph Nader, "Consumerism and Legal Services: The Merging of Movements," *Law and Society Review* 11(1976): 247–256; Nader, "GATT, NAFTA, and the Subversion of the Democratic Process," in *The Case against the Global Economy*, ed. Jerry Mander and Edward Goldsmith (San Francisco: Sierra Club Books, 1997).

49. Donald E. Schwartz, "The Public-Interest Proxy Contest: Reflections on Campaign GM," *Michigan Law Review* 69, no. 3 (1971): 419–538; Ralph Nader, Mark Green, and Joel Seligman, *Constitutionalizing the Corporation: The Case for Federal Chartering of Giant Corporations* (Washington, DC: CARG, 1976); Mark Green, "The Case for Corporate Democracy," *Regulation: AEI Journal on Government and Society* (May–June 1980): 20–25; Nader et al., *Taming the Giant Corporation*, 123; Luther J. Carter, "Campaign GM: Reformers Lose on Vote but Not on Influence," *Science*, May 29, 1970, 1077–1078; James Phelan and Robert Pozen, *The Company State: Ralph Nader's Study Group Report on DuPont in Delaware* (New York: Grossman, 1973). Nader never stopped being a shareholder activist. "Nader, an Adversary of Capitalism, Now Fights as an Investor," *New York Times*, January 15, 2014.

50. Jules Bernstein, Mark Green, Vic Kamber, and Alice Tepper Marlin, "Conceptual Draft of Corporate Democracy Act," in *The Big Business Reader: On Corporate America*, ed. Mark Green (New York: Pilgrim Press, 1983), 500–511; Green, "The Case for Corporate Democracy"; Ralph Nader and Mark Green, "Corporate Democracy," *New York Times*, December 28, 1979; Philip Shabecoff, "Law Against Business Abuse Urged," *New York Times*, December 13, 1979; Donald Feder, "Naderizing the Giant Corporation," *Reason*, August 1980; Benjamin Waterstone, "The Corporate Mobilization against Liberal Reform: Big Business Day, 1980," in *What's Good for Business: Business and American Politics since World War II*, ed. Kim Phillips-Fein and Julian E. Zelizer (New York: Oxford University Press, 2012), 233–248.

51. S. Prakash Sethi and Oliver F. Williams, *Economic Imperatives and Ethical Values in Global Business: The South African Experience and International Codes Today* (New York: Springer, 2000); "It's the Season for Stockholders," *Chemical Week*, March 24, 1982, 14; E. J. Kahn, "Annals of International Trade," *New Yorker*, May 14, 1979, 117–149; Sarah Bernstein, "CalPERS Divestment Research Report," Pension Consulting Alliance, September 2008; Rockefeller, quoted in Anderson, "New American Revolution," 187.

52. Investor Responsibility Research Center, "Shareholder Nomination of Candidates for Director," Analysis no. 7, April 16, 1973; "Wider Audience for Annual Meetings," *Chemical Week*, April 19, 1978, 52; Alice Tepper Marlin and Susan Young, "Prying Open the Clam: On Proxies, Secrecy, and Social Accountability," in Green, *Big Business Reader*, 385–390. For an overview, see David Vogel, *Lobbying the Corporation: Citizen Challenges to Business Authority* (New York: Free Press, 1978).

53. Judith Stein, *Pivotal Decade: How the United States Traded Factories for Finance in the 1970s* (New Haven, CT: Yale University Press, 2010).

54. Barry Bluestone and Bennett Harrison, *The Deindustrialization of America* (New York: Basic Books, 1982); Daniel J. B. Mitchell, "Union vs. Nonunion Wage Norm Shifts," *American*

Economic Review 76, no. 2 (1986): 249–252; William J. Baumol, Alan S. Blinder, and Edward N. Wolff, *Downsizing in America: Reality, Causes, and Consequences* (New York: Russell Sage, 2003); Michael Goldfield, *The Decline of Organized Labor in the United States* (Chicago: University of Chicago Press, 1987); US Bureau of Labor Statistics, "Major Work Stoppages in 2009," February 2010, accessed November 21, 2018, https://www.bls.gov/news.release/archives/wkstp _02102010.pdf

55. Richard B. Freeman and James L. Medoff, *What Do Unions Do?* (New York: Basic Books, 1984), chap. 15; Paul C. Weiler, *Governing the Workplace: The Future of Labor and Employment Law* (Cambridge, MA: Harvard University Press, 1990).

56. Emily Honig, "Women at Farah Revisited: Political Mobilization and Its Aftermath among Chicana Workers in El Paso, Texas, 1972–1992," *Feminist Studies* 22, no. 2 (1996): 425–452; Steven Greenhouse, "Jack Sheinkman, 77, Lawyer Led Clothing Workers' Union," *New York Times*, January 30, 2004; Manheim, *Death of a Thousand Cuts.*

57. Timothy J. Minchin, *Don't Sleep with Stevens! The J. P. Stevens Campaign and the Struggle to Organize the South, 1963–1980* (Gainesville: University of Florida Press, 2005); Manheim, *Death of a Thousand Cuts.* Sometimes corporate campaigns are called "comprehensive campaigns" or "capital campaigns." Research on the campaigns usually discusses the mobilization of workers and communities; less has been said about the campaigns' financial tactics. Kate Bronfenbrenner, Ronald Seeber, and Rudolph Oswald, eds., *Organizing to Win: New Research on Union Strategies* (Ithaca, NY: Cornell University Press, 1998); and Kate Bronfenbrenner, ed., *Global Unions: Challenging Transnational Capital through Cross-Border Campaigns* (Ithaca, NY: ILR Press, 2007); Jane F. McAlevey, *No Shortcuts: Organizing for Power in the New Gilded Age* (New York: Oxford University Press, 2016).

58. After the J. P. Stevens campaign, Ray Rogers started his own consultancy, Comprehensive Campaign, Inc. In later years, his reputation was hurt by perceptions of recklessness. William Serrin, "A Gadfly for Labor: Ray Rogers," *New York Times*, October 6, 1985, 6; Paul Jarley and Cheryl L. Maranto, "Union Corporate Campaigns: An Assessment," *ILR Review* 43 (1990): 506.

59. Charles Madigan, "How Union 'Wrapped' Textile Giant J. P. Stevens," *Chicago Tribune*, October 26, 1980.

60. Minchin, "'Don't Sleep'"; Ed McConville, "5 Years After Union Victory, Battle Goes on at J. P. Stevens," *Washington Post*, August 29, 1979; Warren Brown, "Great Labor War Gains Tallied," *Washington Post*, October 26, 1980; David Vogel, *The Market for Virtue* (Washington, DC: Brookings, 2005), 180–181. In 1995, ACTWU merged with the International Ladies Garment Workers Union (ILGWU) to create UNITE, the Union of Needle Trades, Industrial and Textile Employees.

61. Metcalf quoted in Jeremy Rifkin and Randy Barber, *The North Will Rise Again: Pensions, Politics and Power in the 1980s* (Boston: Beacon Press, 1978), 149.

62. "Shareholders Contest Announced," *PR Newswire*, December 3, 1987; Kenneth Noble, "Organized Labor; Taking the Fight to the Shareholder," *New York Times*, March 20,1988, 4; "Echlin Inc. Opposes Group's Resolutions on Asbestos Issues," *Wall Street Journal*, December 15, 1987; Trudy Ring, "Unions Putting Votes to Work; Corporate Governance Issues Targeted," *Pensions & Investment Age*, September 5, 1988.

63. Andrew J. Hoffman, "A Strategic Response to Investor Activism," *Sloan Management Review* 37, no. 2 (1996): 51–64; Manheim, *Death of a Thousand Cuts*, 195; "Two Labor Unions

Launch an Independent Shareholder Solicitation at Kodak," *PR Newswire*, May 3, 1990; "Exxon Pressed Again," *Reuters News*, April 11, 1990; Michael Useem, *Investor Capitalism: How Money Managers Are Changing the Face of Corporate America* (New York: Basic Books, 1996), 40.

64. Jeffrey Marshall, "Amalgamated Bloodies Irksome Banks," *United States Banker*, October 1, 1991, 14.

65. James A. Craft, "The Employer Neutrality Pledge," *Labor Law Journal* 31 (1980): 753–763; Julius G. Getman, *Restoring the Power of Unions: It Takes a Movement* (New Haven, CT: Yale University Press, 2010), 80; Paul J. Baicich and Lance Compa, "Cooperate, Hell: Unions Get What They Fight For," *Washington Post*, December 1, 1984; Timothy J. Minchin, "A Successful Union in an Era of Decline: Interrogating the Growth of the Service Employees International Union, 1980–1995," *Labor History* (2020): 1–20; Richard B. Freeman, "Contraction and Expansion: The Divergence of Private Sector and Public Sector Unionism in the United States," *Journal of Economic Perspectives* 2, no. 2 (1988): 63–88.

66. Timothy J. Minchin, "A Successful Union in an Era of Decline: Interrogating the Growth of the Service Employees International Union, 1980–1995," *Labor History* (2020): 306–307; Dave Hage, "Organized Labor Learning New Tactics for Future Fights," *Star Tribune*, February 16, 1988; Joann S. Lublin, "Health Care Employees Are Target of Big Organizing Drive," *Wall Street Journal*, February 24, 1984; "The Picket Line Gives Way to Sophisticated New Tactics," *Business Week*, April 16, 1984, 116; "Beverly Enterprises Responds to Union Rights Campaign," *Dow-Jones News Service*, May 4, 1995; Neil Steward, "Hard to Swallow," *Investor Relations*, September 1, 1995; Charles Perry, *Union Comprehensive Campaigns* (Philadelphia: Wharton School Press, 1987). After more than twenty years, the Beverly campaign yielded few new members other than in Pennsylvania, Andy Stern's original bailiwick. After twenty years, there was resistance inside the union to continuing the Beverly effort, given what Stern said were "limited financial and staff resources." Minchin, "A Successful Union," 307.

67. Bank for International Settlements, *Semiannual Over-the-Counter (OTC) Derivatives Markets Statistics* (Basel, CH: 2008); Rajan and Zingales, "The Great Reversals," 13–15; Charles R. Morris, *The Two Trillion Dollar Meltdown: Easy Money, High Rollers, and the Great Credit Crash* (New York: Public Affairs, 2008); Blair, *Ownership and Control*, 46.

68. Milton Friedman, *Capitalism and Freedom* (Chicago: University of Chicago Press, 1962), 133–135, 178–180; Angus Burgin, *The Great Persuasion: Reinventing Free Markets since the Great Depression* (Cambridge, MA: Harvard University Press, 2012).

69. Among the leading proponents of shareholder primacy are Stephen A. Ross, "The Economic Theory of Agency: The Principal's Problem," *American Economic Review* 63, no. 2 (1973): 134–139; Michael C. Jensen and William H. Meckling, "Theory of the Firm: Managerial Behavior, Agency Costs, and Ownership Structure," *Journal of Financial Economics* 3, no. 4 (1976): 305–360; Michael C. Jensen and Richard S. Ruback, "The Market for Corporate Control: The Scientific Evidence," *Journal of Financial Economics* 11 (1983): 5–50; Michael C. Jensen, "Agency Costs of Free Cash Flow, Corporate Finance, and Takeovers," *American Economic Review* 76, no. 2 (1986): 323–329; Henry Hansmann and Reiner Kraakman, "The End of History for Corporate Law," *Georgetown Law Journal* 89, no. 2 (2001): 439–468. The 1919 case *Dodge v. Ford Motor Co.*, 204 Mich. 459, 170 N.W. 668, is often cited as legal justification for shareholder primacy, although the logic and relevance of the case have been repeatedly challenged. Einer R. Elhauge, "Sacrificing Corporate Profits in the Public Interest," *New York University Law Review*

80, no. 3 (2005): 138–140; Lynn M. LoPucki, "The Myth of the Residual Owner: An Empirical Study," *Washington University Law Quarterly* 82 (2004): 1341–1374; Iman Anabtawi and Lynn Stout, "Fiduciary Duties for Activist Shareholders," *Stanford Law Review* 60 (2007): 1255–1308.

70. Martha Derthick and Paul Quirk, *The Politics of Deregulation* (Washington, DC: Brookings Institution, 1985); J. P. Heinz, A. Southworth, and A. Paik, "Lawyers for Conservative Causes: Clients, Ideologies, and Social Distance," *Law and Society Review* 37, no. 1 (2003): 5–50; Cass R. Sunstein, *Radicals in Robes: Why Extreme Right-Wing Courts Are Wrong for America* (New York: Basic Books, 2005); Steven M. Teles, *The Rise of the Conservative Legal Movement* (Princeton, NJ: Princeton University Press, 2010); Philip C. Bobbitt, "The Age of Consent," *Yale Law Journal* 135, no. 7 (2013): 2334–2284; Nancy MacLean, *Democracy in Chains: The Deep History of the Radical Right's Plan for America* (New York: Viking Press, 2017).

71. Margaret M. Blair and Lynn A. Stout, "A Team Production Theory of Corporate Law," *Virginia Law Review* (1999): 247–328; Margaret M. Blair and Lynn A. Stout, "Director Accountability and the Mediating Role of the Corporate Board," *Washington University Law Quarterly* 79, no. 2 (2001): 403–448, at 422; Lynn Stout, *The Shareholder Value Myth: How Putting Shareholders First Harms Investors, Corporations, and the Public* (San Francisco: Berrett-Kohler, 2012), 30. Also see Stephen Bainbridge, "Director Primacy: The Means and Ends of Corporate Governance," *Northwestern University Law Review* 97, no. 2 (2003): 547–606. Firms must decide whether to rely on firm-specific investments or to buy resources from others. Roberts and Van den Steen contend that, when firms take the former approach, it isn't efficient to leave shareholders in charge. Instead, companies must "ced[e] a role in corporate governance to employees in order to motivate their investing in firm-specific human capital." John Roberts and Eric van den Steen, "Human Capital and Corporate Governance," in *Corporate Governance: Essays in Honor of Horst Albach*, ed. Horst Albach and Joachim Schwalbach (Berlin: Springer Verlag, 2001), 128–144.

72. Iman Anabtawi, "Some Skepticism about Increasing Shareholder Power," *UCLA Law Review* 53, no. 3 (2006): 575; Henrik Cronqvist and Rüdiger Fahlenbrach, "Large Shareholders and Corporate Policies," *Review of Financial Studies* 22, no. 10 (2009): 3941–3976.

Chapter 2. The CalPERS Era

1. Michael Useem, *Investor Capitalism: How Money Managers Are Changing the Face of Corporate America* (New York: Basic Books, 1996); Hilary Rosenberg, *A Traitor to His Class: Robert A. G. Monks and the Battle to Change Corporate America* (New York: John Wiley, 1999), 62–66, 97, 135. Monks was a true believer in shareholder primacy, even when evidence challenged his faith. Although he favored independent directors, he scoffed at Ralph Nader's idea of encouraging women and nonwhites to join boards. "A board is not the place to demonstrate a social conscience," he said, even though research showed that board diversity enhanced share prices. He also was dubious of studies showing that practices to empower shareholders had little or no effect on performance. When a prominent governance scholar produced studies critical of his ideas, Monks drubbed them as "academic self-indulgence." Rosenberg, *Traitor*, 288; "A Different Kind of Governance Guru," *Business Week*, August 9, 2004; David A. Carter, Betty Simkins, and W. G. Simpson, "Corporate Governance, Board Diversity, and Firm Value," *Financial Review*,

February 1, 2003; Renee Adams and Daniel Ferreira, "Women in the Boardroom and Their Impact on Governance and Performance," *Journal of Financial Economics* 94 (2009): 291–309.

2. Georgeson, *Annual Corporate Governance Review* (*ACGR*) 1996, 4; Rosenberg, *A Traitor to His Class*, 92.

3. Georgeson, *ACGR* 1996, 4.

4. Rosenberg, *A Traitor to His Class*, 93, 99, 217; Who Runs Your Company Anyway?" *Fortune*, September 12, 1988; "Bill of Rights Seeks to Boost Power of Shareholders," *Washington Post*, April 13, 1986; Mark Roe, "The Modern Corporation and Private Pensions," 41 *UCLA Law Review* (1993); Norman Stein, "Reversions from Pension Plans," *Tax Law Review* 44, no. 259 (1989): 259–334. Monks and his business partner, Nell Minow, put their ideas into practice via LENS, the hedge fund they owned. LENS professed the need for governance reforms to empower investors, such as stock options, independent boards, and removal of poison pills—the cookbook. LENS sometimes behaved like any other corporate raider, seeking to fire CEOS and obtain board seats to press companies to divest units and turn the cash over to shareholders. At Sears, where Monks established his reputation, the company responded to his demands for a board seat by buying back ten percent of its stock. Minow was known as "the CEO killer," credited with ousting twenty-two CEOs from their jobs. Corporations, said Monks, "are our [shareholders'] companies, and we don't have to permit them to do something we don't want done." Bruce Bigelow, "Shareholder Rights Activist Stands Up to Corporations," *San Diego Union-Tribune*, July 21, 2006. Jonathan R. Lainge, "Can You Count On Sears?—Wall Street May Be Overlooking Values in the Retail Giant," *Barron's*, May 18, 1992; Joann S. Lublin, "Dissident Investors Fight for Board Seats Without Seeking Full Control of Firms," *Wall Street Journal*, June 1, 1999; David S. Hilzenrath, "Performance' Options Getting a Second Look," *Washington Post*, April 1, 2001. Monks quoted in David A. Geracioti, "Bob Monks' 30-Year Crusade," *Registered Representative*, February 1, 2003.

5. Christopher Castaneda, "To Retire in Dignity and Comfort: A Decade-by-Decade History of CalPERS, 1920s–1990" (2004), manuscript on file with the CalPERS Library, Sacramento, California; Bill Boyarsky, *Big Daddy: Jesse Unruh and the Art of Power Politics* (Berkeley: University of California Press, 2007); "On Wall Street, More Investors Push Social Goals, *New York Times*, February 11, 2001.

6. Paul Harbrecht, S.J., *Pension Funds and Economic Power* (New York: Twentieth Century Fund, 1959), 204; Christopher Castaneda, "To Retire in Dignity"; Richard Stevenson, "California Battle over State Fund," *New York Times*, June 18, 1991. An excellent history of shareholder activism can be found in Richard Marens, "Inventing Corporate Governance: The Mid-Century Emergence of Shareholder Activism," *Journal of Business and Management* 8 (2002): 365–389.

7. Sanford M. Jacoby, "Convergence by Design: The Case of CalPERS in Japan," *American Journal of Comparative Law* 55, no. 2 (2007): 239–293; Rosenberg, *A Traitor to His Class*; "Bill of Rights Seeks to Boost Power of Shareholders," *Washington Post*, April 13, 1986.

8. Castaneda, "To Retire in Dignity," chaps. 1, 7; Stephen Choi and Jill Fisch, "On Beyond CalPERS: Survey Evidence on the Developing Role of Public Pension Funds in Corporate Governance," *Vanderbilt Law Review* 61 (2008): 315–354. The New York plan accounted for 70 percent of public-pension fund proposals voted on between 1996 and 2002.

9. Interview with Ed Durkin, Director of Corporate Affairs, United Brotherhood of Carpenters, April 2008, Washington, DC; Interview with Jackie Cook, specialist in corporate ESG

disclosure analysis, CERES, April 15, 2013. Valdes was one of several CalPERS officials later investigated for taking bribes from companies seeking CalPERS investments, but he was not indicted. Randy Diamond, "Guilty Plea Opens New Chapter in CalPERS Story," *Pensions and Investments* (hereafter *P&I*), July 21, 2014.

10. Rosenberg, *A Traitor to His Class*, 100, 121; Jacoby interview with Sarah Teslik, former executive director, The Council of Institutional Investors, May 2008, Washington, DC; Council of Institutional Investors, *End of Millennium Report* (Washington, DC: 2000); "Pension Fund Group Faces Its Own Governance Battle," *New York Times*, April 1, 1996; "TRW Leader Is Watchdog," *Cleveland Plain Dealer*, April 14, 1996; Interview with Dr. William D. Crist, former president of the board, CalPERS, February 2007, Turlock, California; Patrick McGurn, "DOL Issues New Guidelines on Proxy Voting," *IRRC Corporate Governance Bulletin* 11 (July–August 1994), 7. Martin Coyle of TRW was the first co-chairman from a corporate plan.

11. Useem, *Investor Capitalism*, 55.

12. Margaret Blair, *Ownership and Control: Rethinking Corporate Governance for the Twenty-First Century* (Washington, DC: Brookings, 1995), 46; Diane K. Denis and John J. McConnell, "International Corporate Governance," *Journal of Financial and Quantitative Analysis* 38 (2000):1–36; Carolyn Kay Brancato, *2007 Institutional Investment Report* (New York: Conference Board, 2007); Alex Edmans and Clifford G. Holderness, "Blockholders: A Survey of Theory and Evidence," ed. Benjamin Hermalin and Michael Weisbach, *Handbook of the Economics of Corporate Governance*, volume 1 (Amsterdam: North Holland, 2017): 541–636; Sanjai Bhagat, Bernard Black, and Margaret Blair, "Relational Investing and Firm Performance," *Journal of Financial Research* 27 (2004): 1–30. CII holdings were calculated on the assumption that its members had fifty percent of their assets in equities. Leslie Wayne, "Have Shareholder Activists Lost Their Edge?" *New York Times*, January 30, 1994.

13. "Seeking to Stay out of Proxy Battles," *New York Times*, August 8, 1991; Teslik interview; Roberta Romano, "Public Pension Fund Activism in Corporate Governance Reconsidered," *Columbia Law Review* 93 (1993): 834; Sanford M. Jacoby, "The Wreckage of U.S. Auto: Who Was Behind the Wheel?" *New Labor Forum* 18 (2009): 27–30. In 1992, GM's embattled board issued a twenty-eight-point set of pro-shareholder governance principles, which CalPERS sent to two hundred CEOs of large companies. "Tales from the Boardroom Wars: CalPERS Hanson on His Long Fight for Shareholders' Rights," *Business Week*, June 5, 1994. On the ascendance of finance, see David Halberstam, *The Reckoning* (New York: Morrow, 1986); Neil Fligstein, *The Transformation of Corporate Control* (Cambridge: Harvard University Press, 1990); Dirk Zorn, Frank Dobbin, Julian Dierkes, and Man-Shan Kwok, "Managing Investors: How Financial Markets Reshaped the American Firm" in *The Sociology of Financial Markets*, ed. Karin Knorr-Cetina and Alex Preda (New York: Oxford University Press, 2006).

14. "Time Warner Feels Force of Shareholder Power," *Business Week*, July 29, 1991; Michael Useem, *Executive Defense: Shareholder Power and Corporate Reorganization* (Cambridge, MA: Harvard University Press, 1993), 202; Teslik interview; Kathleen Day, "Soldiers for the Shareholders," *Washington Post*, August 27, 2000. Fifty-five percent of public-pension plans have pursued litigation at least once. Fisch and Choi, "On Beyond CalPERS."

15. James Sailer, "California PERS (A)," *Harvard Business School Case Study*, August 17, 2000.

16. States varied considerably in their unfunded liabilities. In 2014, the funded ratio of New York State's pension plan stood at 98 percent, whereas, in neighboring New Jersey, it was

42 percent. "State Public Pension Funding Gap Hit $1.1. Trillion in 2015: Pew," *Reuters*, April 20, 2017; Tax Foundation, "How Well Funded Are Pension Plans in Your State?" April 5, 2017.

17. Castaneda, "To Retire in Dignity," chap. 7; Kenneth R. French, "Presidential Address: The Cost of Active Investing," *Journal of Finance* 63, no. 4 (2008): 1537–1573; "US Institutions Show Teeth as Shareholders," *Financial Times*, March 4, 1985. It's been alleged that public-pension officials became activists because they enjoyed the limelight and the opportunities to meet with powerful people in business and government. One should not minimize the veracity of this claim. For example, from 1992 to 1994, CalPERS board members took 101 trips, including twenty-one to foreign countries. "A Boondoggle or Benefit? Public Funds Wrestle with Ethics of Conference Travel," *P&I*, July 24, 1995.

18. Sailer, *California PERS (A)*; Diane Del Guercio and Jennifer Hawkins, "The Motivation and Impact of Pension Fund Activism," *Journal of Financial Economics* 52 (1999): 293, 298; "Corporate Couch Potatoes" *Fortune*, December 24, 1990; "The Search for a Perfect Corporate Board," *New York Times*, August 3, 1997; "Council Unveils List of Underperformers," *P&I*, October 21, 1994; Rakesh Khurana, *Searching for a Corporate Savior: The Irrational Quest for Charismatic CEOs* (Princeton, NJ: Princeton University Press, 2002), 54. High institutional and low inside ownership was associated with successful win rates in proxy contests. Lilli Gordon and John Pound, "Information, Ownership Structure, and Shareholder Voting," *Journal of Finance* 48 (1993): 697–718.

19. "Large Foot in Board-Room Door," *New York Times*, June 6, 1991; Leslie Wayne, "Seeking to Stay Out of Proxy Battles," *New York Times*, August 8, 1991; "Tales from the Boardroom Wars"; John Myers, "How a Governor's Bid to Exert Control over California Public Pensions Backfired, *Los Angeles Times*, October 7, 2016; Kayla J. Gillan, "California 'RAID' History," unpublished speech, February 1997, at http://www.CalPERS-governance.org/viewpoint/speeches/gillan .asp.

It wasn't only Republicans who had their eye on public pension capital. In the late 1980s, more than a dozen Democratic governors, including New York's Mario Cuomo, adopted rules for "economically targeted investments" (ETIs) that would take money from public pension plans to finance commercial and residential construction projects in a state's depressed regions. At the behest of construction unions, the New York plan had a requirement that, for projects in which a pension plan's contribution exceeded 50 percent, the contractor and property managers had to sign a neutrality agreement related to union organizing (see chapter 3). State and local pension funds were leery of ETIs. There was a fear, as in California, that if states meddled with investment decisions, it would be easier to tap their assets to reduce budget deficits, as New York City had done during the 1975 fiscal crisis. Sarah Teslik, speaking for the Council of Institutional Investors, said, "We're concerned about the trend of the states focusing on public fund assets as if they were state tax dollars." Critics charged that ETIs had subpar investment returns. Several studies find this to be true, although the relationship is weak, while others find no negative effects. Gordon L. Clark, *Pension Fund Capitalism* (Oxford: Oxford University Press, 2000); State of New York, *Our Money's Worth: Report of the Governor's Taskforce on Pension Fund Investment* (Albany, June 1989); Adria Scharf, "Labor's Capital: Putting Pension Funds to Work for Workers," *Dollars & Sense*, September 1, 2004; Roberta Romano, "Public Pension Fund Activism in Corporate Governance," *Columbia Law Review* 93 (1993); Teslik in James A. White, "States Seek to Link Pension Investments," *Wall Street Journal*, September 28, 1989; Julia L. Coronado,

Eric M. Emgen, and Brian Knight, "Public Funds and Private Capital Markets: The Investment Practices and Performance of State and Local Pension Funds," *National Tax Journal* 56 (2003): 579. On rates of return see David Hess, "Protecting and Politicizing, Public Pension Fund Assets: Empirical Evidence on the Effects of Governance Structures and Practices," *University of California Davis Law Review* 39 (2005): 207–208, 213–214.

20. Claire E. Crutchley, C. R. Hudson, and M.R.H. Jenson, "Shareholder Wealth Effects of CalPERS' Activism," *Financial Services Review* 7, no. 1 (1998): 1–10; Richard Stevenson, "Huge Fund Turns Up Proxy Heat," *New York Times*, March 21, 1992, at 37; Mark Trumbull, "Who's Running the Company?" *Christian Science Monitor*, August 3, 1992, at 6; Michael J. Clowes, *The Money Flood: How Pension Funds Revolutionized Investing* (New York: Wiley, 2000), 249.

21. Barry Rehfeld, "Low-Cal CalPERS," *Institutional Investor* 31, no. 42 (1997): 41–53; Del Guercio and Hawkins, "Motivation and Impact," 303; Working Group on Corporate Governance, "A New Compact for Owners and Directors," *Harvard Business Review* 69 (1991): 141, 144.

22. Rehfeld, "Low-Cal CalPERS."

23. Michael P Smith. "Shareholder Activism by Institutional investors: Evidence from CalPERS," *Journal of Finance* 51 (1996): 227–252; Roberta Romano, "Less Is More: Making Institutional Investor Activism a Valuable Mechanism of Corporate Governance," *Yale Journal on Regulation* 18 (2001): 174–252; Del Guercio and Hawkins, "Motivation and Impact," 310; "Kayla Gillan: CalPERS' Grand Inquisitor," *Business Week*, February 24, 1997; Crist interview, February 2007.

24. Holly Gregory, *International Comparison of Selected Corporate Governance Guidelines and Codes of Best Practice* (New York: Weil, Gotshal, & Manges, 2005); F. Cuomo, C. Mallin, and A. Zattoni, "Corporate Governance Codes: A Review and Research Agenda," *Corporate Governance* 24 (2016): 222–241; Sanjai Bhagat, Brian Bolton, and Roberta Romano, "The Promise and Peril of Corporate Governance Indices," *Columbia Law Review* 108 (2008): 1803–12; Gustavo Manso, "Motivating Innovation," *Journal of Finance* 65 (2011): 1823–1860. TIAA-CREF was one of CII's most active members. However, other CII members criticized TIAA-CREF for promoting individual retirement accounts at the expense of defined benefit plans. Although once a nonprofit company providing portable pension benefits for college professors, today it is a for-profit company, one of the Fortune 100 financial corporations. Pensions are but one part of its business. The term "cookbook" originated with John Pound, then a Harvard professor and later a consultant to companies and pension plans.

25. James McRitchie, "A Conversation With: Richard Koppes" (1995), *Corporate Governance*, https://corpgo.fatcow.com/forums/conversation/koppes.html; Adam Bryant, "The Search for the Perfect Corporate Board," *New York Times*, August 3, 1997.

26. CalPERS, *Corporate Governance: Core Principles and Guidelines, United States* (April 13, 1998), http://www.boardoptions.com/governance.htm; CalPERS, *Domestic Proxy Voting Guidelines* (February 16, 1999). Also see CalPERS, *Why Corporate Governance Today? A Policy Statement* (August 14, 1995); "CalPERS, CII, Approve Comprehensive Sets of Corporate Governance Standards," *IRRC Corporate Governance Bulletin* 15, January 1998; CalPERS, "U.S. Corporate Governance Core Principles and Guidelines" (Sacramento, 1998); CII, "Corporate Governance Policies," updated April 1, 2015; "Resisting Those Ugly Americans: Contempt in France for U.S. Funds and Investors," *New York Times*, January 9, 2000; Jacoby, "Convergence by Design."

27. Lynn A. Stout, "Share Price as a Poor Criterion for Good Corporate Law," *Berkeley Business Law Journal* 3 (2001): 45–56.

28. Paul Gompers, Joy Ishii, and Andrew Metrick, "Corporate Governance and Equity Prices," *Quarterly Journal of Economics* 118 (2003): 107–155; Lucian Arye Bebchuk, Alma Cohen, and Allen Ferrell, "What Matters in Corporate Governance?" *Review of Financial Studies* 22 (2009): 783–827; Lucian Bebchuk, Alma Cohen, and Charles Wang, "Learning and the Disappearing Association between Governance and Returns," *Journal of Financial Economics* 108 (2013): 323–348.

Takeover barriers are said to protect ("entrench") executives lest a hostile bid lead to their removal. The deterrents allegedly cause a variety of problems, including inefficient spending, especially on acquisitions and labor costs, and failure to prioritize share-price maximization. Conversely, takeovers—or the threat of them— are said to raise equity prices by getting rid of unprofitable divisions and by replacing incumbent CEOs with shareholder-oriented CEOs, unbeholden to workers.

Research critical of the entrenchment hypothesis finds that hostile takeovers are not associated with preexisting governance defects or low returns to shareholders and that they do not lead to improved performance in the long term. Ravenscraft and Scherer, for example, find no evidence of greater profitability nine years after a takeover; instead, profitability declined. An overview of research by Tuch and O'Sullivan concludes that "in the short-run, acquisitions have at best an insignificant impact on shareholders' wealth. Long-run performance analysis reveals overwhelmingly negative returns." David Ravenscraft and F. M. Scherer, "Life after Takeover," *Journal of Industrial Economics* 36 (1987): 147–156; Christian Tuch and Noel O'Sullivan, "The Impact of Acquisitions on Firm Performance: A Review of the Evidence," *International Journal of Management Reviews* 9 (2007): 141–170. Studies that confirm Ravenscraft and Scherer include N. K. Chidambaran, Darius Palia, and Yudan Zheng, "Does Better Corporate Governance 'Cause' Better Firm Performance?" SSRN working paper (draft March 2006); Sanjai Bhagat and Roberta Romano, "Empirical Studies of Corporate Law," *Handbook of Law and Economics* 2 (2007): 945–1012; Ray Fisman et al., "Governance and CEO Turnover: Do Something or Do the Right Thing?" *Management Science* 60 (2013): 319–337; Andrei Shleifer and Lawrence Summers, "Breach of Trust in Hostile Takeovers: Causes and Consequence," in *Corporate Takeovers: Causes and Consequences,* ed. Alan J. Auerbach (Chicago: University of Chicago Press, 1988); Sanjai Bhagat, Andrei Shleifer, and Robert Vishny, "Hostile Takeovers in the 1980s: The Return to Corporate Specialization," *Brookings Papers on Economic Activity: Microeconomics* (1990): 1–84; Andrei Shleifer and Robert Vishny, "Stock Market Driven Acquisitions," *Journal of Financial Economics* 70 (2003): 295–311; Robert Comment and G. William Schwert, "Poison or Placebo? Evidence on the Deterrence and Wealth Effects of Modern Antitakeover Measures," *Journal of Financial Economics* 39 (1995): 3–43; John Core, Wayne Guay, and Tjomme Rusticus, "Does Weak Governance Cause Weak Stock Returns?" *Journal of Finance* 61 (2006): 655–687.

For similar findings from the United Kingdom, see Julian Franks and Colin Mayer, "Hostile Takeovers and the Correction of Managerial Failure," *Journal of Financial Economics* 40 (1996): 163–181; and Rajeeva Sinha, "The Role of Hostile Takeovers in Corporate Governance," *Applied Financial Economics* 14 (2004): 1291–1306.

Sample duration affects results. Studies often use event-history analysis to measure share-price performance during periods as brief as a day, which has obvious limitations when investors are seeking long-run returns. Hostile bids often generate a spike in stock prices immediately after the bid is announced. There is an expectation that the takeover will lead to asset sales (asset sales can command price premia when a purchaser from in the same industry is seeking market power). Hence, it's possible for takeovers to boost share prices but not efficiency, as with takeovers motivated by a search for market power and tax benefits. Concentration ratios—which measure market power—increased during the 1980s. Frederic L. Pryor, "New Trends in U.S. Industrial Concentration, *Review of Industrial Organization* 18, no. 3 (2001): 301–326, at 301; Lawrence J. White, "Trends in Aggregate Concentration in the United States," *Journal of Economic Perspectives* 16 (2001): 137–160.

29. Bhagat, Bolton, and Romano, "Promise and Peril"; Mary O'Sullivan, *Contests for Corporate Control: Corporate Governance and Economic Performance in the United States and Germany* (Oxford: Oxford University Press, 2000), 162–76; Sandra Betton, B. Espen Eckbo, and Karin Thorburn, "Corporate Takeovers," Tuck School of Business, working paper 2008-47, August 2008; Gregor Andrade, Mark Mitchell, and Erik Stafford, "New Evidence and Perspectives on Mergers," *Journal of Economic Perspectives* 15 (2001): 103–120.

30. Critical studies include John A. Wagner, J. L. Stimpert, and Edward Fubara, "Board Composition and Organizational Performance," *Journal of Management Studies* 35 (1998): 655–677; Sanjai Bhagat and Bernard Black, "The Non-Correlation between Board Independence and Long-Term Firm Performance," *Journal of Corporation Law* 27 (2002): 231–274; Bhagat, Bolton, and Romano, "Promise and Peril"; April Klein, "Firm Performance and Board Committee Structure," *Journal of Law and Economics* 41, no. 1 (1998): 275–304; Kenneth Lehn, Sukesh Patro, and Mengxin Zhao, "Determinants of the Size and Composition of US Corporate Boards: 1935–2000," *Financial Management* 38 (2009): 747–780; Vidhan K. Goyal and Chul W. Park, "Board Leadership Structure and CEO Turnover," *Journal of Corporate Finance* 8 (2002): 49–66; D. Dalton, C. M. Daily, A. E. Ellstrand, and J. L. Johnson, "Meta-Analytic Reviews of Board Composition, Leadership Structure and Financial Performance," *Strategic Management Journal* 19 (1998): 269–290; Chia-Wei Chen, J. Barry Lin, and Bingsheng Yi, "CEO Duality and Firm Performance: An Endogenous Issue," *Corporate Ownership and Control* 6, no. 1 (2008): 58–65.

Martijn Cremers and his colleagues find that firms that adopt a staggered board increase in value, while de-staggering is associated with decreased value, which runs counter to the cookbook. They explain that short-term shareholders generate incentives for a firm to underinvest in risky long-term projects. A staggered board insulates directors from opportunistic myopia on the part of investors. The authors show that staggered boards have a strong positive association with R&D spending, and the amount of intangible assets and innovation. Martijn Cremers, Lubomir P. Litov, and Simone M. Sepe, "Staggered Boards and Firm Value, Revisited," working paper, December 19, 2013.

31. Adam Ross Sorkin, "Back to School, but This One Is for Top Corporate Officials," *New York Times*, September 3, 2002; Lorsch in "Shareholder Activists Win Big Ones on Votes at EMC, Mentor Graphics," *Wall Street Journal*, May 9, 2002. For more realistic analyses of board behavior, see Ruth Wageman et al., "The Changing Ecology of Teams: New Directions for Future Research," *Journal of Organizational Behavior* 33, no. 3 (2012): 301–315; Daniel Forbes and Frances Milliken, "Cognition and Corporate Governance: Understanding Boards of Directors as Strategic Decision-Making Groups," *Academy of Management Review* 24 (1999): 489–450; Colin Carter and Jay Lorsch, *Back to the Drawing Board: Designing Corporate Boards for a*

Complex World (Boston: Harvard Business School Press, 2003); Marleen A. O'Connor, "The Enron Board: The Perils of Groupthink," *University of Cincinnati Law Review* 71 (2002): 1233–1320.

32. Data provided by Rakesh Khurana at Harvard Business School; Colin Leinster, "He'll Get You If You Don't Watch Out. The Famous Raider-Manager Believes American CEOs are an Example of Reverse Darwinism—the Survival of the Unfit Test," *Fortune* 117 (February 29, 1988): 58; Mark R. Huson, Robert Parrino, and Laura T. Starks, "Internal Monitoring Mechanisms and CEO Turnover: A Long-Term Perspective," *Journal of Finance* 56, (2001): 2265–2297; Steven Kaplan and Bernadette Minton, "How Has CEO Turnover Changed," working paper, University of Chicago, August 2008.

33. booz&co., *12th Annual CEO Succession Report* (2012), 9; Chuck Lucier, Rob Schuyt, and Junichi Handa, "CEO Succession 2003: The Perils of Good Governance," *strategy + business* 35 (2004) at https://www.strategy-business.com/article/04208; Khurana, *Searching for a Corporate Savior*, chap. 3; Jeffrey A. Krug and Ruth V. Aguilera, "Top Management Team Turnover in Mergers and Acquisitions," *Advances in Mergers and Acquisitions* 4 (2005): 123–151; Yan Zhang and Nandini Rajagopalan, "When the Known Devil Is Better than an Unknown God: An Empirical Study of the Antecedents and Consequences of Relay CEO Successions, " *Academy of Management Journal* 47 (2004): 483–500.

Wiersema discusses K-Mart, where performance worsened after the CEO was fired in 1995. CalPERS was one of the loudest voices calling for the dismissal. Similarly, in 2008 the Laborers' International Union of America (LIUNA), then affiliated with Change to Win, filed resolutions at banks implicated in the financial crisis demanding that their boards create succession plans. LIUNA complained that outsider CEOs had cost companies too much money. Margarethe Wiersema, "Holes at the Top: Why CEO Firings Backfire," *Harvard Business Review*, December 2002, 70; "Union Wants CEO Selection Criteria Made Public," *Globe & Mail*, February 7, 2008.

34. Michael C. Jensen and Kevin J. Murphy, "CEO Incentives—It's Not How Much You Pay, But How," *Harvard Business Review* 68, no. 3 (1990): 138–153; Kevin J. Murphy, "Executive Compensation," in *Handbook of Labor Economics*, ed. Orley Ashenfelter and David Card (Amsterdam: Elsevier, 1999), 6; Lukomnik in "Holders Put the Screws to Wooden Performers," *Footwear News*, November 27, 1995. CalPERS promoted stock options in its guidelines and in meetings with other activists. "The Flap over Executive Pay," *Business Week*, May 6, 1991; CalPERS, "Why Corporate Governance Today? A Policy Statement," August 14, 1995; CalPERS, *Corporate Governance*; CalPERS, *Domestic Proxy Voting Guidelines*.

A perverse effect occurs when board directors receive stock options, as the cookbook recommended. Although intended to align directors with shareholders, the practice is found to raise the odds that the CEO's own option grants will be illegally backdated. Moreover, so-called independent directors manipulate their option grants, just like CEOs. Lucian A. Bebchuk, Yaniv Grinstein, and Urs Peyer, "Lucky CEOs and Lucky Directors," *Journal of Finance* 65, no. 6 (2010): 2363–2401; S. Burcu Avci, Cindy A. Schipani, and H. Nejat Seyhun, "Do Independent Directors Curb Financial Fraud: The Evidence and Proposals for Further Reform," *Indiana Law Journal* 93 (2018): 757–808.

35. Lucian Bebchuk, Jesse Fried, and David Walker, "Managerial Power and Rent in the Design of Executive Compensation," *University of Chicago Law Review* 69 (2002): 751–755; Lucian A. Bebchuk and Jesse M. Fried, *Pay Without Performance: The Unfulfilled Promise of Execu-*

tive Compensation (Cambridge, MA: Harvard University Press, 2004); Hamid Mehran, "Executive Compensation Structure, Ownership, and Firm Performance," *Journal of Financial Economics* 38, no. 2 (1995): 163–184; "Fat Cats Turn to Low Fat," *The Economist*, March 5, 2005, at 14; Jared Harris and Philip Bromiley, "Incentives to Cheat: The Influence of Executive Compensation and Firm Performance on Financial Misrepresentation," *Organization Science* 18, no. 3 (2007): 350–367; Don Warren, May Zey, Tanya Granston, and Joseph Roy, "Earnings Fraud: Board Control vs. CEO Control and Corporate Performance, 1992–2004," *Managerial and Decision Economics* 32 (2011): 17–34; Dan R. Dalton and Catherine M. Daily, "Director Stock Compensation: An Invitation to a Conspicuous Conflict of Interests?" *Business Ethics Quarterly* 11, no. 1 (2001): 89–108; Cynthia E. Devers, Albert A. Cannella Jr., Gregory P. Reilly, and Michele E. Yoder, "Executive Compensation: A Multidisciplinary Review of Recent Developments," *Journal of Management* 33 (2007): 1016.

36. Lifeng Gu and Dirk Hackbarth, "Governance and Equity Prices: Does Transparency Matter?" *Review of Finance* 17 (2013): 1989–2003; Xue Wang, " Increased Disclosure Requirements and Corporate Governance Decisions: Evidence from Chief Financial Officers in the Pre- and Post–Sarbanes-Oxley Periods," *Journal of Accounting Research* 48 (2010): 885–920; Young Jun Cho, "Segment Disclosure Transparency and Internal Capital Market Efficiency: Evidence from SFAS No. 131," *Journal of Accounting Research* 53 (2015): 669–723.

37. Rehfeld, "Low-Cal CalPERS"; Allan A. Kennedy, *The End of Shareholder Value: Corporations at the Crossroads* (Cambridge, MA: Perseus, 2001); Crist interview, February 2007; Fisch and Choi, "On Beyond CalPERS." After retiring from the CalPERS board, Crist maintained his skepticism about research: "I believe in something like this [governance reform] intuitively. You've got to say, 'It makes a difference.' . . . Can you take me to a piece of scholarship which absolutely proves this? No. But can you convince me that it doesn't make a difference on the good side? No, it has. And it does and it will continue to do so." In the early 2000s, Crist became chairman of the advisory committee for a FTSE/ISS corporate governance index fund, which was co-owned by the *Financial Times* and ISS. Glass Lewis, a competitor of ISS, launched a similar fund. Crist interview.

38. Because CalPERS was a client, Wilshire Associates may have felt compelled to tell the pension plan what it wanted to hear. Wilshire had another possible conflict of interest: its consulting work was not independent of its other lines of business. "Concerns Raised over Consultants to Pension Funds," *New York Times*, March 21, 2004; Useem, *Investor Capitalism*, 28; CalPERS, "Facts at a Glance," September 2005; CalPERS, "Why Corporate Governance Today?" at 6.

39. Romano, "Less Is More"; Smith, "Shareholder Activism"; Jonathan M. Karpoff, "The Impact of Shareholder Activism on Target Companies: A Survey of Empirical Findings," unpublished manuscript, University of Washington, School of Business, 1998; Crutchley et al., "Shareholder Wealth Effects"; Philip C. English, T. I. Smythe, and C. R. McNeil, "The 'CalPERS Effect' Revisited," *Journal of Corporate Finance* 10, no. 1 (2004): 157–174; Stuart Gillan and Laura Starks, "Corporate Governance Proposals and Shareholder Activism: The Role of Institutional Investors," *Journal Financial Economics* 57, no. 2 (2000): 275–305; Brad Barber, "Monitoring the Monitor: Evaluating CalPERS Shareholder Activism," *Journal of Investing* 16 (2007): 66–80; James N. Nelson, "The 'CalPERS Effect' Revisited Again," *Journal of Corporate Finance* 12, no. 2 (2006): 187–213; Crist interview, February 2007.

40. Mary O'Sullivan, "Innovation, Industrial Development, and Corporate Governance," PhD diss., Harvard University, 1996. Shad quoted in Gerald F. Davis and Tracy Thompson, "A Social Movement Perspective on Corporate Control," *Administrative Science Quarterly* 39 (1994): 153; Kathleen M. Kahle and René M. Stulz, "Is the US Public Corporation in Trouble?" *Journal of Economic Perspectives* 31 (2017): 67–88; Thomas Bourveau, Thomas, Xinlei Li, Daniele Macciocchi, and Chengzhu Sun, "Do Shareholders' Preferences Affect Share Repurchases? Evidence from Mutual Funds Short-terminism," SSRN working paper 3584004 (2020). For data on payouts, see J. Fred Weston and Juan A. Siu, "Changing Motives for Share Repurchases," UCLA Anderson School, working paper, 2003.

41. In theory, investors should discount any stock-price gains associated with buybacks. But some investors are fooled because they fail to learn from past experience that the gains are transient. One result is that buybacks can lead to higher share prices. Daniel Bens, Venky Nagar, Douglas J. Skinner, and M. H. Franco Wong, "Employee Stock Options, EPS Dilution, and Stock Repurchases," *Journal of Accounting and Economics* 36 (2003): 51–90; Urs Peyer and Theo Vermaelen, "The Nature and Persistence of Buyback Anomalies," *Review of Financial Studies* 22 (2009): 1693–1745; Gregor Andrade, "Do Appearances Matter? The Impact of EPS Accretion and Dilution on Stock Prices," SSRN Working Paper (June 1999); Theo Vermaelen, "Common Stock Repurchases and Market Signalling," *Journal of Financial Economics* 9, no. 2 (1981): 139–183; Konan Chan, David L. Ikenberry, Imoo Lee, and Yanzhi Wang, "Share Repurchases as a Tool to Mislead Investors," *Journal of Corporate Finance* 16, no. 2 (2010): 137–158; Fangjian Fu and Sheng Huang, "The Persistence of Long-Run Abnormal Returns Following Stock Repurchases and Offerings," *Management Science* 62, no. 4 (2016): 964–984. On buybacks and stock-based pay, see George W. Fenn and Nellie Liang, "Corporate Payout Policy and Managerial Stock Incentives," *Journal of Financial Economics* 60, no. 1 (2001): 45–72.

42. On innovation and buybacks, see Florence Honoré, Federico Munari, and Bruno van Pottelsberghe de La Potterie, "Corporate Governance Practices and Companies' R&D Intensity: Evidence from European Countries," *Research Policy* 44, no. 2 (2015): 533–543; Philippe Aghion, John Van Reenen, and Luigi Zingales, "Innovation and Institutional Ownership," *American Economic Review* 103 (2013): 277–304; Lily Nguyen, Le Vu, and Xiangkang Yin, "Share Repurchases and Firm Innovation," *Accounting & Finance* (2020): 1–31; David Bendig, Daniel Willmann, Steffen Strese, and Malte Brettel, "Share Repurchases and Myopia: Implications on the Stock and Consumer Markets," *Journal of Marketing* 82 (2018): 19–41. On investment and buybacks, see Alok Bhargava, "Executive Compensation, Share Repurchases, and Investment Expenditures," *Review of Quantitative Financial Accounting* 40 (2013): 403–422; Dong Lee, Han Shin, and René M. Stulz, "Why Does Capital No Longer Flow More to the Industries with the Best Growth Opportunities?" NBER working paper 22924, 2016. On the effects of buybacks on wages and employment, see Hector Almeida, Vyacheslav Fos, and Mathias Kronlund, "The Real Effects of Share Repurchases," *Journal of Financial Economics* 119 (2016): 168–185; Hector Almeida, "Is It Time to Get Rid of Earnings-per-Share (EPS)?" *Review of Corporate Finance Studies* 8, no. 1 (2019): 174–206; Gutiérrez and Philippon, "Investmentless Growth."

43. Home Depot data in Katy Milani and Irene Tung, "Curbing Stock Buybacks: A Crucial Step to Raising Worker Pay and Reducing Inequality," National Employment Law Project and Roosevelt Institute, July 2018. Also see Lenore Palladino and Adil Abdela, "Making the Case: How Ending Walmart's Stock Buyback Program Would Help to Fix Our High-Profit, Low-Wage Economy," Roosevelt Institute, Washington, DC, May 22, 2018.

44. "G.M. to Buy Back 20% of Stock," *New York Times*, March 4, 1987; James Buchan, "GM Share Plan Cheers Institutions: Reaction to the Largest US Corporate Buyback," *Financial Times*, March 5, 1987; David Halberstam, *The Reckoning* (New York: William Morrow, 1986).

45. "UAW Sees Big Three Cash Reserves as Contract Issue," Reuters, September 18, 1995.

46. Jacoby, "Wreckage of U. S. Auto." German Guitierrez and Thomas Philippon ask why nonfinancial companies since 2000 have underinvested in fixed capital despite their profitability and healthy valuations. Of the seven factors they analyzed, only two had strong explanatory power: reduced competition as a result of market concentration and increases in passive ownership by quasi-indexers like pension funds. Among their explanations for the latter finding are the higher payouts sought by quasi-indexers. Gutierrez and Philippon, "Investmentless Growth."

47. Daniel L. Greenwald, Martin Lettau, and Sydney C. Ludvigson, "How the Wealth Was Won: Factor Shares as Market Fundamentals," NBER working paper 25769, April 2019; B. Hu, D. Wu and X. Zhang "Having a Finger in the Pie: Labor Power and Corporate Payout Policy," *Financial Management* 47 (2018): 993–1027; Sheng-Syan Chen, Yan-Shing Chen, and Yanzhi Wang, "Does Labor Power Affect the Likelihood of a Share Repurchase?" *Financial Management* 44 (2015): 623–653; Jack He, Xuan Tian, and Huan Yang. "Labor Unions and Payout Policy: A Regression Discontinuity Analysis." *SSRN Electronic Journal* (2016).

48. Mark L. Mitchell and J. Harold Mulherin, "The Impact of Industry Shocks on Takeover and Restructuring Activity," *Journal of Financial Economics* 41 (1996): 199; Alfred D. Chandler Jr., *The Visible Hand: The Managerial Revolution in American Business* (Cambridge, MA: Harvard University Press, 1977); Oliver E. Williamson, *Corporate Control and Business Behavior* (Englewood Cliffs, NJ: Prentice-Hall, 1970); Colin Mayer, "Corporate Governance, Competition and Performance," *Journal of Law and Society* 24 (1997): 152–176; "Shad, Regan, at Odds on Bill," *Globe and Mail*, July 18, 1984; *Economic Report of the President*, February 1985, 196.

49. *Unocal Corp. v. Mesa Petroleum Co.*, 493 A.2d 946, 955 (Del. 1985); *Revlon, Inc. v. MacAndrews & Forbes Holdings, Inc.*, 506 A.2d 173 (Del. 1986); Melvin Aaron Eisenberg, "The Legal Roles of Shareholders and Management in Modern Corporate Decision-making," *California Law Review* 57, no. 1 (1969): 5; Lynn Stout, *The Shareholder Value Myth: How Putting Shareholders First Harms Investors, Corporations, and the Public* (San Francisco: Berrett-Kohler, 2012), 30. Also see Lynn A. Stout, "Bad and Not-So-Bad Arguments for Shareholder Primacy," *Southern California Law Review* 75, no. 5 (2001): 1189–1210; Stephen Bainbridge, "Director Primacy: The Means and Ends of Corporate Governance," *Northwestern University Law Review* 97, no. 2 (2002): 547–606; William B. Chandler and Leo E. Strine, "The New Federalism of the American Corporate Governance System," *University of Pennsylvania Law Review* 152, no. 2 (2003): 953–1005; William T. Allen, Jack B. Jacobs, and Leo E. Strine, "The Great Takeover Debate: A Meditation on Bridging the Conceptual Divide," *University of Chicago Law Review* 69 (2002): 1067–1100; Margaret M. Blair, "Financial Restructuring and the Debate About Corporate Governance," in *The Deal Decade: What Takeovers and Leveraged Buyouts Mean for Corporate Governance*, ed. Margaret M. Blair (Washington, DC: Brookings Institution, 1993); Alexandridis C. F. Mavrovitis, and N. G. Travlos, "How Have M&As Changed? Evidence from the Sixth Merger Wave," working paper, Henley Business School, June 2011; G. William Schwert, "Hostility in Takeovers: In the Eyes of the Beholder?" *Journal of Finance* 55 (2000): 2599–2640.

50. Bhagat, Shleifer, and Vishny, "Hostile Takeovers in the 1980s"; Shleifer and Summers, "Breach of Trust"; Martin J. Conyon, Sourafel Girma, Steve Thompson, and Peter W. Wright,

"Do Hostile Mergers Destroy Jobs?" *Journal of Economic Behavior and Organization* 45, no. 4 (2001): 427–440; Shleifer and Vishny, "Stock Market Driven Acquisitions"; Frank R. Lichtenberg and Donald Siegel, "The Effect of Ownership Changes on the Employment and Wages of Central Office and Other Personnel," *Journal of Law and Economics* 33, no. 2 (1990): 383–408; Joshua Rosett, "Do Union Wealth Concessions Explain Takeover Premiums? The Evidence on Contract Wages," *Journal of Financial Economics* 27 (1990): 263–282; Brian Becker, "Union Rents as a Source of Takeover Gains among Target Shareholders," *Industrial & Labor Relations Review* 49 (1995): 3–17; Jagadeesh Gokhale, Erica Groshen, and David Neumark, "Do Hostile Takeovers Reduce Extramarginal Wage Payments?" *Review of Economics and Statistics* 77 (1995): 470–485.

With a pension reversion, a company terminates an allegedly overfunded pension plan, skims off the excess and uses any remaining assets to purchase annuities or set up a defined contribution plan. Regulations adopted in the early 1980s made reversions easier to carry out, and in the mid-1990s Republicans attempted to make it even easier. Teresa Ghilarducci, *Labor's Capital: The Economics and Politics of Private Pensions* (Cambridge, MA: MIT Press, 1992): 97–100; Jeffrey Pontiff, Andrei Shleifer, and Michael S. Weisbach, "Reversions of Excess Pension Assets after Takeovers," *RAND Journal of Economics* 21, no. 4 (1990): 600–613; Mitchell A. Petersen, "Pension Reversions and Worker-Stockholder Wealth Transfers," *Quarterly Journal of Economics* 107, no. 3 (1992): 1033–1056; Margaret M. Blair, "The Great Pension Grab: Comments on Richard Ippolito, Bankruptcy and Workers: Risks, Compensation and Pension Contracts," *Washington University Law Quarterly* 82, no. 4 (2004): 1305–1312; Robert D. Hershey, "Threat is Seen in Pension Shift," *New York Times*, September 28, 1995; Gordon L. Clark, "Contested Terrain: Republican Rhetoric, Pension Funds, and Community Development," *Urban Geography* 20 (1999): 197–225.

51. Rehfeld, "Low-Cal CalPERS," 20, 42; Del Guercio and Hawkins, "The Motivation and Impact of Pension Fund Activism," 312; Mark Huson, "Does Corporate Governance Matter? Evidence from CalPERS Interventions," University of Alberta working paper, 1997; Macht in Floyd Norris, "On Wall Street: For Richer, For Poorer?" *New York Times*, March 9, 1996; Jiwook Jung, "Shareholder Value and Workforce Downsizing, 1981–2006," *Social Forces* 93, no. 4 (2014): 1335–1368; L. Josh Bivens and Christian E. Weller, "Institutional Shareholder Concentration, Corporate Governance Changes, and Diverging Fortunes of Capital and Labor," paper presented at the conference "Pension Fund Capitalism and the Crisis of Old-Age Security in the United States," September 2004, Center for Economic Policy Analysis, The New School, New York; William J. Baumol, Alan Blinder, and Edward N. Wolff, *Downsizing in America: Reality, Causes, and Consequences* (New York: Russell Sage Foundation, 2003), 261. The portion of equities owned by pension funds tripled from 9 percent to 27 percent between 1970 and 1985, and those shares made it easier for hostile bids to achieve critical mass. Blair, *Ownership and Control*, 46.

52. Norris, "On Wall Street," 13. In some states, such as New York, there was political pressure on public pension plans to limit their involvement in hostile takeovers. Governor Mario Cuomo convened a task force on the issue, and, although it never led to formal regulation, it influenced the funds' investment decisions. Romano, "Public Pension Fund Activism," 815.

53. Roberta Romano, "The Political Economy of Takeover Statutes," *Virginia Law Review* 74 (1987): 111–199; Mark Roe, "A Political Theory of American Corporate Finance," *Columbia Law Review* 91 (1991): 10–67; "Pennsylvania's Anti-Takeover Law," *Executive Report*, September 1, 1990, 22; Brian Burrough and John Helyar, *Barbarians at the Gate: The Fall of RJR Nabisco* (New

York: Harper & Row, 1990); "Senate Approves Limits on Golden Parachutes," *New York Times,* June 22, 1988; William Long and David Ravenscraft, "LBOs, Debt, and R&D Intensity," *Strategic Management Journal* 145 (1993): 119–135.

An influential study of constituency statutes by economists Marianne Bertrand and Sendhil Mullainathan found that in adopting states, workers had larger pay increases, especially white-collar workers, and companies had lower investment and productivity than in other states. Their interpretation is that managers and workers sought the statutes to shield themselves from efficiency-oriented shareholders, in order to live a quiet life, undisturbed by takeovers, and spend on themselves money that might more efficiently have gone to shareholders for reinvestment elsewhere. Economist Emilio Catan and law professor Marcel Kahan published a critique of the Bertrand and Mullainathan study that found errors in coding methodology, misspecification of institutional details, and failure to take account of substantial stock holdings of executives. Marianne Bertrand and Sendhil Mullainathan, "Enjoying the Quiet Life? Corporate Governance and Managerial Preferences," *Journal of Political Economy* 111 (2003): 1043–1075; Emiliano M. Catan and Marcel Kahan, "The Law and Finance of Antitakeover Statutes," *Stanford Law Review* 68, no. 3 (2016): 629–680. Also see Michael Koetter, J. W. Kolari, and Laura Spierdijk, "Efficient Competition? Testing the 'Quiet Life' of US Banks with Adjusted Lerner Indices," in *Proceedings of the 44th Bank Structure and Competition Conference, Federal Reserve Bank of Chicago* (2008), 234–252; Aleksandra Kacperczyk, "With Greater Power Comes Greater Responsibility? Takeover Protection and Corporate Attention to Stakeholders," *Strategic Management Journal* 30 (2009): 261–285.

54. Timothy J. Vogus and Gerald F. Davis, "Elite Mobilizations for Anti-Takeover Legislation," in *Social Movements and Organization Theory,* ed. G. F. Davis, D. McAdam, W. R. Scott, and M. N. Zald (Cambridge: Cambridge University Press), 96–121; "Investment Banks, Business at Odds on Takeover Laws," *Washington Post,* September 27, 1987; David Marcus, "Corporate Control Alert," *The Deal,* July 12, 2005; "Unions Seek Takeover Protection," *The Record,* April 9, 1987; Eric W. Orts, "Beyond Shareholders: Interpreting Corporate Constituency Statutes," *George Washington Law Review* 61 (1992): 21; John Hoerr, "ESOPs: Revolution or Ripoff?" *Business Week,* April 15, 1985, 94.

55. Isaac Fox and Alfred Marcus, "The Causes and Consequences of Leveraged Management Buyouts," *Academy of Management Review* 17 (1992): 62–85; Allen Kaufman and Ernest J. Englander, "Kohlberg Kravis Roberts & Co. and the Restructuring of American Capitalism," *Business History Review* 67 (1993): 52–97; Long and Ravenscraft, "LBOs, Debt, and R&D Intensity."

56. Thomas Kochan, Harry Katz, and Robert McKersie, *The Transformation of American Industrial Relations* (New York: Basic Books, 1986), 189–195; Joseph R. Blasi, *Employee Ownership: Revolution or Ripoff?* (New York: Ballinger, 1990); Joseph Blasi and Douglas Kruse, *The New Owners: The Mass Emergence of Employee Ownership in Public Companies and What It Means to American Business* (New York: HarperCollins, 1992); Christine Farrell and John Hoerr, "ESOPs: Are They Good for You?" *Business Week,* May 15, 1989, 116; Jeffrey Gordon, "Employee Stock Ownership in Economic Transition: The Case of United Airlines," in *Comparative Corporate Governance,* ed. Klaus J. Hopt et al. (Oxford: Oxford University Press, 1998), 387–436; National Center for Employee Ownership, *ESOPs and Corporate Governance,* 3rd ed. (Oakland, CA, 2009).

57. Martin Lipton, "Takeover Bids in the Target's Boardroom," *Business Lawyer* (1979): 101–134; The Business Roundtable, "Corporate Governance and American Competitiveness," *Business Law* (November 1990): 241–244.

58. Jörn Block, "Family Management, Family Ownership, and Downsizing: Evidence from S&P 500 Firms," *Family Business Review* 23 (2010): 109–130; Frederick F. Reichheld, *The Loyalty Effect: The Hidden Force behind Growth, Profits, and Lasting Value*, rev. ed. (Boston: Harvard Business Review Press, 2001); Martha Groves, "In Tight Job Market, Software Develops Programs to Keep Employees," *Los Angeles Times*, June, 14 1998; Mark C. Crowley, "How SAS Became the World's Best Place to Work," *Fast Company*, January 22, 2013.

59. SIFMA, *Who Owns Stock in America* (New York: SIFMA, October 2019); Board of Governors of the Federal Reserve System, *Financial Accounts of the United States*, First Quarter, 2020; US Department of Labor, Employee Benefits Security Administration, *Private Pension Plan Bulletin Historical Tables and Graphs, 1975–2017*, September 2019.

60. William J. Wiatrowski, "The Last Private Industry Pension Plans," *Monthly Labor Review*, December 2012, 3–18; *Alicia H. Munnell and Annika Sundén, Coming Up Short: The Challenge of 401(k) Plans* (Washington, DC: Brookings Institution Press, 2004); Teresa Ghilarducci, *When I'm Sixty-Four: The Plot against Pensions and the Plan to Save Them* (Princeton, NJ: Princeton University Press, 2008); Teresa Ghilarducci, Michael Papadopoulos, and Anthony Webb, "Inadequate Retirement Savings for Workers Nearing Retirement," Schwartz Center for Economic Policy Analysis, The New School for Social Research, New York (2017).

61. Alicia H. Munnell, Jean-Pierre Aubry, and Caroline V. Crawford, *Multiemployer Pension Plans: Current Status and Future Trends*, Center for Retirement Research at Boston College, Special Report, December 2017; Harriet Weinstein and William Wiatrowski, "Multiemployer Pension Plans," *Monthly Labor Review* (Spring 1999): 19–23; *NCCMP Multiemployer Pension Facts and the National Economic Impact*, January 5, 2018; GAO, *Multiemployer Pension Plans: Report to Congress Required by the Pension Protection Act of 2006* (Washington, DC, 2013).

62. Doug Sword, "Retirees' Worst Nightmare: Federal Backing of Pension Funds at Risk: Looming Insolvency of Central States Pension Plan Has Stakeholders Calling for Bipartisan Solution," *Roll Call*, February 28, 2020; Teamsters for a Democratic Union, "Central States Pension Fund," December 10, 2019 at http://www.tdu.org/central_states_pension_fund_12_7 _billion_in_asset; https://www.unionfacts.com.

63. John J. Topoleski, Multiemployer Defined Benefit (DB) Pension Plans: A Primer, Congressional Research Service Report, September 24, 2018; U.S. Department of Labor, Private Pension Plan Bulletin; Munnell et al., "Multiemployer Pension Plans"; Mary Williams Walsh, "Congress Saves Coal Miner Pensions, But What About Others?" *New York Times*, December 24, 2019; Milliman, "Milliman Multiemployer Pension Funding Study," Fall 2019; GAO, *Multiemployer Pension Plans*.

Although most DB plans—public and private—were in good health on the eve of the pandemic, a minority were dangerously underfunded; the pandemic further weakened them. Congressional Democrats approved stimulus legislation (the HEROES Act) in May 2020 that would have provided assistance to single-employer and multiemployer DB plans, as well as permit states and localities to spend a portion of their federal relief dollars to shore up their own plans. Senate Republicans were adamantly opposed to helping the public plans, encouraged by the same libertarian groups that had been attacking the plans—and public sector unions—for years.

Erica Werner, "House Democrats Pass $3 Trillion Coronavirus Relief Bill Despite Trump's Veto Threat," *Washington Post*, May 18, 2020; Michael Hiltzik, "Conservatives Use Crisis to Attack Public Workers," *Los Angeles Times*, April 24, 2020; Noam Scheiber and Kenneth P. Vogel, "Web of Donors Sees a Chance to Curb Labor," *New York Times*, February 26, 2018.

64. The General Accounting Office (GAO) in 2016 conducted a review of the Teamsters' Central States Southeast and Southwest Areas Pension Fund, this 35 years after a similar review, and found nothing sufficiently egregious to warrant recommendations to Congress. Back in the 1980s, the Labor Department wrested control of Central States from its trustees and hired Goldman Sachs and Northern Trust to manage the fund's assets. As an investigative journalist discovered, Goldman and Northern Trust took huge risks with the assets and overinvested in equities and in bonds of real estate companies that tanked during the financial crisis. Central States lost over 40 percent of its assets at that time. As the pension plan unraveled, Northern Trust paid for hundreds of its clients to fly to a golf tournament, stay in luxury hotels, and attend a private concert by singer Sheryl Crow. Eliot Blair Smith, "How the Teamsters Pension Disappeared More Quickly Under Wall Street than the Mob," *MarketWatch*, April 6, 2016 at https://www.marketwatch.com/story/how-the-teamsters-pension-disappeared-more-quickly-under-wall-street-than-the-mob-2016-04-04; "Northern Trust Says the Party Is Over," *Financial Times*, December 30, 2009. Also see Dan Moldea, *The Hoffa Wars: Teamsters, Rebels, Politicians, and the Mob* (New York: Paddington, 1978); Michael A. McCarthy, "Turning Labor into Capital: Pension Funds and the Corporate Control of Finance," *Politics and Society* 42 (2014): 455–487.

65. Stuart Dorsey and John Turner, "Union–Nonunion Differences in Pension Fund Investments and Earnings," *ILR Review* 43, no. 5 (1990): 542–555; AFL-CIO Housing Investment Trust, *A Strategy for Creating Union Jobs and Housing for Working Families* (February 2009), http://www.aflcio-hit.com/user-assets/Documents/special_reports/strategy_unionjobs.pdf; Tessa Hebb and Larry Beeferman, "U.S. Pension Funds' Labour-Friendly Investments," Alfred P. Sloan Foundation, working paper, May 2008; McCarthy, "Turning Labor into Capital," 466.

66. João F. Cocco and Paolo F. Volpin, "Corporate Governance of Pension Plans: The UK Evidence," *Financial Analysts Journal* 63, no.1 (2007): 70–83; João F. Cocco and Paolo F. Volpin, "Corporate Pension Plans as Takeover Deterrents," *Journal of Financial and Quantitative Analysis* 48 (2013): 1119–1144; Divya Anantharaman and Yong Gyu Lee, "Managerial Risk Taking Incentives and Corporate Pension Policy," *Journal of Financial Economics* 111, no. 2 (2014): 328–351; US Department of Labor, *Private Pension Plan Bulletin*. Despite ERISA, some single-employer plans still hold significant amounts of the company's own stock. Susan J. Stabile, "Pension Plan Investments in Employer Securities: More Is Not Always Better," *Yale Journal on Regulation* 15 (1998): 61; João F. Cocco, "Corporate Pension Plans," *Annual Review of Financial Economics* 6 (2014): 163–184; John Langbein, Susan Stabile, and Bruce Wolk, *Pension and Employee Benefit Law*, 4th ed. (New York: Foundation Press, 2006), 599–605; Ghilarducci, *Labor's Capital*, chap. 5.

67. Harbrecht, *Pension Funds and Economic Power*, 98.

68. As of 2019, among the larger reserve funds are the AFL-CIO ($95 million), the Teamsters ($235 million), and AFSCME ($125 million).

69. Susan Sterett, "Serving the State: Constitutionalism and Social Spending," *Law and Social Inquiry* 22 (1997): 311–56; U.S. Census Bureau, *2012 Survey of Public Pensions: State & Local Data*; Jeremy Rifkin and Randy Barber, *The North Will Rise Again: Pensions, Politics, and Power in the 1980s* (Boston: Beacon Press, 1978), 150, 167; Richard Freeman, "Unionism Comes to the

Public Sector," NBER working paper 1452, 1984, 33; Castaneda, *To Retire in Dignity*; Alicia Munnell et al., "Why Have Defined Benefit Plans Survived in the Public Sector?" Center for Retirement Research, Boston College, December 2007, 4.

70. Peter F. Drucker, *The Unseen Revolution: How Pension Fund Socialism Came to America* (New York: Harper & Row, 1976); Peter Drucker, "Pension Fund 'Socialism,'" *Public Interest* (Winter 1976): 3–45.

Chapter 3. Labor's Shares

1. Leslie Wayne, "Have Shareholders Lost Their Edge?" *New York Times*, January 30, 1994.

2. Wayne, "Have Shareholders Lost Their Edge?; interview with Carin Zelenko, Director, Capital Strategies Department, International Brotherhood of Teamsters (IBT), Washington, DC, March 2008; Sweeney in "Use Pension Funds to Advance Labor Goals, Union Chief Urges," *Employee Benefit News*, December 1, 1999. An important study of labor's shareholder activities in the 1980s and 1990s is Stewart J. Schwab and Randall S. Thomas, "Realigning Corporate Governance: Shareholder Activism by Labor Unions," *Michigan Law Review* 96 (1998): 1018–1094.

3. Marco Becht, Julian Franks, Colin Mayer, and Stefano Rossi, "Returns to Shareholder Activism: Evidence from a Clinical Study of the Hermes UK Focus Fund," *Review of Financial Studies* 22 (2008): 3093–3129; Silvers quoted in Fabrizio Ferri and James Weber, "AFSCME vs. Mozilo . . . and 'Say on Pay' for All!" Harvard Business School Case 9-109-009, March 18, 2009; "Revolt of the Shareholders," *New York Times*, February 23, 2003. On investor negotiations, see Jeanne Logsdon and Harry Van Buren III, "Beyond the Proxy Vote: Dialogues between Shareholder Activists and Corporations," *Journal of Business Ethics* 87 (2009): 353–65; Willard Carleton, James Nelson, and Michael Weissbach, "The Influence of Institutions on Corporate Governance through Private Negotiations: Evidence from TIAA-CREF," *Journal of Finance* 53 (1998): 1335–1362. A UK union pension plan owned the hedge fund.

4. Interview with Beth Young, July 2008, New York City. Young is an attorney who advises union pension funds on shareholder activities. She was formerly the Shareholder Initiatives Coordinator in the AFL-CIO's Office of Investment and has taught at Harvard Law School.

5. Opponents of labor's shareholder activism claim that acting on collateral interests is inconsistent with fiduciary law. But the law is *not* that trustees must consider only individual stock returns when making decisions. If an investment offers equal *portfolio returns* to another investment, then it is permissible to consider collateral benefits, including the investment's social conscientiousness. Also, an investment may offer a lower expected return than an alternative but still be preferred if it fits the portfolio better, as when it provides diversification. In other words, there is lawful flexibility to exercise collateral interests. Benjamin J. Richardson, an environmental law expert, notes that "in recent years the law appears to have evolved in some jurisdictions to allow fiduciaries to consider collateral interests of beneficiaries, such as their status as employees [or a local community or the natural environment]. . . . The US Department of Labor, which administers ERISA, says that the law's fiduciary standards do not preclude consideration of collateral benefits, such as those offered by a socially-responsible fund." Benjamin J. Richardson, "Do the Fiduciary Duties of Pension Funds Hinder Socially Responsible Investment?" *Banking and Finance Law Review* 22 (2007): 158, 161. Steven L. Wilborn, Nebraska

College of Law, to author, October 16, 2017, and December 7, 2018; Benjamin J. Richardson, "Fiduciary Relationships for Socially Responsible Investing: A Multinational Perspective," *American Business Law Journal* 48 (2011): 597–640.

6. Andrew K. Prevost, Ramesh P. Rao, and Melissa A. Williams. "Labor Unions as Shareholder Activists: Champions or Detractors?," *Financial Review* 47 (2012): 327–349; Yonca Ertimur, Fabrizio Ferri, and Volkan Muslu, "Shareholder Activism and CEO Pay," *Review of Financial Studies* 24 (2010): 535–592; "Prodding for Disclosure of Funds' Proxy Votes," *Washington Post*, April 8, 2001; Imogen Rose-Smith, "Firms Slammed in AFL-CIO Proxy Voting Survey," *Money Management Letter*, March 18, 2002; AFL-CIO, *Key Votes Survey 2010*, https://www.corpgov.net/wp-content/uploads/2011/02/2010-AFL-CIO-Key-Votes-Survey.pdf

7. Young interview.

8. Floyd Norris, "Taking a Strike to the Boardroom," *New York Times*, May 5, 1989; "UMW Takes Contract Dispute to Pittston's Own Turf," *Wall Street Journal*, January 27, 1989.

9. Robert J. LaLonde and Bernard D. Meltzer, "Hard Times for Unions: Another Look at the Significance of Employer Illegalities," *University of Chicago Law Review* 58 (1991): 953–1014; John Schmitt and Ben Zipperer, "Dropping the Ax: Illegal Firings during Union Election Campaigns," Center for Economic and Policy Research, Washington, DC, January 2007; David Moberg, "Labor Fights for Rights," *The Nation*, September 15, 2003; Richard B. Freeman, "Contraction and Expansion: The Divergence of Private Sector and Public Sector Unionism in the United States," *Journal of Economic Perspectives* 2 (1988): 63–88; John Logan, "The Clinton Administration and Labor Law: Was Comprehensive Reform Ever a Realistic Possibility?" *Journal of Labor Research* 28 (2007): 609–628.

10. General Motors early on pledged to remain neutral in its southern plants. GM understood what it was dealing with—there was no fear of the unknown when it came to the UAW—and believed that neutrality would improve relations with the union in other places. Foreign automotive companies operating in the South—such as Mercedes-Benz, Volkswagen, and Nissan—negotiated with unions in their home countries, who pressured the firms to sign neutrality agreements. None did. James Brudney, "Neutrality Agreements and Card Check Recognition: Prospects for Changing Paradigms," *Iowa Law Review* 90 (2005): 819–886; Julius G. Getman, *Restoring the Power of Unions: It Takes a Movement* (New Haven, CT: Yale University Press, 2013), 80; Steve Early, "Organizing Efforts Getting Some Nonunion Help," *Boston Globe*, June 27, 1999; "Developments in Labor Law; Examining Trends and Tactics in Labor Organizing Campaigns," Hearing before the Subcommittee on Employer–Employee Relations," US House of Representatives, 108th Cong. 2nd sess., April 12, 2004.

11. Adrienne Eaton and Jill Kriesky, "Dancing with the Smoke Monster," in *Justice on the Job: Perspectives on the Erosion of Collective Bargaining in the United States*, ed. Richard Block et al. (Kalamazoo, MI: Upjohn Institute for Employment Research, 2006), 157. A careful weighing of the evidence finds that neutrality and card check had the intended effect of curbing management's anti-union activities. Adrienne E. Eaton and Jill Kriesky, "NLRB Elections versus Card Check Campaigns: Results of a Worker Survey," *Industrial and Labor Relations Review* 62 (2009): 157–172.

12. Kyle J. Arnone, "Between Class and Contract: Finance, Law, and 'Justice for Janitors' in the Commercial Real Estate Industry," working paper, UCLA Sociology Department, 2012; "In Court Actions, Employers Fight Back against Union Corporate Campaigns," *CCH HR Management*,

January 2, 2008; Adrienne Eaton, Janice Fine, Allison Porter, and Saul Rubinstein, *Organizational Change at SEIU: 1996–2009*, Rutgers University, courtesy of Saul Rubinstein, n.d.; Testimony by David Bego, President and CEO of Executive Management Services, Inc., Indianapolis in "Corporate Campaigns and the NLRB," Hearing before the Subcommittee on Health, Employment, Labor, and Pensions, US House of Representatives, 112th Cong., 1st Sess., Washington, DC, May 26, 2011; "Labor Pains," *Modern Healthcare*, December 6, 2004; "Healthcare without Harm," *Dow Jones Press Release*, October 6, 1999; Paul Jarley and Cheryl Maranto, "Union Comprehensive Campaigns: An Assessment," *Industrial and Labor Relations Review* 43 (1990): 506; Kim Moody, "Competition and Conflict: Union Growth in the US Hospital Industry," *Economic and Industrial Democracy* 35 (2012): 5–25. SEIU eventually obtained neutrality agreements from Tenet.

13. David Hage, "Unions Launching New, Aggressive Organizing Efforts," *Mpls.-St. Paul Star Tribune*, May 23, 1988; interview with Steve Abrecht, director of Research and Capital Strategies, SEIU and chair of the SEIU National Industry Pension Fund, April 2008, Washington, DC.

14. Steven Greenhouse, *The Big Squeeze: Tough Times for the American Worker* (New York: Anchor Books, 2009), 241–261; Steven Greenhouse, "Janitors' Drive in Texas Gives Hope to Unions," *New York Times*, November 28, 2005; David Moberg, "Union Pension Power," *The Nation*, June 1, 1998, 16–20; Timothy J. Minchin, "A Successful Union in an Era of Decline: Interrogating the Growth of the Service Employees International Union, 1980–1995," *Labor History* 61 (June–August 2020): 300–319. The Houston story is not an entirely happy one for SEIU. In 2016, it lost a lawsuit filed by a cleaning services company that claimed SEIU had made false statements about its employment practices. A jury awarded the company over $5 million, at which point the Texas branch of SEIU filed for bankruptcy. The janitorial contracts in Houston remain in effect, although, by 2016 membership was down substantially. "Texas SEIU Files for Bankruptcy in Wake of Lawsuit Judgment," *Houston Chronicle*, December 6, 2016.

15. See Kate Bronfenbrenner et al., eds., *Organizing to Win: New Research on Union Strategies* (Ithaca, NY: ILR Press, 1998); Getman, *Restoring Power*; Rick Fantasia and Kim Voss, *Hard Work: Remaking the American Labor Movement* (Berkeley: University of California Press, 2004); "Justice for Janitors Calls for Boycott of Lenkin Family Holdings," *U.S. Newswire*, February 13, 1992; Pablo Gaston, "The Industrial Origins of Organizing Models in Two US Unions," IRLE Conference on Strategic Decision-Making in Labor and Social-Movement Organizations, working paper, Department of Sociology, Berkeley, 2010.

One of CarrAmerica's main investors was Equitable Life Insurance. SEIU asked Equitable to help resolve the dispute, but Equitable refused. SEIU then threatened to pull its investments in Equitable, worth $80 million, and to put the company on the AFL-CIO's boycott list. At that point, Equitable became more cooperative. "Equitable Sheds Its Stake in Carr REIT," *Washington Business Journal*, July 29, 1996.

16. W. Morgan Mallard, "Janitors Plan Down Demonstration; Group Asking Pay Raises Is Under Court Injunction," *Atlanta Journal Constitution*, November 22, 1987; "Pension Funds Love to Own New York City Real Estate," *New York Sun*, March 18, 2004; David Bacon, "Four Years of Class War End in a Union Contract," David Bacon: Stories, Photographs (blog), http://dbacon.igc.org/Unions/19SacJan.html; Joshua Bloom, "Ally to Win: Black Community Leaders and SEIU's L.A. Security Campaign," in *Working for Justice: The L.A. Model of Worker Organizing and Advocacy*, ed. Ruth Milkman, Joshua Bloom, and Victor Narro (Ithaca, NY: Cornell Uni-

versity Press, 2010); Benjamin I. Sachs, "Labor Law Renewal," *Harvard Law and Policy Review* 1 (2007): 379; Harold Meyerson, "A Clean Sweep," *American Prospect*, June 19, 2000; "Official of Major Calif. Pension Fund Backs Janitors," *Boston Globe*, September 26, 2002; "6 Firms, Janitors Reach Interim Pact; Contractors Break Ranks," *Boston Globe*, October 5, 2002; Abrecht interview; "Precarious Employment Practices in Property Management," Issue Brief, SHARE, Vancouver, 2007, http://www.share.ca/files/Property_Management_Brief_Public.pdf; Roger Waldinger et al., "Helots No More—A Case Study of the Justice for Janitors Campaign," in *Organizing to Win*, ed. Bronfenbrenner et al., 102–119; "Boston Properties to Face Shareholder Challenge on Corporate Governance," PR Newswire, November 13, 2003; "SEIU Develops New Online, Print Service Tracking Boston Properties, Inc." Business Wire, December 5, 2001; "Janitors' New Voice Mostly Immigrant Women, They Seek Better Wages, Benefits," *Boston Globe*, January 12, 2002; "Stiffed Board: Shareholders Angry about Executive Pay Are Targeting the People Responsible: Directors," *Wall Street Journal*, April 9, 2007.

17. Bacon, "Four Years"; "Janitors Pressure Intel," *San Francisco Business Times*, May 19, 2004; "Intel Shareholders Show Strong Support for SEIU Master Trust Proposal," Business Wire, May 20, 2004; "Bay Area Janitors Vote Overwhelmingly to Authorize Strike," PR Newswire, May 17, 2008.

18. Mallard, "Janitors Plan"; Bacon, "Four Years"; Joshua Bloom, "Ally to Win: Black Community Leaders and SEIU's L. A. Security Campaign," in *Working for Justice*, ed. Milkman, Bloom, and Narro, 167–190; Sachs, "Labor Law Renewal," 379; Harold Meyerson, "A Clean Sweep," *American Prospect*, June 19, 2000; "Official of Major Calif. Pension Fund Backs Janitors"; "6 Firms, Janitors Reach Interim Pact"; Abrecht interview; "Precarious Employment Practices in Property Management"; Roger Waldinger et al., "Helots No More."

19. Jack Fiorito and Paul Jarley, "Union Organizing and Membership Growth: Why Don't They Organize?" *Journal of Labor Research* 33 (2012): 461–486; Michael Piore, "Unions: A Reorientation to Survive," in *Labor Economics and Industrial Relations: Markets and Institutions*, ed. Clark Kerr and Paul Staudohar (Cambridge, MA: Harvard University Press, 1994); Nanette Byrnes, "Blue Collar Blues: Labor Unions Need Reorganization," *Financial World*, November 23, 1993; Richard Hurd and William Rouse, "Progressive Union Organizing: The SEIU Justice for Janitors Campaign," *Review of Radical Political Economics* 21 (1990): 70–75; Abrecht interview; Stephen Lerner and Jono Shaffer, "25 Years Later: Lessons from the Organizers of Justice for Janitors," *The Nation*, June 16, 2015; Steven Henry Lopez, *Reorganizing the Rust Belt: An Inside Study of the American Labor Movement* (Berkeley: University of California Press, 2004), 9; Kim Moody, "The Direction of Union Mergers in the United States: The Rise of Conglomerate Unionism," *British Journal of Industrial Relations* 47 (2009): 676–700; Minchin, "A Successful Union," 312.

20. "One Union Has Begun a First of Its Kind Shareholder Fight on the Internet," *Pensions and Investments* (hereafter *P&I*), October 16, 1995; Eric Brazil, "Hillhaven Workers Win New Contract," *SF Gate*, May 28, 1996.

21. "Shareholders Keep Directors Feeling the Heat," *P&I*, February 9, 1998; "Former Health-South CEO Scrushy Televangelist," *USA Today*, October 26, 2004; Jennifer Caplan, "Workers Claim Scrushy Sold Company Stock Before Releasing Bad News About Earnings," *CFO.com*, April 9, 2003; "Caring for Our Elderly," *Worcester Telegram and Gazette* [Massachusetts], October 12, 1998; "SEIU Pension Funds," http://www.secinfo.com/dvwb6.7a.htm; "SEIU Applauds

Columbia/HCA for Reversing Anti-Shareholder Trend," Business Wire, May 19, 1997; Marleen O'Connor, "Labor's Role in the Shareholder Revolution," in *Working Capital: The Power of Labor's Pensions*, ed. Archon Fung, Tessa Hebb, and Joel Rogers (Ithaca, NY: ILR Press, 2001), 71; Andrew Stern to New Columbia Shareholder Committee, March 23, 1998; interview with John M. Richardson and Rob Kellogg, *JMR Financial*, April 2008, Washington, DC. JMR was an advisor to unions on their capital market activities.

In the post-Enron wave of CEO prosecutions, HealthSouth's CEO, Richard Scrushy, was indicted for fraud, including the cashing in of stock options after reporting false financial results. Although subsequently acquitted, Scrushy was retried and sentenced in 2006. Former Senator Bill Frist's father founded HCA, and Frist was in the Senate at the time of the HealthSouth campaign. See chapter 6.

22. Marc Cooper, "Labor Deals a New Hand," *The Nation*, March 24, 1997.

23. Steven Greenhouse, "Labor Rolls on in Las Vegas," *New York Times*, April 27, 1998; Cooper, "Labor Deals"; Kathy Seal, "Hotel Unions' New Boss Heightens Expectations," *Hotel and Motel Management*, October 5, 1998; David Moberg, "Organization Man: For HERE President John Wilhelm, Building the Union Always Comes First," *The Nation*, July 16, 2001; Nelson Lichtenstein, "Labour, Liberalism, and the Democratic Party: A Vexed Alliance," *Relations Industrielles/Industrial* Relations, 66 (2011): 525. Also see James P. Kraft, *Vegas at Odds: Labor Conflict in a Leisure Economy, 1960–1985* (Baltimore, MD: Johns Hopkins University Press, 2009).

24. "Culinary/MGM Battle Heats Up," *Las Vegas Business Press*, August 23, 1993; Christina Binkley, "At Some Casinos, the Worst Enemy Isn't a Card Counter," *Wall Street Journal*, June 7, 1999; Mike Davis, "Armageddon at the Emerald City," *The Nation*, July 11, 1994; Ricki Fulman, "Matt Walker," *P&I*, October 19, 1998; "National Labor Relations Board Backs Culinary's Version of How It Organized MGM Grand," *Las Vegas Sun*, February 7, 1999. Fiedler's quote is from Getman, *Restoring the Power*, 103.

25. Even without shareholders, privately owned casinos could be vulnerable. When Adelson's company sought to issue bonds, HERE circulated a report questioning its ability to pay back debt. Binkley, "At Some Casinos."

26. "Report Criticizes Santa Fe Hotel," *Business Wire*, December 8, 1993; Binkley, "At Some Casinos."

27. "Executive Options Take Luster of Casino's Shares," *Wall Street Journal*, May 1, 2003; "Las Vegas Casino Group, Union Disagree Amiably on Corporate Governance," *Las Vegas Review-Journal*, May 19, 2005; "Station Casinos' Stockholders Approve Company's Proposals; Union's Non-Binding Proposal Fails," *Business Wire*, May 24, 2006; "Union Wants Insiders to Pull Station from Bankruptcy," *Las Vegas Review-Journal*, November 20, 2009; "Workers from Station Casinos Form Union Organizing Committee," *Business Wire*, February 25, 2010; "Station Workers Seek Refuge with Culinary," *Las Vegas Sun*, March 15, 2009; "U.S. Government Issues Massive Labor Law Complaint against Station Casinos," *Business Wire*, June 24, 2010; Fiorito and Jarley, "Union Organizing," 465; "The Palms Casino Hotel Off Las Vegas Strip Votes to Unionize," *This Day*, May 3, 2018.

28. "100 Best Companies to Work For," *CNN Money*, http://money.cnn.com/magazines/fortune/bestcompanies/2008/snapshots/72.html; "Hotel Housekeepers Report Staggering Job Injury Rate," *New Standard*, May 3, 2006, http://newstandardnews.net/content/index.cfm/items/3122

29. Getman, *Restoring Power*, 103, 105; Lopez, *Reorganizing the Rust Belt*; "Marriott Does It without Unions," *San Francisco Chronicle*, August 14, 1985; Getman, *Restoring the Power of Unions*, 105; "Worker Agreement Seen as Union Model," *Hotel and Motel Management*, November 18, 1996; "S.F. Marriott Concedes to Union," *San Francisco Chronicle*, October 8, 1996; "Marriott Hikes Wages for Its Union Workers," *San Francisco Chronicle*, September 30, 1998.

30. Barry Rehfeld, "A Suite Victory for Shareholders," *Institutional Investor*, July 1, 1998.

31. Rehfeld, "Suite Victory"; Christina Binkley, "Marriott Shareholders Vote Down Plan to Create Two Stock Classes," *Wall Street Journal*, May 21, 1998; "Stock Class Warfare Ends at Marriott," *Washington Times*, May 21, 1998.

32. "Marriott Protest—Scores Arrested," *San Francisco Chronicle*, November 18, 1998; "Brown Leads Call to Boycott S. F. Marriott," *San Francisco Chronicle*, September 5, 2000; "Religious Leaders Take on Labor Dispute," *San Francisco Chronicle*, August 30, 2001; "Marriott Shareholders Force Company to Divest from Burma," *Business Wire*, May 11, 2002; "Hard-Fought Accord for Marriott, Union," *San Francisco Chronicle*, August 30, 2002; Pablo Gaston, "Contention across Social Fields: Manipulating the Boundaries of Labor Struggle in the Workplace, Community, and Market," *Social Problems* 65 (2018): 231–250.

33. "ESOP Fables: UAL Worker-Owners May Face Bumpy Ride if the Past Is Any Guide: Pay and Management Snags Can Hamper Such Firms as Weirton Steel Found but Avis's Switch Pays Off," *Wall Street Journal*, December 23, 1993; Jonathan D. Rosenblum, *Copper Crucible: How the Arizona Miners' Strike of 1983 Recast Labor–Management Relations in America*, 2nd ed. (Ithaca, NY: ILR Press, 1998), 169–84; "Smoking Out Marc Rich," *Institutional Investor*, August 1, 1992; Kate Bronfenbrenner and Tom Juravich, *Ravenswood: The Steelworkers' Victory and the Revival of American Labor* (Ithaca, NY: Cornell University Press, 1999); "The Rich List," *The Guardian*, May 12, 2001; Thomas DiLorenzo, "The Corporate Campaign against Food Lion: A Study of Media Manipulation," *Journal of Labor Research* 17 (1996): 359–375; interview with Peter Rossman, Director of International Campaigns, International Union of Food, Agricultural, Hotel, Restaurant, Catering, Tobacco and Allied Workers' Associations (IUF), Geneva, Switzerland, December 2008. The surprise ending came on Bill Clinton's last day in office, when he pardoned Rich. At the time, Barney Frank, a liberal Congress member from Massachusetts, said the pardon was "contemptible." The pardon, too, remains shrouded in mystery. Peter Schweizer, "Bill Clinton's Pardon of Fugitive Marc Rich Continues to Pay Big Dividends," *New York Post*, January 17, 2016.

34. Mike Beirne, "USW Launches Campaign Against Bayou Steel," *American Metal Market*, August 4, 1993; Mike Beirne, "Bayou Union Tries to Crash Investor Meetings," *American Metal Market*, February 9, 1994; Mike Beirne, "Union Solicits Bayou Owners; "USW Files Lawsuits Seeking Proxy Access, Meeting," October 31, 1994; Amy Geisel, "Bayou Steel Files Suit Against Striking Union," *Knoxville News-Sentinel*, August 11, 1995; and Corinna Petry, "Workers Return to Bayou," November 8, 1996. Mini-mills, mostly nonunion, sprang up in the 1970s and 1980s as low-cost alternatives to primary steel manufacturers, which were mostly unionized.

35. Hilary Rosenberg, *A Traitor to His Class: Robert A. G. Monks and the Battle to Change Corporate America* (New York: Wiley, 1999), 164–175; Jayne Zanglein, "From Wall Street Walk to Walk Street Talk: The Changing Face of Corporate Governance," *DePaul Business Law Journal* 11 (1998): 43–122.

36. AFL-CIO Executive Council, "Model Guidelines for Delegated Proxy Voting Responsibility," February 1991, and "Pension Guidelines for Domestic and International Investment,"

February 1993; Aaron Bernstein, "Working Capital: Labor's New Weapon?" *Business Week,* September 29, 1997; Richardson and Kellogg interview. Michael Jensen was one of the first to use the phrase "imperial CEO." Ian Williams, "Of Corporate Bondage," *Investor Relations,* June 1, 1995.

37. AFL-CIO, *"Exercising Authority, Restoring Accountability: AFL-CIO Proxy Voting Guidelines,"* various; Jayne Elizabeth Zanglein, "Pensions, Proxies and Power: Recent Developments in the Use of Proxy Voting to Influence Corporate Governance," *Labor Lawyer* 7 (1991): 771–809. Short-term shareholding is associated with reduced R&D and patent activity, cutbacks in investment, and a reduction in a firm's value to shareholders. Andrei Shleifer and Robert W. Vishny, "Equilibrium Short Horizons of Investors and Firms," *American Economic Review* 80, no. 2 (1990): 148–153; Brian Bushee, "The Influence Of Institutional Investors on Myopic R&D Investment Behavior," *Accounting Review* 73 (1998): 305–333; Craig W. Holden and Leonard L. Lundstrum, "Costly Trade, Managerial Myopia, and Long-Term Investment," *Journal of Empirical Finance* 16 (2009): 126–135; Kevin Laverty, "Economic 'Short-Termism': The Debate, the Unresolved Issues, and the Implications for Management Practice and Research," *Academy of Management Review* 21 (1996): 825–860; Gregory Jackson and Anastasia Petraki, *Understanding Short-Termism: The Role of Corporate Governance* (Stockholm: Glasshouse Forum, 2011); Richard Davies, Andrew G. Haldane, Mette Nielsen, and Silvia Pezzini, "Measuring the Costs of Short-Termism," *Journal of Financial Stability* 12 (2014): 16–25; Philippe Aghion, John Van Reenen, and Luigi Zingales, "Innovation and Institutional Ownership," *American Economic Review* 103, no.1 (2013): 277–304.

38. Andrea Adelson, "Calpers Chooses a Less Adversarial Voice," *New York Times,* September 17, 1994; Richard A. Oppel Jr., "CalPERS Plans to Invest More Aggressively," *New York Times,* September 1, 1999; Kate Berry, "The CalPERS Machine," *Los Angeles Business Journal,* May 10, 2004; IRRC Institute and Mercer Associates, *Investment Horizons: Do Managers Do What They Say?* (New York: Mercer, 2010), 14; Martijn Cremers and Ankur Pareek, "Patient Capital Outperformance: The Investment Skill of High Active Share Managers Who Trade Infrequently," *Journal of Financial Economics* 122, no. 2 (2016): 288–306. Those who embrace the efficient market hypothesis (EMH) reject the claim that there is a difference between short-term and long-term effects on share price. If management decisions based on current share prices cause harm to a firm's long-term prospects, investors will sell their shares and current prices will fall. In other words, current share prices incorporate future states; there is no wedge. The problem is that the EMH is wanting, empirically, one reason being that markets are rife with informational asymmetries between managers and investors. Current prices are not informationally efficient with respect to the long term. Lynn A. Stout, "The Toxic Side Effects of Shareholder Primacy," *University of Pennsylvania Law Review* 160 (2013): 2016.

39. UN Global Compact and Global Corporate Governance Forum, "Corporate Governance: The Foundation for Corporate Citizenship and Sustainable Business" (2009); UN Principles for Responsible Investment, "Engaging on Director Nominations: An Investor Guide" (2017); Ron Blackwell and Bill Patterson, "The Crisis of Confidence in American Business: Corporate Accountability or Business as Usual," press release, August 6, 2002; Ron Blackwell and Bill Patterson, "Knocking Down the Boardroom Door," *New Labor Forum* 12 (2003): 51–60; Ron Blackwell interview, March 2007, Washington, DC. For critical perspectives on the UN's efforts, see David Vogel, "The Private Regulation of Global Corporate Conduct: Achieve-

ments and Limitations," *Business & Society* 49, no. 1 (2010): 68–87; Jim Baker, "Labour and the Global Compact: The Early Days," in *Learning to Talk: Corporate Citizenship and the Development of the UN Global Compact*, ed. Malcolm McIntosh, Sandra Waddock, and George Kell (London: Routledge, 2004), 168–182.

40. Damon A. Silvers and Michael I. Garland, "The Origins and Goals of the Fight for Proxy Access," at https://www.sec.gov/spotlight/dir-nominations/silversgarland022004.pdf; Damon Silvers, Policy Director, AFL-CIO, interview, March 2007, Washington, DC; Damon Silvers, William Patterson, and J. W. Mason, "Challenging Wall Street's Conventional Wisdom: Defining a Worker-Owner View of Value," in *Working Capital*, ed. Fung et al., 203–221.

41. Eric Becker and Patrick McVeigh, "Social Funds in the United States: Their History, Financial Performance, and Social Impacts," in *Working Capital*, ed. Fung et al., 44–66; Paula Tkac, "One Proxy at a Time: Pursuing Social Change through Shareholder Proposals," *Economic Review* 91 (2006): 1–20; Silvers, Patterson, and Mason, "Challenging Wall Street's Conventional Wisdom," 219. Alliances between labor and environmental movements were fraught during the 1970s and 1980s because of union concerns that environmentalists would undermine well-paid jobs in energy and construction. These concerns persist in the building trades. The Laborers, for example, are leery of solar and other alternative energy sources that may replace well-paid jobs in the oil industry, where the union has members, with nonunion and lower-paid jobs. "Green New Deal," *Labor Notes*, March 2019.

42. "Fidelity Pushes into Managing Payroll, Benefits," *Wall Street Journal*, January 3, 2003; "Looking over Managers' Shoulders, by Law," *New York Times*, July 6, 2003; Jennifer S. Taub, "Able but Not Willing: The Failure of Mutual Fund Advisers to Advocate for Shareholders' Rights," *Journal of Corporate Law* 34 (2008): 843; Federal Reserve, *Flow of Funds Accounts*, 2008; Robert Kuttner, *The Squandering of America: How the Failure of Our Politics Undermines Our Prosperity* (New York: Vintage, 2008), 138; Gerald F. Davis, "The Rise and Fall of Finance and the End of the Society of Organizations," *Academy of Management Perspectives* 23 (2009): 27–44; Gerald F. Davis and E. Han Kim, "Business Ties and Proxy Voting by Mutual Funds," *Journal of Financial Economics* 85 (2007): 562; Rasha Ashraf, Narayanan Jayaraman, and Harley E. Ryan. "Do Pension-related Business Ties Influence Mutual Fund Proxy voting? Evidence from Shareholder Proposals on Executive Compensation," *Journal of Financial and Quantitative Analysis* 47 (2012): 567–588.

43. "Labor Asks Pension Funds: Are You for Us or against Us?" *Pittsburgh Post-Gazette*, June 15, 1996; "Unions Quiz Money Managers," *P&I*, December 8, 1997; "AFL-CIO Joins Consumer Groups on Disclosure," *Investor News*, August 21, 2000; "Prodding for Disclosure of Funds' Proxy Votes."

44. "SEC Chief Pledges Action on Funds," *Wall Street Journal*, November 10, 2003; "S.E.C. Has Found Payoffs in Sales of Mutual Funds," *New York Times*, January 14, 2004; John Plender, "Broken Trust," *Financial Times*, November 21, 2003; "Proxy-Vote Disclosure Draws Critics," *Wall Street Journal*, December 9, 2002; "Social Activists Ride Coattails of Enron Case," *Investor News*, April 8, 2002; "Time to Fess Up Nears for Fund," *Investor News*, September 30, 2002; "SEC Proposal on Proxy Votes Finds Supporters in the House," *Wall Street Journal*, December 17, 2002.

45. Louis Uchitelle, *The Disposable American: Layoffs and Their Consequences* (New York: Vintage Books, 2007); Louis Lavelle, "How Shareholder Votes Are Legally Rigged," *Bloomberg BusinessWeek*, May 19, 2002, 48; "Fidelity Faces Rally by AFL-CIO," *Wall Street Journal*, July 31,

2002; "Unions Targets Corporate Change," *Wall Street Journal*, July 30, 2002; "An Offshore Storm Ends," *Hartford Courant*, August 3, 2002; New York Stock Exchange, Corporate Accountability and Listing Standards Committee, *Report*, June 6, 2002, A-6; "Stanley Decides against Bermuda Reincorporation," *Washington Post*, August 2, 2002; "Don't Short Bermuda," *P&I*, August 19, 2002; "CalPERS Urges Offshore Companies to Return to the U.S.," Reuters, November 18, 2002. On the AFL-CIO's campaign against tax avoidance, see *Accounting Reform and Investor Protection: Hearings before the Senate Committee on Banking, Housing, and Urban Affairs*, 107th Cong., 2nd Sess., 107-948, vol. II, March 2002: 1012, 1016–31 (testimony of Damon A. Silvers); *The Corporate and Auditing Accountability, Responsibility and Transparency Act of 2002: Hearings before the House Committee on Financial Services*, 107th Cong., 2nd Sess., March–April 2002: 107–160, 141–173.

46. Aaron Lucchetti, "Labor Puts Pressure on Funds: AFL-CIO's Trumka Discusses Why Unions Push for More Disclosure," *Wall Street Journal*, March 3, 2003; Interview with Richard Trumka, AFL-CIO Secretary Treasurer and later AFL-CIO President, Washington DC, March 2007.

47. Austan Goolsbee, "The Fees of Private Account and the Impact of Social Security Privatization on Financial Managers," University of Chicago Graduate School of Business, working paper, September 2004; "Labor Unions Enter Social Security Debate," *New York Times*, March 17, 2005; "Blow to Bush Reform Plan," *Financial Times*, March 8, 2005; "AFL-CIO Targets Schwab, Wachovia," *Pittsburgh Post-Gazette*, March 17, 2005; "Social Security Change Faces Labor Muscle," *Wall Street Journal*, March 22, 2005; "Unions Muffle Wall Street Support of Private Accounts," *Washington Post*, March 8, 2005; AFL-CIO Office of Investment, "Retirement Security: How Do Investment Managers Stack Up?" May 11, 2006.

48. Dragana Cvijanović, Amil Dasgupta, and Konstantinos E. Zachariadis, "Ties That Bind: How Business Connections Affect Mutual Fund Activism," *Journal of Finance* 71 (2016): 2933–2966; Jackie Cook, "Corporate Political Spending and the Mutual Fund Vote," Center for Political Responsibility, December 2012; "Governance Rules Need to Be Set by Objective Parties," *Financial Times*, February 6, 2016.

49. Lucian A. Bebchuk and Robert J. Jackson Jr., "Shining Light on Corporate Political Spending," *Georgetown Law Journal* 101 (2012): 923–968; Lucian A. Bebchuk and Robert J. Jackson Jr., "Corporate Political Speech: Who Decides?" *Harvard Law Review* 124 (2010): 83–117; Timothy Kuhner, *Capitalism v. Democracy: Money in Politics and the Free Market Constitution* (Stanford, CA: Stanford Law Press, 2014).

50. *Abood v. Detroit Board of Education*, 431 U.S. 209 (1977); *Public Communications Workers of America. v. Beck*, 487 U.S. 735 (1988).

51. J. C. Coates IV, "Corporate Governance and Corporate Political Activity: What Effect Will *Citizens United* Have on Shareholder Wealth? Harvard Law School, discussion paper no. 684, September 2010; "On Wall Street, More Investors Push Social Goals, *New York Times*, February 11, 2001; "Center for Political Accountability Urges SEC to Require Corporate Political Disclosure," *PR Newswire*, September 8, 2004; Social Investment Forum, *2005 Report on Socially Responsible Investing Trends in the United States*; Heidi Walsh, "Social and Environmental Proposals in 2010," Sustainable Investments Institute, July 22, 2010; Forum for Sustainable and Responsible Investment, *Report on US Sustainable, Responsible and Impact Investing Trends* (Washington, DC: 2014); Vishal P. Baloria, Kenneth Klassen, and Christine I. Wiedman,

"Shareholder Activism and Voluntary Disclosure Initiation: The Case of Political Spending," *Contemporary Accounting Research*, November 15, 2017, doi: 10.1111/1911-3846.12457; M. K. Chin, Donald C. Hambrick, and Linda K. Treviño, "Political Ideologies of CEOs: The Influence of Executives' Values on Corporate Social Responsibility," *Administrative Science Quarterly* 58 (2013): 197–232. Coates finds that corporate spending on politics is negatively associated with firm value. For contrary results, see Michael J. Cooper, Huseyin Gulen, and Alexei V. Ovtchinnikov, "Corporate Political Contributions and Stock Returns," *Journal of Finance* 65 (2010): 687–724.

52. Alicia H, Munnell, Jean-Pierre Aubry, and Mark Cafarelli, "Defined Contribution Plans in the Public Sector: An Update," Center for Retirement Research, Boston College, no. 37 (2014); Hazel Bradford, "Public Plans Surf Wave of Reforms in Aftermath of Crisis," *P&I*, February 18, 2019. For an overview of the libertarian right, including ALEC, see Jane Mayer, *Dark Money: The Hidden History of the Billionaires Behind the Rise of the Radical Right* (New York: Random House, 2016); Nancy MacLean, *Democracy in Chains: The Deep History of the Radical Right's Stealth Plan for America* (New York: Penguin, 2017); and Alex Hertel-Fernandez, *State Capture: How Conservative Activists, Big Businesses, and Wealthy Donors Reshaped the American States—and the Nation* (New York: Oxford University Press, 2019). On pensions and the right, see Beth Almeida, Kelly Kenneally, and David Madland, "The New Intersection on the Road to Retirement: Public Pensions, Economics, Perceptions, Politics, and Interest Groups," in *The Future of Public Employee Retirement Systems*, ed. Olivia S. Mitchell and Gary Anderson (New York: Oxford University Press, 2009); David Webber, *The Rise of the Working-Class Shareholder: Labor's Last Weapon* (Cambridge, MA: Harvard University Press, 2018), 223–227. The same right-wing groups also sought to privatize Social Security. On labor's efforts to protect defined-benefit plans, see Teresa Ghilarducci, "Organized Labor and Pensions," in *The Oxford Handbook of Pensions and Retirement Income*, vol. 13, ed. Gordon Clark, Alicia H. Munnell, and J. Michael Orszag (New York: Oxford University Press, 2006): 381–398.

53. Steven Greenhouse, "Yes, America is Rigged Against Workers," *New York Times*, August 3, 2019; Vishal P. Baloria, Kenneth Klassen, and Christine Wiedman, "Shareholder Activism and Voluntary Disclosure Initiation: The Case of Political Spending" (November 15, 2017). Available at https://ssrn.com/abstract=2079131 or http://dx.doi.org/10.2139/ssrn.2079131; Christopher P. Skroupa, "Investors Want Disclosure of Corporate Political Contributions and Lobbying Expenditures," *Forbes*, April 20, 2012; "Companies See Pitfall of Political Giving," *Washington Post*, April 13 2012; "More Shareholders Push for Transparency in Political Spending," *Washington Post*, May 22, 2012; "Investors Announce New Shareholder Initiative Seeking Disclosure of Company Lobbying Activities," *PR Newswire*, January 19, 2012; AFSCME, "Institutional Investors Press Companies for Disclosure of Lobbying in 2014," February 18, 2014; AFSCME, "Institutional Investors Continue to Press Companies for Disclosure of Lobbying in 2016," March 17, 2017; Georgeson, *Annual Corporate Governance Review (ACGR)*, 2012; Alexander Hertel-Fernandez, "Who Passes Business's 'Model Bills'? Policy Capacity and Corporate Influence in US State Politics," *Perspectives on Politics* 12 (2014): 582–602.

On *Citizens United*, see *Citizens United v. FEC*, 558 U.S. 310 (2010); Adam Winkler, *We the Corporations: How American Businesses Won Their Civil Rights* (New York: Liveright, 2018); Leo Strine Jr. and Nicholas Walter, "Conservative Collision Course: The Tension between Conservative Corporate Law Theory and *Citizens United*," *Cornell Law Review* 100 (2014): 335.

54. "More Boardrooms Targeted for Political Spending; Shareholder Proposals on the Rise to Disclose Corporate Donations," *MarketWatch*, April 19, 2012; "Center for Political Accountability Urges SEC to Require Corporate Political Disclosure," *PR Newswire*, September 8, 2004; Daniel Pedrotty to Elizabeth M. Murphy, secretary, Securities and Exchange Commission, January 18, 2012; "Companies: Show Us the Money," *New York Times*, March 20, 2013. Ten prominent law professors, the AFL-CIO, and others sent letters to the SEC.

55. "S.E.C. Is Asked to Require Disclosure of Donations," *New York Times*, April 24, 2013; "The S.E.C. and Political Spending," *New York Times*, October 29, 2014; Kevin Bogardus, "Capuano Bill Puts 'Citizens Fix' at Risk," *The Hill*, May 12, 2010, https://thehill.com/business -a-lobbying/97363-support-for-capuano-bill-risks-citizens-fix; "More Boardrooms Targeted for Political Spending"; Skroupa, "Investors Want Disclosure"; "The Corporate Disclosure Assault: Unions and Liberal Activists Are Using Proxy Rules to Attack Business Political Speech," *Wall Street Journal*, March 20, 2012; "Servings Shareholders and Democracy," *New York Times*, August 10, 2011; "SEC Will Not Consider Political Spending," *Washington Post*, December 2, 2013; Heidi Walsh and Robin Young, "How Leading U.S. Corporations Govern and Spend on State Lobbying," *SSRN*, April 27, 2017, https://papers.ssrn.com/sol3/papers.cfm?abstract_id =2940518; Bebchuk and Jackson, "Shining Light," 947.

56. "US Labor Dept. Weighs in on Union Pension-Plan Activism," *Wall Street Journal*, January 7, 2008; Louis J. Campagna, US Department of Labor, to David Chavern, US Chamber of Commerce, June 24, 2008; Department of Labor, Employee Benefits Security Administration, 29 CFR 2509, "Interpretive Bulletin Relating to Investing in Economically Targeted Investments" and "Interpretive Bulletin Relating to Exercise of Shareholder Rights," October 9, 2008.

57. Scalia had been appointed as the Labor Department's solicitor by President George W. Bush in April 2001. He served for only eighteen months because Senate Democrats refused to confirm him. One reason was Scalia's opposition to an ergonomics rule to protect worker health and safety. Senator John Edwards (D–NC) said that Scalia did not have "necessary empathy for workers." In 2019, President Trump appointed Scalia to be his Secretary of Labor. He immediately formulated a Labor Department proposal to prevent pension funds from considering collateral issues and defended the idea in a *Wall Street Journal* op-ed. "Democrats Question Bush Policies on Workplace Injuries," *New York Times*, April 19, 2002; "Bush Bypasses Senate on 2 More Nominees," *New York Times*, January 12, 2002; "Suing the Government? Call Scalia," *Bloomberg*, January 26, 2012; Noam Scheiber and Ron Lieber, "Labor Dept. Seeks to Restrict Social Goals in Retirement Investing," *New York Times*, June 24, 2020; Eugene Scalia, "Retirees' Security Trumps Other Social Goals," *Wall Street Journal*, June 24, 2020.

58. Eugene Scalia, "The New Labor Activism," *Wall Street Journal*, January 23, 2008; Ashwini K. Agrawal, "Corporate Governance Objectives of Labor Union Shareholders: Evidence from Proxy Voting," *Review of Financial Studies* 25 (2012): 187–226. The study to which Scalia referred was written when Agrawal was a doctoral student. It first came to light when Agrawal's dissertation chair, Steven Kaplan of the University of Chicago, posted a notice of it at the website, "Harvard Law School Forum on Corporate Governance," two months before Scalia's op-ed appeared. The op-ed was followed by an exchange between Kaplan, Agrawal, and the AFL-CIO's Daniel Pedrotty on the Harvard website. The AFL-CIO published a report seeking to debunk Agrawal's findings. The reader can follow the Harvard thread by starting with the last post and working backward. Harvard Law School Forum on Corporate Governance, "AFL-CIO

Proxy Voting: A Response by Agrawal," April 17, 2008, https://corpgov.law.harvard.edu/2008
/04/17/afl-cio-proxy-voting-a-response-by-agrawal/. Relevant posts are Ashwini Agrawal,
April 17, 2008; Daniel Pedrotty, March 27; Steven Kaplan, March 18; Agrawal, March 18; Pedrotty, March 1; Pedrotty, February 29; Kaplan, November 26, 2007; AFL-CIO, "Facts about
the AFL-CIO's Proxy Votes," March 2008. Agrawal's study finds that for the eighteen months
after the CTW's unions bolted from the AFL-CIO, the AFL-CIO's pension and reserve funds
shifted their votes to favor directors at companies where the CTW had members, while the
Carpenters did the opposite: favoring directors at companies with unions affiliated with the
AFL-CIO. The inference is that considerations other than shareholder value drove how unions
voted on director nominations. Other studies reach different conclusions.

   59. John Dos Santos and Chen Song, "Analysis of the Wealth Effects of Shareholder Proposals," Workforce Freedom Initiative, US Chamber of Commerce, July 22, 2008; "U.S. Chamber
Highlights Drawbacks of Union-Backed Shareholder Activism," *Targeted News Service*, June 23,
2009. "Union Pension Funds' Shareholder Activism Criticized by Chamber of Commerce Officials," *Daily Labor Report*, June 2009; Manhattan Institute, Proxy Monitor, "Special Report:
Labor-Affiliated Shareholder Activism," 2014; Ivan Osorio, "Unions: Political by Nature," Competitive Enterprise Institute, July 10, 2012.

   60. David Cifrino, "ISS and Glass Lewis Update Proxy Voting Guidelines For 2015," *Mondaq
Business Briefing*, November 14, 2014; Prevost, Rao, and Williams, "Labor Unions as Shareholder
Activists," 347. Research that obtains similar results includes Ertimur, Ferri, and Muslu, "Shareholder Activism," 576; Luc Renneboog and Peter G. Szilagyi, "The Role of Shareholder Proposals
in Corporate Governance," *Journal of Corporate Finance* 17 (2011): 168; Andrew K. Prevost, Udo-
msak Wongchoti, and Ben R. Marshall, "Does Institutional Shareholder Activism Stimulate Corporate Information Flow?" *Journal of Banking and Finance* 70 (2016): 105–117. It's worth noting that
financial companies, mutual funds, and corporate pension plans all pursue collateral interests,
either occasionally or systematically. Economists have paid scarce attention to the behavior of
these investors as compared to studies of union and public plans. One explanation is that union
and public plans are more transparent and their data easier to obtain; the other is antipathy to
unions among economists. James A. Brickley, Ronald C. Lease, and Clifford W. Smith Jr., "Ownership Structure and Voting on Antitakeover Amendments," *Journal of Financial Economics* 20 (1988):
267–291; Cvijanović et al., "Ties That Bind"; Davis and Kim, "Business Ties"; Aneel Keswani, David
Stolin, and Anh L. Tran, "Frenemies: How Do Financial Firms Vote on Their Own Kind?" *Management Science* 63 (2016): 631–654. See chapter 2 on corporate plans.

   61. "Power to the Owners," *The Economist*, March 9, 2013.

Chapter 4. Breaking Barriers, Building Bridges

   1. "Push Comes to Shove on Proxy Reform," Institutional Investor, April 1, 1991; "What the
New SEC Rules Do for Activism," *Institutional Investor*, April 1, 1993.

   2. "Breeden Reaffirms Proxy Effort," *Pensions & Investments* (hereafter *P&I*), October 28,
1991; Joel Chernoff and Marlene Givant Star, "Companies Brace for 1993 Proxy Season; SEC's
Long-Awaited Reforms Turn Up the Heat on Directors," *P&I*, October 26, 1992.

   3. Joel Chernoff, "Major Changes of SEC Proxy Reform Outlined," *P&I*, October 26, 1992;
Fran Hawthorne, "What the New SEC Rules Do for Activism," *Institutional Investor*, April 1,

1993. Nell Minow estimated that the new rules would cut legal costs of shareholder activists by two-thirds.

4. Virginia J. Harnisch, "Rule 14a-8 after Reagan: Does It Protect Social Responsibility Shareholder Proposals?" *Journal of Law and Policy* 6 (1989–1990): 415–447.

5. Harnisch, "Rule 14a-8," 423. The SEC's staff, not its commissioners, makes routine decisions on corporate exclusion requests, although commissioners can influence them. The SEC's five commissioners are presidential appointees, but no more than three may come from the same political party. Presidents are not authorized to fire them. Donald C. Langevoort, "The SEC, Retail Investors, and the Institutionalization of the Securities Markets," *Virginia Law Review* 95 (2009): 1025–1083.

6. "Lawmaker Says SEC Discourages Challenges to Executive Pay," *Dow Jones Newswires*, May 15, 1991; "Shareholders Get Say on CEOs' Pay," *Tampa Bay Times*, February 14, 1992; "U.S. Shareholders May Get Vote on Pay," *Wall Street Journal*, February 5, 1992. Also see Andrew K. Prevost and John D. Wagster, "Impact of the 1992 Changes in the SEC Proxy Rules and Executive Compensation Requirements," unpublished paper, September 1999, https://papers.ssrn.com/sol3/papers.cfm?abstract_id=179661

7. Marlene Givant Star, "Suit Seeks to Keep Hiring Policies on Proxies," *P&I*, August 17, 1992; Michelle McCann, "Shareholder Proposal Rule: Cracker Barrel in Light of Texaco," *Boston College Law Review* 39, no. 4 (July 1998): 965–999; Aaron Bernstein, "Labor Flexes Its Muscles as a Stockholder," *Business Week*, July 14, 1994, 79. While secretary of the Department of Labor, Robert Reich had the department issue new guidelines on proxy voting that said pension plans would be permitted to engage companies about their use of so-called high-performance work practices, a cluster including training investments, team-based production, stock ownership, and union-management cooperation. Drawn from Germany and Japan, mostly, the melange was related to industrial policy, about which Reich had once been enthusiastic. Research had shown that the practices raised wages, productivity, and share performance, the latter putting them beyond the business exclusion. Reich promoted the idea in the pension world, giving a speech about it to CII and reaching out to CalPERS, which later announced it would include a company's work practices among the criteria for making investment decisions. Reich was enthusiastic, calling the CalPERS decision a "big deal."

One of the few times Reich's idea was put to use came in 1995, when ACTWU, joined by the LongView Funds, submitted proposals to seven companies, asking them to report on their use of high-performance practices. One was Southwest Airlines, intentionally selected because it was an exemplar of workplace innovation and union-management cooperation. Another was Oshkosh B'Gosh, Southwest's opposite and a company where ACTWU had members. The children's apparel manufacturer was planning to shift production from its unionized factory in Wisconsin to Honduras and Tennessee. The Oshkosh proposal, unlike the other six, contained additional language stating that "high-performance workplace organizations are more often successful at unionized facilities." Twenty-two percent of shares were voted in favor, a strong showing. Stephen Power, "Pension Funds Get Guidelines for Activism," *Wall Street Journal*, July 29, 1994; Patrick S. McGurn, "DOL Issues New Guidelines on Proxy Voting, Active Investing," *IRRC Corporate Governance Bulletin* (July–August 1994); Asra Q. Nomani, "CalPERS Says Its Investment Decisions Will Reflect How Firms Treat Workers," *Wall Street Journal*, June 16, 1994; Marlene Givant Star, "Teamsters May Start Shareholder Lawsuit," *P&I*, January 10, 1994.

On Oshkosh, see Richard Marens, "Extending Frames and Breaking Windows: Labor Activists as Shareholder Activists," *Ephemera* 7 (2007): 448–452.

8. Ricki Fulman, "SEC Rules Blasted as Anti-Shareholder," *P&I*, October 27, 1997; Michael Schroeder, "SEC Backs Off on Shareholder-Resolution Curbs," *Wall Street Journal*, November 20, 1997; "SEC Adopts Modest Changes for Votes on Shareholder Resolutions," *Dow Jones Online News*, May 19, 1998; Mark E. Brossman and Molly J. Tatman, "SEC's Amendments to Shareholder Proposal Rules Are a Victory for Shareholder Advocacy," *Employee Benefits Journal* 23 (1998): 20–24.

9. Timothy J. Minchin, "'Labor Is Back?' The AFL-CIO during the Presidency of John J. Sweeney, 1995–2009," *Labor History* 54 (2013): 399; "AFL-CIO to Push for Wage-Gap Theme in Meeting Series," Reuters, February 20, 1996.

10. John J. Sweeney, Richard Trumka, and Linda Chavez-Thompson, "Rebuilding the American Labor Movement," *NEW SOLUTIONS: A Journal of Environmental and Occupational Health Policy* 6, no. 3 (1996): 82–86; US Chamber of Commerce, "Organized Labor's Growing Militancy," *Nation's Business* 85, June 1, 1997; Dammann quoted in Marc Cooper, "Labor Deals a New Hand," *The Nation*, March 24, 1997; Steve Early, "Organizing Efforts Getting Some Nonunion Help," *Boston Globe*, June 27, 1999. Sweeney had been SEIU's president when the Beverly drive began and also chairman of the union's Master Trust, its large multiemployer plan. For an overview that places these developments in historical context, see Teresa Ghilarducci, "Organized Labor and Pensions," in *The Oxford Handbook of Pensions and Retirement Income*, vol. 13, ed. Gordon L. Clark, Alicia H. Munnell, and Kate Williams (New York: Oxford University Press), 381–398.

11. Taylor E. Dark, "Debating Decline: The 1995 Race for the AFL-CIO Presidency," *Labor History* 40 (1999): 323–344; "Union Chief Has Bold Plans in Bid to Lead AFL-CIO," *Los Angeles Times*, July 17, 1995; Jonathan Cohn, "Hard Labor," *New Republic*, October 6, 1997; "Pension Fund Issues Top Labor Agenda," *P&I*, October 16, 1995.

12. "Labor's Growing Shareholder Activism," *P&I*, March 23, 1998; "Unions Quiz Money Managers," *P&I*, December 8, 1997. Evidence of coordinated voting can be found in Richard Marens, "Going to War with the Army You Have: Labor's Shareholder Activism in an Era of Financial Hegemony," *Business and Society* 47 (2008): 312–342.

13. Phyllis Plitch, "AFL-CIO Steps Up Executive Pay Activism in Cyberspace," Dow Jones News Service, April 4, 2001; Louis Lavelle, "Corporate Compensation Deals Questioned; AFL-CIO Cites Board Ties to CEOs," *Bergen Record*, April 10, 1998. Rees in "Soderquist, Glass Top Paid Executives in Arkansas," Associated Press, July 9, 2000.

14. Lublin, "Poison Pills." Data on proxy submissions are for 1997 and 1998, from Jayne Zanglein, "From Wall Street Walk to Wall Street Talk," 11 *DePaul Business Law Journal* (1998–1999): 77.

15. Leigh Jones, "Teamsters Seek More Shareholding Muscle at Fleming," *Journal Record* [Oklahoma City], September 27, 1996; "Companies in Proxy Battles," *P&I*, April 19, 1993; Randall S. Thomas and Kenneth J. Martin, "Should Labor Be Allowed to Make Shareholder Proposals," *Washington Law Review* 73 (1998): 68–71; Jack Fiorito and Paul Jarley, "Union Organizing and Membership Growth: Why Don't They Organize?" *Journal of Labor Research* 33 (2012): 461–486, at 465; "Shareholder Activism: Shareholders Keep Directors Feeling the Heat," *P&I*, February 8, 1998. On poison pills, see Yonca Ertimur, Fabrizio Ferri, and Stephen Stubben,

"Board of Directors' Responsiveness to Shareholders," *Journal of Corporate Finance* 16 (2010): 53–72.

16. "Managers Vote against Clients," *P&I*, April 20, 1998; Christian E. Weller, "Understanding the Challenges and Opportunities of Increased Shareholder Activism for Workers," Proceedings of the 52nd Annual Meeting of the Industrial Relations Research Association, Boston, 2000, 184–93. The Key Votes Survey is similar to the AFL-CIO's congressional key votes that grade members of Congress.

17. "Unions Quiz Money Managers," *P&I*, December 8, 1997; and "Bill Patterson, AFL-CIO, Says Institutional Investors Should Show Independence from Management," *P&I*, March 8, 1999; Trumka in Frank Swoboda, "Organized Labor to Keep Scorecard on Fund Managers," *Washington Post*, February 19, 1999; "Labor Wins Shareholder Votes," *Washington Post*, March 4, 1999; "Prodding for Disclosure of Funds' Proxy Votes," *Washington Post*, April 8, 2001; "Firms Slammed in AFL-CIO Proxy Voting Survey," *Money Management Letter*, March 18, 2002; Young and Trumka interviews.

18. "AFL-CIO Strikes Out against UAM over Labor Dispute" and "Taft-Hartley: Labor Flexes Muscles on Investment Community," *Money Management Letter*, June 16, 1997 and December 29, 1997; "Unions Pushed to the Wall: Strike Strategies Losing Clout," *Boston Globe*, July 27, 1997; Aaron Bernstein, "Working Capital: Labor's New Weapon?" *Business Week*, September 29, 1997. A different strike involving the Steelworkers took place at Oregon Steel's historic plant in Pueblo, Colorado, site of the Ludlow Massacre. The Office of Investment lent a hand. In addition to pressuring the company's bank (Wells Fargo) to cut back on loans to Oregon Steel, union investors submitted three cookbook proposals that won overwhelming support from other shareholders. After the union won a major NLRB case against Oregon Steel in 2004, the company agreed to pay back wages and rehire some workers. "Labor Wins Shareholder Votes; Decisions at Oregon Steel Reflect Union Pressure on Wall Street," *Washington Post*, March 4, 1999; "Wells Distances Itself from Steel Company," *San Francisco Chronicle*, July 2, 1999. "Steel Settlement: 6½ -Year Strike Ends as Pueblo Workers Agree to $61M Deal," *Rocky Mountain News*, March 17, 2004.

19. "Labor's Role in Capital Market," *P&I*, September 7, 1998; Swoboda, "Scorecard," *Washington Post*, February 19, 1999. Interview with John Marshall, Research Director, SEIU Capital Stewardship Program, July 2008, New York City; Young interview.

20. Jayne Zanglein and Denise Clark, *Capital Stewardship Certificate Program* (Baltimore, MD: National Labor College, 2001); Monami Chakrabarti, "Labor and Corporate Governance: Initial Lessons from Shareholder Activism," *WorkingUSA* 8 (2004): 45–69; Trumka interview. Blackwell quoted in William Greider, "The Soul of Capitalism," *The Nation*, September 29, 2003. Also see Gordon L. Clark, Emiko Caerlewy-Smith, and John C. Marshall, "Pension Fund Trustee Competence," Journal of Pension Economics and Finance 5 (2006).

21. SEIU, "Proposal #14 Adopted by SEIU Delegates at the 22nd International Convention," Pittsburgh, PA, May 2000; Herman Santos, "On Being a Union-Nominated Pension Fund Trustee," *Transfer* 17 (2011): 81–82; Ed Mendel, "CalPERS Board Seat: SEIU Seeks Three in a Row," *Calpensions*, September 28, 2009, http://calpensions.com/2009/09/28/calpers-board -seat-seiu-seeks-three-in-a-row; Barry B. Burr, "AFSCME Succeeds in First Foray into Activism," *P&I*, September 18, 2000; William Greider, "The New Colossus: The New Politics of Capital," *The Nation*, February 28, 2005; Ed Mendel, "Would Aiding Labor Hurt Profits?" *Calpen-*

sions, June 22, 2009, https://calpensions.com/2009/06/22/calpers-would-aiding-labor-hurt -profits/; "CalPERS Post Carries Clout," *Sacramento Bee,* August 21, 2006. Interviews with Sarah Teslik, Steve Abrecht, and Rob Kellogg and John Richardson.

22. Teslik interview; David Hess, "Protecting and Politicizing, Public Pension Fund Assets: Empirical Evidence on the Effects of Governance Structures and Practices," *University of California Davis Law Review* 39 (2005): 206, 215; Barbara A. Haney, Paul A. Copley, and Mary S. Stone, "The Effect of Fiscal Stress and Balanced Budget Requirements on the Funding and Measurement of State Pension Obligations," *Journal of Accounting and Public Policy* 21 (2002): 287–313; Johanna Westar and Anil Verma, "What Makes for Effective Labor Representation on Pension Boards?" *Labor Studies Journal* 32 (2007): 382–410; Joel T. Harper, *Board of Trustees Composition and Investment Performance of US Public Pension Plans,* Rotman International Centre for Pension Management, University of Toronto, February 2008, https://icpm.in1touch .org/document/4313/Joel_Harper_Board_of_Trustee_Composition_and_Investment _Performance_of_US_Public_Pension_Plans_February_2008.pdf

23. Anonymous source; Harper, *Board of Trustees.* Several unions had their own trustee-training programs. During its campaign for responsible-contractor policies, SEIU held trustee workshops on the real estate industry. AFSCME organized annual conferences to educate trustees from state and local plans about how to avoid investments that would be harmful to state and local employees.

24. Abrecht and Zelenko interviews; Burr, "AFSCME Succeeds"; "Labor of Love," *Institutional Investor,* March 14, 2005; Larry W. Beeferman, "Capital Stewardship in the United States," *Transfer* 17 (2011): 43–57; AFSCME, *Best Practice Policies for Trustees and Pension Systems* (Washington, DC, n.d.); Fabrizio Ferri and James Weber, "AFSCME vs. Mozilo . . . and 'Say on Pay' for All! (A)," Harvard Business School, case study 9-109-009, March 18, 2009, 3.

25. Crist interview. Crist accused corporate pension trustees of engaging in similarly self-indulgent activities in contrast to the professionalism of public-plan trustees. Some years later, several of Crist's fellow trustees were investigated for taking kickbacks from companies seeking CalPERS investments. See chapter 8.

26. "Use Pension Funds to Advance Labor Goals, Union Chief Urges," *Employee Benefit News,* December 1, 1999; interview with Steven Sleigh, partner, Yucaipa Companies and former director of Strategic Resources, International Association of Machinists and Aerospace Workers (IAM), Los Angeles, July 2010; Kim Voss and Rachel Sherman, "Breaking the Iron Law of Oligarchy: Union Revitalization in the American Labor Movement," *American Journal of Sociology* 106 (2000): 303–349.

27. Durkin interview; Richard Marens, "Waiting for the North to Rise: Revisiting Barber and Rifkin after a Generation of Union Financial Activism in the US," *Journal of Business Ethics* 52 (2004): 112; Marens, "Going to War"; "Microsoft Shareholders Grill Gates, Ballmer," *Seattle Times,* November 12, 2003; "Grading the Companies," *Seattle-Post Intelligencer,* September 21, 2003; "United Brotherhood of Carpenters and Joiners Worker-Owner Activism White Paper," December 2001, courtesy of Edward Durkin; Jeff Grabelsky, "Building and Construction Trades Unions: Are They Built to Win?" *Social Policy* 35 (2004): 35–39; Abrecht and Durkin interviews.

28. "Union Affiliation by US State," http://en.wikipedia.org/wiki/Union_affiliation_by_U.S. _state. The data are for 2008. Young, Teslik, and Richardson and Kellogg interviews.

29. Murphy quoted in Greider, "The New Colossus"; John Cioffi, *Public Law and Private Power: Corporate Governance Reform in the Age of Financial Capitalism* (Ithaca, NY: Cornell University Press, 2010), 11. Teslik left CII in 2004. According to Robert Monks, she was tired of the council's "array of conflicting interests." Barry Burr, "Tough Decision: Teslik Leaving Stresses of CII to Lead Financial Planners' Group," *P&I*, October 4, 2004.

30. Anonymous interview; Judith H. Dobrzynski, "Pension-Fund Group Faces Its Own Governance Battle," *New York Times*, April 1, 1996; "Top Retirement Funds Plan to Jointly Push Reforms," Reuters, May 28, 2003.

31. Mary Williams Walsh, "Calpers Wears a Party, or Union, Label," *New York Times*, October 13, 2002; "Can CalPERS Afford to Throw Stones?" *Business Week*, June 24, 2002; "CalPERS' Emerging Markets Policy on the Hot Seat," *P&I*, May 13, 2002; Cooper, "Labor Deals"; "Burton Resignation Signals Big Changes for CalPERS," *P&I*, May 27, 2002; Crist interview.

32. Deborah Brewster and Simon London, "Calpers Chief Relaxes in the Eye of the Storm," *Financial Times*, June 2, 2004.

33. Crist interview; Analyst quoted in Aaron Bernstein and Amy Borrus, "Labor Sharpens Its Pension Sword," *Business Week*, November 23, 2003; Walsh, "Calpers Wears a Party."

For a more optimistic account of the Safeway story, see David Webber, *The Rise of the Working-Class Shareholder: Labor's Last Weapon* (Cambridge, MA: Harvard University Press, 2018).

34. Steven Greenhouse, "2 Sides Seem Entrenched in Supermarket Dispute," *New York Times*, November 10, 2003; Mary Williams Walsh, "California Pension Activist Expects to Be Ousted," *New York Times*, December 1, 2004; Mary Williams Walsh, "Calpers Ouster Puts Focus on How Funds Wield Power," *New York Times*, December 2, 2004.

Tom Petruno, "Business Applauds Shakeup at CalPERS," *Los Angeles Times*, December 2, 2004; Union official quoted in Marc Lifsher, "Calpers Removes Chief," *Los Angeles Times*, December 2, 2004; Steven Brull, "A Truly Civil Servant," *Institutional Investor*, June 15, 2005.

35. Young and Durkin interviews. Also see Matthew T. Bodie, "Labor Interests and Corporate Power," *Boston University Law Review* 99 (2019): 1123–1150.

36. "Schwarzenegger Proposes Overhaul of California Pensions," Reuters, January 6, 2005; "Governor Hits State Pensions," *San Diego Union-Tribune*, February 11, 2005.

37. "CalPERS Leads Fight on Pension Proposal," *Sacramento Bee*, January 21, 2005; "Schwarzenegger Aims at State Pension System," *New York Times*, January 23, 2005; "National Fight against California Pension Revamp," Reuters, February 2, 2005; Angelides in Greider, "New Colossus"; "The Saga of the Special Election," *Sacramento Bee*, November 13, 2005.

38. "CalPERS Board Opposes Social Security Privatization," *Business Wire*, December 15, 2004; Lee Conrad, "Government Outsourcers May Lose Calpers Funds," *US Banker*, November 3, 2003; "SEIU Opposes Privatization," *P&I*, January 6, 2003; "Unions Use Big Stock Investors as Weapons," *Wall Street Journal*, September 23, 2003; David Moberg, "How Edison Survived," *The Nation*, February 26, 2004. AFSCME was infuriated by the Edison incident and by the Florida plan's failure to monitor its Enron investments (it lost three times more than any other state fund). It proposed a new board structure with half of its trustees chosen from the ranks of plan participants and retirees. AFSCME, "Inside the Florida State Board of Administration: Mismanagement Made the Enron Loss Inevitable," September 2002.

39. Nancy J. Kim, "Companies Issuing Codes of Conduct," *Bergen Record*, September 10, 1995; "Sweatshops Top Social Activism List," *Investor Relations Business*, February 10, 1997; "The

New Financial Activists," *Institutional Investor*, June 1, 2000; "Finance–U.S. Crisis Prompts Calls for Debate on Global Economy," *Interpress Service*, September 17, 1998; "Ethical Crusaders Aim to Redeem Corporate Sinners," *Financial Times*, March 29, 2002. Whether corporate codes make a difference is another matter. The preponderance of studies finds that they have little effect. See Muel Kaptein and Mark S. Schwartz, "The Effectiveness of Business Codes," *Journal of Business Ethics* 77 (2008): 111–127; David Vogel, "The Private Regulation of Global Corporate Conduct," *Business and Society* 49 (2010): 68–87; Guy Mundlak and Issi Rosen-Zvi, "Signaling Virtue? A Comparison of Corporate Codes in the Fields of Labor and Environment," *Theoretical Inquiries in Law* 12 (2011): 603–663.

40. Sarah Anderson, John Cavanagh, and Thea Lee, "We Can Fight, We Can Win," *The Nation*, December 6, 1999; "USWA Hails Nicaragua Agreement," PR Newswire, May 11, 2001; "The New Kid on the Block"; Investor Statement Urges Business to Do Its Part to Make Modern-Day Slavery History," PR Newswire, June 27, 2011.

41. "Counterpunch: Walmart's Unlikely Role: Corporate Defender in Chief," *Wall Street Journal*, July 26, 2005; LongView Funds, "Amalgamated Bank and Coalition of Religious Funds Urge Walmart Advisory Vote on Compensation," Press Release, New York, June 5, 2008.

42. "Shareholders to Focus on Executive Compensation," *Investor Relations Business*, March 2, 1998; "Proxy Proposals Hit Record High," *Investor Relations Business*, February 24, 2003; "SEC Intent on Investor Rights Review," *Financial Times*, October 14, 2007; "Institutional Investors Press Companies for an Advisory Vote on Executive Pay," AFSCME, Washington, DC, press release, January 24, 2008; "Pay Disparity Disclosure Is Focus of Unprecedented New Shareholder Push," *PR Newswire*, December 1, 2009.

43. US General Accounting Office (GAO), *Corporate Shareholder Meetings: Issues Relating to Firms That Advise Institutional Investors on Proxy Voting* (Washington, DC, June 2007), 13; Stephen Choi and Jill Fisch, "On Beyond CalPERS: Survey Evidence on the Developing Role of Public Pension Funds in Corporate Governance," *Vanderbilt Law Review* 61 (2008): 315–354; Paul Rose, "The Corporate Governance Industry," *Journal of Corporation Law* 32 (2007): 887, 889; Stephen Choi, Jill Fisch, and Marcel Kahan, "The Power of Proxy Advisors: Myth or Reality?" *Emory Law Journal* 59 (2010): 869; Yonca Ertimur, Fabrizio Ferri, and David Oesch, "Shareholder Votes and Proxy Advisors: Evidence from Say on Pay," *Journal of Accounting Research* 51 (2013): 951–996. When ISS recommends a vote against a director, the vote total is estimated to drop by an average of 8–20 percent. ISS is the largest proxy advisor in the United States, with Glass, Lewis & Co. a distant second. Jie Cai, Jacqueline Garner, and Ralph A. Wakling, "Electing Directors," *Journal of Finance* 64 (2009): 2389–2421.

44. RiskMetrics Group, "U.S. Proxy Voting Guidelines," February 25, 2010; Sanjai Bhagat, Brian Bolton, and Roberta Romano, "The Promise and Peril of Corporate Governance Indices," *Columbia Law Review* 108 (2008): 1874; Richardson and Kellogg interview; Monks quoted in Hilary Rosenberg, *A Traitor to His Class: Robert A. G. Monks and the Battle to Change Corporate America* (New York: John Wiley, 1999), 135; Robert Daines, Ian Gow, and David Larcker, "Rating the Ratings: How Good Are Commercial Governance Ratings?" *Journal of Financial Economics* 98 (2010): 439–462.

45. Interview with Donald MacDonald, trustee director, BT Pension Scheme, London, January 2009; Rosenberg, *A Traitor*, passim.

46. Chakrabarti, "Labor and Corporate Governance," 67; Kellogg and Richardson, and Young interviews; ISS, *2011 Taft-Hartley International Proxy Voting Guidelines*, January 2011.

47. RiskMetrics Group, "2010 SRI U.S. Proxy Voting Guidelines," January 2010; RiskMetrics Group, *Corporate Social Issues Reporter*, November 2008; "ISS Recommends Unocal Shareholders Vote for Global Labor Standards," *PR Newswire*, May 13, 2002; "ISS Backs Shareholder Proposal to Restore Pension, Retiree Benefits at IBM," *PR Newswire*, April 13, 2000; Jeffrey McGuiness, president LPA to LPA Company Representatives, "Key Labor-Backed Shareholder Resolutions Supported by 'Independent' Shareholder Service Firm," June 7, 2002. When companies sell only to other companies and not to consumers—as in chemicals, metals, mining, and oil and gas extraction—the reputational effects are less threatening.

48. Leslie Wayne, "Have Shareholder Lost Their Edge?" *New York Times*, January 30, 1994; Patrick McGurn, "The Role of Proxy Advisory Firms in the Shareholder Proxy Process," *Investor Relations Business*, February 16, 1998; "Controversy Ignites Competition in Proxy Advisory Business," *Dow Jones News Services*, June 11, 2007; "A Proxy Advisor's Two Sides; Some Question Work of ISS for Companies It Scrutinizes," *Washington Post*, January 23, 2006; GAO, *Corporate Shareholder Meetings*; European Commission, "Green Paper: The EU Corporate Governance Framework," Brussels, April 5, 2011. When the GAO investigated conflicts of interest among ISS and other proxy advisors, it found no major violations. In 2012, the Justice Department and the SEC investigated ISS for selling confidential shareholder voting data over several years to Georgeson, a proxy solicitor. With this information, boards can game the system by pressuring those who have not yet voted to support management. The business community and its supporters regularly attack ISS and other proxy advisors, whose recommendations they often disagree with, as when ISS and Glass, Lewis endorsed proposals on disclosure of political spending. Recently the NAM demanded that advisors be required to tell a company their voting recommendations before sending them out to clients, a burden for the advisors and a threat to their independence. GAO, *Corporate Shareholder Meetings*; "Vote Solicitor Georgeson Ensnared in Scandal," *New York Post*, April 16, 2012; James R. Copland, David F. Larcker, and Brian Tayan, "Proxy Advisory Firms: Empirical Evidence and the Case for Reform," Manhattan Institute, May 21, 2018.

Between 2006 and 2020, ISS had no less than five different owners: RiskMetrics; Morgan Stanley Capital International, Warburg Pincus, and Hermes Investment Management; Thomson Reuters; Genstar Capital (a private equity fund); and Deutsche Börse, owner of the Frankfurt Stock Exchange. Most of the owners have been financial institutions whose profits are related to robust shareholder capitalism. Whether this influenced ISS's recommendations, or its general orientation, has never been studied.

Chapter 5. From Exuberance to Enron

1. Michael Mandel, *The High-Risk Society* (New York: Crown Books, 1996); "Rugged Individualism?" *Institutional Investor*, January 1, 1996; Daniel Yergin and Joseph Stanislaw, *The Commanding Heights: The Battle for the World Economy* (New York: Free Press, 1998).

2. James Flanigan, "Employee-Owned United Airlines May Prove to Be Good Buy," *Austin American-Statesman*, December 19, 1993; Michael J. McCarthy, "Administration Looks Favorably on Idea of Employee Ownership," *Wall Street Journal*, December 23, 1993.

3. Jon Talton, "Jon Talton Column," *Charlotte Observer*, May 24, 1998; Patrick Wintour, "Blair Defends His Vision of Stakeholder Economy," *The Guardian*, January 1996; John Cioffi and Martin Höpner, "The Political Paradox of Finance Capitalism: Interests, Preferences, and Center-Left Party Politics in Corporate Governance Reform," *Politics and Society* 34 (2006): 463–501. Near the end of Blair's term, one of his advisors, David Pitt-Watson, and Jon Lukomnik, manager of New York City's pension plans in the 1990s, co-authored a book hailing "citizen investors" who would "foster a culture of competitiveness and performance, producing more wealth and employment." Stephen Davis, Jon Lukomnik, and David Pitt-Watson, *The New Capitalists* (Boston: Harvard Business School, 2006), 230.

4. "Executive Pay: An Embarrassment to Free Marketers," *Wall Street Journal*, January 10, 1992; "What's Your Boss Worth? 35 Times Your Salary? 1,000 Times? The Workforce Gets Angry," *Washington Post*, August 5, 1990; "Japan Takes Aim at U.S. Executives' Pay," *Asian Wall Street Journal*, December 30, 1991; "CEOs' Presence in Bush Party Draws Attention to Their Pay," *San Diego Union-Tribune*, January 13, 1992. A book that caught the spirt of the times is Graef Crystal, *In Search of Excess: The Overcompensation of American Executives* (New York: Ecco Press, 1991).

5. Sylvia Nasar, "The Richest Getting Richer: Now It's a Top Political Issue," *New York Times*, May 11, 1992.

6. Rick Wartzman, "The Clinton Budget: Tax Plan Gives Shareholders a Voice in How Companies Pay Top Executives," *Wall Street Journal*, April 9, 1993; David Hilzenrath, "White House Unveils Plan to Rein in Corporate Pay," *Washington Post*, April 9 1993. "Clinton Victory Wouldn't Slash Top Officer Pay," *Wall Street Journal*, November 30, 1992; Thomas B. Edsall, "Tsongas Message Called Strongest in TV Debate," *Washington Post*, February 2, 1992. Ten years after leaving the cabinet, Reich described the Clinton White House as "one of the most pro-business administrations in American history." Robert Reich, *Supercapitalism: The Transformation of Business, Democracy, and Daily Life* (New York: Vintage, 2007), 137.

7. Matthew Sherman, "A Short History of Financial Deregulation in the U.S.," Center for Economic and Policy Research, Washington, DC, July 2009, http://cepr.net/documents /publications/dereg-timeline-2009-07.pdf; Nicholas Confessore, "Lost Causes," *American Prospect*, September 25, 2000; Simon Johnson and James Kwak, *13 Bankers: The Wall Street Takeover and the Next Financial Meltdown* (New York: Random House, 2010), 91; G. William Domhoff, *The Myth of the Liberal Ascendancy* (Boulder, CO: Paradigm Books, 2013), 268; Jacob Hacker and Paul Pierson, *Winner-Take-All Politics* (New York: Simon & Schuster, 2010). Summers quoted in "Congress Passes Wide-Ranging Bill Easing Bank Laws," *New York Times*, November 5, 1999.

8. Robin Blackburn, "The Subprime Crisis," *New Left Review*, March 2008; "Gramm and the Enron Loophole," *New York Times*, November 17, 2008. Weill kept a plaque in his office labeling himself "The Shatterer of Glass-Steagall," *New York Times*, July 25, 2012.

9. Robert J. Shiller, *Irrational Exuberance* (Princeton, NJ: Princeton University Press, 2000), 8, 39; Markus Brunnermeier, *Asset Prices under Asymmetric Information* (New York: Oxford University Press, 2001); Investment Company Institute, *401(k) Plans: A 25-Year Retrospective* (Washington, DC, 2006), 3; Charles A. Jeszeck, *Private Pensions: Long-Standing Challenges Remain for Multiemployer Pension Plans* (Washington, DC: General Accounting Office), 2010; Sushil Bikhchandani, David Hirshleifer, and Ivo Welch, "A Theory of Fads, Fashion, Custom,

and Cultural Change in Informational Cascades," *Journal of Political Economy* 100 (1992): 992–1026.

10. "CalPERS Puts $100 Million into Kline's Venture Fund," *Los Angeles Business Journal*, January 31, 2000; "Calpers Adds to Alternatives Funds," *Pensions & Investments* (hereafter *P&I*), February 21, 2000; letter to author from Susan Kane, CalPERS, March 10, 2006; "CalPERS Ups Allocation for RE, Alternative Invest," Dow Jones, May 16, 2000; Mark Sarney, "State and Local Pension Plans' Equity Holdings and Returns," *Social Security Bulletin* 63 (2000): 12–26; "Telecommunications Industry Too Devastated Even for Vultures," *New York Times*, December 17, 2001. Quote from Ricki Fulman, "The Best of Times for Tech: Heady Internet Valuations Draw Pension Funds into Venture Cap," *P&I*, March 20, 2000.

11. Sweeney quoted in "Fed Faces Pressure to Deflate Markets," *Washington Times*, April 4, 2000. Data on benefit provisions of public plans come from annual reports of the National Association of State Retirement Plan Administrators.

12. Shiller, *Irrational Exuberance*; John Cassidy, *Dot.con: How America Lost Its Mind and Money in the Internet Era: The Greatest Story Ever Sold* (New York: Harper Collins, 2002). Accounts of the frothy stock market emphasize investor psychology, what Greta Krippner terms "the speculative mania hypothesis." Psychological factors, though important, achieved their potency through financial deregulation and the bipartisan endorsement of stock ownership. Greta Krippner, *Capitalizing on Crisis: The Political Origins of the Rise of Finance* (Cambridge, MA: Harvard University Press, 2011).

13. SEC, press release 2003-54, "Ten of Nation's Top Investment Firms Settle Enforcement Actions Involving Conflicts of Interest between Research and Investment," https://www.sec .gov/news/press/2003-54.htm; *Investment News*, February 10, 2001; William W. Bratton, "Enron and the Dark Side of Shareholder Value," *Tulane Law Review* 76 (2002): 1275, 1334; *Analyzing the Analysts: Hearings before the Subcommittee on Capital Markets, Insurance, and Government Sponsored Enterprises, of the House Committee on Financial Services*, 107th Cong. 53-61 (2001), testimony of Damon A. Silvers; "Unions Put Pressure on Wall Street over Analysts' Conflicts of Interest," *Wall Street Journal*, October 29, 2001

14. It was easier for large public plans to meet with directors and executives than it was for union investors. Their assets were vastly greater than those of even the largest union plans. In addition to informal meetings and letters, public plans began to file an increasing but small number of derivative lawsuits, which, if successful, would require the company to comply with the intent. Institutional investors, when they are dissatisfied, are most likely to meet with top management (63%) followed by discussions with boards at which management is not present (45%). Stephen Choi and Jill Fisch, "On Beyond CalPERS: Survey Evidence on the Developing Role of Public Pension Funds in Corporate Governance," *Vanderbilt Law Review* 61 (2008): 335–338; Barry S. Burr, "Support Growing: All Investor Eyes on Busy Proxy Season," *P&I*, June 14, 2004; "Shareholders Rise Up," *New York Times*, October 10, 2002; Joseph McCahery, Zacharias Sautner, and Laura T. Starks, "Behind the Scenes: The Corporate Governance Preferences of Institutional Investors," *Journal of Finance* 71 (2016). Also see Andrew K. Prevost and Ramesh P. Rao, "Of What Value Are Shareholder Proposals Sponsored by Public Funds?" *Journal of Business* 73 (2000): 177–204.

15. Gretchen Morgenson, "A Bubble That Enron Insiders and Outsiders Didn't Want to Pop," *New York Times*, January 14, 2002; Steven Greenhouse, "Public Funds Say Losses Top $1.5 Billion," *New York Times*, January 29, 2002.

Enron claimed that it ranked seventh in the Fortune 500. But after it failed, a study measured its revenue based on accepted accounting principles—not Enron's—and found that the company was actually 287th on the list, about the same size as General Mills. William R. Bufkins and Bala G. Dharan. "Red Flags in Enron's Reporting of Revenues and Key Financial Measures," in *Enron: Corporate Fiascos and Their Implications*, ed. Nancy B. Rapoport and Bala G. Dharan (New York: Foundation Press, 2004), 97–110.

16. "Prepared Statement of Damon A. Silvers, Associate General Counsel, AFL-CIO," in *An Overview of the Enron Collapse: Hearings before the Committee on Commerce, Science, and Transportation*, US Senate, S. Hrg. 107–724, December 18, 2001, 87; "Statement of Damon A. Silvers," *Hearings before the Committee on Financial Services*, US House of Representatives, 107th Cong., 2nd Sess. April 9, 2002, 141. In December 2002, ten banks reached preliminary settlements with the SEC and New York State Attorney General Eliot Spitzer. Although they were fined $1.4 billion, the largest fine ever levied in a regulatory settlement, it would not be enough to deter recidivism. "Wall Street Brokers Fined $1.4 Billion," *Bloomberg*, December 21, 2002; "AFL-CIO Targets Investment Banks with Proxy Question," *Dow Jones News Service*, December 10, 2002; "Wall Street Firms Settle Charges over Research in $1.4 Billion Pact," *Wall Street Journal*, April 29, 2003; Dan Jamieson, "Forgotten in the Fix: Why Aren't Brokers Included in Plans to Overhaul Firms' Research Practices?" *Wall Street Journal*, July 1, 2002.

17. Robert Kuttner, *The Squandering of America: How the Failure of Politics Undermines Our Prosperity* (New York: Vintage Books, 2008), passim.

18. Data on investors and Enron from Factiva; Michael Useem, *Investor Capitalism: How Money Managers Are Changing the Face of Corporate America* (New York: Basic Books, 1996), 5–6; John C. Coffee Jr., "What Caused Enron? A Capsule Social History of the 1990s," *Cornell Law Review* 89 (2004): 269–309; "The Crisis in Corporate Governance," *Business Week*, May 6, 2002; John Byrne, "Restoring Trust in Corporate America," *New York Times*, June 24, 2002; S. Burcu Avci, Cindy A. Schipani, and H. Nejat Seyhun, "Do Independent Directors Curb Financial Fraud: The Evidence and Proposals for Further Reform," *Indiana Law Journal* 93 (2018): 757–808; Blackwell interview.

19. Bratton, "Enron and the Dark Side," 1334, 1340; Kathleen Pender, "CalPERS Had Enron Because Many Did," *San Francisco Chronicle*, December 9, 2001; Crist interview; Joshua Green, "What Has Become of Enron's Former Directors?" *American Prospect*, June 17, 2002, 14–15; Brunnermeier, *Asset Pricing*; Markus Brunnermeier and Dilip Abreu, "Synchronization Risk and Delayed Arbitrage," *Journal of Financial Economics* 66 (2003): 41–36; Anat Admati, "A Skeptical View of Financialized Corporate Governance," *Journal of Economic Perspectives* 31 no. 3 (Summer 2017): 136.

20. Loren Fox, *Enron: The Rise and Fall* (New York: Wiley, 2004), 120–123; Sanford M. Jacoby, "Convergence by Design: The Case of CalPERS in Japan," *American Journal of Comparative Law* 55 (2007): 239–293; Bratton, "Enron and the Dark Side," 1308; "CalPERS Had Enron because Many Did," *San Francisco Chronicle*, December 9, 2001; "Can CalPERS Afford to Throw Stones?" *Business Week*, June 24, 2002.

21. Jerry W. Markham, *A Financial History of Modern U.S. Corporate Scandals* (Armonk, NY: M.E. Sharpe, 2006); "Crisis," *Business Week*, May 6, 2002; "WorldCom's Collapse: The Overview," *New York Times*, July 22, 2002; Ellen Frank, "The Great Stock Illusion," *Dollars & Sense*, November 1, 2002; Ana Radelat, "Labor Pushes Campaign for Laid-Off WorldCom Workers," *Gannett News Service*, September 7, 2002; Shawn Young, "Without a Net: In Bankruptcy, Getting

Laid Off Hurts Even Worse," *Wall Street Journal*, September 30, 2002; Nomi Prins, "Whose Jobs? Our Jobs!" *Dollars & Sense*, March 2003.

Tyco's Dennis Kozlowski was among the era's most egregious CEOs. The first hint of trouble at Tyco came in January 2002, shortly after Enron's bankruptcy. It turned out that Kozlowski had defrauded Tyco of hundreds of millions of dollars, for which he later served eight years in prison. He is infamously remembered for throwing a $2 million toga party for his wife's birthday. Held at an Italian villa, it was replete with Roman guards and goddesses. Tyco, like Enron, adhered to the cookbook, duping even savvy investors like Robert Monks. Two years before its problems came to light, Monks said, "Dennis has all the qualities you look for in a great CEO, whether it's superior operating performance or pro-shareholder corporate governance. Dennis is the best at his job that I've ever seen. He's in a class with General Electric's Jack Welch, and the funny thing is that so few folks have caught on to him yet," in retrospect an ironic remark. Monks was on Tyco's board for ten years, evidence that independent directors—as at Enron— were not a panacea. Jessica Sommar, "Kozlowski Billed Firm for $2.1 Million Bash," *New York Post*, September 18, 2002; Jonathan R. Laing, "Tyco's Titan: How Dennis Kozlowski Is Creating a Lean, Profitable Giant," *Barron's*, April 12, 1999.

22. Joe Nocera, "Donaldson: The Exit Interview," *New York Times*, July 23, 2005; Silvers in Radelat, "Labor Pushes."

23. Leigh Strope, "Ex-Enron Workers before Congress," AP News, January 30, 2002; Aaron Bernstein, "Bracing for a Backlash: After Enron, Business May Be Subjected to a New Wave of Regulation," *Business Week*, February 4, 2002; "Former Enron Workers to Get More Severance Pay," *Washington Post*, June 12, 2002; Kris Axtman, "Unions Look to 'Enron Effect' for Growth," *Christian Science Monitor*, September 19, 2002; Young, "Without a Net."

24. Bernstein, "Bracing for a Backlash"; "U.S. Pundits Ponder If Market Crisis Presages 1930s-Style Overhaul," *Asian Wall Street Journal*, July 25, 2002; Prins, "Whose Jobs"; Greenhouse, "Public Funds"; "Labor Pushes Campaign for Laid-Off WorldCom Workers," Gannett News Service, September 7, 2002; "Without a Net," *Wall Street Journal*, September 30, 2002; "AFL-CIO President Demands More Corporate Reform," *Securities Litigation and Regulation Reporter*, August 14, 2002; Axtman, "Unions Look."

25. "How to Fix Corporate Governance," *Business Week*, May 6, 2002; Bratton, "Enron and the Dark Side," 1284; "Greed and Fear Return," *Financial Times*, June 8, 2002; AFL-CIO, Executive Council statement, August 6, 2002, Chicago; Patterson in Kaja Whitehouse, "Satisfied with Change, AFL-CIO Backs Down from Goldman," *Wall Street Journal*, February 21, 2002.

It turned out that one of the bad apples was Grasso himself. In September 2003, word leaked out that he was under investigation by the SEC for fraudulent reporting of his own compensation. Shortly thereafter, James Needham, a former New York Stock Exchange (NYSE) chairman, called for Grasso's resignation. The heads of major Wall Street firms wanted Grasso out as well, at which point CalPERS (Harrigan and Angelides) and the New York City funds chimed in. It was only a week between the investigation's announcement and Grasso's resignation. "Grasso Giving Up $48 Million in Benefits," *New York Times*, September 10, 2003; "Officials in 2 States Urge Big Board Chief to Quit," *New York Times*, September 17, 2003; "Chairman Quits Stock Exchange in Furor over Pay," *New York Times*, September 18, 2003.

26. Byrne, "Restoring Trust in Corporate America"; quote in Phyllis Plitch, "Unions Flex Muscle through Increased Investor Activism," Associated Press, April 24, 2002; "Labor Groups

Take Stock: Activists Push Corporations for Reforms," *Washington Times*, April 28, 2002; "Howls of Corporate Watchdogs Wake Up Shareholders," *St. Louis Post-Dispatch*, September 22, 2002.

27. "Unions Urge Groups to Act on Enron Directors," *Financial Times*, January 26, 2002; "AFL-CIO Asks SEC to Bar Enron Directors from Boards," Reuters, February 4, 2002; "AFL-CIO Announces Broad Program to Address Conflicts of Interest in the Capital Markets & the Collapse of Enron," PR Newswire, December 12, 2001.

28. Stephen M. Bainbridge, *The Complete Guide to Sarbanes-Oxley* (Avon, MA: Adams Media, 2007); John Bostelman, Mark Teviño, and Robert E. Buckholtz, *Public Company Deskbook: Sarbanes-Oxley and Federal Governance Requirements* (New York: Practicing Law Institute, 2003); "Unions Flex Muscle"; John C. Coates, "The Goals and Promise of the Sarbanes-Oxley Act," *Journal of Economic Perspectives* 21 (2007): 91–116; Pamela Yip, "Plans to Save Workers from Future Enron Get Tied Up in Congress," *Dallas Morning News*, August 19, 2002. Sarbanes-Oxley had been preceded by new listing requirements from the major stock exchanges that were, in some respects, more stringent than SOX. They called for a majority of independent directors and fully independent compensation and nominating committees. There also was a provision, not in SOX, for boards to hold periodic meetings without management present. See "Testimony of Damon A. Silvers," presentation to the New York Stock Exchange Special Committee on Corporate Accountability and Listing Standards, New York, May 23, 2002.

29. John W. Cioffi, *Public Law and Private Power: Corporate Governance Reform in the Age of Finance Capitalism* (Ithaca, NY: Cornell University Press, 2010), 116; Roberta Romano, "The Sarbanes-Oxley Act and the Making of Quack Corporate Governance," *Yale Law Journal* 114 (2005): 1521, 1569; Jesse M. Fried, "Rationalizing the Dodd-Frank Clawback," European Corporate Governance Institute (ECGI), law working paper No. 314 (2016); interview with David A. Smith, advisor to Representative Barney Frank and former director, AFL-CIO Policy Department, Washington, DC, April 2008; "Sarbanes-Oxley: A Pussycat on Clawbacks," Dow Jones News Service, June 9, 2006; "Enron Executives Protected Pensions with Partnerships," *Wall Street Journal*, February 7, 2002; "CA Shareholder Asks CA to 'Recoup' Executive Bonuses," Dow Jones News Service, April 27, 2004; Alison Frankel, "Sarbanes-Oxley's Lost Promise: Why CEOs Haven't Been Prosecuted," Reuters, July 27, 2012. There is research examining whether SOX affected governance outcomes. It did, albeit modestly. It increased executive departures when fraud occurred and made CEOs slightly more responsive to shareholder demands. Denton Collins, Adi Masli, Juan Manuel Sanchez, and Austin L. Reitenga, "Earnings Restatement, Sarbanes-Oxley, and the Disciplining of Chief Financial Officers," *Journal of Accounting, Auditing, and Finance* 24 (2009): 1–34; J. K. Land, "CEO Turnover around Earnings Restatement and Fraud," *Pacific Accounting Review* 22 (2010): 180–198; Vidhi Chhaochharia and Yaniv Grinstein, "Corporate Governance and Firm Value: The Impact of the 2002 Governance Rules," *Journal of Finance* 63 (2007): 1789–1825.

30. Sweeney disappointed more than a few in the labor movement by chairing a June 2002 dinner at which former Treasury Secretary Robert Rubin was feted as the National Housing Conference's "Housing Person of the Year." Rubin had been the mastermind of financial deregulation in the Clinton administration and later lobbied on Enron's behalf when the company began to fall apart. Sweeney's involvement may have been realpolitik; Rubin remained a powerful figure in the Democratic Party. "House Lawmakers Pass Accounting Reform Bill," Knight-Ridder,

April 25, 2002; "Robert Rubin to Be Honored," PR Newswire, June 13, 2002; William Greider, "Not Wanted: Enron Democrats," *The Nation*, April 8, 2002; Robert Kuttner, "By Common Consent," *American Prospect*, March 18, 2007.

31. "AFL-CIO President John J. Sweeney Demands Corporate Reform in Major Wall Street Address," AFL-CIO press release, July 30, 2002; "Labor to Press for Changes in Corporate Governance," *New York Times*, July 30, 2002.

32. "Deloitte to Settle Bear Stearns Case," *Wall Street Journal*, June 12, 2012; "Sarbanes-Oxley Harpoons the Whale," *Wall Street Journal*, September 19, 2013; David Moberg, "End of Business as Usual," *The Nation*, April 18, 2002; Blackwell interview; "SEC Chairman Makes Exit," *Globe and Mail* (Canada), June 2, 2005.

33. Testimony of Damon A. Silvers, Hearing before the Subcommittee on Regulatory Affairs of the Committee on Government Reform, U.S. House, 109th Cong., 2nd Sess., April 5, 2006.

34. "Backlash in the Executive Suite," *Business Week*, June 14, 2004; "Here It Comes: The Sarbanes-Oxley Backlash," *New York Times*, April 17, 2005; "Panel of Executives and Academics to Consider Regulation and Competitiveness," *New York Times*, September 13, 2006; "Businesses Seek New Protection on Legal Front," *New York Times*, October 29, 2006; "Sharply Divided Reactions to Reports on U.S. Markets," *New York Times*, December 1, 2006; Robert Kuttner, "Friendly Takeover," *American Prospect*, March 18, 2007; "We Need to Regulate Smarter—Not Less," *American Public Media*, November 22, 2006; "Cheney Expresses Doubts about Sarbanes-Oxley," *Information Week*, October 31, 2006; AFL-CIO to Robert Pozen, 2006, courtesy of Dan Pedrotty; Walter Hamilton, "Stock Rules Irk NYC as Wall Street Parties On," *Los Angeles Times*, April 23, 2007; "Sharply Divided Reactions to Report on U.S. Markets," *New York Times*, December 1, 2006; "Chairman Cox and Colleagues Urge No Congressional Action on SOX Auditing Costs," *The Deal*, June 28, 2007. Silvers quoted in Siobhan Hughes, "Ex-SEC Commissioner: U.S. Markets Not Losing Competitiveness," *Dow Jones Newswire*, May 8, 2007. The academics on the Committee on Capital Markets Regulations included Hal Scott from the Harvard Law School and Luigi Zingales of the University of Chicago's business school. Another member was Wilbur J. Ross Jr., who later became Donald Trump's controversial commerce secretary.

35. "AFL-CIO President Demands More Corporate Reform," *Securities Litigation Reporter*, August 14, 2002; "Union Targets Corporate Change," *Wall Street Journal*, July 30, 2002; Ron Blackwell and Bill Patterson, "The Crisis of Confidence in American Business: Corporate Accountability or Business As Usual," AFL-CIO press release, August 6, 2002.

36. "Grand Jury Reviews Stock Transactions by Insurance Firm," *Wall Street Journal*, March 15, 2002; "Labor-Owned Insurer Urged to Release Inquiry Report," *New York Times*, March 28, 2003; *The ULLICO Scandal and Its Implications for U.S. Workers: Hearing before the Committee on Education and the Workforce*, 107th Cong., 1st Sess., 09-19 (2003); *Self-Dealing and Breach of Duty at ULLICO*, US Senate, Committee on Intergovernmental Affairs, Majority Staff Report, June 2, 2004; "Stock Dealing at Union-Owned Insurer Creates Schism within Labor Movement," *New York Times*, April 8, 2003; "Uproar over Stock Deals Divides Labor Leaders," *Washington Post*, February 23, 2003.

37. Hassan Khalil, "The Future of the Labor Left," *Monthly Review* 52 (2000): 60–83; Kris Papp, *Working Construction: Why White Working-Class Men Put Themselves—and the Labor Movement—in Harm's Way* (Ithaca, NY: ILR Press, 2006).

38. "The Picket Line Gives Way to Sophisticated New Tactics," *Business Week*, April 16, 1984; "Cheers, and Boos, at Archer-Daniels Meeting," *New York Times*, October 20, 1995; interviews with Durkin and Young. On Durkin see Richard Marens, "Waiting for the North to Rise: Revisiting Barber and Rifkin after a Generation of Union Financial Activism in the US," *Journal of Business Ethics* 52 (2004): 109–123.

39. Durkin interview.

40. "Public Funds, Unions Putting Pressure on Some Managers to Back Defined Benefit Plans," *P&I*, March 21, 2005; Durkin and Abrecht interviews; anonymous interview, 2012.

41. Mark Erlich and Jeff Grabelsky, "Standing at a Crossroads: The Building Trades in the Twenty-First Century," *Labor History* 46 (2005): 421–445; "Bush's Labor Buddy," *Wall Street Journal*, January 14, 2003; Herman Benson, "The New Unity Partnership," *New Politics* 10 (2004): 106–109; David Moberg, "The Seven-Year Itch," *The Nation*, September 3, 2001; "Bush Courts Unions to Split Off Votes," *Washington Post*, March 31, 2002; David Moberg, "Labor Plays Its Hand," *The Nation*, November 11, 2002; William Johnson and Chris Kutalik, "New Unity Partnership: Five Union Presidents Launch Bid to 'Revolutionize' AFL-CIO," *Labor Notes*, September 30, 2003; Richard Dorrough, "Building Delusions at the Carpenters," *Labor Notes*, November 10, 2009.

42. Erlich and Grabelsky, "Standing at Crossroads"; Ruth Milkman and Kent Wong, "Organizing the Wicked City: The 1992 Southern California Drywall Strike," in *Organizing Immigrants: The Challenge for Unions in Contemporary California*, ed. Ruth Milkman (Ithaca, NY: ILR Press, 2000), 169–190; Southwest Carpenters, "The Legacy of the 1992 Drywall Movement," June 16, 2017, https://www.swcarpenters.org/the-legacy-of-the-1992-drywall-movement; "Pension Fund Takes Auditor Term Limit Battle to Proxies," *Wall Street Journal*, December 9, 2011; Harry Kelber, "Corporate Unionism (2)," *Labor Educator*, September 13 2004; David Correia, "Welcome to the Business-Friendly Carpenters' Union," *Counterpunch*, September 11, 2009.

43. Durkin in Barry B. Burr, "Joint Effort: Union Funds Using Proxy Resolution as Lobbying Tool," *P&I*, June 9, 2003; Alicia H. Munnell, Jean-Pierre Aubry, and Caroline V. Crawford, *Multiemployer Pension Plans: Status and Future Trends*, Center for Retirement Research at Boston College, special report, December 2017; "New Study Shows Skilled Craft Unions and Biopharmaceutical Industry Partnership Resulted in $14 Billion in Major Construction Project Investment," *Business Wire*, December 13, 2018; "Firms and Investors Trying More Talk, Less Acrimony," *Wall Street Journal*, July 16, 2007; Katie Thomas, "Industry's Unlikely Ally in Drug-Pricing Battle: Unions," *New York Times*, December 4, 2019; United Brotherhood of Carpenters and Joiners, "A Shareowner-Management Dialogue on Governance Issues and Long-Term Corporate Value," Worker-Owner Activism White Paper, December 2001," courtesy of Ed Durkin; Marens, "Waiting for the North"; Joann S. Lublin and Phred Dvorak, "The Insiders: How Five New Players Aid Movement to Limit CEO Pay—Mainstream Figures Mix With Activists," *Wall Street Journal*, March 13, 2007. Also see Papp, *Working Construction*. Durkin created a small organization that competes with ISS, ProxyVote Plus, this after he had a falling out with ISS. Its clients came from the building trades. "A Proxy Adviser's Two Sides: Some Question Work of ISS for Companies It Scrutinizes," *Washington Post*, January 23, 2006.

44. David Moberg, "Union Pension Power," *The Nation*, June 1, 1998; Erik Loomis, *Empire of Timber: Labor Unions and the Pacific Northwest Forests* (Cambridge: Cambridge University Press, 2015); "The Case against the Junk Bond Emperor," *Financial Times*, September 9, 1988;

"PERS Stake in Maxxam Questioned," *Press Democrat Santa Rosa,* January 4, 1997; Durkin and Young interviews. To its credit, CalPERS supported two candidates for Maxxam's board proposed by the Steelworkers, but by then it was an end-game situation. In a 1994 interview, Durkin said public plans had played a role in the mass layoffs of the 1980s and early 1990s by pressuring management to prioritize share prices. It would make more sense for the funds, he said, "not to be encouraging this kind of cannibalizing and downsizing." Mitchel Benson, "Maxxam, Calpers Talk About Board," *Wall Street Journal,* March 8, 2000; John Hall, "Board Revamp Voted Down," *Times-Picayune,* May 7, 1994.

45. United Brotherhood of Carpenters and Joiners, "Shareowner-Management Dialogue," 3; Durkin interview.

46. ISS releases, *PR Newswire,* June 16, 2004; William Baue and Mark Thomsen, "Publicity Conscious Companies Seek to Resolve Shareholder Differences before Annual Meeting," Associated Press, April 19, 2004; *ACGR,* 2004, i–iii; interview with Jackie Cook, CERES, April 2013; *ACGR,* data on voted proposals at S&P 1,500 companies, various years. For research on withdrawals, see Yonca Ertimur, Fabrizio Ferri, and Stephen Stubben, "Board of Directors' Responsiveness to Shareholders," *Journal of Corporate Finance* 16 (2010): 53–72; Rob Bauer, Frank Moers, and Michael Viehs, "Who Withdraws Shareholder Proposals and Does It Matter? *Corporate Governance* 23 (2015): 472–488; Maggie Foley, Richard J. Cebula, Chulhee Jun, and Bob Boylan, "An Analysis of Withdrawn Shareholder Proposals," *Corporate Governance* 15 (2015): 546–562; Diane Del Guercio and Tracie Woidtke, "Do the Interests of Public Pension Fund and Labor Union Activists Align with Other Shareholders'? Evidence from the Market for Directors," Working Paper, University of Oregon, October 2012; Jayne Zanglein, "No More Business as Usual: Using Pension Activism to Protect Workers' Rights," in *Justice on the Job: Perspectives on the Erosion of Collective Bargaining in the United States,* ed. Richard N. Block, Sheldon Friedman, Michelle Kaminski, and Andy Levin (Kalamazoo, MI: W.E. Upjohn Institute, 2006). Studies of shareholder activism usually do not include withdrawn and omitted proposals, which truncates the sample and biases the results.

47. Harvard Law School Forum on Corporate Governance and Financial Regulation, GMI Ratings, "Corporate Director Elections and Majority Withhold Votes" (2012), at http://blogs .law.harvard.edu/corpgov/2012/09/01/corporate-director-elections-and-majority-withhold -votes; J. Cai, L. Garner, and R. A. Walkling, "Electing Directors," *Journal of Finance* 64 (2009): 2389–2421; Stephen J. Choi, Jill E. Fisch, Marcel Kahan, and Edward B. Rock, "Does Majority Voting Improve Board Accountability?" *University of Chicago Law Review* 83, no. 3 (Summer 2016): 1119–1180.

48. Yonca Ertimur, Fabrizio Ferri, and Volkan Muslu, "Shareholder Activism and CEO Pay," *Review of Financial Studies* 24, no. 2 (2010): 535–592; Barry B. Burr, "Support Growing: All Investor Eyes on Busy Proxy Season," *P&I,* June 14, 2004; Louis Lavelle, "Governance: Backlash in the Executive Suite," *Business Week,* June 14, 2004.

49. Kay in Kaja Whitehouse, "Stiffed Board: Shareholders Angry about Executive Pay Are Targeting the People Responsible: Directors," *Wall Street Journal,* April 9, 2007; "Pension Plans Step Up Corporate Governance Effort," *P&I,* April 19, 2004; Yonca Ertimur, Fabrizio Ferri, and David Oesch, "Does the Election System Matter? Evidence from Majority Voting," working paper, 2013; Stephen Choi, Jill Fisch, and Marcel Kahan, "The Power of Proxy Advisors: Myth or Reality?" *Emory Law Journal* 59 (2010): 869–918; Diane Del Guercio, Laura Seery, and Tracie

Woidtke, "Do Boards Pay Attention When Institutional Investor Activists 'Just Vote No'?" *Journal of Financial Economics* 90 (2008): 84–103; GMI Ratings, "The Election of Directors"; Cai, Garner, and Walkling, "Electing Directors"; Cooke interview.

50. Joseph Grundfest, "Just Vote No: A Minimalist Strategy for Dealing with Barbarians inside the Gates," *Stanford Law Review* 45 (1993): 857–937; ACGR, 2004, 2008; "Just Vote No," *St. Louis Post-Dispatch*, November 3, 1992; "What the New SEC Rules Do for Activism," *Institutional Investor*, April 1, 1993; "CalPERS Is Planning to Change Its Focus," *New York Times*, August 16, 1995; Cooke interview; Hanson in Robert A. G. Monks and Nell Minow, *Corporate Governance*, 5th ed. (New York: Wiley, 2011), 212; Young interview; Barry B. Burr, "Support Growing: All Investor Eyes on Busy Proxy Season," *P&I*, June 14, 2004.

51. "Union Funds Get Serious with Proxy Voting," *P&I*, April 5, 1993; "Board Members Too Are Getting Scrutiny," *New York Times*, March 12, 1996; Louis Lavelle, "SEC May Ask Directors, CEOs, to Disclose Ties; Finance Rule Could Help Ensure Independence," *Bergen Record*, June 22, 1999; "AFL-CIO Calls Boards Too Cozy with CEO on Pay," *Washington Post*, April 7, 1999; "AFL-CIO Launches Vote No Drive against Directors over Pay," Dow Jones Newswire, April 15, 2004; "AFSCME to Withhold Votes," Dow Jones Newswire, April 20, 2004.

52. Ertimur, Ferri, and Muslu, "Shareholder Activism and CEO Pay."

53. "AFL-CIO, CWA, and IBEW Announce Vote No Campaign against Comcast Directors," PR Newswire, May 5, 2004; "AFL-CIO Cintas Chairman Farmer to Leave Nominating Committee," Dow Jones Newswire, October 14, 2003; "AFL-CIO Announces Vote No Campaign against Cintas Chairman," PR Newswire, October 3, 2003; "Union Notches Rare Win at Comcast," *Labor Notes*, May 4, 2010; "Labor Shareholder Activism: 2006," ISS Background Report, 36.

54. Choi, Fisch, and Kahan, "Power of Proxy Advisors"; Cai, Garner, and Walkling, "Electing Directors"; Ertimur, Ferri, and Muslu, "Shareholder Activism"; Del Guercio, Seery, and Woidtke, "Do Boards Pay Attention?" Paul Fischer, Jeff Gramlich, Brian Miller, and Hal White, "Investor Perceptions of Board Performance: Evidence from Uncontested Director Elections," *Journal of Accounting and Economics* 48 (2009): 172–189; Whitehouse, "Stiffed Board."

55. James Westphal and Poonam Khanna, "Keeping Directors in Line: Social Distancing as a Control Mechanism in the Corporate Elite," *Administrative Science Quarterly* 48 (2003): 361–399, quotation at 365. Also see James Westphal and Edward Zajac, "Defections from the Inner Circle: Social Exchange, Reciprocity, and the Diffusion of Board Independence in U.S. Corporations," *Administrative Science Quarterly* 42 (1997): 161–183; James Westphal and Edward Zajac, "Who Shall Govern? CEO/Board Power. Demographic Similarity, and New Director Selection," *Administrative Science Quarterly* 40 (1995): 60–83. Recent studies report that director networks are shrinking. Mark Mizruchi, *The Fracturing of the American Corporate Elite* (Cambridge, MA: Harvard University Press, 2013); Richard A. Benton, "The Decline of Social Entrenchment: Social Network Cohesion and Board Responsiveness to Shareholder Action," *Organization Science* 28 (2017): 262–282.

56. Ertimur, Ferri, and Stubben, "Board of Directors' Responsiveness," 54; New Hampshire official quoted in Louis Lavelle, "Commentary: How Shareholder Votes Are Legally Rigged," *Bloomberg Businessweek*, May 20, 2002. Also see IRRC Institute and GMI Ratings, *The Election of Corporate Directors: What Happens When Shareowners Withhold a Majority of Votes from Director Nominees?* New York, August 2012; Luc Renneboog and Peter G. Szilagyi, "The Role of Shareholder Proposals in Corporate Governance," *Journal of Corporate Finance* 17 (2011): 167–188;

Randall S. Thomas and James F. Cotter, "Shareholder Proposals in the New Millennium: Shareholder Support, Board Response, and Market Reaction," *Journal of Corporate Finance* 13, nos. 2–3 (2007): 368–391.

Chapter 6. Executive Pay

1. An earlier version of this chapter appeared as Sanford M. Jacoby, "Executive Pay and Labor's Shares: Unions and Corporate Governance from Enron to Dodd-Frank," *Accounting, Economics, and Law: A Convivium* (February 2020). "The Great CEO Pay Heist: Executive Compensation Has Become Highway Robbery," *Fortune*, June 25, 2001; Minow in Conor Dougherty, "Board Members of L.A.'s Top Companies Get Around," *Los Angeles Business Journal*, May 6, 2002; "Eisner's New Pay Plan Could Top $200 Million," *Chicago Tribune*, February 26, 1997; "Investors Grow Restive over Lavish Boardroom Pay," *Financial Times*, May 4, 2003. Minow was a pivotal figure in the investing world. With Robert Monks, she was a co-founder of LENS, president of Institutional Shareholder Services (ISS), and founder of The Corporate Library, a source of information on corporate governance.

2. Charles S. Clark, "Weighing Options Pay Disparity Between Executives, Workers, At Record Levels," *Rocky Mountain News*, August 3, 1997; Robert Rose, "Call to Action: Labor Has Discovered the Perfect Issue for Galvanizing Workers," *Wall Street Journal*, April 9, 1998; Charles Clark "Executive Pay: Do CEOs Get Paid Too Much," *Congressional Quarterly Researcher* 7 (July 11, 1999): 603–604; "Unions Take Fight over CEO's Pay to Shareholders," *Knight-Ridder Business News*, April 11, 1999; "AFL-CIO Links Some Executives' Big Paychecks to Cronyism," *Washington Post*, April 10, 1998; Lucian Bebchuk and Yaniv Grinstein, "The Growth of Executive Pay," *Oxford Review of Economic Policy* 21 (2005): 283–303.

3. Rose, "Call to Action."

4. David Vogel, *Lobbying the Corporation* (New York: Basic Books, 1978), 14.

5. Carola Frydman and Raven E. Saks, "Executive Compensation: A New View from a Long-Term Perspective, 1936–2005," *Review of Financial Studies* 23 (2010): 2099–2138; Lawrence Mishel and Alyssa Davis, "Top CEOs Make 300 Times More than Typical Workers: Pay Growth Surpasses Stock Gains and Wage Growth of Top 0.1 Percent," Economic Policy Institute, June 21, 2015; Bebchuk and Grinstein, "The Growth of Executive Pay."

6. Alex Edmans and Xavier Gabaix, "Is CEO Pay Really Inefficient? A Survey of New Optimal Contracting Theories," *European Financial Management* 15, no. 3 (2009): 486–496; Xavier Gabaix, Augustin Landier, and Julien Sauvagnat, "CEO Pay and Firm Size: An Update after the Crisis," *Economic Journal* 124 (2014): F-60-F89; Steven N. Kaplan, "Are U.S. CEOs Overpaid?" *Academy of Management Perspectives* 23 (2008): 5–20; Michael C. Jensen and Kevin J. Murphy, "Performance Pay and Top-Management Incentives," *Journal of Political Economy* 98 (1990): 225–264; Kevin J. Murphy, "The Politics of Pay: A Legislative History of Executive Compensation," Marshall School of Business working paper no. FBE 1 (2011); Steven N. Kaplan and Joshua Rauh, "Wall Street and Main Street: What Contributes to the Rise in the Highest Incomes?" NBER working paper 13270 (2007); Xavier Gabaix and Augustin Landier, "Why Has CEO Pay Increased So Much?" *Quarterly Journal of Economics* 123, no. 1 (2008): 49–100.

Regarding the relationship between firm size and CEO pay, Frydman and Saks observe that it is highly sensitive to the sample period (there is almost no correlation from the 1940s to the early 1970s). It's difficult to determine whether there is causality in the post-1970s relationship. In the financial sector, firm size explains about one-fifth of the pay premium for bankers. Carola Frydman and Dirk Jenter, "CEO Compensation," Working Paper No. 16585, National Bureau of Economic Research, 2010; Thomas Philoppon and Ariell Reshef, "Wages and Human Capital in the US Finance Industry: 1909–2006," *Quarterly Journal of Economics* 127 (2012): 1551–1609.

As for the skill story, Murphy and Zabojnk conjecture that "over the past three decades, general managerial skills (i.e., the skills transferable across companies, or even industries) became relatively more important for the CEO job, perhaps as a result of the steady progress in economics, management science, accounting, finance, and other disciplines which, if mastered by a CEO, can substantially improve his [sic] ability to manage any company. At the same time, certain types of knowledge specific to one particular firm, like information about its product markets, suppliers, clients, and so forth, which 30 years ago was not easily communicable to outsiders and therefore required a manager to spend time within the firm acquiring this information, is nowadays available in computerized form at the tip of the CEO's fingers. It may therefore be less important that a present-day CEO candidate possesses these types of firm-specific knowledge." Cremers and Grinstein offer strong evidence contrary to this view. Also, MBA-CEOs are less prevalent than is commonly said. Only a third of the top one hundred CEOs of public companies have MBA degrees. Kevin J. Murphy and Jan Zabojnik, "CEO Pay and Appointments: A Market-Based Explanation for Recent Trends," *American Economic Review* 94 (2004): 192–196; K. J. Martijn Cremers and Yaniv Grinstein, "Does the Market for CEO Talent Explain Controversial CEO Pay Practices?" *Review of Finance* 18 (2013): 921–960; "Map: See Where the Top CEOs Got MBA Degrees," *U.S. News & World Report*, August 6, 2019, https://www.usnews.com/education/best-graduate-schools/top-business-schools/articles/2018-07-06/map-see-where-top-ceos-in-the-fortune-500-got-mba-degrees

A recent study by Song et al. considers two types of employment-related inequality: within-firm and between-firm pay dispersion. They find that two-thirds of rising pay inequality is due to between-firm dispersion, which, they say, is caused by the concentration of highly educated and highly productive workers in companies with rents to share. Think Amazon or Apple. The remaining one-third is due to within-firm inequality. The implication is that the CEO-employee pay gap is not the primary driver of employment-related inequality, although it matters. But the finding fails to take account of corporate outsourcing of low-wage jobs to overseas suppliers, contractors, and franchisees. Today, Amazon's janitors and drivers are independent contractors, while subcontracting firms manufacture Apple products in China and elsewhere. Sharing in Amazon's or Apple's monopoly rents isn't an option for these low-wage workers. If they were directly employed, the Song et al. results would be different. Jae Song, David J. Price, Faith Guvenen, Nicholas Bloom, and Till Von Wachter, "Firming Up Inequality," *Quarterly Journal of Economics* 134 (2018): 1–50. On contracting, see David Weil, *The Fissured Workplace: Why Work Became So Bad and What Can Be Done to Improve It* (Cambridge, MA: Harvard University Press, 2014).

7. "Neither Rigged Nor Fair," *The Economist*, June 25, 2016; Lawrence Mishel and Natalie Sabadish, "CEO Pay in 2012 Was Extraordinarily High Relative to Typical Workers and Other High Earners," Economic Policy Institute, June 26, 2013; Mishel and Davis, "Top CEOs Make 300 Times More"; Qianqian Huang, Feng Jiang, Erik Lie, and Tingting Que, "The Effect of Labor Unions on CEO Compensation," *Journal of Financial and Quantitative Analysis* 52, no. 2 (2017): 553–582; John DiNardo, Kevin Hallock, and Jorn-Steffen Pischke, "Unions and Managerial

Pay," Working Paper no. 6318, National Bureau of Economic Research, 1997; Rafael Gomez and Konstantinos Tzioumis, "What Do Unions Do to CEO Compensation?" discussion paper 720, Centre for Economic Performance, London School of Economics, May 2006; Sheng-Syan Chen, Yan-Shing Chen, and Yanzhi Wang, "Does Labor Power Affect the Likelihood of a Share Repurchase?" *Financial Management* 44 (2015): 623–653; Richard Freeman and James Medoff, *What Do Unions Do?* (New York: Basic Books, 1984), 186; Brian Becker, "Union Rents as a Source of Takeover Gains among Target Shareholders," *Industrial & Labor Relations Review* 49 (1995): 3–17; Ian Dew-Becker and Robert J. Gordon, "Where Did the Productivity Growth Go? Inflation Dynamics and the Distribution of Income," National Bureau of Economic Research Working Paper no. w11842, 2005; Martin J. Conyon and Kevin J. Murphy, "The Prince and the Pauper? CEO Pay in the United States and United Kingdom," *Economic Journal* 110, no. 467 (2000): 640–661; Lucian A. Taylor, "CEO Wage Dynamics: Estimates from a Learning Model," *Journal of Financial Economics* 108, no. 1 (2013): 79–98.

8. Carola Frydman and Dirk Jenter, "CEO Compensation," *Annual Review of Financial Economics* 2 (2010): 75–102; Lucian Bebchuk and Jesse Fried, *Pay without Performance: The Unfulfilled Promise of Executive Compensation* (Cambridge, MA: Harvard University Press, 2004); Gretchen Gavett, "CEOs Get Paid Too Much, According to Nearly Everyone in the World," *Harvard Business Review*, September 23, 2013; Claudia Deutsch, "Behind Big Dollars, Worrisome Boards," *New York Times*, April 9, 2006; "Tax Savvy Execs Work for $1, Get Paid Millions as Capital Gains," *Forbes*, May 2, 2016; Taekjin Shin, "Fair Pay or Power Play? Pay Equity, Managerial Power, and Compensation Adjustments for CEOs," *Journal of Management* 42 (2016): 419–448; "House Committee Probes Executive-Pay Consultants," *CFO.com*, December 5, 2007; Gretchen Morgenson, "How Big a Payday for the Pay Consultants?" *New York Times*, June 22, 2008.

9. Barry B. Burr, "Union Funds Champs of the Proxy Season," *Pensions & Investments* (hereafter *P&I*), February 5, 2007; Majority votes matter because, when pay proposals receive a majority vote, implementation of their contents rises from 5 percent to 32 percent. Yonca Ertimur, Fabrizio Ferri, and Volkan Muslu, "Shareholder Activism and CEO Pay," *Review of Financial Studies* 24 (2011): 535–592. On labor's targets, see Andrew K. Prevost, Ramesh P. Rao, and Melissa A. Williams, "Labor Unions as Shareholder Activists: Champions or Detractors?" *Financial Review* 47 (2012): 327–349. Data are from Georgeson's *Annual Corporate Governance Review (ACGR)*.

10. Ertimur et al., "Shareholder Activism and CEO Pay," 566. Ertimur et al. carve up pay proposals differently than I do in table 6.1. They distinguish among "rules of the game" (disclosure, shareholder approval of pay), "pay design" (expensing options, tying them to performance), and "pay philosophy" (restricting the level of executive pay, giving shareholders the right to vote on compensation). Because large investors were disinclined to micromanage companies, they gave more support to rules of the game—on average, 41 percent of those proposals received "yes" votes—than to those related to pay design, where the average was 25 percent. Luc Renneboog and Peter Szilagyi, "The Success and Relevance of Shareholder Activism through Proxy Proposals," European Corporate Governance Institute—Finance Working Paper, 275/2010, March 2010; Luc Renneboog and Peter Szilagyi, "The Role of Shareholder Proposals in Corporate Governance," *Journal of Corporate Finance* 17 (2011): 167–188.

11. Yaniv Grinstein, David Weinbaum, and Nir Yehuda, "Perks and Excess: Evidence from the New Executive Compensation Disclosure Rules," working paper no. 04-09, Cornell University, Johnson School Research Paper Series, 2008.

12. Beth Young interview; "Heads I Win, Tails I Win: More Companies Offer Bonus Payments That Aren't Tied to Performance," *Wall Street Journal*, April 6, 2000. Meetings were more diplomatic than open conflict, but there was the risk of being manipulated. One study found that in private meetings with major investors, CEOs engaged in ingratiation and persuasion that deterred the investors from seeking strong-form changes in corporate governance. James D. Westphal and Michael K. Bednar, "The Pacification of Institutional Investors," *Administrative Science Quarterly* 53 (2008): 29–72.

13. Industrial Union Department, AFL-CIO, *The Stock Option Scandal* (Washington, DC, 1959), 23.

14. Silvers interview; Kevin J. Murphy and Michael C. Jensen, "The Flap Over Executive Pay: Beware the Self-Serving Critics," *New York Times*, May 20, 1984; William Sanders and Donald C. Hambrick, "Swinging for the Fences: The Effects of CEO Stock Options on Company Risk Taking and Performance," *Academy of Management Journal* 50 (2007): 1055–1078; Michael J. Cooper, Huseyin Gulen, and Raghavendra Rau, "Performance for Pay? The Relation Between CEO Incentive Compensation and Future Stock Price Performance," SSRN Working Paper 1572085, November 1, 2016; Adam J. Wowak, Michael J. Mannor, and Kaitlin D. Wowak, "Throwing Caution to the Wind: The Effect of CEO Stock Option Pay on the Incidence of Product Safety Problems," *Strategic Management Journal* 36 (2014): 1082–1092. CalPERS, Robert Monks, and ISS were among the early advocates for stock options. So was the AFL-CIO. Its 1991 Model Guidelines endorsed stock-based incentive pay for managers but cautioned against providing additional stock compensation that might diminish the incentive effect. Elizabeth Fowler, "On General Mills Agenda, Stock Options as Merit Pay," *New York Times*, September 17, 1990; AFL-CIO Executive Council, "Model Guidelines for Delegated Proxy Voting Responsibility," February 1991.

15. Lucian Bebchuk, Jesse Fried, and David Walker, "Managerial Power and Rent Extraction in the Design of Executive Compensation," *University of Chicago Law Review* 69 (2002): 751–755; Bebchuk and Fried, *Pay without Performance*; Lin Peng and Ailsa Röell, "Executive Pay and Shareholder Litigation," *Review of Finance* 12, no. 1 (2008): 141–184; Jared Harris and Philip Bromiley, "Incentives to Cheat: The Influence of Executive Compensation and Firm Performance on Financial Misrepresentation," *Organization Science* 18, no. 3 (2007): 350–367; "Bush Failed to Stress Need to Rein in Stock Options," *Wall Street Journal*, July 11, 2002; Alex Edmans, Xavier Gabaix, and Dirk Jenter, "Executive Compensation: A Survey of Theory and Evidence," in *The Handbook of the Economics of Corporate Governance* vol. 1, ed. Benjamin Hermalin and Michael Weisbach (Amsterdam: North-Holland, 2017), 383–539. None other than the Federal Reserve Bank of New York released a report concluding, "There is presently no theoretical or empirical consensus on how stock options affect . . . firm performance." "An Expense by Any Other Name," *The Economist*, April 6, 2002.

16. David Leonhardt, "Battle Lines Drawn on Stock Options," *New York Times*, March 17, 2002; "Bush Failed"; Sanford M. Jacoby, "For More Honesty with Stock Options," *Christian Science Monitor*, July 29, 2002.

17. Timothy Egan, "Microsoft's Unlikely Millionaires," *New York Times*, June 28, 1992; William Greider, "Not Wanted: Enron Democrats," *The Nation*, April 8, 2002; "FASB Caves in on Stock Options," *Practical Accountant*, February 1, 1995.

18. Andrew K. Prevost and John D. Wagster, "Impact of the 1992 Changes in the SEC Proxy Rules and Executive Compensation Requirements," unpublished paper, September 1999; Floyd

Norris, "Accounting Board Yields on Stock Options," *New York Times*, December 15, 1994; Harlan Wells, "U.S. Executive Compensation in Historical Perspective," in *Research Handbook on Executive Compensation*, ed. Randall S. Thomas and Jennifer G. Hill (Cheltenham, UK: Elgar, 2012), 41–57; Vineeta Anand, "Council Toughens Stance," *P&I*, February 21, 1994.

19. Gretchen Morgenson, "Business Lobby Seeks to Limit Investor Votes on Options," *New York Times*, June 6, 2002.

20. "The Campaign to Keep Options Off the Ledger," *Bloomberg News*, July 14, 2002; Lucian Bebchuk, "Insider Luck and Governance Reform," presentation for Capital Matters, May 2007; Boston Consulting Group in "Fat Cats Turn to Low Fat," *The Economist*, March 3, 2005. For a review of the correlation between executives' stock and options holdings and earnings manipulation, see Alex Edman, Xavier Gabaix, and Dirk Jenter, "Executive Compensation: A Survey of Theory and Evidence," NBER working paper 23596, July 2017, 85.

21. David Hilzenrath, "How Congress Rode a Storm to Corporate Reform," *Washington Post*, July 28, 2002; "AFL-CIO Head Calls for Grass-Roots Campaign against Corporate Greed," AP Newswire, July 30, 2002; "Statement by AFL-CIO President John J. Sweeney on the Need for New Rules to Ensure Corporate Accountability," PR Newswire, July 9, 2002. During the congressional hearings leading up to Sarbanes-Oxley, Damon Silvers testified that "[a]nyone familiar with the political pressures brought to bear on FASB around accounting for executive stock options in the mid-1990s, not to mention the decade-long paralysis on SPE accounting [Special Purpose Entities, which were crucial to Enron's deception], knows that FASB is too open to pressures from issuers and those beholden to issuers." Silvers quoted in Donna M. Nagy, "Playing Peekaboo with Constitutional Law: The PCAOB and its Public/Private Status," *Notre Dame Law Review* 80 (2004): 988.

22. Liz Pulliam Weston, "Despite Recession, Perks for Top Executives Grow," *Los Angeles Times*, February 1, 2002; "Corporate Reform, Back on the Front Burner," *National Journal*, March 1, 2003; "Excessive Executive Pay Eroding Investor Confidence," Associated Press, May 20, 2003; *CEO Compensation in the Post-Enron Era: Hearing before the Committee on Commerce, Science, and Transportation*, 108th Cong., 1st Sess., May 20, 2003 (Washington, DC: US GPO, 2006). The destruction of the World Trade Center put a dent in commercial air travel, to which the federal government responded with loans and short-term assistance to the airlines, as at the start of the 2020 pandemic.

23. *CEO Compensation*, 15–17; "Investors Grow Restive over Lavish Boardroom Pay." The AFL-CIO's recommendations on stock options are discussed in its proxy guidelines, *Exercising Authority, Restoring Accountability* (Washington, DC: AFL-CIO, 2003), 12–14.

24. "Corporate Reform, Back on the Front Burner"; "Congress, FASB in Stock Option Flap," *CFO.com*, June 6, 2003; "This Options-Expensing Bill Is No Reform," *Business Week*, November 25, 2003; Doerr quoted in Michael Liedtke, "Tech Industry Challenges Reform," *Los Angeles Times*, May 20, 2003.

25. Floyd Norris, "Coke to Report Options as an Expense," *New York Times*, July 15, 2002; Robert Guth, "Tarnished Gold: Microsoft Ushers Out Era of Options," *Wall Street Journal*, July 9, 2003; "AFL-CIO Asks Others to Follow Microsoft on Options," Reuters, July 9, 2003.

26. "Shareholders Have the Floor," *Boston Globe*, January 2, 2003; "Joint Effort: Union Funds Using Proxy Resolution as Lobbying Tool," *P&I*, June 9, 2003; Durkin interview; Fabrizio Ferri and Tatiana Sandino, "The Impact of Shareholder Activism on Financial Reporting and Com-

pensation: The Case of Employee Stock Option Expensing," *Accounting Review* 84 (2009): 433–466. Durkin quoted in Phyllis Plitch, "Teamsters Enter Options War with Battle Against Tech Co," Dow Jones News Service, October 17, 2002.

27. "Cisco and FASB: Options Showdown," *CFO.com*, May 24, 2004; "Shareholders Demand a Voice in Issuing of Stock Options," *New York Times*, May 9, 2002; "Letter Campaigns Try to Sway FASB on Option Expensing," Dow Jones Newswires, May 18, 2004; "Group of Big Pension Funds, Unions, Urges Option Expensing," Dow Jones Newswire, May 19, 2004; *FASB Proposals on Stock Option Expensing: Hearing before the Subcommittee on Commerce, Trade, and Consumer Protection of the Committee on Energy and Commerce*, US House of Representatives, Serial 108-99, July 8, 2014; Fabrizio Ferri, Garen Markarian, and Tatiana Sandino, "Stock Options Expensing: Evidence from Shareholders' Votes," European Accounting Association Annual Congress, Goteborg, 2005. See also Murphy, "The Politics of Pay."

28. Mark Maremont, "HealthSouth Founder Is Charged with Fraud," *Washington Post*, November 5, 2003; "Former HealthSouth CEO, Richard Scrushy, Gets Prison Sentence Reduced," *Forbes*, January 26, 2012; "GE Executive Pay under Spotlight at Annual Meeting," Reuters, April 22, 2003; "Investors Grow Restive"; "GE Settles with SEC over Welch Retirement Perks," Reuters, September 23, 2004.

29. "Long-Awaited Option Vote Rule about to Become Reality," Dow Jones Newswire, June 27, 2003; "SEC Passes Rule Changes for Options," *New York Times*, July 1, 2003.

30. L. D. Brown and Y. Lee, "The Impact of SFAS 123R on Changes in Option-Based Compensation," SSRN Working Paper 930818 (2007); Equilar, *2016 CEO Compensation Pay Trends* (Redwood City, CA, 2016); "Citigroup Payouts of Chiefs Irk Holders," *Wall Street Journal*, August 25, 2006; David Kocieniewski, "Its Chief's Big Tax Bill May Benefit Facebook," *New York Times*, February 4, 2012; Douglas L. Kruse, Joseph R. Blasi, and Rhokeun Park, "Prevalence, Characteristics, and Employee Views of Financial Participation in Enterprises," in *Shared Capitalism at Work*, ed. Douglas Kruse, Joseph Blasi, and Richard Freeman (Chicago: University of Chicago Press, 2010), 50. Despite the hoopla about companies like Microsoft, 75 percent of a company's stock options went to its top five executives, and more than half the remainder went to the next fifty managers. Only three million workers—about 2 percent of the US labor force—were granted stock options at the turn of the century, and they received a relative pittance. Roger Lowenstein, *Origins of the Crash: The Great Bubble and Its Undoing* (New York: Penguin, 2004), 45.

31. "Why the Get-Rich-Quick Days May Be Over," *Wall Street Journal*, April 14, 2003; Michael C. Jensen, "How Stock Options Reward Managers for Destroying Value and What to Do about It," Harvard Business School Working Paper No. 04-27, April 2001; Miller in "Weighing the Options," *Business Mexico*, November 1, 2002; Anat R. Admati, "A Skeptical View of Financialized Corporate Governance," *Journal of Economic Perspectives* 41 (Summer 2017): 131–150. Another apostle of stock options who later confessed her mistakes was Nell Minow. Not long after stepping down from LENS, she said, "In my young and innocent days, I really did think that stock options would be a good thing . . . I really did think that if . . . a higher percentage of the CEO's pay was in stock options, the CEO would pay more attention to long-term value for shareholders." David Hilzenrath, "'Performance' Options Getting a Second Look," *Washington Post*, April 1, 2001.

32. Erik Lie, "On the Timing of CEO Stock Option Awards," *Management Science* 51 (2005): 802–881; Randall A. Heron and Erik Lie, "What Fraction of Stock Option Grants to Top Executives

Have Been Backdated or Manipulated?" *Management Science* 54 (2009): 513–525; "The Perfect Payday," *Wall Street Journal*, March 18, 2006; "Perfect Payday: Options Scorecard," *Wall Street Journal*, September 4, 2007 at http://online.wsj.com/public/resources/documents/info -optionsscore06-full.html; Mark Maremont, "Authorities Probe Improper Backdating of Options," *Wall Street Journal*, November 11, 2005; Yonca Ertimur, Fabrizio Ferri, and David A. Maber, "Reputation Penalties for Poor Monitoring of Executive Pay: Evidence from Option Backdating," *Journal of Financial Economics* 104 (2012): 118–144; "Options Scandal in U.S. Set to Grow Further," *Bloomberg News*, August 4, 2006; "Silicon Valley Was Calming Down. Now an Options Scandal," *New York Times*, July 22, 2006; "Lehman Sued over Alleged Backdating," *Wall Street Journal*, April 14, 2007; Bebchuk, "Insider Luck and Governance Reform."

33. "Funds Urge SEC to Rethink Pay-for-Performance Disclosures," Dow Jones Newswires, April 12, 2006; "Executive Pay Debate Highlights Minimal Power of Shareholders," *Wall Street Journal*, February 7, 2006; "Stock Option Timing: The Scrutiny Intensifies, *Mondaq Business Briefing*, July 31, 2006; testimony of Brandon J. Rees, *Protecting Investors and Fostering Efficient Capital Markets: Hearings before the Committee on Financial Services*, US House of Representatives, 109th Cong., 2nd Sess. (May 25, 2006); Cornish Hitchcock (attorney for Amalgamated Bank) to SEC, April 10, 2006, courtesy of Scott Zdrazil; "Shareholders to Target Options Backdaters in 2007 Proxies," Dow Jones Newswire, October 26, 2006; *ACGR*, 2006, 2007; "Perfect Payday: Stock Option Practices Newest in Long Line of CEO Pay Abuses," *AFL-CIO NOW*, June 30, 2006; "SEC Issues Rules on Executive Pay, Options Grants," *Wall Street Journal*, July 27, 2006; "SEC Votes to Adopt Changes to Disclosure Requirements concerning Executive Compensation and Related Matters," SEC Press Release 2006-123, July 26, 2006; "Options Scandal in U.S. Set to Grow Further." The SEC disclosure rules filled over four hundred pages and can be found at https://www.sec.gov/rules/final/2006/33-8732a.pdf. For a summary, see "SEC Votes to Adopt Changes to Disclosure Requirements Concerning Executive Compensation and Related Matters," SEC Press Release 2006-123, July 26, 2006.

34. "Business Leaders Welcome Tighter Rules but Now Some Claim the Reforms Are Doing More Harm than Good," *Financial Times*, June 1, 2004; "Donaldson Ends SEC Tenure," *Wall Street Journal*, June 2, 2005; "SEC Chairman Makes Exit," *Globe and Mail* (Canada), June 2, 2005; "Donaldson: The Exit Interview," *New York Times*, July 23, 2005; William J. Samuel, AFL-CIO Dept. of Legislation, to Senators Richard Shelby and Paul Sarbanes, July 27, 2005; "Labor Unions Urge Members to Oppose Cox as SEC Chairman," Dow Jones Newswire, July 12, 2005. A careful study finds that the SEC over time reduced the intensity of its backdating investigations and became less likely to scrutinize individual executives. One of the indicted executives was Bruce Karatz of KB Home, who had been a major fundraiser for the Democrats during the Clinton years. Karatz insisted that unreported backdating was a victimless crime, but the claim is false: Firms accused of backdating illegalities subsequently had large negative and abnormal returns. Stephen J. Choi, Anat Wiechman, and A. C. Pritchard, "Scandal Enforcement at the SEC: The Arc of the Option Backdating Investigations," *American Law and Economics Review* 15 (2013): 542–577; "Former KB Home CEO Bruce Karatz Sentenced to Five Years' Probation," *Los Angeles Times*, November 11, 2010; Gennaro Bernile and Gregg A. Jarrell, "The Impact of the Options Backdating Scandal on Shareholders," *Journal of Accounting and Economics* 47 (2009): 2–26.

35. "Congress Is Urged to Hold Off Acting on Options and Pay," *New York Times*, September 7, 2006; "Investor Outcry over Exec Pay Retreat," *Business Week*, December 28, 2006; "Inves-

tors Oppose SEC's Exec-Pay Disclosure Change," Dow Jones Newswire, January 31, 2007; Interview with David Smith; "CEO Politics," *Wall Street Journal*, January 9, 2007; "President Bush Delivers State of the Economy Report," January 31, 2007, https://georgewbush-whitehouse .archives.gov/news/releases/2007/01/20070131-1.html

36. Kaja Whitehouse, "Report Points to Directors for Spreading Stock Options," Dow Jones Newswires, October 19, 2006; "Meet Mr. Labor Union," *Barron's*, October 29, 2007; Leslie P. Norton, "Velvet Handcuffs," *Barron's*, July 24, 1994. When Obama announced Johnson's appointment, Republicans charged that Johnson was unfit, having received three mortgages on favorable terms directly from the CEO of Countrywide Financial, Angelo Mozilo. Johnson left the committee after only a few days. On average, however, Republicans were more likely than Democrats to back business on issues related to stock options. One of the companies whose compensation committee Johnson chaired was KB Homes, Bruce Karatz's company.

"Republican National Committee: Obama's Disgraceful Duo," PR Newswire, June 10, 2008; "Vetting a Vetter: Obama's Pick Fuels GOP Criticism," *New York Times*, June 11, 2008; John M. Broder and Leslie Wayne, "Obama Aide Quits Under Fire for Business Ties," *New York Times*, June 12, 2008; David B. Farber, Marilyn F. Johnson, and Kathy R. Petroni, "Congressional Intervention in the Standard-Setting Process: An Analysis of the Stock Option Accounting Reform Act of 2004," *Accounting Horizons* 21 (2007): 1–22.

37. "New SEC Rules Make Pay More Transparent," *Washington Post*, July 16, 2007; "How Much Does Your CEO Really Make? Go Figure," *Washington Post*, February 8, 2009; Anne Saker, "When the Price Is Right: Yes, Proxy Statements Are Hard to Read—Intentionally," *USA Today*, June 21, 1992; Silvers in Barry B. Burr, "Disclosure Rule to Ease Executive Pay Comparisons," *P&I*, September 4, 2006.

Say on pay had precedents. During the takeover wave of the 1980s, the Senate passed a bill stipulating that, at the time of a takeover vote, shareholders could vote on the severance pay— golden parachutes—promised to executives. It was not enacted. Severance pay again became an issue after the NASDAQ scandals, when SEIU, Amalgamated Bank, the Teamsters, and others filed proxy proposals demanding shareholder voting on golden parachutes. Dodd-Frank made this mandatory.

A related issue was voting on supplemental executive retirement plans (SERPS), which permit executives to circumvent IRS ceilings on the amount of permissible DB benefits. Unions were incensed that executives enjoyed lavish DB pensions at the same time that companies were eliminating the plans for their employees; most SERP proposals came from union investors. The peak years were 2007 and 2008, during which time four of twenty-one of labor's SERP proposals received majority votes. See table 6.1. "Senate Approves Limits on 'Golden Parachutes,'" *New York Times*, June 22, 1988; Peter Fiss, Mark T. Kennedy, and Gerald F. Davis, "How Golden Parachutes Unfolded: Diffusion and Variation of a Controversial Practice," *Organization Science* 23 (2012): 1077–1099; "SEC Says Shareholders Must Vote on Stock-Based Pay," *Reuters*, June 30, 2003; "GE and Coca Cola Will Reduce Executive Retirement Benefits," *Wall Street Journal*, February 13, 2003; "Firing at Golden Parachutes," *Wall Street Journal*, May 21, 2013; ACGR, voted proposals, S&P 1500 companies, various years. Executive pensions are valuable. Bebchuk and Jackson were among the first to point out that omitting their worth from CEO pay underestimates the latter by a whopping 34 percent. Lucian Bebchuk and Robert L. Jackson Jr., "Executive Pensions," NBER working paper 11907, December 2005.

38. "The Day Investors Said Enough Is Enough," *The Guardian*, May 20, 2003; "Vodafone Board Faces TUC Opposition over Pay Awards," Dow Jones Newswires, July 20, 2002; "Calif., Other States Urge More Corporate Reforms," Reuters, June 30, 2003; interview with Janet Williamson, Senior Policy Officer, Trades Union Congress (TUC), January 2009, London; "Executive Pay Is at Issue," *Wall Street Journal: Europe*, July 11, 2002; Randall S. Thomas and Christoph Van der Elst, "Say on Pay around the World," *Washington University Law Review* 92 (2015): 653–731.

39. Ted Cornwell, "Union Challenges Mozilo's Compensation Plan," *National Mortgage News*, June 19, 2006; Consultant quoted in Todd Davenport, "Countrywide Shareholders to Vote on Exec-Pay Proposal," *American Banker*, June 14, 2006; On Countrywide and its role in the financial crisis, see Charles Ferguson, *Inside Job: The Financiers Who Pulled Off the Heist of the Century* (London: Oneworld, 2014) and Neil Fligstein and Alexander F. Roehrkasse, "The Causes of Fraud in the Financial Crisis of 2007 to 2009: Evidence from the Mortgage-backed Securities Industry," *American Sociological Review* 81, no. 4 (2016): 617–643.

40. "With Links to Board, Chief Saw His Pay Soar," *New York Times*, May 24, 2006; "Home Depot CEO Nailed over Pay," Associated Press, May 26, 2006; "Groups Blast Home Depot over Stock Option Mistake," Associated Press, June 29, 2006; "Home Depot Annual Meeting Ground Zero in Pay Debate," *Wall Street Journal*, May 24, 2006; "AFL-CIO: Meeting with Home Depot Dir. Hill Productive," Dow Jones News Service, September 7, 2006; "Home Depot Defends CEO Pay but Reviewing Policies," Dow Jones News Service, September 18, 2006; "Home Depot May See Fallout Over Options Backdating," Reuters, January 20, 2007; "Behind Nardelli's Abrupt Exit," *Wall Street Journal*, January 4, 2007; Pedrotty interview; Harold Meyerson, "Hard Labor," *American Prospect*, July 31, 2004; Jim Irwin, "Detroit-area Home Depot Workers Reject Union Representation," Associated Press, July 1, 2006.

41. Fabrizio Ferri and James Weber, "AFSCME vs. Mozilo . . . and "Say on Pay" for All! (A)," Harvard Business School, case study 9-109-009, March 18, 2009; statement of Thomas J. Lehner, "Written Testimony and Comments for the Record," House Financial Services Committee, May 25, 2006. In the UK, firms responded to negative say-on-pay votes by moderating rewards for failure (less generous severance contracts) and by increasing the sensitivity of pay to performance, but there was no effect on the level of CEO pay. Martin Conyon and Graham Sadler, "Shareholder Voting and Directors' Remuneration Report Legislation: Say on Pay in the UK," *Corporate Governance* 18 (2010): 296–312; Fabrizio Ferri and David A. Maber, "Say-on-Pay Votes and CEO Compensation: Evidence from the UK," *Review of Finance* 17, no. 2 (2013): 527–563; Jeffrey Gordon, "'Say on Pay': Cautionary Notes on the UK Experience and the Case for Shareholder Opt-In," *Harvard Journal on Legislation* 46 (2009), 323.

42. "Frank's Bill Seeks Greater Disclosure of Executive Pay," *Boston Globe*, November 11, 2005; "Frank Introduces Legislation to Protect Shareholders from Abuse of Executive Compensation," US Federal News Service, November 10, 2005; "Bill Targets Executive Compensation," *Los Angeles Times*, November 11, 2005. "Even with Disclosure, Investors Have Little Say on Pay," Dow Jones Newswires, January 31, 2006; letter from William Samuel, director, AFL-CIO Department of Legislation to Senators Chris Dodd and Richard Shelby, April 24, 2007, courtesy of Dan Pedrotty.

43. "Frank's Bill Seeks Greater Disclosure"; Siobhan Hughes and John Godfrey, "House Democrat Targets Executive Pay," *Wall Street Journal*, November 10, 2005; "New SEC Rules to Lift the Veil on CEO Pay," Kiplinger, December 9, 2005; "AFSCME Urges US Companies to

Curb Executive Pay," Reuters, December 7, 2005; "Labor of Love," *Institutional Investor*, March 14, 2005; "Union Funds Champs of Proxy Season," *P&I*, February 5, 2007; Ferri and Weber, "AFSCME vs. Mozilo"; "U.S. House Lawmakers Clash on Issue of CEO Pay," Dow Jones Newswires, May 26, 2006; statement of Thomas J. Lehner, "Written Testimony and Comments for the Record." At Davos, Frank "received flak" from CEOs antagonistic to his bill. He replied, "Shareholders have virtually no influence and I think boards of directors are not doing their job." Frank returned to Davos in 2007 and on that visit warned business leaders that "if they want to go forward with globalization, they have to pay more attention to questions of equity and fairness." "Gathering of World's Rich and Powerful Wraps Up with Appeal to Help World's Poor," Associated Press, January 28, 2007.

44. Damian Paletta, "US Rep Frank Calls on Businesses for Wages, Trade Deal," Dow Jones Newswires, January 3, 2007; "Behind Nardelli's Exit"; Smith interview; Gallup, "Confidence in Institutions" at https://news.gallup.com/poll/1597/Confidence-Institutions.aspx

45. Robin Toner, "A New Populism Spurs Democrats on the Economy," *New York Times*, July 16, 2007; "President Bush Delivers State of the Economy Report," *White House Press Releases and Documents*, January 31, 2007; Ben Feller, "Bush Takes Aim at Companies' Lavish Executive Pay," Associated Press, January 31, 2007.

46. "Give It Back, Hank," *Washington Post*, December 21, 2006. Regarding conservative views on inequality, see Paul Krugman, *Peddling Prosperity: Economic Sense and Nonsense in the Age of Diminished Expectations* (New York: W.W. Norton, 1994), chap. 5.

47. "Everyone from Pres. Bush to Union Activists Asks: How Can CEO Pay Be Brought Down to Earth?" Associated Press Newswires, February 9, 2007; Joann S. Lublin, "Behind Nardelli's Abrupt Exit," *Wall Street Journal*, January 4, 2007; Gretchen Morgenson, "Roadblocks to Greater Say on Pay," *New York Times*, January 21, 2007; "Most CFAs Back the Vote on Executive Pay," *Investment News*, April 2, 2007; "Director Elections and Majority Voting," *ISS Governance Weekly*, July 13, 2007.

48. "U.S. Rep. Frank: Say-on-Pay Would Test Directors," Reuters, March 19, 2007; "AFL-CIO's PayWatch Website Exposes Rigged CEO Pay System," PR Newswire, April 5, 2007.

49. "House Votes to Have Shareholders Weigh in on Exec Pay," *Los Angeles Times*, April 21, 2007; "Presidential Rivals Differ on Senate 'Say on Pay' Bill," *Best's Insurance News*, June 4, 2007; "Obama Pushes Say on Pay," *CFO.com*, April 11, 2008; "Say on Pay Bills More Cudgel than Reality," Associated Press, June 15, 2008.

50. Ertimur et al., "Shareholder Activism and CEO Pay"; Riskmetrics, *2007 Postseason Report*; "CEO Compensation Survey," *Wall Street Journal*, April 9, 2007.

51. Rob Bauer, Frank Moers, and Michael Viehs, "The Determinants of Withdrawn Shareholder Proposals," SSRN working paper, 2012; "Shareholders Push for Vote on Executive Pay," *Wall Street Journal*, February 26, 2007; Edward Iwata, "Backdated Options May Snare Some Directors as Critics Blast Rubber-Stamping," *USA Today*, March 29, 2007; Riskmetrics, *2007 Postseason Report*; Jie Cai, Jacqueline L. Garner, and Ralph A. Walkling, "Electing Directors," *Journal of Finance* 64, no. 5 (2009): 2389–2421; "New Breed of Directors Reaches Out to Shareholders," *Wall Street Journal*, July 21, 2008.

52. "Institutional Investors to Press Companies," *Global Proxy Watch*, February 9, 2007; ISS, "Director Elections'; Erin White, "Firms, Investors Trying More Talk, Less Acrimony—Annual-Meeting Fights Are Reduced by Forums On Hot-Button Issues," *Wall Street Journal*, July 16, 2007.

53. Richard Marens, "Going to War with the Army You Have: Labor's Shareholder Activism in an Era of Financial Hegemony," *Business and Society* 47 (2008): 312–342; Ertimur et al., "Shareholder Activism and CEO Pay," 543, 581; Kara Scannell, "Policy Makers Work to Give Shareholders More Boardroom Clout," *Wall Street Journal*, March 26, 2009.

54. Baird Webel and Marc Lebonte, *Troubled Asset Relief Program (TARP): Implementation and Status*, report by the Congressional Research Service, June 27, 2013; Barry S. Burr, "Shareholders See Victory in Obama Administration," *P&I*, November 10, 2008.

55. Webel and Lebonte, "TARP." Two TARP recipients (one being American Express) reached an agreement with a social investor, Calvert Group, to start say on pay immediately. Congressional Research Service, TARP; text of ARRA at https://www.gpo.gov/fdsys/pkg/PLAW-111publ5/html/PLAW-111publ5.htm

56. Social Investment Forum, "Socially Responsible Investors, Labor, Pension Funds Agree: Bail-Out Recipients Facing Say on Pay Resolutions Should Adopt Policy," February 24, 2009; "Wall St. Pay Moves in Cycles. (Guess Where We Are Now)," *New York Times*, February 5, 2009; "U.S. Targets Excessive Pay for Top Executives," *Washington Post*, June 11, 2009; "Investors Say Yes on Pay at TARP Firms," *Wall Street Journal*, September 2, 2009; "Shareholders Challenge Goldman Sachs as It Prepares to Pay Record Bonuses," *Investment Weekly News*, October 21, 2009.

57. Interview with Damon Silvers, January 2009, Chicago; *ACGR 2009*; "Shareholders to Focus on Executive Compensation," *Wall Street Journal*, January 12, 2009; "Senator Schumer and the SEC Separately Propose Action on Corporate Governance Matters," *Mondaq*, May 22, 2009; Stephen Labaton, "In Victory for Obama, House Panel Approves Restraints on Executive Pay," *New York Times*, July 29, 2009. Consistent with his views, Ed Durkin opposed say on pay's inclusion in Dodd-Frank, saying it would impede "thoughtful investigative work on comp plans." Scannell, "Policy Makers."

58. Randall S. Thomas, Alan R. Parmiter, and James F. Cotter, "Dodd-Frank's Say on Pay: Will It Lead to a Greater Role for Shareholders in Corporate Governance?" *Cornell Law Review* 97 (2012): 1248; James F. Cotter, Alan R. Palmiter, and Randall S. Thomas, "The First Year of Say-on-Pay under Dodd-Frank: An Empirical Analysis and Look Forward," *George Washington Law Review* 91 (2013): 967–1011; Gretchen Morgenson, "When Shareholders Make Their Voices Heard," *New York Times*, April 7, 2012.

59. Noam Noked, "The State of Engagement between U.S. Corporations and Shareholders," Harvard Law School Forum on Corporate Governance, March 15, 2011 at https://corpgov.law.harvard.edu/2011/03/15/the-state-of-engagement-between-u-s-corporations-and-shareholders/; AFL-CIO in Steven Greenhouse, "Labor Puts Executive Pay in the Spotlight," *New York Times*, April 9, 2011; Gretchen Morgenson, "Shareholders' Votes Have Done Little to Curb Lavish Executive Pay," *New York Times*, May 16, 2015; Jesse Eisinger, "In Shareholder Say-on-Pay Votes, More Whispers Than Shouts," *New York Times*, June 26, 2013.

Studies finding that positive say-on-pay votes restrain executive pay include: Ricardo Correa and Ugur Lel, "Say on Pay Laws, Executive Compensation, CEO Pay Slice, and Firm Value around the World," *FBR International Finance Discussion Paper* no. 1084 (2013); Steven Balsamet, Jeff Boone, Harrison Liu, and Jennifer Yin, "The Impact of Say-on-Pay on Executive Compensation," *Journal of Accounting and Public Policy* 35, no. 2 (2016): 162–191; Ferri and Maber, "Say on Pay Votes"; Walid Alissa, "Boards' Response to Shareholders' Dissatisfaction: The Case of Shareholders' Say on Pay in the UK," *European Accounting Review* 24 (2015): 727–752. For opposite findings, see Vicente Cuñat, Mireia Gine, and Maria Guadalupe, "Say Pays! Shareholder Voice and Firm Performance," *Review of Finance* 20 (2016): 1799–1834; Kelly Brunarski, T. Colin Campbell, and Yvette Harman, "Evidence on Outcome of Say-on-Pay Votes: How Managers, Directors and Shareholders Respond," *Journal of Corporate Finances* 30 (2015): 132–149; Peter Iliev and Svetla Vitanova, "The Effect of the Say-on-Pay Vote in the United States," *Management Science* 65 (2019): 4505–4521; Christopher S. Armstrong, Ian D. Gow, and David F. Larcker, "The Efficacy of Shareholder Voting: Evidence from Equity Compensation Plans," *Journal of Accounting Research* 51, no. 5 (2013): 909–950.

60. Peter F. Drucker, *Frontiers of Management* (1986; New York: Routledge, 2011), 138–143; Drucker, "Reform Executive Pay or Congress Will," *Wall Street Journal*, April 24, 1984; Lawrence Mishel and Jessica Schieder, "Stock Market Headwinds Meant Less Generous Year for Some CEOs," Economic Policy Institute, July 12, 2016.

61. Joani Nelson-Horchler, "What's Your Boss Worth? 35 Times Your Salary? 1,000 Times? The Workforce Gets Angry," *Washington Post*, August 5, 1990; Robert Borosage, "Buchanan's Challenge: Is Anyone Listening? *The Nation*, March 18, 1996; "Sabo Fights Lonely Fight of Old-Fashioned Liberal," *Minneapolis Star-Tribune*, February 10, 1997; "Rep. Sabo Introduces Income Equity Act of 2005," *US Federal News*, July 12, 2005; Sabo quote in Martin Sabo, "No One Should Be Left Behind in Our Nation's New Economy," *Tax Foundation's Tax Features*, October 1, 1999.

62. "Wealth of Titans: Fat Stock Options, Payouts Fortify Execs' Compensation," *USA Today*, April 7, 1999; United for a Fair Economy, *Executive Excess 1998: CEOs Gain from Massive Downsizing*, Fifth Annual Executive Compensation Survey, Boston, April 23, 1998; "Shareholders Revolt: Is Your CEO Worth $39 Million?" *Workforce Management*, January 1, 1999.

63. "U.S. Senator Offers Say on Pay, Bonus Clawback Bill," *Reuters*, February 26, 2010; "Pay Rule Still Unwritten Amid Corporate Push," *Washington Post*, July 7, 2013; "Firms Resist New Pay Equity Rules," *Wall Street Journal*, June 28, 2012; "Some See Benefits in Publicized Comparisons," *International New York Times*, August 7, 2015; "Rewarding or Hoarding? An Examination of Pay Ratios Revealed by Dodd-Frank," a report prepared by the staff of Representative Keith Ellison, May 20, 2018; Lawrence Mishel and Julia Wolfe, "CEO Compensation Has Grown 940% Since 1978; Typical Worker Compensation Has Risen Only 12% During that Time," Economic Policy Institute, August 14, 2019. Business and its congressional supporters fought against pay ratio reporting. Twenty-two industry groups worked with Representative Nan Hayworth of New York (R), a Tea Party enthusiast, to pass the "Burdensome Data Collection Relief Act," which sought to excise the provision from Dodd-Frank. It was introduced four times, first in 2011, but never enacted. Damon Silvers said it should have been called the "Promote CEO Pay Secrecy Act." Peter Whoriskey, "Some Companies Are Reporting Big Raises, But They're Not Real," *Washington Post*, March 19, 2020; Testimony of Damon A. Silvers, *Legislative Proposals to Promote Job Creation, Capital Formation, and Market Certainty: Hearings before House Subcommittee on Capital Markets and Government-Sponsored Enterprises*, March 16, 2011, p. 3. Recently, legislatures in California, Connecticut, Illinois, and Massachusetts have considered legislation that would tie a corporation's tax rates to its pay ratio. "Should Congress Rescind the Pay Ratio Rules?" *Wall Street Journal*, February 28, 2016; "A CEO Pay Regulation Is about to Be Scuttled," *Huffington Post*, February 9, 2017; HR Policy Organization, "California (Re)Introduces Pay Ratio Corporate Tax Bill with Unique Calculation," April 13, 2018; conversation with Damon Silvers, Chicago, 2016. The California bill can be found at https://leginfo.legislature.ca.gov/faces/billTextClient.xhtml?bill_id=201920200SB37

64. Steven N. Kaplan, "Are US CEOs Overpaid?" *Academy of Management Perspectives* 22 no. 2 (2008): 9. Data on payouts courtesy of Howard Silverblatt, McGraw Hill Companies, New York.

Chapter 7. Shareholder Democracy

1. Blackwell interview; Elson quoted in Joanne S. Lublin, "Corporate Funding for Shareholder Activism?" *Wall Street Journal,* July 3, 2006; Ferlauto in Barry B. Burr, "Shareholders See Victory in Obama Administration," *Pensions and Investments,* November 10, 2008.

2. Joseph A. Dear, CIO, CalPERS, to Elizabeth M. Murphy, secretary, SEC, January 19, 2010; "Theory and Practice: Investors May Get More Say in Selecting Directors," *Wall Street Journal,* April 16, 2007; Lucian A. Bebchuk, "The Myth of the Shareholder Franchise," *Virginia Law Review* 93 (2007): 687. Choi and Fisch report a higher figure for nominations by public plans. Stephen J. Choi and Jill E. Fisch, "On Beyond CalPERS: Survey Evidence on the Developing Role of Public Pension Funds in Corporate Governance," *Vanderbilt Law Review* 61 (2008): 326–332.

3. Jill E. Fisch, "From Legitimacy to Logic: Reconstructing Proxy Regulation," *Vanderbilt Law Review* 46 (1993): 1129–1200; Donald E. Schwartz, "The Public-Interest Proxy Contest: Reflections on Campaign GM," *Michigan Law Review* 69 (1971): 519. Mark Green, an associate of Ralph Nader's, said proxy access was necessary because shareholders were "powerless." It wasn't only Naderites who favored proxy access. Melvin Eisenberg, the distinguished corporate law professor, endorsed it too. Mark Green, "The Case for Corporate Democracy," *Regulation: AEI Journal on Government and Society* 4 (1980): 20–25; Eisenberg, *The Structure of the Corporation: A Legal Analysis* (Boston: Little, Brown 1976), 117–121; Jules Bernstein, Mark Green, Vic Kamber, and Alice Tepper Marlin, "Conceptual Draft of Corporate Democracy Act," in *The Big Business Reader: On Corporate America,* ed. Mark Green (New York: Pilgrim Press, 1983), 503.

4. "The Board Battle: Who's in Charge Here?" *Washington Post,* June 29, 1989; "Shelby to Introduce Pro-Shareholder Tender-Offer Bill in Senate," *Securities Week,* July 10, 1989; "Pension Plan Raids Hotly Debated in the Senate," *American Metal Market,* February 16, 1990; "Democracy for Shareholders," *St. Louis Post-Dispatch,* June 11, 1990; ; Jayne W. Barnard, "Shareholder Access to the Proxy Revisited," *Catholic University Law Review* 40 (1990): 37–105; "Shareholders Stand Up and Are Heard," *Financial Times,* March 4, 1991; Michael K. Molitor, "Crucial Role of the Nominating Committee: Re-Inventing Nominating Committees in the Aftermath of Shareholder Access to the Proxy," *UC Davis Business Law Journal* 11 (2010): 97–180; Kathleen Day, "Soldiers for the Shareholder," *Washington Post,* August 27, 2000.

5. "AIG Shareholder Group to Ask That More Seats on Board Be Created," *Bestwire,* May 16, 2000. Also see J. Robert Brown Jr., "The SEC, Corporate Governance and Shareholder Access to the Boardroom," *Utah Law Review* 2008, no. 1339 (2008): 1339–1393; Michael E. Murphy, "The Nominating Process for Corporate Boards of Directors," *Berkeley Business Law Journal* 5 (2008): 131–193. Responsible Wealth is a nonprofit created in the 1990s to reduce inequality. Working with wealthy inheritors, it has sought higher taxes on the rich and filed shareholder proposals related to executive pay. It's part of United for a Fair Economy, mentioned in chapter 6.

6. "Enron's Many Strands: Public Funds Say Losses Top $1.5 Billion," *New York Times,* January 29, 2002; "Investors Mull Wider Board Role; Group May Seek Power to Nominate Direc-

tors," *Washington Post*, March 27, 2002; "AFSCME Calls for Increased Activism, Details Proxy Access Campaign to Public Pension Funds," PR Newswire, November 26, 2002; "Proxy Contest: AFSCME Fund Leading Battle over Candidate Nominations," *Pensions & Investments* (hereafter *P&I*), March 17, 2003; "AOL—You've Got Mail," PR Newswire, May 15, 2003; Zucker in Phyllis Plitch, "Investors Push for a Director of One's Own on Proxies," Dow Jones News Service, February 14, 2003.

7. "CalPERS to Ask SEC to Let Shareholders Choose Directors," Dow Jones News Service, March 18, 2003; Phyllis Plitch, "Investors, Stirred Up by Scandals, Rally for Corporate Democracy," *Wall Street Journal*, July 9, 2003; Judith Burns, "Shareholder Advocates Applaud SEC's Proxy-Access Plan," Dow Jones News Service, July 15, 2003.

8. "Business Group Asks SEC to Halt Director-Election Rules," Dow Jones News Service, December 22, 2003; Teslik in "Investors Mull"; "Corporate 'Democracy' on Trial before U.S. SEC," Reuters, July 6, 2003; Damon A. Silvers and Michael I. Garland, "The Origins and Goals of the Fight for Proxy Access," 2004, https://www.sec.gov/spotlight/dir-nominations /silversgarland022004.pdf; Sarah Teslik interview; *CEO Compensation in the Post-Enron Era: Committee on Commerce, Science, and Transportation*, US Senate, testimony of Damon Silvers, May 20, 2003; "SEC May Study NYSE Proxy Rule," *Wall Street Journal*, July 30, 2003; "Labor of Love," *Institutional Investor*, March 14, 2005.

9. SEC, Division of Corporate Finance, "Staff Report: Review of the Proxy Process regarding the Nomination and Election of Directors," July 15, 2003, https://www.sec.gov/news/studies /proxyrpt.htm; Kevin Drawbaugh, "SEC Debates Proxy Plan to Wire, Poll Shows Support," Reuters News, October 6, 2003; "Creating Triggers for Board Proxy Access Has Challenges," Dow Jones News Service, July 24, 2003; CII Research and Education Fund, Proxy Access by Private Ordering, February 2017, https://www.cii.org/files/publications/misc/02_02_17 _proxy_access_private_ordering_final.pdf

10. Broc Romanek, "Doing the Math: How Many Proxy Access Comment Letters This Decade?" TheCorporateCounsel.net, February 12, 2010, https://www.thecorporatecounsel.net /blog/2010/02/math-of-comment-letters.html; SEC, Division of Corporate Finance, "Staff Report"; Henry A. McKinnell, Chairman, The Business Roundtable, to Jonathan Katz, Securities and Exchange Commission, December 22, 2003, at https://www.sec.gov/rules/proposed /s71903/s71903-381; Rock Center for Corporate Governance, Stanford University, "SEC Proxy Access Reform," April 21, 2010; remark on activist investors from Wachtell, Lipton, Rosen & Katz to SEC at https://www.sec.gov/rules/proposed/s71903/wachtell111403.htm; journalist quoted in David Marcus, "The Great Motivator," *Daily Deal*, October 20, 2003.

11. Martin Lipton and A. D. Rosenblum, "Election Contests in the Company's Proxy: An Idea Whose Time Has Not Come," *Business Lawyer* 59 (2003): 67–94; Richard L. Trumka to Jonathan G. Katz, secretary, SEC, December 19, 2003, at https://www.sec.gov/rules/proposed /s71903/aflcio121903.htm

12. CFA Institute, *Proxy Access in the US: Revisiting the Proposed SEC Rule* (Charlottesville, VA, 2014); "Investors Suggest Look to Europe on Proxy Vote Issue," Dow Jones News Service, October 31, 2006; Organization for Economic Co-operation and Development, *Board Member Nomination and Election* (Paris, 2012).

13. William B. Chandler and Leo E. Strine, "The New Federalism of the American Corporate Governance System," *University of Pennsylvania Law Review* 152 (2003): 1000; "SEC Could Face

Legal Fight If Investors Win Proxy Access," Dow Jones News Service, July 14, 2003; Lucian Arye Bebchuk, "The Case for Increasing Shareholder Power," *Harvard Law Review* 118 (2004): 833–914; "Campaign against Proxy Access Moves into High Gear," *Corporate Governance*, September 9, 2009; Joseph A. Grundfest, "SEC's Proposed Proxy Access Rules: Politics, Economics, and the Law," *Business Law* 65 (2009): 361–394.

14. Pedrotty interview.

15. Interview with Tom Powdrill, Pensions & Investments Research Council (PIRC), London, October 2008; Pedrotty and Trumka interviews. As evidence of the traditional union view, Appelbaum and Hunter quote from a 1976 speech by Thomas Donahue, then AFL-CIO Secretary-Treasurer: "Because American unions have won equality at the bargaining table, we have not sought it in corporate boardrooms. We do not seek to be a partner in management—to be, most likely, the junior partner in success and the senior partner in failure. We do not want to blur in any way the distinctions between the respective roles of management and labor in the plant. We guard our independence fiercely—independent of government, independent of any political party, and independent of management." Eileen Appelbaum and Larry W. Hunter, "Union Participation in Strategic Decisions of Corporations," in *Emerging Labor Market Institutions for the Twenty-First Century*, ed. Richard B. Freeman, Joni Hersch, and Lawrence Mishel (Chicago: University of Chicago Press, 2005), 267.

16. Appelbaum and Hunter, "Union Participation in Strategic Decisions of Corporations." Research on German companies finds that employee directors improve the bottom line. Larry Fauver and Michael Fuerst, "Does Good Corporate Governance Include Employee Representation? Evidence from German Corporate Boards," *Journal of Financial Economics* 82 (2006): 673–710; Simon Jäger, Benjamin Schoefer, and Jörg Heining, "Labor in the Boardroom," NBER Working Paper 26519 (November 2019); E. Han Kim, Ernst Maug, and Christoph Schneider, "Labor Representation in Governance as an Insurance Mechanism," *Review of Finance* 22, no. 4 (2018): 1251–1289.

17. "Investors of the World, Unite," *The Deal*, April 2, 2004; "AFL-CIO Targets Directors," *The Deal*, April 19, 2004; "Death by Proxy? Vote on Eisner Causes a Stir," *Wall Street Journal*, March 4, 2004; "Discontent Remains High after Disney's Moves on Eisner," *New York Times*, March 4, 2004; "SEC Reverses Walt Disney Proxy Decision," *Wall Street Journal*, December 29, 2004; "SEC Rebuffs Investors on Board Votes," *New York Times*, February 8, 2005. Representing Disney at the SEC was Martin Lipton.

18. "Here It Comes: The Sarbanes-Oxley Backlash," *New York Times*, April 17, 2005; Joseph Nocera, "Donaldson: The Exit Interview," *New York Times*, July 23, 2005; "Campaigning for the Board"; *Implementation of the Sarbanes-Oxley Act of 2002: Hearings before the Committee on Banking, Housing, and Urban Affairs*, US Senate, 108th Cong., 1st Sess. (2003), 165, 167.

19. Blackwell and Young interviews.

20. AFSCME, "AIG, Proxy Access and Executive Pay Reforms Lead AFSCME List of Shareholder Proposals for 2005 Annual Meetings," January 6, 2005, https://www.afscme.org/news/press-room/press-releases/2005/aig-proxy-access-and-executive-pay-reforms-lead-afscme-list-of-shareholder-proposals-for-2005-annual-meetings; Durkin interview. There were few proposals in support of majority voting until 2005, when CalPERS began seeking it. Phyllis Plitch, "CalPERS Majority Vote Push Could Propel Issue Forward," Dow Jones News Service, March 15, 2005.

21. Gretchen Morgenson, "Who's Afraid of Shareholder Democracy?" *New York Times*, October 2, 2005; Lucian A. Bebchuk and Scott Hirst, "Private Ordering and the Proxy Access Debate," *Business Lawyer* 65 (2010): 329–359; "Boardrooms Open Up to Investors' Input," *USA Today*, September 6, 2007; Council of Institutional Investors, "Majority Voting Primer— Making Shareowners' Votes Count: Majority Voting in Director Elections," February 27, 2006; "Teamsters Shareholders Score Majority Vote Victory at FedEx," PR Newswire, March 13, 2007. Boards became more responsive to shareholder proposals after the adoption of majority voting. Yonca Ertimur, Fabrizio Ferri, and David Oesch, "Does the Director Election System Matter? Evidence from Majority Voting," *Review of Accounting Studies* 20, no. 1 (2015): 1–41.

22. Ertimur, Ferri, and Oesch, "Does the Director Election System Matter?"; CII, "FAQ: Majority Voting for Directors," https://www.cii.org/files/issues_and_advocacy/board _accountability/majority_voting_directors/CII%20Majority%20Voting%20FAQ%201-4-17 .pdf; Randall Smith, "Some Big Public Pension Funds Are Behaving like Activist Investors," *New York Times*, November 28, 2013.

23. "US Rep. Frank: Say-on-Pay Would Test Directors," Reuters, March 19, 2007; "Barney Frank's Grand Bargain," *Business Week*, January 8, 2007; Stephen Taub, "Appeals Court Revives Proxy-Access Issue," *CFO.com*, September 7, 2006; "US Senate Eyes Proxy Access, Targets Hearing," Reuters, March 20, 2007; "Investors May Get More Say in Selecting Directors," *Wall Street Journal*, April 16, 2007; "Proxy Season Pre-Empted by Peace," *P&I*, May 14, 2007; "SEC Faces Scrutiny on Governance," *Financial Times*, May 11, 2007; "Open Season: Why America's Boards Face Awkward Times in the Auditorium," *Financial Times*, April 1, 2007; interview with Brishen Rogers, Change to Win Investment Group, April 2008, Washington, DC.

24. "SEC Proxy Study to Look at Overseas Rules," *Financial Times*, February 23, 2007; "Proxy Season Pre-Empted," and "Frank: SEC Needs to Start Over on Proxy Access," Dow Jones News Service, September 27, 2007; "Investors Blast SEC's 5% Proxy Threshold," *Corporate Governance*, September 12, 2007; "US Activists Launch Online Opposition to SEC Proxy-Access Plans," *CNN Money*, August 29, 2007; *SEC Proxy Access Proposals: Implications for Investors: Hearing before the Committee on Financial Services*, US House of Representatives, 110th Congress, 1st Sess., September 27, 2007; *Hearing on Shareholder Rights and Proxy Access*, Committee on Banking, Housing, and Urban Affairs, U.S. Senate, 110th Cong. 1st Sess., November 14, 2007, testimony of Anne Simpson, 169, 179; "Democrats Mull Short List of US SEC Candidates," Reuters, November 9, 2007; Richardson and Kellogg, interview; Judith Burns, "SEC Votes 3-1 to Maintain Companies' Prerogative on Proxy Access," *Corporate Governance*, December 5, 2007; "AFL-CIO: CEOs' Pay Packages Played Role in Mortgage Crisis," Dow Jones News Service, April 14, 2008; "AFL-CIO's Executive PayWatch Website Shows How CEO Pay Packages Helped Create Mortgage Crisis," PR Newswire, April 14, 2008.

25. "Ex-SEC Chief Says Time Has Come for Proxy Access," Reuters, July 1, 2008; "Nader Calls for Crackdown on Corporate Crime," Targeted News Service, August 8, 2008; "Lifting the Lid: Investor Activists Pin Hope on New President," Reuters, February 22, 2008; Young interview; "SEC Allows Firms to Exclude Proxy Access Proposals," Reuters, February 12, 2008; "Home Run for the SEC," *P&I*, September 6, 2010.

26. Joanna Chung, "Schapiro Pledges Tougher SEC Action," *Financial Times*, January 15, 2009; Arthur Levitt Jr., "How to Boost Shareholder Democracy," *Wall Street Journal*, July 1, 2008.

On Schapiro, see Stephen Taub, "Mary Schapiro Puts SEC Back in Business," *Institutional Investor*, November 3, 2009.

27. "SEC Announces Creation of Investor Advisory Committee," *SEC News Digest*, June 3, 2009; "U.S. Business Challenges SEC Power to Grant Proxy Access," *Bloomberg*, April 30, 2009; Kara Scannell, "Fight Brews as Proxy-Access Nears," *Wall Street Journal*, August 26, 2009; "Companies, Funds Spar over Need for Nomination Rule," *P&I*, August 24, 2009; "Where Are the Funds?" *P&I*, March 5, 2012; Durkin interview. The 2009 SEC proposal is at http://www.sec.gov/rules/proposed/2009/33-9086.pdf.

28. "Senator Schumer and the SEC Separately Propose Action on Corporate Governance Matters," *Mondaq*, May 22, 2009; Chase Cole, "New Corporate Governance Legislation," *Mondaq*, June 12, 2009. The Shareholder Bill of Rights can be found at https://www.gpo.gov/fdsys/pkg/BILLS-111s1074is/pdf/BILLS-111s1074is.pdf. See chapter 6 on Schumer and Cantwell.

29. Jeffrey Toobin, "The Senator and the Street," *New Yorker*, August 2, 2010; Ryan Grimm, "Senate Dems Hold EFCA Strategy Session," *Huffington Post*, June 21, 2009; Kellogg and Richardson interview.

30. "New SEC, Congressional Weapons Could Threaten Directors," *Corporate Governance*, September 23, 2009; Jia Lin Yang, "Opponents of 'Shareholder Bill of Rights' Reach Out to Sen. Schumer," *Washington Post*, April 30, 2009.

31. Jia Lin Yang, "CEOs Far and Wide Band against Regulatory Provision," *Washington Post*, May 14, 2010; "Corporate Governance Legislation Passes Senate," *Mondaq*, June 7, 2010; "House–Senate Conference Committee Holds a Meeting on the Wall Street Reform and Consumer Protection Act," *SEC Wire*, June 16, 2010; David A. Katz and Laura A. McIntosh, "Senate Bill Adversely Affects the Landscape," *New York Law Journal* 243 (May 27, 2010). On the NDC, see Stephen K. Medvic, "Old Democrats in New Clothing? An Ideological Analysis of a Democratic Party Faction," *Party Politics* 13 (2007): 587–609.

32. "Corporate Governance Legislation Passes Senate"; "House–Senate Conference Committee Holds a Meeting"; "White House Intervenes on Shareholder Rights," Reuters, June 17, 2010; "Group Targets Obama Adviser Jarrett on Proxy Access," Dow Jones News Service, June 17, 2010; "Americans for Financial Reform Holds a Teleconference to Discuss Growing Evidence of Public Demand for Wall Street Reform," Financial Market Regulatory Wire, June 24, 2010; "Factbox: Keys to US House–Senate Panel on Wall St. Reform," Reuters, June 24, 2010; "Conferees Go Down to the Wire on Last Tough Issues," *CongressDaily/AM*, June 25, 2010.

33. "Investors Get Board Boost with Proxy Rule," *Wall Street Journal*, August 23, 2010; "SEC Gives Big Investors More Say over Corporate Boards," *NationalJournal.com*, August 25, 2010; "US Investors Win Right to Challenge Runaway Boardroom Pay Packets," *The Guardian* (UK), August 26, 2010; "New Rule on Proxies Puts Heat on Firms," *Corporate Governance*, August 25, 2010.

34. "SEC Gives Big Investors"; "SEC Votes to Propose Pro-Shareholder Proxy Rules," Dow Jones News Service, May 20, 2009; "Alinsky Wins at the SEC," *Wall Street Journal*, August 30, 2010; "Proxy Access Draws Mixed Reactions," *Compliance Weekly*, October 31, 2010; Sheri Qualters, "Split SEC Votes to Ease Nomination of Board Directors by Shareholders," *New York Law Journal* 244, August 27, 2010. In its defense, the SEC said that it had considered and rejected the hijack argument. It reasoned that any harm would be limited because ownership and holding requirements would "allow the use of the rule by only holders who demonstrated a significant, long-term commitment to the company" and who would therefore be unlikely to risk a dimin-

ishment of shareholder value. SEC, "Facilitating Shareholder Director Nominations, Part 4 of 5," *Federal Register*, 75 no. 179, September 16, 2010.

35. "Business Trade Groups Fight New Proxy Rules," *Washington Post*, September 30, 2010.

36. *Business Roundtable and Chamber of Commerce of the United States v. Securities and Exchange Commission*, U.S. Court of Appeals, District of Columbia Circuit, July 22, 2011, 7–12; Proxy Access Invalidated on APA Grounds" at http://www.professorbainbridge.com /professorbainbridgecom/2011/07/proxy-access-invalidated-on-apa-grounds.html; "Is Proxy Access Dead? Ask Boards, CEOs and Shareholders," *Fortune*, September 26, 2011. After the court ruled against the SEC, share prices fell at companies who likely would have been the first recipients of shareholder nominations. It was a sign that investors viewed proxy access as value-enhancing. Bo Becker, Daniel Bergstresser, and Guhan Subramanian, "Does Shareholder Proxy Access Improve Firm Value? Evidence from the Business Roundtable's Challenge," *Journal of Law and Economics* 56, no. 1 (2013).

37. Stephen Foley, "BlackRock at Odds with Its Investors Over Shareholder Rights," *Financial Times*, April 28, 2015; Ronald Orol, "How One Gadfly Investor Opened Up Corporate Board Elections," *The Deal*, March 20, 2015; Latham & Watkins, "Proxy Access in the 2015 Season," September 3, 2015; "Zombie Directors and Failed Boards: An Interview with Scott Stringer," *Proxy Insight: Proxy Monthly*, February 2015; David Webber, *The Rise of the Working-Class Shareholder: Labor's Last Weapon* (Cambridge, MA: Harvard University Press, 2018), 65-70; ACGR, 2014–2017.

38. Attracta Mooney, "Vanguard, Fidelity Face Proxy Access Row," *Financial Times*, February 1, 2016; Diana Medland, "Deep Division Among Mutual Funds on Proxy Access, *Forbes*, January 31, 2016; Yafit Cohen, "The 2016 Proxy Season: Proxy Access Proposals," Harvard Law School Forum on Corporate Governance and Financial Regulation, August 26, 2016; "Proxy Access Update: Current Status and Outlook," *Bloomberg Law*, May 23, 2017; Marc S. Gerber, "Proxy Access: Highlights of the 2017 Season," Harvard Law School Forum on Corporate Governance and Financial Regulation, July 1, 2017; Holly J. Gregory, Rebecca Grapsas, and Claire Holland, "The Latest on Proxy Access," Harvard Law School Forum on Corporate Governance and Financial Regulation, February 1, 2019, https://corpgov.law.harvard.edu/2019/02/01/the -latest-on-proxy-access

39. Cydney Posner, "Does Proxy Access Create Leverage—Even If No One Uses It?" *Mondaq Business Briefing*, October 18, 2019; Smith interview. Research is divided on the relationship between proxy access and shareholder returns. Studies finding a negative association include Siona Robin Listokin, "Institutional Investor Composition and Proxy Access Proposals," SSRN working paper 2017188 (2012); David F. Larcker, Gaizka Ormazabal, and Daniel J. Taylor, "The Market Reaction to Corporate Governance Regulation," *Journal of Financial Economics* 101 (2011): 431–448; and Yijiang Zhao and Kung H. Chen, "The Influence of Takeover Protection on Earnings Management," *Journal of Business Finance & Accounting* 35 (2008): 347–375. Studies that find a positive relationship include Joanna Campbell, T. Colin Campbell, David R. Sirmon, Leonard Dierman, and Chris S. Tuggle, "Shareholder Influence over Director Nomination via Proxy Access: Implications for Agency Conflict and Stakeholder Value," *Strategic Management Journal* 33 (2012): 1431–1451; Becker, Bergstresser, and Subramanian, "Does Shareholder Proxy Access Improve Firm Value?; Jonathan B. Cohn, Stuart L. Gillan, and Jay C. Hartzell, "On Enhancing Shareholder Control: A (Dodd-) Frank Assessment of Proxy Access," *Journal of Finance* 71 (2016): 1623–1668.

Chapter 8. Organizing Finance

1. Brian Burrough and John Helyar, *Barbarians at the Gate: The Fall of RJR Nabisco* (New York: Harper Collins, 1988). Private equity funds also purchase privately owned companies; some funds specialize in this part of the industry. It's important to keep in mind the variety of private equity firms: there are more than three thousand of them that vary in size, profitability, and strategies.

2. "The Uneasy Crown," *Economist*, February 10, 2007; L. W. Beeferman, "Private Equity and American Labor", *Journal of Industrial Relations* 51, no.4 (2009): 543–556; "These 15 Charts Illustrate the Current U.S. Private Equity Landscape," *PitchBook*, July 19, 2016; "The Money Binge," *New York Times*, April 4, 2007. An excellent overview of private equity is Eileen Appelbaum and Rosemary Batt, *Private Equity at Work: When Wall Street Manages Main Street* (New York: Russell Sage Foundation, 2014). Carried interest is the profit received by a fund's general partners when they sell an investment. Favorable tax treatment is a large part of what makes private equity so lucrative. Critics charge that profits earned with other people's money are equivalent to performance-based fees paid to the general managers for their acumen; therefore, they are ordinary income and should be taxed as such.

3. Viral V. Acharya, Oliver F. Gottschalg, Moritz Hahn, and Conor Kehoe, "Corporate Governance and Value Creation: Evidence from Private Equity," *Review of Financial Studies* 26, no. 2 (2012): 368–402. A different study reports that 10% of the funds do not return any money while 25% have internal rates of return over 50%. CalPERS made 90% of its return from 40% of its investments in private equity. Florencio Lopez-de-Silanes, Ludovic Phalippou, and Oliver Gottschalg, "Giants at the Gate: Investment Returns and Diseconomies of Scale in Private Equity," *Journal of Financial and Quantitative Analysis* 50, no. 3 (2015): 377–441.

4. Fidelity official in "Buy-out Boom Draws Sharp Criticism," *New Zealand Herald*, February 12, 2007; Appelbaum and Batt, *Private Equity*, chap. 7; Nicholas Bloom, Raffaella Sadun, and John Van Reenen, "Do Private Equity Owned Firms Have Better Management Practices?" *American Economic Review* 105, no. 5 (2015): 442–446; Patrick A. Gaughan, "How Private Equity and Hedge Funds Are Driving M&A," *Journal of Corporate Accounting and Finance* 18, no. 4 (2007): 55–63; Lerner in "In Private Equity, the Limits of Apollo's Power," *New York Times*, December 7, 2008. On leverage, see Peter Folkman, Julie Froud, Karel Williams, and Sukhdev Johal, "Private Equity: Levered on Capital or Labour?" *Journal of Industrial Relations* 51, no. 4 (2009): 523. It's not uncommon for one private equity fund to flip an investment to another fund, which then can play the same tax-advantaged leverage game, and sometimes flip to a third fund, or even more.

5. "Private Equity's Bottom Line for Workers," *Washington Post*, April 4, 2007; James O'Shea, *The Deal From Hell: How Moguls and Wall Street Plundered Great American Newspapers* (New York: Public Affairs Press, 2011); interview with Maria Ludkin, attorney, GMB Union, London, January 2009; Williamson interview.

6. Ludovic Phalippou and Oliver Gottschalg, "The Performance of Private Equity Funds," *Review of Financial Studies* 22, no. 4 (2008): 1747–1776; "Pension Funds Fail to Reap Private Equity's Rewards," *New York Times*, April 3, 2010.

7. "How US Public Funds Fuel Private Equity," *Financial Times*, August 28, 2006; "Why Unions Cozy Up to Buyout Kings," *Wall Street Journal*, February 28, 2007; Wilshire Consulting,

"Report on State Retirement Systems," 2007; "Public Pension Funds Fail to Reap"; "Entering the Secret Garden of Private Equity," *New York Times*, December 28, 2014; John Adler and Jay Youngdahl, "The Odd Couple: Wall Street, Union Benefit Funds, and the Looting of the American Worker," *New Labor Forum* 19 (2010): 83; "How US Public Funds Fuel Private Equity," *Financial Times*, August 28, 2006; In 2013, the twenty-nine largest US public pension funds had $236 billion invested in private equity. Funds with assets over $5 billion had an average portfolio allocation of 13 percent to private equity, less for smaller funds. Appelbaum and Batt, *Private Equity, Private Equity*, 34, 2182–20, 244.

8. "Big Unions' Funds Still Avoiding Private Equity," *Pensions & Investments* (hereafter *P&I*), May 4, 1998; "Slowly, Private Equity Begins to Work for Unions," *Buyouts*, May 3, 1999; Justin Dini, "Private Labors: Union Pension Funds Are Jumping into Private Equity," *Institutional Investor*, April 1, 2002; interview with Michael Musaraca, Assistant Director, District Council 37, AFSCME and Designated Trustee, New York City Employees Retirement System (NYC-ERS), July 2008, New York City.

9. "US Public Funds Fuel Private Equity"; "Wells Fargo Isn't the Only Firm That Needs a Lesson," *New York Times*, October 7, 2016; "When Private Equity Firms Give Retirees the Short End," *New York Times*, June 13, 2015. Phalippou quoted in Chris Flood, "CalPERS' Support of Private Equity 'Propaganda' Slammed," *Financial Times*, September 6, 2015.

10. Caught up in the scandal at CalPERS was its former board chair, William Crist. He maintained his innocence and was not indicted. However, the fund's CEO was sentenced for fraud and bribery, while a board member committed suicide before his trial. None of their activities involved Relational Investing. "At CalPERS, a Revolving Door of Fees for Influence," *Wall Street Journal*, January 15, 2010; Craig Karmin, "Calpers Set to Document Middleman Payments," *Wall Street Journal*, January 14, 2010; Alexandra Stevenson, "Calpers's Disclosure on Fee Uncertainties Brings Surprises, and Scrutiny," *New York Times*, June 26, 2015. Also see "Lawsuit Seeks Details on Failed $100 Million CalPERS Investment," *San Francisco Public Press*, July 23, 2010.

11. AFL-CIO, *Report of the Investment Product Review Group*, October 1999; AFL-CIO, *Investment Product Review: Private Capital 2002*, November 2002.

12. "Unions Grasp for Influence over Private Equity," *Labor Watch*, published by Capital Research Center, October 2007; "Labor of Love," *Daily Deal*, June 27, 2005. Bill Clinton became a consultant to Yucaipa in 2002; on at least one occasion, he persuaded a union to do business with the firm. "Controversy by the Truckload: Battle for Car Hauler Puts Spotlight on Burkle's Dealings," *Wall Street Journal*, May 2, 2007.

13. Ross in Dale Russakoff and David Cho, "New Labor Strikes Deals with Private Equity," *Washington Post*, June 10, 2007; "Cerberus's Sharp-Toothed Ways," *Washington Post*, May 15, 2007; "Jobs, Wages, Health Care, Pensions: All in Jeopardy as Chrysler Is Sold to Private Firm," *Labor Notes*, May 28, 2007; Sleigh interview; Beeferman, "Private Equity," 552; Appelbaum and Batt, *Private Equity at Work*, 206–209, 233–234. Many called Ross a "vulture investor."

14. Interview with Zelenko; "How a Blackstone Deal Shook Up a Workforce," *Wall Street Journal*, July 27, 2007; Appelbaum and Batt, *Private Equity*, 74–76; "Gluttons at the Gate," *Business Week*, October 30, 2006; James Taylor, "Hertz Backers Cash in $1 Billion of Shares," *Private Equity International*, June 7, 2007; Nathan Bromey, "Pandemic Wreaking Havoc on Stores," *USA Today*, May 28, 2020; Robert Kuttner, "The Real Villain in Bankruptcies: Private Equity," *American Prospect*, May 27, 2020.

15. "German Business Alarmed as SPD Chairman Munterfering Denounces Capitalist Locust List," *Financial Times*, May 2, 2005; "Reshaping Germany's Companies," *BBC News*, September 15, 2005; interview with Babette Frölich, Head of Strategy, and Thomas Klebe, Legal Adviser, I. G. Metall, December 2008, Frankfurt, Germany; Socialist Group in the European Parliament, *Hedge Funds and Private Equity: A Critical Analysis* (Brussels: PSE, April 2007); interview with Poul N. Rasmussen, member of the European Parliament, Brussels, December 2008.

16. It's been said that pension plans found a replacement for their own activism by investing with and supporting activist hedge funds. The two types of activism—shareholder and hedge fund—are not the same, however. Hedge funds are relatively myopic with a laser-like focus on payouts. Improvements in operating performance are not on their agenda, according to Klein and Zur. By contrast, pension funds have longer time horizons and target companies based on governance practices instead of cash holdings, and monitor their investments to see if operating performance and other measures improve over time.

In 2014, CalPERS shocked the investing world when it announced it would unwind its hedge fund investments. Cited reasons included high fees and low returns. Another was recent revelations of bribery and insider trading at several well-known hedge funds. In some blue places, public pension trustees were appalled, this coming on top of negative articles in *The Atlantic* and the *New York Times*, about the human wreckage left behind after hedge funds exited a target. In 2016, Letitia James, then New York City's second-highest public official, asked fellow NYCERS trustees to dump hedge funds. "Let them sell their summer homes and jets and return those fees to their investors."

But some pension plans remained with activist funds. CalSTRS tripled the size of its activist portfolio from 2012 to 2015, this at the time CalPERS exited. The split surfaced in 2015, when CalSTRS backed a hedge fund seeking board seats at DuPont. CalPERS sided with management and criticized the hedge fund for "short-term thinking." Private equity, whatever its blemishes, was less controversial and offered higher returns after 2010 than hedge funds.

Diane Del Guercio and Jennifer Hawkins, "The Motivation and Impact of Pension Fund Activism, " *Journal of Financial Economics* 52 (1999): 293–340; April Klein and Emanuel Zur, "Entrepreneurial Shareholder Activism: Hedge Funds and Other Private Investors," 64 *Journal of Finance* (2009): 187–229; Alon Brav, Wei Jiang, and Hyunseob Kim, "Hedge Fund Activism: A Review," 4 *Foundations and Trends in Finance* (2010): 185–246; Telephone interview, Alon Brav, Professor of Finance, Fuqua School of Business, Duke University, February 2, 2016; Alon Brav, Wei Jiang, Frank Partnoy, and Randall Thomas, "Hedge Fund Activism, Corporate Governance, and Firm Performance," *Journal of Finance* 63 (2008): 1729–1775; Jon Hartley, "Why CalPERS Exiting the Hedge Fund Space," *Forbes*, September 22, 2014; Robert Teitelman, "Will Public Pensions Regret Dumping Hedge Funds?" *Institutional Investor*, February 15, 2017; Liz Hoffman, "Largest U.S. Pensions Divided on Activism," *Wall Street Journal*, May 19, 2015; Alana Semuels, "Can America's Companies Survive America's Most Aggressive Investors?" *The Atlantic*, November 18, 2016; Nelson D. Schwartz, "How Wall Street Bent Steel," *New York Times*, December 6, 2014; Merryn Somerset Webb, "Fund Managers Are Having Far Too Much Fun," *Financial Times*, April 23, 2016; Gretchen Morgenson, "New York's Teamsters May Have Their Pensions Cut. What Went Wrong?" *New York Times*, December 30, 2016. Data on hedge funds are from Alon Brav, Wei Jiang, and Hyunseob Kim, *Hedge Fund Activism* (Hanover, MA: now-publishers, 2010); Brav, Jian, and Kim, "Hedge Fund Activism: Updated Tables and Figures," Unpublished manuscript, Duke University, Fuqua School of Business, available at https://faculty. fuqua. duke. edu/~ brav/HFactivism_September_2013. pdf (2013).

17. "American Coin Has New Chairman, Job Cuts," Reuters News, April 14, 1999; Don Clark, "Sun Micro Slashes Jobs; Fallen Silicon Valley Star to Shed Up to 6,000 More Workers," *Wall Street Journal*, November 15, 2008; Phred Dvorak and Joann S. Lublin, "Boards Give Up Taming Act; Activist Investors Take Seats Increasingly Without Fight," *Wall Street Journal*, April 7, 2008; Al Lewis, "How Corporate Raiders Can Trash Credit Ratings; Shareholder Activists Aren't Always Altruistic White Knights," *Marketwatch*, March 12, 2014; Schwartz, "Wall Street Bent Steel"; David Schuyler, "Manitowoc Co. Plans to Split Its Cranes, Food-Service Businesses," *Milwaukee Business Journal*, January 30, 2015.

In 2004, after leading CalPERS into battle on behalf of Safeway workers, Sean Harrigan recommended Ralph Whitworth for a directorship on the New York Stock Exchange. After he left CalPERS, Harrigan did not return to his union but instead stayed in the investing world. For two years he was president of the Los Angeles Fire and Police Pensions Fund. Harrigan was implicated in a placement fee scandal and resigned his position at the fund. Phyllis Plitch, "Calpers Nominates Fmr SEC Chair Levitt to NYSE Board," *Wall Street Journal*, March 25, 2004; "CalPERS Proves Fees Paid in Pay-to-Play Deal," Reuters, October 15, 2009.

18. Schwartz, "How Wall Street Bent Steel"; Randy Diamond, "CalSTRS Takes Bold Step in Governance," *P&I*, April 29, 2013; Randall Smith, "Some Big Public Pension Funds Are Behaving Like Activist Investors," *New York Times*, November 28, 2013; Randall Smith, Ed Mendel, "Pension Shareholder Clout Reshapes Corporations," February 2, 2015 at https://calpensions.com/2015/02/02/pension-shareholder-clout-reshapes-corporations/; Anup Agrawal and Yuree Lim, "The Dark Side of Hedge Fund Activism: Evidence from Employee Pension Plans," *29th Annual Conference on Financial Economics & Accounting*, Tulane University, 2018.

In 2007, the AFL-CIO and public plans found themselves at loggerheads when TCI, the British hedge fund, targeted CSX, a railroad. Public plans were among TCI's largest investors. TCI had accumulated 20 percent of CSX stock and demanded that the railroad cut back on capital spending and use the savings to buy back shares. CSX had bargaining contracts with fourteen different unions, who were concerned that if TCI won the fight, it would lead to job losses and a decline in the company's long-term prospects. Those supporting TCI included CalPERS and CalSTRS. Kellogg and Richardson interview; "Fears over Surge in Corporate Activism," *The Guardian*, October 14, 2007; "Stoking the Fires at CSX," *Kiplinger Washington Editors*, November 2, 2007; "Anticlimax in Long-Running CSX Railroad Court Case," *New York Times*, July 19, 2011.

19. Abrecht interview; Stern in "Labor Leader, Buyout Kings Speak Same Language," *Wall Street Journal*, May 30, 2007; "New Labor Strikes Deals."

20. Peter Dreier, "Divorce-Union Style: Can the Labor Movement Overcome UNITE HERE's Messy Breakup?" *The Nation*, August 12, 2009; "Private Equity's Bottom Line"; "Labor Leader, Buyout Kings."

21. Service Employees International Union, "Behind the Buyouts: Inside the World of Private Equity," April 20, 2007; "Private Equity's Bottom Line"; "Labor Leader, Buyout Kings"; "Q&A: A Union's New Cause: The SEIU's Stephen Lerner Details What Exactly the Union Wants from the Private Equity Industry," *Investment Dealer Digest*, June 18, 2007; "Congress

Hints at Regulating Private Equity," *Investment News*, May 29, 2007. KB Toys went bankrupt nine years after Bain's purchase.

22. "Rep. Frank Says Sox Goes Overboard, but No Legislation Is Necessary," *Investment News*, March 26, 2007; Steven N. Kaplan and Joshua Rauh, "It's the Market: The Broad-based Rise in the Return to Top Talent," *Journal of Economic Perspectives* 27, no. 3 (2013): 35–56; *Private Equity's Effects on Workers and Firms: Hearing before the Committee on Financial Services*, US House of Representatives, 110th Cong., 1st Sess., May 16, 2007; "Unkind Cut for Janitors at Hilfiger," *New York Times*, May 16, 2007; "Labor Leader, Buyout"; "Sound and Fury over Private Equity," *New York Times*, May 20, 2007; "Union Takes Anti-Buyout Campaign Worldwide," *New York Times*, June 4, 2008; "For Schumer, the Double-Edged Sword of Cozying Up to Hedge Funds," *New York Times*, June 22, 2007; Danielle Fugazy, "A Union's New Cause," *M&As*, July 1, 2007. Also see Matthew T. Bodie, "Mother Jones Meets Gordon Gekko: The Complicated Relationship between Labor and Private Equity," *University of Colorado Law Review* 79 (2008): 1317–1354. A *New York Times*–Equilar study found that publicly owned private equity firms had the best-paid CEOs of any major industry. Blackstone's Stephen Schwarzman received a cool $800 million. Ben Protess and Michael Corkery, "Just How Much Do the Top Private Equity Earners Make?" *New York Times*, December 10, 2016.

23. "Blackstone Fears Union Pressure Will Hit Returns," Dow Jones News Service, May 28, 2007; Richard L. Trumka to John White, Director of Corporation Finance, and Andrew Donohue, Chief of Staff, Securities and Exchange Commission, May 15, 2007; and June 12, 2007, courtesy of Dan Pedrotty; Sara Hansard, "Private Equity; Legislative Pressure Would Make Unions Happy," *Investment News*, May 29, 2007.

24. "Private Equity and Hedge Funds," AFL-CIO Executive Council Statement, Chicago, August 8, 2007; "Paulson Warns of 'Unintended' Fallout in Taxing Funds," *Bloomberg*, June 27, 2007; Aviva Aron-Dine, "An Analysis of the Carried Interest Controversy," Center on Budget and Policy Priorities, Washington, DC, August 1, 2007; *Carried Interest, Part 1: Hearing before the Senate Committee on Finance*, 110th Cong., July 11, 2007; "For Schumer, the Double-Edged Sword"; "Congress Weighs End to Private Equity Tax Break," *New York Times*, June 21, 2007; "Schumer's Tax Gambit," *Wall Street Journal*, August 16, 2007; "US Union Attacks Private Equity 'Tax Dodges,'" *Financial Times*, August 16, 2007; "Private Equity Tax Hike Loses Steam in Senate," *Los Angeles Times*, October 10, 2007; "Tax Proposal Baton Passed to the Senate," *Investment Dealer Digest*, November 19, 2007.

25. "Pension Group Changes View on Private Equity," *Reuters*, September 5, 2007; "Minority Group Fights 'Carry' Tax Plan," *Wall Street Journal*, September 5, 2007. An interesting debate over carried interest took place between Damon Silvers and Steven Kaplan, the University of Chicago economist. See "Trading Shots: Taxing Private Equity; Experts Debate Whether Firms Are Getting an Unfair Tax Break," *Wall Street Journal Online*, June 25, 2007.

26. Alec MacGillis, "The Billionaires' Loophole," *New Yorker*, March 14, 2016; "Registration Reality," *Private Equity Manager*, June 18, 2010; "Recovery Trumps Proposed Tax on Carried Interest," *P&I*, February 8, 2010; "Democrats Shift Focus Back to Jobs Creation," *New York Times*, May 18, 2010; "Showdown on Fund Taxes," *Wall Street Journal*, June 9, 2010.

27. "Rep. Barney Frank Holds a Hearing on Regulation of Systemic Risk in the Financial Services Industry," House Financial Services Committee Hearing, *Financial Markets Regulation Wire*, March 17, 2009; "American Federation of Labor and Congress of Industrial Organizations

President Richard Trumka Prepared Testimony before the House Financial Services Committee Hearing on Systemic Regulation, Prudential Matters, Resolution Authority and Securitization," *Financial Markets Regulation Wire*, October 29, 2009; "Labor: We'll Storm Wall St.," *New York Post*, April 10, 2010; "Late Push to Hike Taxes on Private Equity Firms Foiled," *CongressDaily/PM*, February 17, 2009.

28. "GOP Ramps Up Attack on Dodd Bill," *CongressDaily/PM*, April 13, 2010; Richard Trumka, "It's Time to Restrict Private Equity," *Wall Street Journal*, April 13, 2010; "Left-Wing Senators to Propose Amendments to Financial Reform Bill," *Theflyonthewall.com*, May 3, 2010; "A Backlash against Obama's Budget," *Business Week*, March 5, 2009; Eileen Appelbaum, "Dodd-Frank at Five: Private Equity and the SEC," *Huffington Post*, July 21, 2015; "Schwarzman's Unfortunate War Analogy," *New York Times*, August 16, 2010.

29. Marick F. Masters, Ray Gibney, and Tom Zagenczyk, "The AFL-CIO v. CTW: The Competing Visions, Strategies, and Structures," *Journal of Labor Research* 27 (2006): 473–504; "SEIU Is Now the Fastest Growing Union in America," HR.com, 2000, https://www.hr.com/hr/communities/labor_relations/unions_-_collective_bargaining/the_seiu_is_now_the_fastest_growing_union_in_north_america_eng.html; Robert J. Grossman, "Reorganized Labor," *HRMagazine*, January 1, 2008; Paula B. Voos, "Trends in Union Organizing Expenditures, 1953–1977," *ILR Review* 38, no. 1 (1984): 52–63; Zelenko interview. A proportional or larger share of the two-thirds increase in CTW's dues went to the national office to support organizing.

30. "SEIU Is Now the Fastest Growing Union"; Adrienne Eaton, Janice Fine, Allison Porter, and Saul Rubenstein, *Organizational Change at SEIU: 1996–2009*, Rutgers University, n.d.; John B. Judis, "Drill Sergeant," *New Republic*, December 15, 2002; "Resolution #14, Adopted by SEIU Delegates at the 22nd International Convention, Pittsburgh, May 2000"; Anonymous union source, 2009.

31. Shai Bernstein, Josh Lerner, Morten Sorensen, and Per Stromberg, "Private Equity and Industry Performance," *Management Science* 63 (2016): 1198–1213; Abrecht interview; David Hall, "Private Equity and Employment: The Davos/WEF/Harvard Study," Public Services International Research Unite, University of Greenwich, London, January 29, 2008; Steven J. Davis, John Haltiwanger, Kyle Handley, Ben Lipsius, Josh Lerner, and Javier Miranda, "The Economic Effects of Private Equity Buyouts," Becker-Friedman Institute, University of Chicago, working paper no. 2019–122, 2019.

32. Timothy J. Minchin, "A Successful Union in an Era of Decline: Interrogating the Growth of the Service Employees International Union, 1980–1995," *Labor History* (2020): 307; "Service Employees End California Nursing Home Partnership," *Labor Notes*, June 25, 2007; Andy Stern, *A Country That Works: Getting America Back on Track* (New York: Free Press, 2006), 107; Edward V. Jeffrey, "SEIU International President Outlines Allegations of Misconduct by Head of California Local," jacksonlewis, March 31, 2008; "Union Disunity," *San Francisco Weekly*, April 11, 2007; "Labor Leader, Buyout Kings"; Steve Early, *The Civil Wars in U.S. Labor: Birth of a New Workers Movement or Death Throes of Old?* (Chicago: Haymarket Press, 2011).

33. Smith interview; Appelbaum and Batt, *Private Equity at Work*, 71–72; "The Barbarian Establishment," *The Economist*, October 22, 2016; Stern, *Country That Works*, xiv. After a private equity firm purchased Beverly in 2006, its name changed to Golden Living. The new owners reduced staffing levels, sold facilities and leased them back, and then flipped the company to

another private equity firm. It was the same old story. Aline Bos and Charlene Harrington, "What Happens to a Nursing Home Chain When Private Equity Takes Over? A Longitudinal Case Study" 54 INQUIRY: *The Journal of Health Care Organization, Provision, and Financing* (2017).

34. Tim Shorrock, "Crony Capitalism Goes Global," *The Nation*, March 14, 2002; "Spies for Hire: Carlyle Group to Become Owner of 'One of America's Largest Private Intelligence Armies,'" *Democracy Now*, May 19, 2008, https://www.democracynow.org/2008/5/19/spies_for_hire_the_secret_world

35. "Looks Like Rain," *Institutional Investor*, December 1, 2011; "Manor Care LBO a Tall Order for Rattled Lenders," Reuters, November 9, 2007; "HCP and Carlyle's ManorCare in $6bln Asset Deal," Reuters, December 13, 2010; "CtW Investment Group Challenges HCP Board Re: $6.1 Billion ManorCare Deal Citing Questionable Billing Practices," PR Newswire, February 16, 2011.

36. Kate Sheppard, "Taking on the Buyout Guys," *American Prospect*, November 13, 2007; Ian Clark, "Owners and Managers: Disconnecting Managerial Capitalism? Understanding the Private-Equity Business Model," *Work, Employment and Society* 23 (2009): 775–786; "Post-Buyout, ManorCare Does Job Out of Spotlight," *Toledo Blade*, March 28, 2010; "Carlyle-ManorCare Facing New Federal Charges for Breaking the Law," PR Newswire, August 27, 2008; "Not All Buyers Avoid the Union Label," Bank Loan Report, July 6, 2009; "Nation's Largest Healthcare Workers Union Calls for Congressional Hearings into Private Equity Ownership of Nursing Homes," PR Newswire, October 2, 2007; "PE Still Nursing Its Wound," *Investment Dealer Digest*, October 29, 2007. At the time, Carlyle was planning to buy ailing banks. The union set up a website, BigBadBanks.org, and Andy Stern published two op-eds in the *Wall Street Journal* opposing bank takeovers by private equity, not only Carlyle but also TPG. Andy Stern, "Keep Private Equity Away from Our Banks," *Wall Street Journal*, July 7, 2008; Andy Stern, "Private Equity and the Banks: Their Idea? Government Risk but Private-Sector Rewards," *Wall Street Journal*, August 3, 2009.

37. Andrew L. Stern's prepared statement in *Private Equity's Effects on Workers and Firms*, 58; "Private Equity Ownership of Nursing Homes to be Probed," *CongressDaily/PM*, October 23, 2007; "At Many Homes, More Profit and Less Nursing," *New York Times*, September 2, 2007; "Lawmakers Question Private-Equity Impact on Nursing Homes," *Washington Post*, November 16, 2007; "Carlyle Manor Care Deal at Center of Nursing Home Debate," Dow Jones News Service, November 12, 2007; "Pair of Proposals Take Aim at Carlyle Group," *Washington Post*, February 15, 2008; Smith interview.

38. "Labor Leader, Buyout Kings"; "SEIU Launches Ad Campaign Opposing Corporate Raiders' Plans to Buy Mich. Nursing Homes," PR Newswire, October 3, 2007; "Post-Buyout, ManorCare Does Job Out of Spotlight"; Labor Union Airs Concerns about Private Equity," Dow Jones News Service, August 15, 2007; "Sale of Nursing Homes to Carlyle Group Concerns State Officials," Associated Press, October 14, 2007; "Union Asks State Regulators to Examine Nursing Home Chain Buyout," Associated Press, October 10, 2007; Martha Raffaele, "Pa. Lawmakers to Examine Nursing Home Buyout by Carlyle Group," Associated Press, November 7, 2007. Charging nursing homes with fraud was an old SEIU tactic, first used at Beverly in the 1980s. At Universal Health Services, a public nursing home company SEIU was trying to organize, CtW Investment Group sent a twelve-page letter to the board containing evidence of Medicare billing fraud as well as "entrenched and unresponsive" corporate governance. "CtW

Investment Calls for Governance Changes at Universal Health Services," *Dow Jones Institutional News*, March 29, 2017.

39. Sheppard, "Taking on the Buyout Guys"; "Union Protests Carlyle's Bid for Manor Care," *Washington Post*, September 20, 2007; Carl Horowitz, "SEIU Steps Up Campaign against Private Equity Funds," National Legal & Policy Center, June 2, 2008; Lerner in Thomas Heath, "Ambushing Private Equity," *Washington Post*, April 18, 2008; "Manor Care Protesters Disrupt Rubenstein Speech at Conf.," Dow Jones News Service, January 18, 2008; Smith interview. Because the nurse was nervous, her words were a bit garbled. After she left the stage, Rubenstein imperiously said, "I think a remedial English course would be helpful." The nurse, a union supporter, was disciplined by Manor Care, often a prelude to dismissal. But the union filed charges with the NLRB that were later upheld. "Carlyle-Manor Care Facing New Federal Charges for Breaking the Law," PR Newswire, August 27, 2008.

40. L. W. Beeferman, "Private Equity and American Labor: Multiple, Pragmatic Responses Mirroring Labor's Strengths and Weaknesses," *Journal of Industrial Relations* 51, no. 4 (2009): 544; "CalPERS Goes for Private Equity," *Global Investor*, October 1, 2008; "CalPERS Resets Private Equity Allocation," *FINalternatives*, December 19, 2007; "Blackstone Fears Union Pressure Will Hit Returns," Dow Jones News Service, May 28, 2007; Shorrock, "Crony Capitalism"; "Wall Street Pushes to Relax Pension Rules," *Business Week*, October 10, 2005; American Bar Association, *When ERISA Meets Private Equity* (Chicago, 2016). By 2013, CalPERS's private equity investments had risen to 16 percent of its portfolio. The following year it began reducing its portfolio allocation until it reached 8 percent, although in 2020 it announced that it once again planned to increase its share of the asset class. Alex Lynn, "CalPERS Posts Lowest PE Returns of the Decade After 'Precipitous' Drop," *Private Equity International*, March 10, 2020.

41. "Carlyle Group Embrace of Abu Dhabi Undermining Respect for Human Rights," PR Newswire, December 10, 2007; "Ambushing Private Equity," *Washington Post*, April 18, 2008; SEIU, "Sovereign Wealth Funds and Private Equity: Increased Access, Decreased Transparency," April 2008; "California's Stern Rebuke," *Wall Street Journal*, April 21, 2008.

42. "Stern Rebuke"; "CalPERS Tackles PE Legislation," *Investment Dealer Digest*, March 24, 2008; "Backlash Against Obama's Budget." CalPERS had been investing with Carlyle since the mid-1990s as well as with Wilbur Ross. Tim Shorrock, "CalPERS and Carlyle," *The Nation*, March 14, 2002.

43. "Taking on the Buyout Industry," *New York Times*, March 10, 2008; "Pounding Private Equity," *Wall Street Journal*, August 23, 2008; Chris Zappone, "Union Takes Aim at Private Equity," *CNNMoney*, June 27, 2007; Abrecht and Young interviews. Carlyle threw SEIU a bone when in 2009 it signed a thirty-five-year deal with the state of Connecticut to operate highway service stops. As part of the deal, it gave SEIU permission to organize the restaurants. Thomas Heath, "Carlyle to Run Conn Roadside Service Stops," *Washington Post*, November 20, 2009.

44. Zappone, "Union Takes Aim"; Rossman, Richardson and Kellogg, and Abrecht interviews. Ironically, in 2002 SEIU was among the union pension funds with the largest investments in private equity. Shorrock, "CalPERS and Carlyle."

45. "Overdoses, Bedsores, and Broken Bones: What Happened When a Private Equity Firm Sought to Care for Society's Most Vulnerable," *Washington Post*, November 25, 2018; "Carlyle Manor Care Deal at Center of Nursing Home Debate," Dow Jones News Service, November 12, 2007; "Nursing Home CEO Wants $100M Payout amid Bankruptcy Threat," *New York Post*,

June 2, 2017; "Carlyle Group Cedes Control of Nursing Home Chain," *New York Post*, June 11, 2017; "Carlyle Group's Founders Step Back for New Leaders in Shakeup," *New York Post*, October 25, 2017;"Nursing Home Chain's Collapse Has Been a Decade in the Making," *New York Post*, March 5, 2018; "HCR Manor Care Strategy to Exit Bankruptcy Gets OK; Will Sell 74 Facilities," *McKnights*, April 17, 2018; "Despite Recent Troubles, HCR Manor Care Has a Rich History," *Toledo Blade*, July 27, 2018.

46. "Union Takes Anti-Buyout Campaign"; Appelbaum and Batt, *Private Equity*, 228; "$7.1 Billion KKR and CD&R Buyout of U.S. Foodservice Raises Questions about Job Safety and Food Safety," PR Newswire, May 10, 2007. Labor first locked horns with KKR in 1989, when the AFL-CIO opposed the firm's infamous buyout of RJR Nabisco. In 1994, KKR proposed a buyout of Borden, the food and chemical company, for which it would exchange shares in RJR Nabisco to investors who tendered their Borden shares. At the time, the Teamsters had 7,000 members at Borden and feared for their jobs. The point person for the Teamsters was Bill Patterson, who sent letters to Borden shareholders asking them not to tender. Early sellers to KKR included the LENS fund, the hedge fund founded by Robert Monks, and the Ohio Teachers fund. Jon Lukomnik of New York City's pension funds opposed the KKR deal because it gave KKR overly large fees and the right to buy Borden at a low price even if the deal fell apart. KKR ended up buying Borden, divested some of its businesses and pocketed the cash, and then sold the company to a different private equity firm, Apollo, nine years later. Apollo combined Borden with two other firms to create a new company, Hexion. Come 2020, Hexion went bankrupt. Each stage in the process exemplifies the facets of private equity: large fees, tax-advantaged debt, cash withdrawals, sale to another private equity firm, and bankruptcies. In *Private Equity*, Appelbaum and Batt dissect the logic of the private equity business model. Stan Hinden, "Union Official Hits Kohlberg Kravis Takeover Activities," *Washington Post*, February 10, 1989; Glenn Collins, "Borden Deal Is Opposed by Teamsters," *New York Times*, September 21, 1994; Steve Bailey, "Borden Inks Agreement with KKR," *Boston Globe*, September 24, 1994.

47. "Crocodile Tears for Private Equity Titan," *Financial Times*, August 29, 2007; "Union Takes Anti-Buyout Campaign"; "Equity Firms Face Global Protest on Tax Benefits," *New York Times*, June 5, 2008; "Protesting a Private Equity Firm (With Piles of Money)," *New York Times*, October 10, 2007; SEIU, "Winners and Losers: Fallout from KKR's Race for Profit," n.d.; "SEIU Steps Up Campaign"; "Union's Concerns Don't Change Board's Vision," *The Spokesman-Review* (Spokane), September 11, 2007.

48. David Moberg, "Translating Solidarity," *American Prospect*, November 5, 2010; UNI Global Union website; interview with Michael Laslett, European campaign director, SEIU, October 2008, London. UNI Global is one of ten global union federations (GUFs) organized around different industries. First known as UNI, it was created in 2000 out of several transnational predecessors whose origins went back to the formation of the International Labour Organization after the First World War. It has signed more framework agreements than any other GUF. Michael Fichter and Jamie K. McCallum, "Implementing Global Framework Agreements: The Limits of Social Partnership," *Global Networks* 15 (2015): S65–S85.

49. Thao Hua and Arleen Jacobius, "Unions Balk, Buyouts Bend; Fight Between Unions, Private Equity May Affect Returns, Investment Flow," *Pensions & Investments*, May 14, 2007; "KKR Portfolio Companies Could Put Consumers, Workers, and the Environment at Risk," *PR Newswire*, February 26, 2008; "Union Takes Anti-Buyout Campaign"; interview with Gabriele

Fulton, UNI Global Union, November 2008, Geneva; UNI, "Global Unions Response to Private Equity," November 2008; UNI Global, "Hedge Funds: Issues for Trade Unionists," August 2008; UNI Private Equity conference announcement, December 3, 2008.

50. Laslett interview; "Union Targets Private Equity Firms over Pensions," *Guardian*, July 17, 2008; UNI Global Union, "Pension Fund Investment in Private Equity," July 2008; "Private Equity Workshop Advances Union Bargaining Agenda," December 4, 2007, http://www.iufdocuments.org/buyoutwatch/2007/12/; "Unite Warns Private Equity: Act Responsibly or Risk Losing Our Pensions Investments," PR Newswire Europe, July 16, 2008; "Private Equity Will Be the Next Bubble to Burst," *Guardian*, February 4, 2009.

51. Interview with Colin Meech, Head of Capital Stewardship, UNISON, and Ben Rudder, Adviser, UNISON, November 2008, London; interviews with Alan MacDougall, PIRC, November 2008, and Ludkin, MacDonald, and Williamson; Ian Clark, "The Private Equity Business Model and Associated Strategies for HRM: Evidence and Implications?" *International Journal of Human Resource Management* 20 (2009): 2030–2048.

Another campaign based on a UNI-SEIU partnership took place at Wackenhut, which, after a series of mergers, became part of G4S, a giant multinational employer of security guards. UNI and SEIU took advantage of the Principles for Responsible Investment (PRI), discussed in chapter 3, which contained the ILO's labor standards. Some of the largest pension funds in northern Europe and the Anglo world were signatories, as was G4S. PRI did not have relationships with individual unions, only with pension plans, but its staff worked with UNI to arrange meetings between G4S and SEIU and GMB, a British union. After a six-year campaign, an agreement was reached in 2008 that required G4S to respect organizing rights, provide a mechanism for union complaints, and give SEIU the right to card check in nine US cities. During the campaign, SEIU improvised a variety of tactics to lead G4S to an agreement. A critical part was outreach to G4S's institutional investors, such as F&C, a socially responsible asset manager in Britain, and a Norwegian pension fund, which subsequently divested its G4S stock. UNI estimated that UK and US pension funds owned ten million G4S shares, although this was less than 1 percent of outstanding stock. On the other hand, signatories to the PRI agreement owned an additional 7 percent. Because investors and the general public would be more sympathetic to a campaign focused on human rights in the poor countries where G4S operated, SEIU worked with unions in India, Africa, and Southeast Asia to organize anti-G4S protests. Criticism of SEIU came from GMB, whose concerns mirrored UNISON's, namely, that SEIU was overbearing and overly tactical. Interviews with Rob Lake, APG Asset Management, December 2008, Amsterdam; interview with Elsa Bos and Marcel Jeucken, PGGM Pension Funds (now PFZW), December 2008, Amsterdam; Rossman interview; Fichter and McCallum, "Implementing Global Framework"; Moberg, "Translating Solidarity"; "Workers of the World Unite," *Guardian*, August 12, 2006; Harold Meyerson, "Where Are the Workers?" *American Prospect*, February 16, 2009; "A Global Agreement between UNI and G4S: Ethical Employment Partnership," December 11, 2008; Ergon Associates, "European Institutional Investors and Labour Issues: Report to the SEIU," May 2006. The best overview of the G4S story is Jamie K. McCallum, *Global Unions, Local Power: The New Spirit of Transnational Organizing* (Ithaca, NY: ILR Press, 2013). Thanks to John Logan.

52. "Las Vegas Council Mulls Ways to Use Voice to Speak for Workers," *National Catholic Reporter*, June 4, 1999; "Getting Organized; HCA Agreement Gives Way to More Unions,"

Modern Healthcare, November 29, 2010; "Hospital Unions Make Inroads through Neutrality Deals," *Labor Notes*, November 8, 2010; Jane McAlevey, *No Shortcuts: Organizing for Power in the New Gilded Age* (New York: Oxford University Press, 2016); "Unions Enter Pacts to Boost Members," *Wall Street Journal*, January 29, 2011; "New Labor Strikes Deals"; Appelbaum and Batt, *Private Equity*, 227–232.

53. "How a Blackstone Deal Shook Up a Work Force." Carlyle was the last of the big three to do an IPO, this in 2012.

54. "Blackstone Group Taking Hilton Hotels Private for $20.1 Billion," Associated Press, July 3, 2007; "Hotel Workers Union Applauds Blackstone-Hilton Combination," PR Newswire, July 3, 2007; Michael S. Mitchell, "Union Organizing Trends in the Hospitality Industry," HospitalityNet, July 24, 2007, https://www.hospitalitynet.org/opinion/4032340.html

55. Smith and Zdrazil, interviews; Ed Mendel, "CalSTRS, CalPERS Pressure Hilton in Labor Dispute," Calpensions, November 15, 2010, https://calpensions.com/2010/11/15/calstrs-calpers-pressure-hilton-in-labor-dispute

56. Dreier, "Divorce"; "Labored Negotiations: Many Acquirers to Try to Avoid Unionized Targets," *Mergers & Acquisitions*, June 1, 2009; Raynor in "New Labor Strikes Deals."

57. Stephen Foley, "American Union Targets Blackstone to Expose Private Equity Ills," *The Independent* (London), April 2, 2007; "Blackstone Admits Union Pressure in New Filings," *Financial News*, May 28, 2007; "Blackstone Group Goes Public," *New York Times*, June 23, 2007.

58. Patterson in "Union Shop," *The Deal.com*, April 20, 2007; Richardson and Kellogg interview.

59. Rogers interview; "CVS/Caremark Director Resigns," *Washington Post*, July 4, 2007; Riskmetrics Group, *2007 Postseason Report*; CtWIG, "Corporate Transactions 2007."

60. "Union Shop."

61. "Where the Action Is: Forget the Audit Committee: The New Hot Seat on Boards Is the Nominating Committee," *Wall Street Journal*, January 14, 2008; "CtW Investment Group Forum for Caremark Institutional Shareholders," New York, February 2, 2007; *ISS Governance Weekly*, July 11, 2007; William B. Patterson to Caremark Shareholders, February 12, 2007; Patterson to Michael D. Ware, director and member of Audit Committee, Caremark Board of Directors, December 21, 2006; "CVS Caremark and United Food and Commercial Workers Union Announce Cooperation Agreement in 500 Stores," CISION PR Newswire, January 17, 2013, https://www.prnewswire.com/news-releases/cvs-caremark-and-united-food--commercial-workers-union-announce-cooperation-agreement-in-500-stores-187320751.html. Amalgamated Bank's LongView Funds, now linked to CTW via UNITE HERE, submitted a proposal demanding changes in Caremark's option-granting procedures. It received 48 percent of the votes.

62. "Banks on List of Union Targets," *Crain's New York Business*, February 23, 2009; "White-Collar Blues Play Well with US Labor Unions," Reuters, January 28, 2009; "Next Up: Bank Employee Unions," *American Banker*, October 1, 2009; "Labor Banks on It: Service Union Eyes Organizing Financial Workers," *New York Post*, December 10, 2008; Stephen Lerner, "An Injury to All: Going beyond Collective Bargaining as We Have Known It," *New Labor Forum*, Spring 2010. An earlier effort to organize banks was led by the labor-backed group 9to5. Lane Windham, *Knocking on Labor's Door: Union Organizing in the 1970s and the Roots of a New Economic Divide* (Chapel Hill: University of North Carolina Press, 2017).

63. "Citing Bailout, Union Wants to Organize Bank Workers," *CNN*, December 9, 2008; Morgan Lewis, "SEIU Organizing Efforts at Financial Services Companies," white paper, Philadelphia, April 2009; "Is BofA Planning the Mother of All Layoffs?" *Moneywatch*, December 11, 2008.

64. "Change to Win Calls for Audit of Financial Services Industry's Use of Public TARP Funds," PR Newswire, April 14, 2009; "Union Seeks to Capitalize on Anger at Banks," *Philadelphia Inquirer*, March 19, 2009; "CtW Calls on B of A Shareholders to Oust Chairman and CEO Ken Lewis; Also Opposes Directors Tom Ryan and Temple Sloan," PR Newswire, March 26, 2009; "Pressure Mounts on BofA CEO before Annual Meeting," *Reuters*, April 17, 2009; "CtW Welcomes RiskMetrics/ISS and Glass Lewis Recommendations against B of A's Ken Lewis," PR Newswire, April 17, 2009; "SEIU Master Trust Leads Successful Shareholder Resolution Forcing Ken Lewis to Resign as Bank of America Chair," PR Newswire, April 29, 2009.

65. "Anti-AIG Demonstrations Draw Small, Animated Crowds," Reuters, March 19, 2009; "Protesters Converge on Goldman's Washington Office," Dow Jones News Service, November 16, 2009; Nina Easton, "What's Really Behind SEIU's Bank of America Protests?" *CNN Money*, May 19, 2010.

66. "SEIU Calls on Financial Firms to Probe $5B in Executive Pay," *Corporate Governance*, April 22, 2009; "SEIU: More than 5,000 Converge on American Bankers Association Convention," *Politics and Government Weekly*, November 12, 2009.

67. "Next Up"; Morgan Lewis, "SEIU Organizing Efforts"; "Shut Up, They Said: Big Labor Threatens Banks on Card Check," *Wall Street Journal*, February 13, 2009.

68. "Marching on the Moneymen," *New York Times*, March 25, 2010; Josh Nathan-Kazis, "Former Union President Andy Stern Says He Was Too Tough on Banks at SEIU," *The Forward*, June 29, 2011.

69. *Labor Union Report*, November 13, 2010; "Caught on Tape: Former SEIU Official Reveals Secret Plan to Destroy JPMorgan, Crash the Stock Market, and Redistribute Wealth in America," *Business Insider*, March 22, 2011; Wade Rathke, "Stephen Lerner, the Banks, and the Right-Wing Scare Machine," March 25, 2011, http://chieforganizer.org/2011/03/25/stephen-lerner-the-banks-and-the-right-wing-scare-machine; "Wade Rathke's Startling Admission: 'Economic Terrorism' Engineer Stephen Lerner Is Still on SEIU Payroll," *The Blaze*, March 28, 2011; Stephen Lerner, "On the Contrary: A New Insurgency Can Only Arise Outside the Progressive and Labor Establishment," *New Labor Forum*, October 2011. In 2013, CWA launched its own campaign to organize bank workers under the aegis of a new organization, "The Committee for Better Banks." The effort was similar to SEIU's, with Santander Bank as its main target. "Behind the Business Attire, Many Bank Workers Earn Poverty Wages," *In These Times*, August 27, 2015; Greg Ryan, "Union Protest Briefly Shuts Down Santander's Headquarters Branch in Boston," *Boston Business Journal Online*, March 28, 2017.

70. "Former AFL-CIO Unions Hit Hurdles," *Wall Street Journal*, April 11, 2007; Harold Meyerson, "Back in the Labor Fold," *American Prospect*, August 12, 2013; telephone interview with John Borsos, Secretary Treasurer, National Union for Healthcare Workers (NUHW), January 2012; "Did a Union Double-Cross Its College Activists?" *Inside Higher Ed*, August 22, 2008; "Union Courting Aramark Workers Coast to Coast," *Houston Chronicle*, November 10, 2007; Harold Meyerson, "Can the Workers of the World Unite?" *American Prospect*, December 1, 2010; Kris Maher, "Unions Forge Secret Pacts with Major Employers," *Wall Street Journal*, May 10,

2008; Yair Lisotkin, "Management Always Wins the Close Ones," *American Law & Economics Review* 10 (2008): 159–184; Jane McAlevey, *Raising Expectations (and Raising Hell): My Decade Fighting for the Labor Movement* (London: Verso, 2012), 58, 98.

71. "UNITE HERE Meeting Acts Out Deep Rifts," *Labor Notes*, March 2009; Early, *The Civil Wars*; Borsos interview; Harold Meyerson, "Hard Labor," *American Prospect*, June 18, 2006; Meyerson, "Back in the Labor Fold"; "Did a Union Double-Cross Its College Activists?"

72. Borsos interview; "Unions Battle over Health Care," *San Francisco Chronicle*, December 7, 2008; Bill Fletcher Jr. and Nelson Lichtenstein, "SEIU's Civil War," *In These Times*, December 16, 2009.

73. Meyerson, "Where Are the Workers"; Masters, Gibney, and Zagenczyk, "The AFL-CIO v. CTW." Kim Voss, a sociologist at Berkeley, is skeptical of rank-and-filist criticisms like those levied against SEIU. "I suggest that union democracy has too often been framed in singular terms, as only involving the curbing of the illegitimate accumulation of power by union leaders. Yet a key problem faced by unions today—how they might best aggregate the interests of diverse workers and represent new constituencies—is also fundamentally a democratic concern, one that can be addressed only by broadening our understanding of union democracy. Kim Voss, "Democratic Dilemmas: Union Democracy and Union Renewal," *Transfer: European Review of Labour and Research* 16, no. 3 (2010): 369–382, at 369; Robert Hickey, Sarosh Kuruvilla, and Tashlin Lakhani, "No Panacea for Success: Member Activism, Organizing and Union Renewal," *British Journal of Industrial Relations* 48, no. 1 (2010): 53–83.

74. Eaton et al., *Organizational Change*; Borsos interview; "For Unions, a Time of Opportunity and Worry," *Wall Street Journal*, September 15, 2009; Rachel Aleks, "Estimating the Effect of 'Change to Win' on Union Organizing," *Industrial & Labor Relations Review* 68 (2015): 584–605; Maher, "Unions Forge." One proviso: The Cornell study did not include results from card checks that circumvented the NLRB and the National Mediation Board.

75. Tom Rosentiel, "What Was—and Wasn't—On the Public's Mind in 2007," Pew Research Center, December 18, 2007.

Chapter 9. The Financial Crisis and Dodd-Frank

1. "40-Year Low in America's View of Wall Street," *CNN*, October 4, 2011; Lindsay A. Owens, "The Polls—Trends: Confidence in Banks, Financial Institutions, and Wall Street, 1971–2011," *Public Opinion Quarterly* 76 (2012): 142–162.

2. "Private Pensions: Timely Action Needed to Address Impending Multiemployer Plan Insolvencies," Report to Congressional Committees, GAO-13-240, US Government Accountability Office, March 2013, 11; "Progress on Many High-Risk Areas, While Substantial Efforts Needed on Others," Report to Congressional Committees, GAO-17-317, US Government Accountability Office, February 2017; NCCMP, "Multiemployer Pension Facts and the National Economic Impact," January 5, 2018; "Steep Losses Pose Crisis for Pensions," *Washington Post*, October 1, 2009; "Pension Funds Still Waiting for Big Payoff from Private Equity, *New York Times*, April 2, 2010; "Pensions Get Funding Relief," *Journal of Accountancy* 73 (2010), https://www.journalofaccountancy.com/issues/2010/sep/lineitems.html; Kevin M. Campe, Rex Barker, Robert A. Behar, Timothy L. Connor et al., "Multiemployer Pension Funding Study: Fall 2017," Milliman, http://careers.milliman.com/insight/Periodicals/multiemployer-pfs

/Multiemployer-Pension-Funding-Study-Fall-2017. Thanks to Charles Jeszeck of the GAO for advice and assistance.

3. "Calpers Prepares First CDO Investment, *Derivatives Week*, November 10, 2002; Jacqueline Doherty, "Bond Funds Gone Wild? A Pension-Plan Dilemma," July 30, 2007; David Evans, "U.S. Pension Funds are Big Buyers of Riskiest Debt," *Bloomberg News*, June 4, 2007; "Banks Sell Toxic Waste CDOs to CalPERS, Texas Teachers Fund," *Bloomberg*, May 31, 2007; Andrew Hill, "Buffett Warns of Derivatives 'Time Bombs,'" *Financial Times*, March 4, 2003.

Good studies of the Great Recession include Michael Lewis, *The Big Short: Inside the Doomsday Machine* (New York: W.W. Norton, 2010); Andrew Ross Sorkin, *Too Big to Fail* (New York: Penguin, 2010); Bethany McLean and Joe Nocera, *All the Devils Are Here: The Hidden History of the Financial Crisis* (New York: Portfolio, 2011); Simon Johnson and James Kwak, *13 Bankers: The Wall Street Takeover and the Next Financial Meltdown* (New York: Vintage, 2011); Adam Tooze, *Crashed: How a Decade of Financial Crises Changed the World* (New York: Viking, 2018); and Atif Mian and Amir Sufi, *House of Debt: How They (and You) Caused the Great Recession, and How We Can Prevent It from Happening Again* (Chicago: University of Chicago Press, 2015).

4. "Fund Files Investor Proposals with Banks, Builders," Reuters, November 15, 2007; Sondra Albert, "The 'Subprime Crisis' Impact on Fixed-Income Funds," AFL-CIO, November 13, 2007; Damon Silvers, "How We Got into This Mess," *American Prospect*, May 1, 2008; Damon Silvers and Heather Slavkin, "The Legacy of Deregulation and the Financial Crisis—Linkages between Deregulation in Labor Markets, Housing Finance Markets, and the Broader Financial Markets," *Journal of Business and Technical Law* 4 (2009): 301. Also see *The Financial Crisis Inquiry Report: Final Report of the National Commission of the Causes of Financial and Economic Crisis in the United States* (Washington, DC: US Government Printing Office, 2011). It was the result of an inquiry led by Phil Angelides that some called the New Pecora Commission.

5. "Union Leaders Denounce Bailout Plan," *New York Times*, September 25, 2008; "Labor Unions Protest in New York against Bailout," Reuters, September 26, 2008; "AFL-CIO President at Wall Street Rally Calls for Reform," Dow Jones News Service, September 22, 2009.

6. "Marching on the Moneymen," *New York Times*, March 15, 2010; "Big Banks Targeted in Protest as Labor Calls for Action on Jobs," *Buffalo News*, March 19, 2010; "Union Plans Rally at Local Brokerage," *Charleston Gazette*, March 16, 2010; Art Levine, "Financial Industry Gives 250% More to Sway Key Legislators," *Huffington Post*, March 18, 2010.

7. "Activists Plan Pro-Financial Reform Rallies, Lobby Days," *Roll Call*, April 12, 2010; "Unions Hold a Rally to Protest Wall Street," *New York Times*, April 29, 2010; "Unions Face Off vs. Wall Street," *New York Post*, April 30, 2010; "Main Street Slams Wall Street," *Washington Post*, April 30, 2010; "SEIU Members Join Thousands of Workers, Clergy, Families in March on Wall Street," Targeted New Service, April 29, 2010; "Thousands March on Wall Street, Calling for Jobs," Labor Notes, April 30, 2010; "In New Ads, SEIU Tells Senate Hopeful Roy Blunt: Reform Wall Street, Don't Reward It," Targeted News Service, April 29, 2010.

8. Zelenko and Teslik interviews; "AFL-CIO: Pay Packages Played Role in Mortgage Crisis," Dow Jones News Service, April 14, 2008; Damon Silvers, "Some Thoughts on the Progressive Reform of the Financial Regulatory Structure," memo for the Obama-Biden Transition Project, n.d.; testimony of Damon Silvers, *Hearing before the Senate Committee on Banking, Housing, and Urban Affairs*, US Sen., 111th Cong, 1st Sess., March 10, 2009, 20. On Paulsen, see Harold Meyerson, "Wall Street's Man in Washington," *Washington Post*, September 25, 2008.

9. "A Need to Reconnect," *Financial Times*, March 13, 2009; "Marching on the Moneymen"; "AFL-CIO Associate General Counsel Damon A. Silvers Prepared Testimony before the House Foreign Affairs Subcommittee on Terrorism, Nonproliferation, and Trade, "Hearing on Foreign Policy Implications of U.S. Effort to Address the Financial Crisis," *Financial Market Regulatory Wire*, June 10, 2009; "Elizabeth Warren Holds a Hearing on America's Financial Regulatory Structure," *Financial Market Regulatory Wire*, January 14, 2009; House Ways and Means Committee Hearing, "Campaign for America's Future and Institute for America's Future Hold a Panel Discussion of the Banks, Banksters [*sic*], and the Reckoning," *Financial Market Regulatory Wire*, June 2, 2009.

10. Alan Beattie, "Outrage at Big Bonuses for AIG Managers," *Financial Times*, March 15, 2009; Deborah Solomon, "Bailout Anger Undermines Geithner," *Wall Street Journal*, February 21, 2010; *Wall Street Fraud and Fiduciary Duties: Can Jail Time Serve as an Adequate Deterrent for Willful Violations: Hearing before the Subcommittee on Crime and Drugs*, US Senate Judiciary Committee, 111th Cong., 2nd Sess., May 4, 2010; "AIG Default Swap Repayments Criticized," *National Underwriter Property and Casualty*, May 27, 2010; "The AFL-CIO Holds a Conference Call and Webinar to Discuss the AFL-CIO's 2009 Executive Paywatch Website," *Financial Market Regulatory Wire*, April 14, 2009. On prosecution and punishment of Wall Street executives, see "Why Only One Top Banker Went to Jail for the Financial Crisis," *New York Times*, April 30, 2014; "Goldman Sachs Finally Admits It Defrauded Investors during the Financial Crisis," *Fortune*, April 11, 2016; Jesse Eisinger, *The Chickenshit Club: Why the Justice Department Fails to Prosecute Executives* (New York: Simon & Schuster, 2017). After Lehman Brothers fell apart, its former CEO, Richard Fuld, appeared in front of Representative Henry Waxman's House Committee on Oversight and Government Reform. Waxman had documents indicating that Fuld committed fraud over the previous eight years, a period during which he received compensation worth nearly $500 million. As he left the hearing, Code Pink, a left-leaning group, shouted that Fuld should go to jail. He never did. "Lehman CEO under Fire from Lawmakers, Protesters," Dow Jones News Service, October 6, 2008; "Lehman Managers Portrayed as Irresponsible," *New York Times*, October 6, 2008.

11. "Campaign '08: Big Pay for Big Bosses under Fire," *Wall Street Journal*, September 22, 2008; "U.S. Targets Excessive Pay for Top Executives," *Washington Post*, June 11, 2009; "The AIG Controversy," *Wall Street Journal*, April 1, 2009; "Dissecting the AIG Bonus," *New York Times*, March 18, 2009; "The AIG Controversy: AIG's Board's Pay Panel Falls under Shareholder Fire," *Wall Street Journal*, April 1, 2009; "Wall Street and Its Bonuses," Dow Jones News Service, May 13, 2009; "Bailout Anger Undermines Geithner," *Wall Street Journal*, February 21, 2010; "Federal Report Faults Banks on Huge Bonuses," *New York Times*, July 22, 2010; "TARP Pay Czar Criticizes Big Bank Bonuses but Won't Seek Refunds of Bailout Money," *Los Angeles Times*, July 24, 2010; "US Faulted over Pay at Rescued Firms," *New York Times*, January 24, 2012; Gallup Poll, "Most Americans Favor Gov't. Action to Limit Executive Pay," June 16, 2009, http://www.gallup.com/poll/120872/americans-favor-gov-action-limit-executive-pay.aspx

12. "Lawmakers to Revisit Wall Street Oversight," *Dow Jones News Service*, July 23, 2008; "Testimony of Damon A. Silvers, Hearing before the Subcommittee on Terrorism, Nonproliferation and Trade of the Committee on Foreign Affairs, House of Representatives," 1st Sess., 111th Cong., June 10, 2009, pp. 11–25; Dennis K. Berman, "The Future of Finance: The New Role of Private Money," *Wall Street Journal*, March 30, 2009; "Rep. Barney Frank Holds a Hearing on

Regulation of Systemic Risk in the Financial Services Industry," Financial Market Regulatory Wire, March 17, 2009; Congressional Oversight Panel, "Modernizing the American Financial Regulatory System," Special Report on Regulatory Reform, January 2009; "U.S. Economists, Officials Urge Financial Regulatory Changes," Dow Jones News Service, January 14, 2009.

13. Richardson and Kellogg, Abrecht, and Zelenko interviews; Larry Kirsch and Robert N. Mayer, *Financial Justice: The People's Campaign to Stop Lender Abuse* (Santa Barbara, CA: Praeger, 2013), 36–49; "Banks, Consumer Groups, at Odds over New Watchdog," *St. Louis Post-Dispatch*, July 11, 2009; "Americans for Financial Reform," *Targeted News Service*, June 17, 2009; "Financial Lobbyists Man the Battle Stations," *Roll Call*, November 16, 2009; "Big Banks Are Back in the Game," *National Journal*, December 14, 2009; Robert N. Mayer and Larry Kirsch, "To Speak in One Voice: Dynamics of a Cross-Movement Coalition for Financial Reform," in *Shopping for Change: Consumer Activism and the Possibilities of Purchasing Power*, ed. Louis Hyman and Joseph Tohill (Ithaca: ILR Press, 2017): 279–294.

14. Heather Slavkin, "Systemic Risk Regulation," *Americans for Financial Reform*, July 2009; Eileen Appelbaum and Rosemary L. Batt, *Private Equity at Work: When Wall Street Manages Main Street* (New York: Russell Sage Foundation, 2014), 279–282; "How House Bill Would Dismantle an Array of Dodd-Frank Reforms," *New York Times*, June 8, 2017; Robert Kuttner, "Too Big to be Governed?" *American Prospect*, December 1, 2010. Her name today is Heather Slavkin Corzo. She later ran the AFL-CIO's Office of Investment.

15. Kuttner, "Too Big"; Jim Kuhnhenn, "Emerging Democratic Voices: Bill to Rein in Banks Is Not Tough Enough," Associated Press, May 3, 2010; "Senate Democrats Hold a News Conference to Discuss Financial Reform," Financial Market Regulatory Wire, April 21, 2010; Simon Johnson, "Does the U.S. Really Have a Fiscal Crisis?" *New York Times*, February 24, 2011; Ezra Klein, "Summers Lost Because Liberals Don't Trust Obama on Financial Reform," *Washington Post*, September 22, 2013; Bill Swindell, "House Dems Splitting Over Regulating Derivatives Market," *Congress Daily/A.M.*, July 22, 2009; Richard Trumka in Simon Johnson, "AFL-CIO: Stronger Financial Reform Would Have Saved Jobs," *Baseline Scenario*, August 19, 2010, https://baselinescenario.com/2010/08/19/afl-cio-stronger-financial-reform-would-have-saved-jobs/#more-7925

16. Janet Hook and Dan Morain, "Democrats Are Darlings of Wall Street," *Los Angeles Times*, March 21, 2008; Alison Vekshin and Dawn Kopecki, "Not So Radical Reform," *Bloomberg BusinessWeek*, January 11, 2010; "Inside Obama's Bank CEOs Meeting," *Politico*, April 3, 2009; Simon Johnson, "When Populism Is Sound," *New York Times*, March 15, 2012; Obama in Simon Johnson and James Kwak, "Teddy Showed the Banks Who's Boss. Will Obama?" *Washington Post*, April 4, 2010; JP Morgan quote in James Gasparino, "Wall Street Still Doesn't Love the GOP," *Wall Street Journal*, November 2, 2010. Conflict surfaced repeatedly between progressives and administration members. At a meeting of the Congressional Oversight Panel, an exchange took place between the Treasury Department official in charge of TARP, the CEO of Citigroup, Elizabeth Warren, and Damon Silvers. The official, formerly president of Merrill Lynch, denied that the government ever offered a too-big-to-fail guarantee, whereas Warren countered that the market "clearly perceived" that such a guarantee had existed. Michael R. Crittenden, "Clash over Too Big to Fail," *Wall Street Journal*, March 4, 2010.

17. Edward Wyatt, "Veto Threat Raised Over Derivatives," *New York Times*, April 17, 2010; Gretchen Morgenson, "Strong Enough for Tough Stains?" *New York Times*, June 26, 2010; Peter

Eavis, "A Banking Rule with Few Friends Struggles to Survive," *New York Times*, December 10, 2014. A giant loophole in Dodd-Frank was its failure to require banks to disclose their offshore derivatives holdings, leaving large parts of the shadow market shrouded in secrecy. "U.S. Banks Moved Billions of Dollars in Trades beyond Washington's Reach," Reuters, August 21, 2015; Emily Flitter, "Decade after Crisis, A $600 Trillion Market Remains Murky to Regulators," *New York Times*, July 22, 2018.

18. John Cassidy, "The Volcker Rule," *New Yorker*, July 19, 2010; "Who's In and Who's Out in the Bailout Bunch," *MarketWatch*, January 22, 2010; Bill Swindell, "After More Than a Year of Lead-Up, Conference Begins," *Congress Daily/A.M.*, June 10, 2010; "Elizabeth Warren, Chair of Congressional Oversight Panel on TARP, Holds a Teleconference to Discuss the House and Senate Wall Street Reform Bills," *Financial Market Regulatory Wire*, June 4, 2010; Michael R. Crittenden, "US Union, Liberal Groups, Push to Toughen Financial Bill," *Wall Street Journal*, June 4, 2010; "Americans for Financial Reform Holds a Teleconference to Discuss Growing Evidence of Public Demand for Wall Street Reform," *SEC Wire*, June 24, 2010.

What shifted the dynamic around the Volcker Rule was an SEC lawsuit against Goldman Sachs in April 2010. The agency alleged that Goldman had failed to disclose that a hedge fund had played a role in selecting the contents of one of Goldman's CDO portfolios that the fund subsequently shorted. The AFL-CIO's Dan Pedrotty called the lawsuit "a game changer." Bill Swindell, "Goldman Suit Will Boost Reform," *Congress Daily/A.M*, April 16, 2010; Richard Wolffe, *Revival: The Struggle for Survival Inside the Obama White House* (New York: Broadway Paperbacks, 2010), 170–173.

19. "Wall Street Plans $38 Billion of Bonuses as Shareholders Lose," *Bloomberg*, November 20, 2007; Eric Dash, "For Ousted Citigroup Chief, a Bonus of $12.5 Million," *New York Times*, November 12, 2007; Rachel Beck and Ellen Simon, "Departing CEO O'Neal to Leave Merrill Lynch with Exit Package Worth $161.5 Million," Associated Press, October 30, 2007; "Congress Questions Executives on Pay," *New York Times*, March 7, 2008; "Panel to Review Payouts Given by Troubled Firms," *New York Times*, March 7, 2008; "Chiefs Pay under Fire at Capitol," *New York Times*, March 8, 2008; "Executives Defend Pay Packages before U.S. House Panel," *Wall Street Journal*, March 7, 2008; "Nearly 700 at Merrill in Million-Dollar Club," *New York Times*, February 11, 2009; Gretchen Morgenson, "Gimme Back Your Paycheck," *New York Times*, February 22, 2009.

20. Elson and McGurn in "Shareholders See Victory in Obama Administration," *Pensions & Investments* (hereafter *P&I*), November 10, 2008; Martha Graybow, "Lifting the Lid: Angry Investors Take Aim at US Bank Boards," Reuters, March 31, 2009; Craig Karmin, "Shareholders Renew Push to Regulate Executive Pay," *Wall Street Journal*, February 13, 2009. A survey found that Americans were in favor of government stepping in to regulate bankers' pay. See *Protecting Shareholders and Enhancing Public Confidence by Improving Corporate Governance: Hearing before the Subcommittee on Securities, Insurance, and Investment*, 111th U.S. Congress, 1st Sess., July 29, 2009, p. 15.

21. Jon Bakija, Adam Cole, and Bradley T. Heim, "Jobs and Income Growth of Top Earners and the Causes of Changing Income Inequality: Evidence from US Tax Return Data," working paper, Williams College, April 2012; Thomas Philoppon and Ariell Reshef, "Wages and Human Capital in the US Finance Industry: 1909–2006," *Quarterly Journal of Economics* 127 (2012): 1551–1609; Ken-Hou Lin and Donald Tomaskovic-Devey, "Financialization and US Income

Inequality, 1970–2008," *American Journal of Sociology* 118 (2013): 1284–1329; Anat Admati and Martin Hellwig, *The Bankers' New Clothes: What's Wrong with Banking and What to Do about It* (Princeton, NJ: Princeton University Press, 2013), 125; Louise Story, "On Wall Street, Bonuses, Not Profits, Were Real," *New York Times*, December 18, 2008; Alfred Rappaport, "The Economics of Short-Term, Performance Obsession," *Financial Analysts Journal* 61 (2005): 65–77; Prince in Michiyo Nakamoto and David Wighton, "Bullish Citigroup is 'Still Dancing' to the Beat of the Buy-out Boom," *Financial Times*, July 10, 2007.

22. Sanjai Bhagat, *Financial Crisis, Corporate Governance, and Bank Capital* (Cambridge: Cambridge University Press, 2017), 24–72.

23. Testimony of Damon A. Silvers, in "Rep. Barney Frank Holds a Hearing on Regulation of Systemic Risk in the Financial Services Industry." The original TARP regulations required that a recipient review its incentive pay methods to eliminate those that encouraged "unnecessary and excessive" risk-taking. A written plan had to be prepared, but it would not be reviewed by the government. Parts of this were incorporated into Dodd-Frank.

24. Sanjai Bhagat, Brian Bolton, and Roberta Romano, "Getting Incentives Right: Is Deferred Bank Executive Compensation Sufficient?" *Yale Journal on Regulation* 31 (2014): 523–564; Anat R. Admati, "Statement for the Senate Committee on Banking, Housing and Urban Affairs' Subcommittee on Financial Institutions and Consumer Protection, Hearing on Examining the GAO Report of Government Support for Bank Holding Companies," July 31, 2014; "SEC Plan Aims to Better Foretell Risks," *Wall Street Journal*, July 2, 2009; "New Rules Curbing Wall Street Pay Announced," *Wall Street Journal*, April 21, 2016; "Wall Street Battle Heats Up as US Election Looms," *Financial Times*, July 15, 2016; "Wall Street Spends Record $2bn on US Election Lobbying," *Financial Times*, March 8, 2017; Gretchen Morgenson, "Want Change? Shareholders Have a Tool," *New York Times*, March 26, 2017; "Regulators Drop Pursuit of Banker, CEO Pay Restrictions," Dow Jones News Service, July 20, 2017; Mishel in Steve Lohr, "Wall Street's High Pay: Episodic Phenomenon," *New York Times*, February 6, 2009.

25. Nicholas Chan, Mila Getmansky, Shane M. Haas, and Andrew W. Lo, "Systemic Risk and Hedge Funds," National Bureau of Economic Research, working paper w11200, 2005; Roger Lowenstein, "Long-Term Capital Management: It's a Short-Term Memory," *New York Times*, September 8, 2008; "The Case for Regulating Derivatives," *San Diego Union-Tribune*, November 13, 2003; "SEC May Start to Regulate Hedge Funds; Staff Proposal Reflects Concerns of Chairman," *Washington Post*, September 26, 2003; Lynn A. Stout, "Derivatives and the Legal Origin of the 2008 Credit Crisis," *Harvard Business Law Review* 1 (2011): 1–38; Photis Lysandrou, "The Primacy of Hedge Funds in the Subprime Crisis," *Journal of Post Keynesian Economics* 34, no. 2 (2011): 225–254. Skeel in "Financial Steroids," *New York Times*, November 30, 2010.

There were a few Cassandras who early on raised red flags about the shadow banking system and its effects on systemic risk. One was the Economic Policy Institute. It noted that the 1987 market downturn could have been worse had Glass-Steagall not provided a firebreak against problems jumping from one segment of the financial industry to another, which was exactly what happened in 2008. Jane D'Arista and Tom Schlesinger, "The Parallel Banking System," EPI Briefing Paper, June 1993. Also see "The Predators' Ball Resumes: Financial Mania and Systemic Risk: An Interview with Damon Silvers," *Multinational Monitor*, May 7, 2007.

26. "CalPERS Fine-Tuning Hedge Fund Investment Policy," Dow Jones News Service, February 13 2003; "Hedge Funds Lure Big Pension Funds despite Amaranth," Dow Jones News

Service, October 3, 2004; Wilshire Consulting, "2007 Wilshire Report on State Retirement Systems," Santa Monica, California, 2007; "Investors Say: Supersize It; More Than 30 U.S. Institutions Invest $1 Billion or More Each," *P&I*, May 1, 2006; "Pennsylvania Pours Another $2 Billion in Hedge Funds," *HedgeWorld News*, July 20, 2006; "Pennsylvania Pension Fund's 17 Percent Return Tough to Copy," Associated Press, April 17, 2008; "Service Employees Likely to Seek Hedge Fund of Funds," *Money Management Letter*, September 10, 2004; "Rich Plan, Poor Plan," *Institutional Investor*, January 13, 2006; "Once-Shy Union Plans Begin to Warm Up to Non-Traditional Investments," *P&I*, August 21, 2006; "White Paper: Institutional Interest and Allocation," *Infovest21*, March 7, 2007; "Pension Plans Play Catch-up," *Barron's*, October 29, 2007; "Marco Sees Big Future Ahead as an Independent Fiduciary," *P&I*, April 2, 2007.

Marco Consulting Group is devoted to Taft-Hartley clients. It offers proxy services and guidance on everything from picking investments to finding union-friendly asset managers. Its business has the effect of aligning several hundred Taft-Hartley funds around common investments, making it easier for them to share information and form voting blocs. "Firms Slammed in AFL-CIO Proxy Voting Survey," *Money Management Letter*, March 18, 2002; "Union Muscle Fuels Morgan Stanley Settlement," *Investment Management Weekly*, May 23, 2011; "Marco Consulting Group Chairman Jack Marco Prepared Testimony before the House Education and Labor Subcommittee Hearing on Creating Greater Accounting Transparency for Pensioners," *Financial Market Regulatory Wire*, July 20 2010; "Companies, Funds, Spar Over Nomination Rule," *P&I*, August 24, 2009.

27. Richard L. Trumka, AFL-CIO, to Hon. Richard C. Shelby and Senator Paul Sarbanes, July 24, 2006, courtesy of Dan Pedrotty; Silvers interview.

28. Gregory Crawford, "Securities Lending: Activist Hedge Funds 'Borrowing' Votes?" *P&I*, April 4, 2005; David Yermack, "Shareholder Voting and Corporate Governance," *Annual Review of Financial Economics* (2010): 2–23; Henry T. C. Hu and Bernard Black, "The New Vote Buying," *University of Southern California Law Review* 79 (2006): 811–908; Silvers interview.

Hedge funds made a mint in the early days of disaster by shorting bank shares, including AIG, J. P. Morgan, Goldman Sachs, and Lehman Brothers. Short selling drove down share prices, making it more difficult for the banks to stave off disaster. After Lehman's collapse, Andrew Cuomo, the New York attorney general, launched an investigation of the short-sellers, while the SEC briefly banned short-selling of nearly one thousand financial institutions. Pension plans— including major activists like CalPERS, CalSTRS, and the New York City pension funds—were among those who had lent their bank shares to hedge funds for short-selling purposes. "U.S. Attorney General to Probe Share Deals," *Financial Times*, September 19, 2008; "Short-Sale Ban Ends to Poor Reviews," *Wall Street Journal*, October 9, 2008; Sebastian Mallaby, *More Money than God: Hedge Funds and the Making of the New Elite* (New York: Penguin Press, 2010), 350–352.

29. American Federation of Teachers, *All That Glitters Is Not Gold: An Analysis of U.S. Public Pension Investments in Hedge Funds* (Washington, DC: AFT, 2015); "Public Pension Plans Bet Their Future on Hedge Funds," *Institutional Investor*, June 1, 2011; Brian R. Cheffins and John Armour, "The Past, Present, and Future of Shareholder Activism by Hedge Funds," *Journal of Corporate Law* 37 (2011): 93; "'Alpha' Bets Turn Sour—Pennsylvania Pension Now Faces Billions in Losses," *Wall Street Journal*, December 1, 2008.

In testimony to Congress, Damon Silvers said, "The decline of defined benefit pension plans has meant that those plans that remain . . . have been forced to look for higher rates of return than are available through buy and hold strategies. The fact that these higher rates of return are illusory has not stopped individuals and institutions from pursuing them"; testimony of Damon A. Silvers, US Senate Banking Committee, Housing and Urban Affairs Subcommittee on Economic Policy, Hearing on Short-Termism in Financial Markets, April 29, 2010.

30. John D. Rogers, "There Is a Future of Finance (and It's Called Fiduciary Capitalism)," *Huffington Post*, May 16, 2014; *Myners Principles for Institutional Investment: Review of Progress* (London: HM Treasury, 2004); IRRC Institute, "Investment Horizons: Do Managers Do What They Say?" 2010; Dominic Barton and Mark Wiseman, "Focusing Capital on the Long-Term," *Harvard Business Review* 92 (2014): 44–51. The Kay Review found that the period in which asset managers held companies is less than ten months. *The Kay Review of UK Equity Markets and Long-Term Decision Making*, final report, July 2012.

31. Henrik Cronqvist and Rüdiger Fahlenbrach, "Large Shareholders and Corporate Policies," *Review of Financial Studies* 22 (2008): 3941–3976; OECD, *The Role of Institutional Investors in Promoting Good Corporate Governance* (Paris, 2011), 31; Martijn Cremers and Ankur Pareek, "Patient Capital Outperformance: The Investment Skill of High Active Share Managers Who Trade Infrequently," *Journal of Financial Economics* 122, no. 2 (2016): 288–306; Bidisha Chakrabarty, Pamela C. Moulton, and Charles Trzcinka, "The Performance of Short-Term Institutional Trades," Cornell University, HSA (January 2016); Kenneth R. French, "The Cost of Active Investing," *Journal of Finance* 63 (2008): 1537–1573. In recent years, ETFs have hastened short-term trading; their average holding period is five days. Jake Zamansky, "The Death of the Buy and Hold Investor," *Fortune*, July 5, 2012; "ETFs Are Eating the US Stock Market," *Financial Times*, January 24, 2017; Joanne Hill, "The Evolution and Success of Index Strategies in ETFs," *Financial Analysts Journal* 72 (2016): 8–13; and Andrew McCollum, "Active Strategies, Indexing, and the Rise of ETFs," Greenwich Associates 2016 Global Exchange-Traded Funds Study, Q3, 2017.

32. The Aspen Institute, *Long-Term Value Creation: Guiding Principles for Corporations and Investors* (New York, 2007); Silvers interview; "Experts to Boards: Think Long Term, Not Short," *Plastics News*, November 12, 2007; Aspen Institute, *Overcoming Short-Termism: A Call for a More Responsible Approach to Investment and Business Management* (New York, 2009).

33. Aspen, *Overcoming Short-Termism*; Lawrence Summers and Victoria Summers, "When Financial Markets Work Too Well: A Cautious Case for a Securities Transactions Tax," *Journal of Financial Services Research* 3 (1988): 261–266.

34. Groupe de Travail, Présidé par Jean-Pierre Landau, "Les Nouvelles Contributions Financieres Internationales" (Paris: La Documentation Française, 2003): Interview with Jacques Cossart, Esther Jeffers, and Bruno Jetin, ATTAC, Paris, December 2009; "Germany, France Press EU on Transactions Tax," *Wall Street Journal*, September 9, 2011; "The Need for a Tax on Financial Trading," *New York Times*, January 28, 2016; "Labor Pledges 'Robin Hood' Tax on City," *Investors Week*, May 14, 2017. The issue was still alive in 2020, when a group of Parliament members proposed that a transactions tax be used to fund the EU's pandemic-related spending. "A Financial Transaction Tax Deal Worth Fighting For," *EurActiv.com*, July 16, 2020.

35. Robert Pollin, Dean Baker, and Marc Schaberg, "Securities Transaction Taxes for US Financial Markets," *Eastern Economic Journal* 29 (2003): 527–558; Roundtable in "Tobin Tax Advocates Pile Pressure on US," *The Guardian*, November 23, 2009; "Brown Fails to Rally 'Tobin Tax' Allies, *Financial Times*, November 8, 2009; "US Lawmakers Weigh a Wall Street Tax," Dow Jones News Service, December 18, 2009; testimony of Damon A. Silvers, "Short-Termism in

Financial Markets," Hearing before the Subcommittee on Economic Policy of the Committee on Banking, Housing, and Urban Affairs, US Senate, 111th Cong., 2d. Sess., April 29, 2010; Richard Trumka, "Make Wall Street Pay for Creating New Jobs," *HuffPost*, May 16, 2010; "Tax on Financial Trades Gains Advocates," *Pittsburgh Post-Gazette*, December 11, 2010.

During the 2016 presidential campaign, Bernie Sanders and Hillary Clinton regularly talked up the Tobin tax, and the *New York Times* editorial board endorsed it too.

36. "Senator Schumer and the SEC Separately Propose Action on Corporate Governance Matters," *Mondaq*, May 22, 2009; "SEC Votes to Propose Pro-Shareholder Proxy Rules," Dow Jones News Service, May 20, 2009; Chase Cole, "New Corporate Governance Legislation," *Mondaq*, June 12, 2009; Booth in Jeffrey Toobin, "The Senator and the Street," *New Yorker*, August 2, 2010; Martin Lipton, Jay W. Lorsch, and Theodore N. Mirvis, "Schumer's Shareholder Bill Misses the Mark," *Wall Street Journal*, May 12, 2009; Dealbook, "Friend to Wall Street, Schumer Falls Quiet," *New York Times*, April 23, 2010; Francine Kiefer, "Is Chuck Schumer's Vision for America Realistic?" *Christian Science Monitor*, November 26, 2014. The text of the Bill of Rights may be found at https://www.cooley.com/news/insight/2009/draft-of-schumer-shareholder-bill-of-rights and Dodd-Frank at https://cftc.gov/sites/default/files/idc/groups/public/@swaps/documents/file/hr4173_enrolledbill.pdf

37. Rudiger Fahlenbrach and René M. Stulz, "Bank CEO Incentives and the Credit Crisis," *Journal of Financial Economics* 99 (2011): 11–26; Andrea Beltratti and René M. Stulz, "The Credit Crisis around the Globe: Why Did Some Banks Perform Better?" *Journal of Financial Economics* 105 (2012): 1–17; David Erkens, Mingyi Hung, and Pedro Matos, "Corporate Governance in the 2007–2008 Financial Crisis: Evidence from Financial Institutions Worldwide," *Journal of Corporate Finance* 18 (2012): 389–411; Simon Deakin, "Corporate Governance and Financial Crisis in the Long Run," Centre for Business Research, University of Cambridge, working paper no. 417, December 2010; William W. Bratton and Michael L. Wachter, "The Case Against Shareholder Empowerment," *University of Pennsylvania Law Review* 158, no. 3 (2010): 653–728.

38. Teresa Kroeger, Tanyell Cooke, and Elise Gould, "The Class of 2016," report of the Economic Policy Institute, Washington, DC, April 21, 2016; "Protests Offer Obama Opportunity to Gain, and Room for Pitfalls," *New York Times*, October 7, 2011; Mark Tremayne, "Anatomy of Protest in the Digital Era: Social Media Gives Wall Street Protests a Global Reach," *New York Times*, October 15, 2011; Brad Chase, "Have the Youth Given Up on Obama?" CNN, December 30, 2011, http://globalpublicsquare.blogs.cnn.com/2011/12/30/have-the-youth-given-up-on-obama; Mark Tremayne, "Anatomy of Protest in the Digital Era: A Network Analysis of Twitter and Occupy Wall Street," *Social Movement Studies* 13 (2014): 110–126; Zeynep Tufekci, *Twitter and Tear Gas: The Power and Fragility of Networked Protest* (New Haven, CT: Yale University Press, 2017). According to one report, three-fourths of the New York protesters had a college degree; see Jillian Berman, "Occupy Wall Street Actually Not at All Representative of the 99 Percent, Report Finds," *HuffPost*, January 29, 2013, http://www.huffingtonpost.com/2013/01/29/occupy-wall-street-report_n_2574788.html. During the 2009–2012 recovery, the top 1% saw its real incomes increase by 35%, whereas the other 99% lost 12%. Emmanuel Saez, Emmanuel Saez, "Striking It Richer: The Evolution of Top Incomes in the United States," *Real-world Economics Review*, 65, September 27, 2013.

39. "Occupy Wall Street: The Draft Manifesto," *Daily Caller*, October 17, 2011, http://dailycaller.com/2011/10/17/occupy-wall-street-the-draft-manifesto/; "Protestors Debate What

Demands, If Any, to Make," *New York Times*, October 17, 2011; Justin Elliott, "Judith Butler at Occupy Wall Street," *Salon*, October 24, 2011, http://www.salon.com/2011/10/24/judith_butler _at_occupy_wall_street/; John Cassidy, "Wall Street Protests: Signs of the Times," *New Yorker*, October 6, 2011. Also see Todd Gitlin, *Occupy Nation: The Roots, the Spirit, the Compromise* (New York: itbooks, 2012); and Craig Calhoun, "Occupy Wall Street in Perspective," *British Journal of Sociology* 64 (2013): 26–38.

40. Occupy the SEC to Ben Bernanke et al., January 13, 2012, https://www.sec.gov /comments/s7-41-11/s74111-230.pdf; Alternative Banking Group, *Occupy Finance*, http:// altbanking.net/projects/our_book.

41. I calculated the number of *Factiva* articles from September 2011 to September 2014 containing a keyword plus a mention of Occupy or the AFL-CIO. The keywords related to finance (finance, Goldman Sachs, banking, banks, and mortgages); regulation (Senate Committee on Finance, Barney Frank, and SEC); inequality (wealth inequality, income inequality, inequality, top 1 percent or one percent, and 99 percent or ninety-nine percent); and executive pay (executive pay, CEO pay, executive compensation, CEO compensation).

42. Steven Greenhouse, "Occupy Movement Inspires Unions to Embrace Bold Tactics," *New York Times*, November 8, 2011.

43. Thomas Piketty and Emmanuel Saez, "Income Inequality in the United States, 1913–1998," *Quarterly Journal of Economics* 118 (2003): 1–41; Wojciech Kopczuk, Emmanuel Saez, and Jae Song, "Uncovering the American Dream: Inequality and Mobility in Social Security Earnings Data since 1937," National Bureau of Economic Research, working paper 13345 (2007); "Super-Help for the Super-Rich," *The Economist*, December 15, 2018; Dennis P. Quinn and Robert Y. Shapiro, "Business Political Power: The Case of Taxation," *American Political Science Review* 85 (September 1991): 851–874. Robert Reich, "We're Witnessing a Revolt Against the Ruling Class," *Newsweek*, August 3, 2015. The figures on the top 1 percent are interpolated from Piketty and Saez. They do not include capital gains.

44. "How Occupy Wall Street Could Succeed," *Washington Post*, October 3, 2011; "Transaction Tax on Financial Speculation Gets Boost from Occupy Wall Street," *Huffington Post*, October 26, 2011; "AFL-CIO Eyes 'Financial Speculation Tax' to Finance Job Packages," Dow Jones News Service, April 12, 2010; "Occupy Wall Street Backs a Nationwide Boycott against Banks," CNBC, October 7, 2011; "Amidst All the 'Transfers,' Much Has Been Learned," *Credit Union Journal*, October 29, 2010. An advisor of Barack Obama's said that the president tried "not just to respond to the public fury but to tamp it down." In his joint address to Congress, Obama said that he knew how unpopular it was to help banks when everyone was suffering from their decisions. But, he added, "In a time of crisis we cannot govern out of anger." "Obama Dials Down Wall Street Criticism," *Wall Street Journal*, March 24, 2009.

45. "Seeking Energy, Unions Join Protest against Wall Street," *New York Times*, October 5, 2011; "Lending a Little Organized Labor to Occupy Wall Street," *Washington Post*, October 21, 2011; "Unions Look to Protesters for Future Supporters," *Wall Street Journal*, October 29, 2011; "Democrats Adopt 'Occupy' Rhetoric," *Boston Globe*, November 2, 2011; "At Labor Group, a Sense of a Broader Movement," *New York Times*, September 14, 2013; "Liberal Groups Plan to Protest at Shareholder Meetings," Dow Jones News Service, April 24, 2012; "Two Unions Push for Resignation of Armstrong from Citi's Board," *Wall Street Journal*, January 19, 2010. Also see "'We Haven't Had a Shortage of Demands and Solutions. We've Had a Shortage of Mass Movements': Stephen

Lerner on Occupy Wall Street," *Washington Post*, October 4, 2011; Penny Lewis and Stephanie Luce, "Labor and Occupy Wall Street," *New Labor Forum* 21 (2012): 43–40; Charles Heckscher and John McCarthy, "Transient Solidarities: Commitment and Collective Action in Post-Industrial Societies," *British Journal of Industrial Relations* 52 (2014): 627–657.

46. "Obama Signs Overhaul of Financial System," *New York Times*, July 21, 2010; Trumka in "US Interest Groups Praise, Blast New Financial Regulations," Dow Jones News Service, July 21, 2010; "JPMorgan and Other Banks Repay TARP Money," *New York Times*, June 17, 2009; "US Union, Liberal Groups Push to Toughen." The labor movement in 2016 funded a coalition group, Take on Wall Street, to close the carried-interest loophole, but it fizzled out. Eileen Appelbaum, *Private Equity and the SEC after Dodd-Frank* (Washington, DC: Center for Economic and Policy Research, 2015); Ludovic Phalippou, Christian Rauch, and Marc Umber, "Private Equity Portfolio Company Fees," *Journal of Financial Economics* 129 (2018): 559–585. Renae Merle, "The Occupy Movement Has Grown Up—and Looks to Inflict Real Pain on Big Banks," *Washington Post*, May 24, 2016.

47. Daniel Indiviglio, "5 Ways Lobbyists Influenced the Dodd-Frank Bill," *The Atlantic*, July 5, 2010; Kevin Drum, "Capital City," *Mother Jones*, January–February 2010; "Remarks by Senator Warren to the AFL-CIO Convention," *Congressional Documents and Publications*, September 8, 2013; Matt Taibbi, "How Wall Street Killed Financial Reform," *Rolling Stone*, May 10, 2012; "Dodd-Frank's Limitations on Risk Taking," *Mondaq*, July 27, 2010; Gary Rivlin, "How Wall Street Defanged Dodd-Frank," *The Nation*, May 20, 2013; "Scrutiny Puts Banks on Defense," *RollCall*, May 24, 2012; "Obama Signs a Bill That Lets Wall St. Have US over a Barrel Once More," *Daily Telegraph*, July 25, 2010.

48. Rivlin, "How Wall Street Defanged"; Slavkin in "Financial Reform Law Offers Look at Lobbyists' Efforts to Shape It," *Los Angeles Times*, November 15, 2010; "Encouraging Public Service through Wall Street's Revolving Door," *New York Times*, December 1, 2014; Public Citizen, "Just Not Us: Wall Street's 'Two Cents' on Pay Rule: Self-Preservation, Not Principle," July 2011, https://www.citizen.org/our-work/financial-reform/just-not-us-wall-streets-two-cents-pay-rule-self-preservation-not. Three years after Dodd-Frank's enactment, Citigroup sought to gut the Lincoln clause on derivatives, a cause taken up by House Republicans. It turned out that seventy of the eighty-five lines in the Republican bill were written by Citigroup's lobbyists. "Bank Lobbyists Help in Drafting Financial Bills," *New York Times*, May 23, 2013.

49. Bachus in Dana Milbank, "Pork Is Back on the Menu," *Washington Post*, December 15, 2010; "A Wall Street Favorite May Lose His Congressional Seat Tonight," *The Nation*, March 30, 2012; "Regulators Decry Proposed Cuts in C.F.T.C. Budget," *New York Times*, February 24, 2011; Silvers in "Business Groups to Argue for Dodd-Frank Fixes," *Wall Street Journal*, March 16, 2011; "Dodd-Frank Act a Favorite Target for Republicans Laying Blame," *New York Times*, September 20, 2011.

50. "Give Us Tougher Financial Reform, Americans Say," *Investment Advisor*, August 26, 2013; Matt Taibbi, "How Wall Street Killed Financial Reform," *Rolling Stone*, May 24, 2012; Pamela Ban and Hye Young You, "Presence and Influence in Lobbying: Evidence from Dodd-Frank," *Business and Politics* 21, no. 2 (2019): 267–295; Eavis, "Banking Rule with Few Friends"; "Wall St. Banks Ask Fed for Five More Years to Comply with Volcker Rule," Reuters, August 11, 2016; "Wall Street Finds Relief in Court from SEC Rules," *Washington Post*, August 12, 2011; "Suing the Government? Call Scalia," *Bloomberg*, January 26, 2012; "Judge Nixes Trading Curbs," *Wall*

Street Journal, September 28, 2012. Scalia's cases were filed in the DC Circuit Court, a pro-business venue whose decisions on the cost-benefit standards were judged "dramatically inconsistent with the standard enacted by Congress." James D. Cox and Benjamin Baucom, "The Emperor Has No Clothes: Confronting the DC Circuit's Usurpation of SEC Rulemaking Authority," *Texas Law Review* 90 (2011): 1813.

51. "U.S. Banks Gear Up to Fight Dodd-Frank Act's Volcker Rule," Reuters, January 3, 2017; Ben Protess, "Republicans' Paths to Unraveling the Dodd-Frank Act," *New York Times*, January 30, 2017; "Key Provisions of the Financial Choice Act," Dow Jones News Service, June 8, 2017; "Rewarding or Hoarding? The Finance 202: Wall Street Betting on Treasury, Not Congress, for Regulatory Rollback," *Washington Post*, June 14, 2017; "How House Bill Would Dismantle an Array of Dodd-Frank Reforms," *New York Times*, June 8, 2017; "Top Republican Outlines Plan to Rip Up Dodd-Frank," *Financial Times*, June 7, 2016; "Bill to Erase Some Dodd-Frank Banking Rules Passes in House," *New York Times*, June 8, 2017; Mara Stein, "Choice Act Fuels Debate Over Shareholder Proposals," Dow-Jones News Service, June 20, 2017; "When Wall Street Writes Its Own Rules," *New York Times*, February 9, 2018; "Congress Eases Banking Curbs Set After Crisis," *New York Times*, May 23, 2018.

52. Testimony by Damon Silvers, special counsel, AFL-CIO, "The Dodd-Frank Act Five Years Later: We Are More Stable," Hearings, House Financial Services Committee, *Congressional Documents and Publications*, July 9, 2015; conversation with Damon Silvers, Chicago, 2016; Francine McKenna, "A Decade After the Crisis, the SEC Still Hasn't Passed Executive Compensation Rules," September 14, 2018, at https://www.marketwatch.com/story/a-decade-after-the-crisis -the-sec-still-leaves-executive-compensation-rules-unwritten-2018-09-10; Jamie Hopkins, "SEC Brings Increased Confusion for Investors with New 'Best Interest' Rule," *Forbes*, June 5, 2019; SEC Commissioner Robert J. Jackson Jr., "Statement on Volcker Rule Amendments," September 19, 2019 at https://www.sec.gov/news/public-statement/statement-jackson-091919

53. US Bureau of Economic Analysis, "Corporate Profits with Inventory Valuation and Capital Consumption Adjustments, Domestic Industries: Financial," retrieved from FRED, Federal Reserve Bank of St. Louis, at https://fred.stlouisfed.org/series/A587RC1Q027SBEA; "How the Mighty Goldman Has Fallen," *The Economist*, January 30, 2020; "Is Dimon's Work Done at JPMorgan Chase?" *The Economist*, March 14, 2020. Profits in the financial sector as a share of total domestic profits went from 19.1% (1980s) to 25.6% (1990s) to 28.3% (2000s). From 2010 to 2018, the figure dropped to 26.7%. *Economic Report of the President*, February 2020, table B-54.

Epilogue

1. Barry T. Hirsch and David A. Macpherson, *Union Membership and Coverage Database from the CPS*, at https://www.unionstats.com; US Bureau of Labor Statistics, "Union Members—2019," news release, January 22, 2020. One bright spot for labor was home-based healthcare, where membership gains were the result of AFSCME and SEIU nudging state governments to enact enabling legislation. Eileen Boris and Jennifer T. Klein, "Labor on the Homefront: Unionizing Home-Based Care Workers," *New Labor Forum* 17 (Summer 2008): 32–34. The 1929 denominator was calculated as total civilian employment minus government employment. Bureau of the Census, *Historical Statistics of the United States: Colonial Times to 1957* (Washington, DC, 1960), 170, 97, 710–711. Also see table I.A in the introduction.

2. Kris Maher, "Big Union to Step Up Recruiting," *Wall Street Journal*, February 11, 2011; "#FastFoodGlobal: Thousands Demand Fair Wages from McDonalds," *Deutsche Welle*, May 15, 2014; Lydia DePillis, "Why Labor Groups Genuinely Believe They Can Unionize McDonald's One Day," *Washington Post*, June 9, 2015. CtWIG and Amalgamated Bank teamed up to remove Chipotle's CEO. Ben Miller, "Activist Investors Want Ells out as Chipotle Chairman," *New York Business Journal Online*, November 3, 2016.

3. Hadley Malcolm and Jayne O'Donnell, "Scraping by at Walmart," Gannett News Service, June 7, 2012; Jenny Brown, "In Walmart and Fast Food, Unions Scaling Up a Strike-First Strategy," *Labor Notes*, January 23, 2013; Joann S. Lublin, "Wal-Mart Board Criticized by ISS; More Independence Needed on Pay and Handling of Bribe Probe, ISS Says," *Wall Street Journal*, May 26, 2014; Clare O'Connor, "As Walmart Annual Meeting Looms, Investor Campaigns Against 'Outsized' Executive Pay," *Forbes*, May 19, 2015; Steven Greenhouse, "How Walmart Persuades Its Workers Not to Unionize," *The Atlantic*, June 9, 2015; Peter Olney, "Where Did OUR Walmart Go Wrong," *In These Times*, December 14, 2015. UFCW cut its financial ties to OUR Walmart in 2015.

4. "Walmart Hikes Minimum Wage, Announces Layoffs on Same Day," Reuters, January 11, 2018; Karen Weise, "Amazon to Raise Minimum Wage to $15 for All U.S. Workers," *New York Times*, October 2, 2018; Matt Stevens, "McDonald's Cedes in Minimum-Wage Fight," *New York Times*, March 28, 2019; Sheryl Gay Stolberg, "House Backs a $15 Minimum Wage," *New York Times*, July 19, 2019; US Bureau of Labor Statistics, "25 Major Work Stoppages in 2019," *TED: The Economics Daily*, February 14, 2020. On minimum wages and inequality, see Zsófia L. Bárány, "The Minimum Wage and Inequality: The Effects of Education and Technology," *Journal of Labor Economics* 34 (2016): 237–274. Also see Steven Greenhouse, *Beaten Down, Worked Up: The Past, Present, and Future of American Labor* (New York: Alfred A. Knopf, 2019), chap. 16; David Rolf, *The Fight for Fifteen: The Right Wage for a Working America* (New York: New Press, 2016).

5. Rachel Aleks, "Estimating the Effect of 'Change to Win' on Union Organizing," *Industrial & Labor Relations Review* 68 (2015): 584–605; Samantha Winslow, "Beware of the 'Easy Way,'" *Labor Notes*, July 2019; Katie Johnson, "Bracing for Trump, Union Cuts Spending," *Boston Globe*, December 28, 2016; Hamilton Nolan, "AFL-CIO's Budget Is a Stark Illustration of the Decline of Organizing," *Splinter*, May 16, 2019; Harold Meyerson, "Labor at a Crossroads: The Seeds of a New Labor Movement," *American Prospect*, Fall 2014, 36–45; Rich Yeselson, "Fortress Unionism," *Democracy: A Journal of Ideas* (2013), https://democracyjournal.org/magazine/29/fortress-unionism/; John Logan, San Francisco State University, to author, October 6, 2013.

6. Proxy data from Georgeson, *Annual Corporate Governance Review*, various.

7. Peter Clapman and Richard Koppes, "Time to Rethink 'One Share, One Vote'?" *Wall Street Journal*, June 23, 2016; Katherine Guthrie, Jan Sokolowsky, and Kam-Ming Wan, "CEO Compensation and Board Structure Revisited," *Journal of Finance* 67 (2012): 1149–1168; Pradnya Joshi, "Golden Parachutes Are Still Very Much in Style," *New York Times*, June 29, 2013; Albert H. Choi, Andrew Lund, and Robert J. Schonlau, "Golden Parachutes and the Limits of Shareholder Voting," *Vanderbilt Law Review* 73 (2020): 223–266; Theo Francis and Joann S. Lublin, "Close Ties in the Boardroom; Corporate Boards Get More Independent, But Directors' Connections with the Companies Endure," *Wall Street Journal*, January 20, 2016; Mary S. Hill, Thomas J. Lopez, and Austin L. Reitenga, "CEO Excess Compensation: The Impact of Firm Size and Managerial Power," *Advances in Accounting* 33 (2016): 35–46; Ilia D. Dichev,

John R. Graham, Campbell R. Harvey, and Shiva Rajgopal, "Earnings Quality: Evidence from the Field," *Journal of Accounting and Economics* 56, no. 2–3 (2013): 1–33; Per-Ola Karlsson, DeAnne Aguirre, and Kristin Rivera, "Are CEOs Less Ethical Than in the Past?" *strategy+business* 87 (2017): 56–59. The figures on fraud are a lower bound, given that normally only one-third of corporate fraud is detected. Alexander Dyck, Adair Morse, and Luigi Zingales, "How Pervasive Is Corporate Fraud?" University of Toronto, Rotman School of Management, working paper no. 2222608 (April 2017).

8. Anna Bernasek, "Robert AG Monks, Crusading Against Corporate Excess," *New York Times*, July 6, 2013.

9. Radhakrishnan Gopalan, Todd Milbourn, Fenghua Song, and Anjan V. Thakor, "Duration of Executive Compensation," *Journal of Finance* 69, no. 6 (2014): 2777–2817; Martijn Cremers and Ankur Pareek, "Patient Capital Outperformance: The Investment Skill of High Active Share Managers Who Trade Infrequently," *Journal of Financial Economics* 122, no. 2 (2016): 288–306. Another disconnect is the gap between CEOs and workers in time they spend working for a firm. In 2018, 52 percent of CEOs of S&P 500 companies had job tenures of 5 years or more versus 72 percent of male workers employed for 3 years or more in large (more than a thousand employees) private sector companies in 2008. It's a very rough comparison that understates the CEO-to-worker tenure gap because worker job tenure steadily increases with firm size. The average S&P company employed 54,000 workers in 2018.

Dan Marcec, "CEO Tenure Rates," Harvard Law School Forum on Corporate Governance, February 12, 2018, https://corpgov.law.harvard.edu/2018/02/12/ceo-tenure-rates/#more-104815; Matthew J. Bidwell, "What Happened to Long-term Employment? The Role of Worker Power and Environmental Turbulence in Explaining Declines in Worker Tenure," *Organization Science* 24, no. 4 (2013): 1061–1082. S&P 500 firm-size data courtesy of Howard Silverblatt, S&P Global. For the period 1995–2015, I searched Factiva for joint mentions of buybacks or repurchases and individual labor leaders, unions, and union organizations. On the consequences of buybacks, see chapter 2.

10. William Lazonick, "Profits Without Prosperity: Stock Buybacks Manipulate the Market and Leave Most Americans Worse Off," *Harvard Business Review* 92, no. 9 (September 2014): 46–55; Amy Chozick, "Report by Clinton Adviser Proposes 'Rewriting' Decades of Economic Policy," *New York Times*, May 12, 2015; William A. Galston and Elaine C. Kamarck, "More Builders and Fewer Traders: A Growth Strategy for the American Economy," Center For Effective Public Management, Brookings Institution, June 2015; Katy Milani and Irene Tung, "Curbing Stock Buybacks: A Crucial Step to Raising Worker Pay and Reducing Inequality," National Employment Law Project and Roosevelt Institute, July 2018; Joseph A. Stiglitz, "Rewriting the Rules of the American Economy: An Agenda for Growth and Shared Prosperity," Version 1.1, Roosevelt Institute, May 2015; Joseph E. Stiglitz, *People, Power, and Profits: Progressive Capitalism for an Age of Discontent* (New York: W.W. Norton, 2020). Annual data on buybacks and global employment at the S&P 500 courtesy of Dr. Edward Yardeni, Yardeni Research, Inc., and Howard Silverblatt, S&P Global. The per-employee figure is an aggregate.

11. UAW Retiree Medical Benefits Trust, "Bridging the Disclosure Gap: An Engagement Guide," Detroit, November 2016; interview with Meredith A. Miller and Cambria Allen-Ratzlaff of the RMBT, October 6, 2020. The regulatory analogue to these proposals was a petition to the SEC from twenty organizations, including the AFL-CIO, asking the agency to curb open-market

buybacks that manipulated earnings per share. SEC Commissioner Robert J. Jackson Jr., a Democrat, was on record in favor of the idea. Robert J. Jackson, Jr., "Stock Buybacks and Corporate Cashouts," June 11, 2018, https://www.sec.gov/news/speech/speech-jackson-061118; "Wary Investors Applauding SEC Call to Examine Stock Buybacks," *Pensions & Investments* (*P&I*), June 25, 2018; Cydney Posner, "Rulemaking Petition Seeks to Rein in Stock Buybacks," *Mondaq Business Briefing*, July 11, 2019.

12. Miller and Allen-Ratzlaff interview; "BlackRock's Voting Record Clashes with CEO's Tough Talk on Buybacks," Reuters, August 4, 2016. The three companies cited in the text voted in favor of buybacks more than half the time at shareholder meetings in the United States, UK, France, Germany, and Japan from 2012 to 2017. Jan Fichtner and Eelke M. Heemskerk, "The New Permanent Universal Owners: Index Funds, (Im)patient Capital, and the Claim of Long-termism," SSRN working paper, 3321597 (2018).

13. Paul Waldman, "Democrats Do Have an Agenda, and Even Some Big Ideas," *Washington Post*, August 15, 2018; Chuck Schumer and Bernie Sanders, "Limit Corporate Buybacks," *New York Times*, February 3, 2019; Sydney Ember, "Bernie Sanders Says 'No' to Incrementalism, Highlighting Divide among Democrats," *New York Times*, March 29, 2019; Tara Go lshan, "Bernie Sanders's Wealth Tax Proposal, Explained," *Vox*, September 24, 2019 at https://www.vox.com/policy-and-politics/2019/9/24/20880941/bernie-sanders-wealth-tax-warren-2020

Matthew Yglesias, "Elizabeth Warren's Proposed Tax on Enormous Fortunes, Explained," *Vox*, January 24, 2019, at https://www.vox.com/policy-and-politics/2019/1/24/18196275/elizabeth-warren-wealth-tax; Ganesh Setty, "Cory Booker Reignites Stock-Buyback Fight on the 2020 Campaign Trail," September 19, 2019, CNBC, at https://www.cnbc.com/2019/09/19/cory-booker-aims-to-reignite-stock-buyback-fight-on-2020-campaign-trail.html; interview with Professor Lenore Palladino, University of Massachusetts, Amherst, October 23, 2020; "CII Members Focus 2016 Efforts on Curbing Stock Buybacks," CII Governance Alert, January 21, 2016. On taxes see Emmanuel Saez and Gabriel Zucman, *The Triumph of Injustice: How the Rich Dodge Taxes and How to Make Them Pay* (New York: W.W. Norton, 2019).

14. Raghuram Rajan, "Value Workers as Much as Shareholders," *Bloomberg*, May 1, 2019; Klaus Schwab, "What Kind of Capitalism Do We Want?" *Time*, December 2, 2019; Warren quoted in David Leonhardt, "American Capitalism Isn't Working," *New York Times*, December 2, 2018. Rajan's ideas were influential but hardly new. For example, see Margaret M. Blair, *Ownership and Control: Rethinking Corporate Governance for the Twenty-first Century* (Washington, DC: Brookings Institution, 1995), chap. 6, and John Roberts and Eric van den Steen, "Human Capital and Corporate Governance," in *Corporate Governance: Essays in Honor of Horst Albach*, ed. Horst Albach and Joachim Schwalbach (Berlin: Springer Verlag, 2001), 128–144.

15. Business Roundtable, "Statement on the Purpose of a Corporation," September 2019, https://opportunity.businessroundtable.org/wp-content/uploads/2019/09/BRT-Statement-on-the-Purpose-of-a-Corporation-with-Signatures.pdf; "Business Roundtable Redefines the Purpose of a Corporation to Promote 'An Economy That Serves All Americans,'" August 19, 2019; Jena McGregor, "Group of Top CEOs Says Maximizing Shareholder Profits No Longer Can Be the Primary Goal of Corporations," *Washington Post*, August 19, 2019.

16. CII in Sarah Kaplan, "Are Companies Right to Abandon the Shareholder-first Mantra?" *Financial Times*, August 28, 2019. The statement is an instance of symbolic management, a common phenomenon in politics and business. In the corporate world, symbolic management "is

an agentic, political process by which organizational actors leverage norms, values, beliefs, and assumptions in the broader culture to exert influence over the perceptions and behaviors of organizational stakeholders. . . . firm leaders adopt governance policies and structures that symbolize conformity to prevailing cultural values, while decoupling them from actual processes in ways that serve their political interests." James Westphal and Sun Hyun Park, *Symbolic Management: Governance, Strategy, and Institutions* (New York: Oxford University Press, 2020), 1. On the disjuncture between what the Roundtable companies said and did, see Lucian Bebchuk and Roberto Tallarina, "The Illusory Promise of Stakeholder Governance," (February 26, 2020), forthcoming, *Cornell Law Review*, December 2020; Peter S. Goodman, "Big Business Pledged Gentler Capitalism: It's Not Happening in a Pandemic," *New York Times*, April 16, 2020.

17. Danielle Kurtzleben, "From Amazon to Walmart, 2020 Candidates Take on Big Corporations by Name," *NPR Morning Edition*, https://www.npr.org/2019/06/05/729735727/from-amazon-to-walmart-2020-candidates-take-on-big-corporations-by-name; "Unseating an Old Idea," *The Economist*, February 1, 2020; Warren Staples, "Giving Workers a Voice in the Boardroom Is a Compelling Corporate Governance Reform, *The Conversation*, May 9, 2019 at https://theconversation.com/giving-workers-a-voice-in-the-boardroom-is-a-compelling-corporate-governance-reform-115463; Lenore Palladino, "Worker Representation on U.S. Corporate Boards," working paper, University of Massachusetts, Amherst, October 28, 2019; Thomas Piketty, *Capital and Ideology* (Cambridge, MA: Harvard University Press, 2020), chap. 11.

A step beyond proxy access occurred when CtW Investment Group asked Alphabet, Google's parent, to have its board nominate a nonexecutive employee to be elected directly by shareholders. Jena McGregor, "This Investor Wants to Put an Employee on Google's Board," *Washington Post*, February 20, 2019; Andrea Vittorio, "Workers from Alphabet to Walmart Want a Voice in the Boardroom," *Bloomberg*, June 3, 2019; Nitasha Tiku, "Alphabet Shareholders Demand Accountability," *Wired*, June 19, 2019.

18. Sarah Jones, "With PRO Act, Democrats Commit to Dramatic Labor Reforms," *New York Magazine*, May 3, 2019; Alexia Fernandez Campbell, "Democrats Have an Ambitious Plan to Save American Labor Unions," *Vox*, May 14, 2019, https://www.vox.com/policy-and-politics/2019/5/14/18536789/right-to-work-unions-protecting-the-right-to-organize-act-bill; Jeffrey M. Jones, "As Labor Day Turns 125, Union Approval Near 50-Year High," *Gallup Politics*, August 28, 2019, https://news.gallup.com/poll/265916/labor-day-turns-125-union-approval-near-year-high.aspx; Henry S. Farber, "Employment, Hours, and Earnings Consequences of Job Loss: US Evidence from the Displaced Workers Survey," *Journal of Labor Economics* 35, no. S1 (2017): S235–S272; Moritz Kuhn, Moritz Schularick, and Ulrike I. Steins, "Income and Wealth Inequality in America, 1949–2016," *Journal of Political Economy* 128, no. 9 (2020): 3469–3519; Steven H. Lopez and Lora A. Phillip, "Unemployed: White-Collar Job-Searching after the Great Recession," *Work and Occupations* 46, no. 4 (2019): 470–510; Lydia Saad, "Socialism as Popular as Capitalism Among Young Adults in U.S.," Gallup, November 25, 2019, at https://news.gallup.com/poll/268766/socialism-popular-capitalism-among-young-adults.aspx; Andrew Edgecliffe-Johnson, "Capitalism Keeps CEOs Awake at Night," *Financial Times*, April 23, 2019.

On the effect of unions on inequality, see Henry Farber, Daniel Herbst, Ilyana Kuziemko, and Suresh Naidu, "Unions and Inequality Over the Twentieth Century: New Evidence from Survey Data," National Bureau of Economic Research, working paper 24587 (2018); Bruce

Western and Jake Rosenfeld, "Unions, Norms, and the Rise in US Wage Inequality," *American Sociological Review* 76 (2011): 513–537.

At the time Obama was elected, unions again looked forward to labor law reform through the Employee Free Choice Act (EFCA). Obama was friendly to unions, the Democrats had a filibuster-proof Congress, and union members had gone all out for the incoming president. But the president had different priorities: restoring the economy and enacting healthcare reform. Another problem were centrist Democrats who did not support the bill. Politically it was a replay of Clinton's first term. Disinterest existed outside of Congress too. Several members of Americans for Financial Reform endorsed EFCA—Public Citizen and the National Consumers' League, for example—but other members, including AARP and Common Cause, were silent. The moment passed when Republicans took control of the House. It was an old story: Unions could find allies around issues other than their own. "Unions Flexing Muscles: Hoping for Passage of Hotly Contested Card Check Bill," *The Record*, February 15, 2009; "President Tells Unions Organizing Act Will Pass," *Wall Street Journal*, March 4, 2009; Cindy Hall, Florida AFL-CIO, "Time to Put Workers First," *Tampa Bay Times*, April 30, 2009; "Democrats Drop Key Part of Bill to Assist Unions," *New York Times*, July 17, 2009; "Stalled Agenda Irks Labor Leaders," *Boston Globe*, October 12, 2009.

19. Leo Strine, "Toward Fair and Sustainable Capitalism: A Comprehensive Proposal to Help American Workers, Restore Fair Gainsharing Between Employees and Shareholders, and Increase American Competitiveness by Reorienting Our Corporate Governance System Toward Sustainable Long-Term Growth and Encouraging Investments in America's Future," *Penn Law: Legal Scholarship Repository* (2019), https://scholarship.law.upenn.edu/faculty_scholarship/2104; "Workplace Investor Disclosure Act of 2020," courtesy of Cambria Allen-Ratzlaff.

20. Thomas A. Kochan and William T. Kimball. "Unions, Worker Voice, and Management Practices: Implications for a High-Productivity, High-Wage Economy," *RSF: The Russell Sage Foundation Journal of the Social Sciences* 5, no. 5 (2019): 98; Benjamin J. Newman and John V. Kane, "Economic Inequality and Public Support for Organized Labor," *Political Research Quarterly* 70, no. 4 (2017): 918–932; Gregory Lyon, "Intraparty Cleavages and Partisan Attitudes Toward Labor Policy," *Political Behavior* 42, no. 2 (2020): 385–413.

INDEX

A NOTE ON THE TYPE

This book has been composed in Arno, an Old-style serif typeface in the classic Venetian tradition, designed by Robert Slimbach at Adobe.